Behind Embassy Walls

★ ★ ★ ★

Behind Embassy Walls

The Life and Times of an American Diplomat

BRANDON GROVE

University of Missouri Press
Columbia and London

An ADST-DACOR Diplomats and Diplomacy Book

Copyright © 2005 by Brandon Grove
University of Missouri Press, Columbia, Missouri 65201
Printed and bound in the United States of America
All rights reserved
5 4 3 2 1   09 08 07 06 05

Library of Congress Cataloging-in-Publication Data

Grove, Brandon, 1929-
Behind embassy walls : the life and times of an American
diplomat / Brandon Grove.
        p.   cm.
"An ADST-DACOR diplomats and diplomacy book."
Includes bibliographical references (p.   ) and index.
Summary: "Autobiography of American diplomat Brandon
Grove's career in the U.S. Foreign Service through the Cold
War, McCarthyism, and Somalia crisis. Includes assess-
ments of Chester Bowles; George Herbert Walker Bush;
Robert Kennedy; George Kennan; Omar Torrijos; John
Sherman Cooper; Philip Habib; Willy Brandt; Mobutu;
Vernon Walters; Jimmy Carter; and Ronald Reagan"—
Provided by publisher.
ISBN 0-8262-1573-4 (alk. paper)
1. Grove, Brandon, 1929-   2. Diplomats—United
States—Biography.   3. United States—Foreign Service—
Biography.   4. United States—Foreign relations—1945-
1989. 5. United States—Foreign relations—1989-1993.
6. United States—Politics and government—1945-1989.
7. United States—Politics and government—1989-1993.
8. Politicians—United States—Biography.   I. Title.
E840.8.G76G76   2005
327.73'0092—dc22
2005000624

★ ★ ★ ★

DESIGNER: KRISTIE LEE
TYPESETTER: PHOENIX TYPE, INC.
PRINTER AND BINDER: THE MAPLE-VAIL BOOK MANUFACTURING GROUP
TYPEFACES: GOUDY OLD STYLE AND TIMES

To Mariana

Our existence is but a brief crack of light
between two eternities of darkness.

—Vladimir Nabokov, *Speak, Memory*

CONTENTS

ILLUSTRATIONS

"...and what is the use of a book," thought Alice,
"without pictures or conversations?"

—Lewis Carroll

Illustrations are from the author's collection, unless otherwise indicated in the captions.

FOREWORD

For more than 225 years, extraordinary men and women have represented the United States abroad under all kinds of circumstances. What they did and how and why they did it remain little known to their compatriots. In 1995 the Association for Diplomatic Studies and Training (ADST) and Diplomatic and Consular Officers, Retired (DACOR) created a book series to increase public knowledge and appreciation of the involvement of American diplomats in world history. The series seeks to demystify diplomacy by telling the story of those who have conducted our foreign relations, as they lived, influenced, and reported them.

In his candid autobiography, *Behind Embassy Walls: The Life and Times of an American Diplomat*, Brandon Grove recounts his thirty-five-year career in the U.S. Foreign Service under nine presidents and twelve secretaries of state, focusing on behind-the-scenes diplomacy. Grove opened the first U.S. embassy to East Germany in 1974, served as consul general in Jerusalem in the early 1980s during the war with Lebanon, and was ambassador to Zaire during three years of Mobutu Sese Seko's infamous reign. As director of the Foreign Service Institute, he played a principal role in the successful struggle to build the State Department's National Foreign Affairs Training Center.

Woven into the narrative are observations about the impact of McCarthyism; career versus political appointees to ambassadorships; lawyers as diplomats; CIA stations at U.S. embassies; congressional delegations traveling abroad; relations with the media; and crisis management in Washington, including gripping accounts of how the U.S. government dealt with the 1978 mass suicides in Jonestown, Guyana, and the 1992 humanitarian crisis in Somalia. A concluding chapter spells out the personal and professional qualities required for America's diplomats to make diplomacy succeed in today's world.

Grove openly voices criticism of the Foreign Service and the State Department, while at the same time revealing the human face of diplomacy. In vivid firsthand commentaries he recounts his service as personal assistant to the legendary ambassador to India, Chester Bowles, at the time of Nehru's death and reveals behind-the-scenes diplomatic maneuvers during the Cold War. He offers discerning assessments of such notable personalities as Ethel and Robert Kennedy, George F. Kennan, John Kenneth Galbraith, George Ball, Willy Brandt, Omar Torrijos, Teddy Kollek, Philip Habib, Lorraine and John Sherman Cooper, Mobutu, Vernon Walters, Kofi Annan, Richard A. Clarke, Jimmy Carter, and Ronald Reagan, along with communist diplomats he encountered in Berlin and in Africa.

In retirement Brandon Grove actively serves on leading foreign affairs councils. He has chaired the editorial board of the *Foreign Service Journal,* is the author of an essay on Zaire in the *Encyclopedia of U.S. Foreign Relations* (Oxford University Press, 1997), and, as Sol M. Linowitz Professor of International Affairs, taught a course on diplomacy at Hamilton College in Clinton, N.Y. In characterizing his life in and out of the Foreign Service, Brandon Grove reveals a fine sense of time and place—and of humor—while contributing throughout to the historical record.

Kenneth L. Brown, President
Association for Diplomatic Studies and Training

Robert L. Funseth, President
Diplomatic and Consular Officers, Retired

ACKNOWLEDGMENTS

Here I acknowledge those whose support has been broad and deep. In the Notes on Sources I thank many others who have helped me with my book. The Association for Diplomatic Studies and Training, having placed its imprimatur on this work, honors the author. A clear-thinking Margery Thompson, in charge of the association's book program, aided me throughout the final stages with her valuable advice, her skillful editing, and her informed search for a publisher.

James O'Shea Wade, a friend and retired editor, guided me in my writing without, I hope, letting me sound too much like a starchy diplomat. Marshall and Pamela Sanders Brement, Foreign Service friends and authors themselves, advised me wisely on the manuscript as a whole. Dr. Matthew Bowen, an author in another field, read an early version, and I profited from his insights. I thank Elizabeth Langworthy for legal advice and Tara Sonenshine for helping to promote my book. Susan Fels compiled the index.

At the University of Missouri Press a number of people made this book possible: Beverly Jarrett, the director and editor in chief; Jane Lago, the managing editor, who worked with me on the manuscript; Karen Renner, the marketing manager; Beth Chandler, the assistant marketing manager for events and publicity; and Kristie Lee, the book's designer. They could not have been more helpful or able associates. I am greatly in their debt.

My gratitude goes to my children: Jack, Catherine, Paul, Mark, and Michele, and to the people they married—Hannah, Paul Wayne Jones, Martha, and David. Their love and presence, and the private joys they gave me without knowing, made the obstacles I faced in diplomacy seem less daunting. And now there are the best of grandchildren. I thank my son Mark for agreeing to write the epilogue with me, and then carrying out his part of the bargain so eloquently.

I am grateful to my wife, Mariana, for her love and loveliness, her patience, encouragement, and support. While writing this book I gained a deeper appreciation of my family and its place in my life. How often, traveling alone, had I returned at the end of a day to the silence of an empty room and asked myself: "Where *is* everybody?"

Behind Embassy Walls

★ ★ ★ ★

PROLOGUE

In May 1958, while waiting to enter the Foreign Service and staying with my parents living in London, I visited the Soviet Union and Poland, remaining for a few days in Warsaw to spend some time with my uncle Wladek and his family.

From Warsaw I took an evening train to Berlin, traveling during the night along a rail corridor controlled by Russian military authorities, a plane ticket in my pocket for my flight from West Berlin to London the following afternoon. Behind the Iron Curtain foreigners often were obliged to travel at night, only deepening the mystery of what lay beyond the tracks.

East German border guards making their way through the train at Frankfurt on the Oder River, near Berlin, asked to see my transit visa. The government-run travel office in Warsaw had failed to provide me one. No one had told me I needed a visa, and I wasn't planning to stay in East Germany. I was just passing through. After checking with the responsible Soviet officer, the soldiers, who were polite and at first wanted to let me proceed, escorted me off the train to a Red Cross shack on the platform with a guard soon posted outside. Held captive and watching incredulously as the train slowly gathered speed without me on board, I foolishly asked to speak to the American consul.

At the time there was, of course, no such person in the Soviet Zone of Occupation. What now, I wondered. After waiting several hours, I was put on a Russian furlough train to Moscow that would stop briefly in Warsaw to let me off. I sat alone in an officers' compartment, drinking tea from a charcoal-heated samovar at the end of the coach and trying to concentrate on a book. The officers and their families in the other compartments were not unfriendly and seemed amused by my predicament.

In the Warsaw station the train did not stop at a platform, as I had expected, but alongside another train. The Russian coach attendant told me to get off. I squeezed through a long, tight space between the cars, wrestling my bags across lumps of gravel and hoping neither train would start to move. Using dollars, I took a taxi to the Bristol Hotel, where I was told by the desk clerk that every room was occupied. On learning I was half-Polish and a casualty of Russo-Prussian red tape, he found a bed for me in a spare maid's room in the attic. He also found bread, sausage, cheese, and beer.

In the travel office the next morning, feeling absurd, I obtained the necessary visa and again set off for Berlin. My visa was inspected with feigned care and dutifully stamped by the same border guards with whom I had argued the day before. We smiled knowingly. When my anxious mother met me at Heathrow Airport she exclaimed with relief, but in the way of mothers, "I knew you'd be arrested on this trip!"

Fifteen years later, staring vacantly out my window at the blanket of rain clouds below on a flight taking me from Copenhagen to East Berlin, late in the afternoon of October 20, 1974, I recalled the ironic aspects of my detention by East German border guards.

I sat in a nearly empty plane making its cautious way through bad weather toward the communist capital of East Berlin. Fellow passengers, men from the West in business suits, read or slumped listlessly in their seats during our short journey. My mission, as the first American diplomat to be accredited to the Soviet-occupied "other Germany," was to establish an embassy in Berlin. Beside me in my briefcase was a letter from Secretary of State Henry Kissinger to Foreign Minister Otto Winzer announcing my appointment. "Mr. Grove," it stated in the arch language of diplomacy, "has been charged to conduct the affairs of the Embassy in a manner that will further strengthen the friendship between the peoples of the United States of America and the German Democratic Republic. Therefore, I entrust him to your confidence."

As our aircraft began its descent, dark clouds suddenly near buffeted my window at great speed, and raindrops left horizontal streaks on the pane. Breaking through the cloud layer into the dusk of a real world of roads, farmlands, villages, and church spires below, our plane bounced and veered uncomfortably.

Feeling vaguely uneasy, and without the pleasant tingling that usually accompanied my arrival to take up a new assignment in the Foreign Service, I was returning to East Germany to become, in effect, a contemporary version of the unavailable American consul. How I got to that position and all that followed is the story of this book.

1

SETTING OFF

1929 to 1942

Vladimir Nabokov in *Speak, Memory* characterized our existence as but a brief crack of light between two eternities of darkness. In the early hours of Monday, April 8, 1929, I was delivered into my personal crack of light in Chicago, where my education in life and its unpredictability began.

Herbert Hoover was our president. The stock market crash and Great Depression were six months away. That year, having failed to support Woodrow Wilson's League of Nations, Congress ratified a toothless Kellogg-Briand Pact intended to abolish war. Sixty-two nations, including Germany and Japan, signed the charter; World War II lay a decade ahead. Five years before, in 1924, Congress had passed the Rogers Act creating a career-based Foreign Service of the United States, in which I would invest thirty-five years of my working life.

The Teapot Dome bribery investigation was at its height, and Herblock began drawing political cartoons for the *Chicago Daily News*. "Scarface" Capone gained control of Chicago's underworld after the St. Valentine's Day massacre during which his syndicate gunned down seven of Bugs Moran's men. Blondie and Popeye first appeared in the funny papers, and the new yo-yos were becoming a national obsession. Cole Porter asked life's burning question: "What is this thing called love?" Coca-Cola put up its first gigantic, illuminated advertising display in New York's Times Square, selling its secret recipe in sassy green-tinted bottles with corrugated metal caps that became American icons at six for a quarter. Long, luscious candy bars were three for a dime. The local movie shows in black and white cost about the same: double features, one "pipperoo," one "stinkeroo," with an adventure serial tagged on to lure one back.

Sound pictures replaced silent film, and with *Sally*, which featured "Singin' in the Rain," the Hollywood musical was born as the Great Depression began.

Much of what I know about the family of my Polish mother, Helen, I learned from Uncle Wladislaw "Wladek" Gasparski and my cousin Wojciech, a professor of humanities in Warsaw. Family records were destroyed during the German air raids of World War II. My grandfather Jan worked at the turn of the century as a furniture craftsman, an upholsterer. He and my grandmother Franciszka had four children. Mother, the youngest, was born in 1898, five years before my father. Her brother Stanislaw was killed in World War I. Her sister Maria was a schoolteacher who died of tuberculosis at twenty-six, and mother referred to her tenderly. Her brother Wladek became a typographer, a journalist, and an actor on the stage. In 1910 he moved from Warsaw, then under Russian domination, to Galicia in southeastern Poland, which was under Austro-Hungarian rule, thus avoiding service in the Russian army.

I would come to know Uncle Wladek. He visited my parents in London during several months of 1958, when I also was staying with them while waiting to enter the Foreign Service. His status as a pensioner allowed him to leave communist Poland. Our common language was German, and together we explored London. After living under Nazi and Soviet oppression, Wladek was deeply affected by British freedoms and prosperity. Yet he bought few things, saying he feared they would be confiscated at the Polish border. Toward the end of his visit he became anxious to return to Warsaw and a small family farm nearby. We had a favorite pub in Brompton Road, near Harrods, where we usually ended our morning excursions with a lager. The pub is no longer there, but when I pass by the Brompton Oratory I remember Wladek.

My cousin Wojciech has two books in English left behind in Warsaw by my mother when she came to the United States in 1923. "H. Gasparska" is written in each. One is about calisthenics. She taught gymnastics in Warsaw and admired Isadora Duncan. To her delight, she was awarded a scholarship by the American YWCA to study and teach gymnastic dance in Chicago. The other book is *The Charm of the Impossible*, by Margaret Slattery, which my mother apparently read to learn English. Did she feel the title echoed her hopes for the future as she prepared to sail—a daring woman of twenty-five changing her life and language—to a continent about which she knew little and where she had no friends? This prospect, if she thought of it at all, must have seemed "impossible" until the YWCA took an interest in her.

Mother felt a passion for America typical of many first-generation immigrants. At movie theaters during World War II, as people rose to sing the national anthem once the lights had dimmed and our flag rippled across the screen, my mother's voice became louder than the rest when she reached for the high notes, disconcerting my father and me. In her love of music she preferred Chopin and the tangos of Argentina. From her Polish nature I inherited pride, a tendency toward romance, and an inclination to daydream. She was superstitious in her Slavic fashion. To her, spilled grains of salt symbolized tears to come, and at meals I brush away salt on a table. Mother had a morbid fear of cats, becoming hysterical when she saw one. An affectionate woman devoted to her children's well-being and trying to teach them good manners, she was not intellectually inclined and stubbornly held on to the anti-Semitic prejudices of middle-class Warsaw.

My American grandparents came from Scotland, Pennsylvania. My father, the first of eight children in the marriage of a civil engineer, Harper Grove, to Elizabeth Hambright, was born in New York in 1903. A photograph of the home in Brooklyn shows a lawn with trees and flowers and a white picket fence. During her first pregnancy my grandmother spent an evening at the theater and was so taken by the work of a British playwright, Brandon Tyne, that she named her firstborn after him, which is how I, too, acquired the name. Until recently this was an unusual first name for an American. A young woman I met at a cocktail party in graduate school told me Brandon Grove sounded like a seaside resort in England, and I agreed.

Forebears on my father's side came from Switzerland, Holland, and Germany, with a bit of Irish mixed in. They settled into Lancaster County, Pennsylvania, and also into parts of Virginia near Luray in the Shenandoah Valley. Some were Mennonites who had fled to American shores to avoid religious persecution. One of these was Hans Graf, born in Switzerland in 1661, who laid out Earl Township on land he bought from the sons of William Penn. He established a trading post for the Indians, exchanging wool blankets for furs, which he then "hauled to Philadelphia on a stout wagon drawn by six powerful horses."

My ancestors stemmed from solid, frugal, and prolific families who raised their children strictly and taught them right from wrong. They came from the ranks of farmers, dairy owners, millers, merchants, pastors, and especially teachers, as did so many other fledgling Americans who settled in Pennsylvania and Virginia. They were proud of their origins in the European homeland, preserving their heritage as they established church schools and built printing presses, developed skills as potters and furniture craftsmen, and perpetuated a musical culture they loved. Above all, my ancestors cherished their personal and religious freedoms. Their Protestantism remained strong until my father's generation. The parents of my great-grandfather named him Martin Luther

Grove. Antecedents of my grandmother Hambright set sail from Rotterdam on the *St. Andrew,* which landed in Philadelphia during October 1738, a year that saw an influx of pioneers. According to a newspaper account, conditions on board were terrible. "The love for great gain caused [Captain] Steadman to lodge the poor passengers like herrings, and as too many had not room between decks, he kept abundance of them upon deck; and sailing to the Southward, where people were at once out of their climate, and for want of water and room, became sick and died very fast."

After the French defeated Generals Braddock and Washington in 1775, Indian marauders roamed the frontiers of Pennsylvania where some of the Hambrights had settled, burning their cabins and scalping their families. Captain John Hambright, a frontier Indian fighter, was ordered the following year "to march with a party of two sergeants, two corporals, and 38 private men under your command to attack, burn and destroy any Indian town or towns, with their inhabitants, on the West Branch of the Susquehanna."

Because we lived abroad when I was a boy, and later on in Washington, I did not know my grandparents well. I associate my grandfather Harper Grove with a bulky hearing aid and my grandmother with meat loaf and baked beans, always topped with ketchup. She was captain of the neighborhood women's bowling team. Grandfather Grove, a stubborn man of principle, relinquished his engineering responsibilities on the Chicago subway construction project because he believed that the mayor's office was cheating on the quality of cement for the tunnel walls and that one day they would collapse. His superiors did not share his alarm, and as far as I know the walls have not collapsed.

Relatives have fought and sometimes died in every major American war from the Revolution to "Desert Storm." Colonel Frederick Hambright was a member of the Continental Congress; Benjamin Franklin at that Congress signed Captain Henry Hambright's commission. Wars later, my uncle Fred Grove volunteered as a pilot trainer in the Royal Air Force and was stationed at a base in England. In July 1941 he wrote to his parents in Chicago. "There is really nothing to worry or fret about. . . . Please ask Philip to give Harriet my Fraternity pin. I promised her she could wear it until I am in a position to offer her a better substitute." Soon afterward, America not yet at war, Fred was killed in a training accident.

My mother and father met at the University of Chicago, where he was a graduate student sorting mail at the post office at night to add to his income. Soon they married, and ten months later I appeared. My younger brother, Lloyd, was also born in Chicago. He is now a professor of languages and a translator of Baudelaire, but, because he values his privacy, this is nearly the last the reader will hear of him. Mother, whose English became accentless and fluent, worked at a federal relief center during the Depression where Polish speakers were needed to communicate with first-generation immigrants. Because she and my father had steady government incomes and modest needs, they fared better than many others in dispiriting years.

At four I attended the University of Chicago's experimental Lab School run according to the principles of John Dewey, which also shaped the educational philosophy of Bard College, from which I graduated. Outside school, boys sported Lindbergh-style flying helmets strapped below the chin, goggles on the forehead ready to pull down as the engine revved up. Charles A. Lindbergh's flight to Paris in 1927 was that era's equivalent of landing on the moon. The kidnapping of his son five years later would haunt families for a long time. On many a night before falling asleep in a fetal position I feared a kidnapper would climb through the window or, worse yet, was waiting under the bed, his clammy hand about to grab my ankle. My leading kindergarten memory is of being thrilled and terrified by Indians who visited us in feathered array to speak and dance before the class. Indian culture was then a more immediate part of life in Illinois. Another memory is of embarrassment when I dropped my lunch tray the day my father came to visit.

Later, when I was about ten and we were home from Europe for a while, we lived for nearly a year in Oklahoma City, where I went to the first of three schools I would attend named in honor of the late Woodrow Wilson. My father, by this time a petroleum geologist, worked and bunked at Socony-Vacuum Oil Company's camps in the drilling fields of Oklahoma and Texas to learn the oil business at the source. I grew up in a time of corduroy knickers making whooshing sounds as the baggy parts above the knees rubbed together when you walked; somehow at least one long sock managed to fall to an ankle. In cold weather fathers and sons wore leather jackets lined with sheepskin whose tightly curled wool collars had an oily smell that was sweet and reassuring. Friends and I played on vacant lots near school called prairies after those swaying fields of tall grass in the heartland. The games we played, our cap guns giving off manly fumes of gunpowder, were Cowboys and Indians, or Cops and Robbers, and the girls were nurses.

The world around us was a grownups' world in which we were youngsters striving to become adults, who seemed to be having more fun because it appeared they could do whatever they wanted. Radio programs like *The Shadow* and *The Lone Ranger*, reaching us through sound cabinets carved to look like

Gothic windows, excited our imaginations as we sat on the floor and listened. The mental images I created of the characters in my books and of their adventures were vivid and stayed with me. I lost all sense of the world around me, immersed in *Treasure Island*, *The Three Musketeers*, *Penrod*, *The Wizard of Oz*, and *The Last of the Mohicans*. I heard Aunt Polly calling out to Tom Sawyer and felt a rush of puppy love through Tom's enchantment with Becky Thatcher. Protagonists in these tales, men and boys of action, were not given to self-analysis, and nothing lastingly bad seemed to happen to good people.

Hitler's Germany, the Queen's Holland, and Franco's Spain

After receiving his doctorate from Chicago in geology and paleontology, my father was hired as a field geologist for Socony-Vacuum Oil Company, with its logo of Pegasus, the flying red horse. Proud of a hard-gained education, he kept his diploma with him as we moved about. He enjoyed recounting the story of his job interview. The chief geologist was looking for someone who could speak German, and my father had met the pro forma language requirement for his degree. Asked whether he knew German, my father said "Ja," adding in English, "We might continue this discussion in German if you'd like." "That won't be necessary," the chief geologist replied. Years later Socony became Mobil, and then ExxonMobil. I recall its headquarters behind the curved façade of 26 Broadway at Bowling Green on the tip of Manhattan, and the building's revolving doors that turned too fast for me. This was the most famous—and for its early history infamous—oil address in the world.

Dad was sent to Germany, and during 1935–1938 we lived in Hamburg. My formal schooling as a six-year-old began in German and archaic German script at the Bertram Schule, the last private school in Hamburg the Nazis allowed to remain open. Gym classes focused on skills useful to military service, among them developing accuracy in throwing dummy wooden hand grenades of World War I design. My classmates, all boys, included another American named Arthur Corwin, whose father also worked for Socony, and a Jewish boy, Ralf Cohen. Arthur was a straw-haired Tom Sawyer with an eye for mischief in which I usually joined for the fun and the scolding later on. Feeling like social outcasts as we struggled to learn German, Arthur and I befriended Ralf, who was bullied by our classmates but held his ground as a rough-and-tumble boy himself.

Built, probably, for a Hanseatic merchant out of a novel by Thomas Mann, our home was an Italianate villa on Harvestehudeweg, with a terrace overlooking the garden and the Alster beyond. From this lake's edges I guided branches, pretending they were ships, and admired the real sailboats on their tacks across the water. I often played there alone and in the rock garden behind our home, using a boy's powers of imagination to invent stories to explain my world to myself. Circumstances forced me to become self-reliant, a close but somewhat guarded observer of my surroundings, and inclined toward introspection. "We are made of time," observed the writer Octavio Paz. Hamburg was where my flow of memories began.

Christmas in Hamburg was like nowhere else, although I no longer believed in Santa Claus. There was snow and cake, and the nights came early. Our Christmas tree was decorated with candles lit by my father, a pail of water nearby for emergencies. I recall the smell of pine and tallow, the serenity of candlelight and shadows dancing on the ceiling, a feeling of being safe and happy in the bosom of my family.

One evening while my parents were out, our German maid Heidi called me into her bathroom to further my education, if only by a bit. Heidi was lying on her back, soaking in the tub. "I want to show you what I show my boyfriend," she said, but with residual modesty kept her knees together and hid from me the mystery of her womanhood. I gazed in admiration at two raspberry-nippled breasts and a blond thatch below her belly. That was all Heidi revealed, and I assumed no secrets remained. Women peed through their behinds, I figured, and you could hear them doing it when they sat down. This impression survived visits to museums where statues of unclad ladies showed similar restraint. There wasn't anything of further interest, a lad like me was led to believe.

By the mid-1930s a Nazi imprint defined Germany. Flags with swastikas flew everywhere. Men in uniform—storm troopers in brown shirts, SS guards wearing black coats—and civilians with Nazi armbands greeted each other on the streets with "Heil Hitler!" Martial music boomed during parades of goose-stepping soldiers; at bonfire rallies in the dark these troops sang in their jubilant voices, "Die Fahne Hoch...!" Raise high the flag...! Citywide air raid drills, initiated by the mournful, undulating wail of sirens, became part of life. Adolf Hitler's shrill voice and Joseph Goebbels's propaganda flooded the airwaves. Huge banners proclaimed "Ein Volk! Ein Reich! Ein Führer!" To me they made as much sense as the ubiquitous soap ads, "Ata! Imi! Persil!" At the Bertram Schule we sang "Deutschland, Deutschland über Alles" every morning.

All of this overwhelmed and thrilled me. Once Arthur and I managed to glimpse Hitler as his train crawled into Hamburg's station and from a window he held out his arm in the Nazi salute. My parents made it a point to tell me that what the Nazis were doing was wrong, and I took this on faith. The German mother of a schoolmate found a different way to explain Hitler. "In America you have President Roosevelt," she said; "in Germany we have Hitler." I knew about Roosevelt, who had responded to an economic crisis in my country, so at the time this seemed to make at least some sense. I played with lead soldiers that included brown-shirted troops and figures of Hitler, Himmler, Goebbels, and Göring to review them. In cautious tones my parents talked about concentration camps with a few of their German acquaintances, or with American friends who could discuss the subject more openly. For me that remained a forbidden topic. There were rumors of a camp for Jews near Hamburg, which turned out to be a grim reality, as we learned after the war. If foreigners knew this, certainly Germans did.

These experiences inspired a lifelong fascination with the complexities and contradictions of German history and culture. In the Foreign Service I was to live in Germany for six years more. When I studied to relearn the language, however, my vocabulary was capped at a boy's level and frustratingly did not include terms such as *value added tax*.

My parents would return to Hamburg for Socony soon after the war ended. In 1946 I found a city nearly devastated, hills of rubble piled up along its streets. A broken spirit had replaced Nazi arrogance. The merchant's home on Harvestehudeweg was undamaged. The Bertram Schule nearby had become a Red Cross headquarters. I managed to find my former headmaster, Claus Bertram, to whom I brought coffee, sugar, flour, cigarettes, and other luxuries from the British Post Exchange. I was embarrassed by the effusion of his thanks and, into my teens, felt awkward about the change in our roles. A warm, proud, and formal man, Herr Bertram had expected us to doff our berets to him on the playground; he had kept his school as liberal as he could until the Nazis closed it down. I was learning what war could do.

In 1938 my father was transferred to Holland, where I attended the English School at The Hague. Here was a language I could speak. My best friend, Ben Chang, son of the Chinese ambassador, told me one day that his father had forbidden him to invite me again to his home to play. Ben couldn't explain why and felt as awkward about this as I. We were learning an early lesson in the consequences of relations among nations. China was roiling in political turmoil, and Ambassador Chang apparently wanted to separate his family from friendships with Americans. There was also, I saw, a certain arrogance and racial prejudice on the part of my classmates toward Ben.

At school we learned in textbooks called *Our Island's Story* about a grand and imperial Britain of kings and queens, castles and dungeons, and possessions all over the world on which, we were proudly told, the sun never set. Large areas of wall maps in our classrooms were colored in imperial red. I took it for granted that the Prince of Wales was in charge of whales, which sounded like interesting work. I met entrancingly beautiful Elaine, my age as well, whose father worked at the British Embassy. Sometimes, as we sat together on a school step bent over a book, our heads would touch and remain touching, each knowing the other knew.

Before the war our travel was mostly by train, relatively little by automobile. Europe's main railroad stations, built at commercial hubs near grand hotels, were huge halls with glass-domed ceilings that let in light and kept the weather out. They were modern-day cathedrals, rib-vaulted architectural symbols of the iron and power of the Industrial Revolution. People rushing in every direction, the whistles, shrieks, and billowing steam, pushcart vendors closing their last sales—all conveyed the excitement of an adventure ready to unfold. Inside a coach compartment the windows slid down halfway so you could lean out as the train gave an initial, thrilling lurch and, with gasps from the engine, slowly gathered speed. Below these windows were brass signs with warnings in several languages not to lean out. My favorite was a scary injunction in Danish, *Laen dem ikke ud*, with its threat of having your head bashed in by a telegraph pole racing toward you and then going straight to Hell.

Socony moved us from The Hague to Madrid, and once more we rode on railroad tracks. The Palace Hotel was a splendid establishment in which we, as foreigners, lived. Spain had been torn apart by a civil war bringing General Francisco Franco to power with Hitler's and Mussolini's support. I was disconcerted to encounter Nazi officers with their shiny boots, swastika armbands, and peaked hats swaggering through the halls. In the hospitable environment of Franco's Spain they were at ease, smoking and bantering, appearing all the more startling without the goose-steps. Avoiding their eyes I shot past.

The fighting in and around Madrid had been fierce and had ended not long before we arrived. Buildings were in ruin and poverty widespread. Bullets had chipped façades throughout the city, and I re-created scenes of street fighting. Those scars and bullet holes have since been patched, leaving blemishes shades lighter than the gray stone building fronts themselves. You can find them around doors and windows if you look. I was troubled to see women in black, their children in ragged clothing, who huddled with outstretched palms in front of restaurants and watched us through the windows while we ate paella.

My parents enrolled me in the French Lycée, where I studied in another new language while picking up street Spanish. Children do their best language learning on playgrounds because they need to. At the Lycée a fellow student who spoke little English, but as an Italian in a French school understood my plight, helped me as much as he could in adjusting to the Lycée's culture. Having to study Spanish in a class taught in French and finding myself without American friends was a discouraging experience. I felt unhappy about having to live in a huge hotel, when no one else I knew did. As in previous schools I was teased about being from Chicago, the gangster capital of the world, something that made me feel guilty.

Moving at an early age from country to country and school to school created a life that was lonely. My younger brother and I were nearly six years apart. Lasting friendships were hard to make. Few youthful experiences were more intimidating than being the new boy in class, the outsider. Feeling like an oddball, I wanted to please everyone, to be accepted by the group. I rebelled and played hooky. Before reaching college I went to sixteen schools and learned to function in three languages. Solitude fostered independence and a way of looking at the world with greater knowledge, insight, and empathy. Forced to rely on my wits, I learned to amuse myself through my imagination and to find the comedy in life. Later I would discover the absurdity.

Coming Home

My mother, my brother, and I left Europe early in 1941 on one of the last transatlantic passenger liners carrying civilians to the United States before war made such crossings too dangerous. My father stayed behind in Spain to complete his exploration for oil, but soon he would be working at 26 Broadway and we would live in Bronxville until America entered the war and we were drawn to Washington. As we sailed from the continent under darkened ship conditions with a British destroyer escort part of the way, I understood that the Germans among whom we lived had invaded my mother's native Poland and the Holland we knew. The pageantry of the Nazis that I had experienced in Hamburg had turned into something evil and threatening whose implications I could not yet grasp. I had been living in a world beyond American shores where the seeds of a diplomatic life were sown, something I would recognize many years later.

We were embarked on one of my family's many voyages across the Atlantic, and I had acquired a love of the ocean and ships and the freedom of open waters. I was thrilled each time to reach the red *Ambrose* lightship off America's shore and to sight Coney Island's parachute-jump tower. Then, on the final leg to our berth in "luxury liner row," we glided past the Statue of Liberty, Ellis Island, and Manhattan's stately skyscrapers, presided over by the Empire State Building. They told me I was coming home.

Fathers and Sons

While I was finishing this memoir my uncle Henry Grove, who lives in Skokie, Illinois, sent me a letter he and his wife, Alice, had come upon while rummaging through old files. It was from my father in Madrid to my grandfather in Chicago, written on February 9, 1941. Dad was still living at the Palace Hotel after we sailed for New York, as recounted above. "Since my family is gone I am frequently lonely, and it is much easier to find time to write letters." Reading his clear and familiar handwriting (he was left-handed and worked at this) I discovered a new dimension to my father—how, at thirty-seven, he related to *his* Dad. I found an effort to please and to make his father proud of him, just as I related to my own father. Dad described an incident I do not remember but was moved to hear him tell because it brought him back and made me admire him again, feel his fatherly love again. "Just this morning I received a letter from Brandon Jr., the first since he reached America. It consisted of an introductory paragraph, and the whole of Van Dyke's poem, 'America for Me.' That poem means more after one has lived in Europe, and it meant a lot to me that my son, who has lived more than half his life abroad, should turn to it spontaneously and so quickly."

2

WAR, PEACE, AND MORE WAR

1942 to 1954

Washington, a provincial city in the north of the South defined by small-scale architecture, tree-lined avenues, and historical monuments, was transforming itself in 1942 into the strategic and bureaucratic command center for a two-front war.

Construction of the Pentagon to house the headquarters of a rapidly expanding American military establishment was nearing completion. This would be the largest office building in the world. Un-air-conditioned barracks along the Mall, built during World War I, were converted into spaces for people like my father on sabbatical from corporate life to do war-related work. From the Board of Economic Warfare he would help plan Allied measures, mainly through bombing raids, to deny oil to the Axis Powers. A lifelong Democrat, a patriot, and too young to have participated in the First World War, he relished being part of the current effort. Now *his* war had come.

My friends and I flocked to vast pep rallies, called "Back the Attack," staged on the Mall. They featured the top bands and vocalists of the day and the latest military equipment, including Jeeps, and they promoted the sale of war bonds. The streets of Washington filled with people saluting each other, civilians learning to identify them by insignia and rank. In a practice originated by Woodrow Wilson during World War I, homes displayed small white banners with blue stars in their windows to proclaim husbands, sons, and daughters in military service. Soon blue stars changed to gold for those who had died.

We knew who our enemies were and what would be required to defeat them. Norman Rockwell's sturdy, cheeky Rosie the Riveter with her lunch pail, a woman in overalls doing a man's job because he had gone off to war, exemplified new vitality in a post-Depression America. Many a Rosie would refuse afterward to revert to the monotonous existence of a "housewife" and would compete with returning veterans searching for what used to be men's work.

Where would we live? Homes and even hotel rooms for people like us pouring into Washington from every part of the country became difficult to find. My parents finally rented a two-bedroom apartment in McLean Gardens, a sprawling project built to meet the housing shortage "for a white war worker." From there I rode the Wisconsin Avenue streetcar a few stops to Alice Deal Junior High, and later to Woodrow Wilson High School. Both were racially segregated, something we took for granted. Meat, butter, sugar, and canned goods, as well as nylon stockings, tires or anything else made of rubber, cigarettes, soap, and gasoline were rationed and required tokens and stamps from coupon books to pay for the points they cost along with the purchase price. With only an "A" sticker for three gallons of gasoline a week, we hardly used our car.

Washingtonians were required to hang blackout shades in their windows so the capital would be more difficult for enemy bombers to find, and local snoopers were on the lookout for cracks of light shining around the edges. School-children were drilled in "duck and cover" exercises, taking shelter under their desks to avoid potential bomb injuries. My father volunteered to be an air raid warden on our block and was issued a white helmet, a flashlight, an armband, and a whistle. During drills he and his companions were in the streets checking blackout compliance in McLean Gardens. The havoc of bombs dropped by Hitler's Luftwaffe on London during sixty-seven consecutive nights in 1940 was on people's minds.

At Woodrow Wilson High I did my part by joining the cadet corps. We were instructed in close-order drill by a retired infantry officer and marched around the neighborhood with World War I rifles when we weren't carrying wooden ones. Cadets were proud of their dark blue uniforms with brass buttons and white web belts worn twice a week to class for drill afterward. Even we thought it odd, however, that the regulation white shirts required detachable collars with studs and that garters were prescribed to hold up our socks. By high school graduation in June 1945, we young men had every reason to expect we soon would be fighting "the Japs" on remote Pacific islands or on the Japanese mainland itself, likely getting killed in the effort. My own war was inching closer. It did not occur to any of us to avoid this prospect as our families and we listened to news of the war on the radio every night. Ironically, the honored guest at our wartime graduation was Edith Galt Wilson, the elderly widow of the former president whose concept of a League of Nations to insure peace had failed. Two atomic bombs dropped on Japan brought hostilities to an end.

Fordham to Vienna

I tried to get into college. This proved difficult as, having skipped a year of high school in an accelerated academic program, I was only a few weeks past sixteen. The GI Bill would provide 2.3 million veterans subsidized educations. Colleges, whose student bodies had shrunk and become increasingly female during the war, suddenly found their admissions offices swamped by applications from GIs in their early twenties and older. Turned down by Columbia and NYU, I was accepted at Fordham University in the Bronx. Living on campus in soulless Dealy Hall, I came to resist what I perceived as the rigid discipline and narrow, arid outlook of the Jesuits at Fordham. The floors of this dormitory's high corridors were covered with worn linoleum, and the doors to our rooms had transoms above them to circulate the air. At ten o'clock the Jesuit living on each landing conducted a bed check.

My devout mother raised me to be a Roman Catholic. Although I was stirred by the mystery of a mass intoned in Latin, I objected to confessing to priests, to an Index of proscribed books, to an infallible pope, and to a deity who permitted such misery in a world of its own creation. I found the concepts of an immaculate conception, transubstantiation, and resurrection beyond my grasp. The gimmickry bothered me: I sometimes felt treated like a fool. Our instructor in religion, for example, told us that if we penciled the initials MJJ, standing for Mary, Jesus, and Joseph, at the bottom of our blue books during exams, this would be taken as a favorable sign, but by whom was not clear. Did I do this? You bet I did.

My year at Fordham convinced me Catholicism was not a religion I could embrace, and at this Jesuit institution I became detached from my faith. My view of human existence had shifted toward Nabokov's image of the brief crack of light. I was becoming a secular humanist, as good a characterization as any of my outlook on life. But when an opportunity in a church somewhere presents itself I light a candle for my mother.

In 1946, taking what would have been my sophomore year off, I accompanied my parents to Vienna, where my father for a while was an assimilated colonel wearing an army uniform and offering an unmilitary salute. He soon reverted to suits and patterned ties to become petroleum attaché at our legation in the Boltzmanngasse. His chief task was to prevent the Soviets from dismantling the Zistersdorf oil refineries, located in their zone of occupation, and then shipping the pieces to Russia. Once again he had been seconded to our government as a petroleum expert. The European winter of 1946–1947 was among the harshest, and the Viennese suffered bitterly as coal supplies dwindled. We lived in an imposing but sparsely furnished and underheated villa in the Blaas Strasse, requisitioned for us by the army. Its former occupant had been the Hitler Youth leader for Austria.

As I explored Vienna with newly found friends, some from our legation, we learned about Four Power occupation responsibilities, opulent PXs and black markets, cigarettes as currency, demimonde liaisons between prostitutes and the military, Four Power street patrols in Jeeps, and the significance of sectors within a city and zones within a country. Even with good intentions, occupiers acquire an arrogant cast through their unlimited powers and contrasting cultures and lifestyles. We youngsters jitterbugged in the nightclub downstairs at the "American" Bristol Hotel while the Viennese froze and scavenged for food and lumps of black coal dropped in the snow as delivery trucks were unloaded. The customary tip for a waiter was a single cigarette per person. I had my first encounter with Soviet forces, an unmilitary, brutish, and ignorant lot. The Viennese called them *Uhr Raueber*, or watch thieves. Impoverished and rubble-strewn, Vienna acquired a postwar aura of decay and decadence. As Harry Lime in the 1949 film of Graham Greene's *The Third Man*, with its haunting zither theme, Orson Welles captured the tawdriness and cynicism of the time.

A few of the people I knew were budding musicians, and we turned to the city's lively musical scene, finding seats in crowded, unheated concert halls where we wore our coats and boots to performances. Earlier I recounted losing my faith at a Jesuit college; in further irony, my boredom with opera originated in Vienna. A young Polish pianist, Andrzej Wasowski, already acclaimed for his interpretations of Chopin, became a lifelong friend. We met during an evening of piano playing at an American major's home, and afterward my Polish mother practically adopted Andrzej.

At the end of the summer of 1947, and with my return to studies in the United States imminent, Andrzej and I concocted a reckless scheme to smuggle him out of Austria. Our plan involved the Arlberg Orient Express as it crossed the Soviet Zone on its way to Switzerland, a journey of twenty hours. Boarding in Vienna, we would have tickets to Paris. Andrzej, behaving like the high-strung and disorganized artist he already was, would pretend to Russian border guards examining our documents on the train that he had misplaced the Gray Pass required to exit their zone, with its official stamps from the Soviet Kommandatura he could not as a Pole have obtained. He would search frantically through his luggage to find it. I would attest to its existence by waving my own pass and berating Andrzej for his carelessness. In a winner-take-all effort to find the right moment, I would express our apologies and offer cartons of American cigarettes as tokens of remorse.

In the event, this was a tense business. In the middle of the night we awaited the arrival of two inspecting border guards, weapons strapped to their shoulders. Alongside the tracks in the countryside I could make out shadowy figures of other guards with automatic weapons posted at intervals to prevent anyone from getting off the train. They wore high boots, baggy trousers, tunics gathered with a belt, red stars on their caps. Only steam hissing from our train broke the silence. The inspectors moved slowly through a hushed coach toward our compartment as they opened and then slammed shut the sliding doors along the way. We heard one of the Russians demanding "Dokumenti!" at each compartment and wondered what they looked like in the flesh. Our fears when they appeared and uttered that terrifying word were genuine, as were Andrzej's hysterics as he searched for his nonexistent Gray Pass. As we went through our paces, these young, pimply, rough-cut Russian farm boys rebuked us in broken German, staring all the while at Andrzej. I pictured him being dragged off the train. In the end nicotine won out. The guards left with our cigarettes safely in their briefcases, the train crept forward, and Andrzej, by then in tears of relief, gained his freedom eventually to become a pianist of world renown. He settled in the United States and died in 1993, at the age of seventy-four.

Bard

Determined in the fall of 1947 not to return to Fordham, and at the urging of my boyhood friend Sam Allen, I applied to Bard, a small "progressive" college for some 270 students in New York's Hudson Valley. Sam and I first got together in the fifth grade at the Brookside School in Montclair, New Jersey, while my father was exploring for oil—this time in the Magdalena Valley of Colombia. Soon we were soul mates deciding to become archaeologists and go on digs in Egypt. We spent many hours poring over Howard Carter and A. C. Mace's account of the discovery, in 1922, of the tomb of Tutankhamen in the Valley of the Kings. Afterward we remained in touch through our letters.

Bard was a pioneering institution during America's midcentury revolution in higher education. Courses were taught in seminars, and the student-teacher ratio was often two or three to one. The Hoffman Library came alive as its librarian, the history professor Felix Hirsch, guided students in all disciplines through the stacks and loaded them up with books. Winter field periods provided opportunities to work and study in the world beyond the college—in my case two internships at the State Department. With an interest in foreign relations, I was allowed to major for one year each in history, economics, and government. My Senior Project was a thesis entitled "Foreign Policy Coordination in the Executive Branch of the Government," researched in Washington through interviews and written under the tutelage of the presidential scholar Louis W. Koenig. Bard, so unlike many other colleges, existed for the individual student, not the other way around. I felt for the first time an awareness of the presence of knowledge I needed to acquire and understand. And yet Bard was constantly on the verge of going broke and having to close its doors.

In America's institutions of higher learning during the immediate postwar period the average age of men was four or five years above my own seventeen. For the most part they knew about hardship, combat, death, drink, sex, and partying and were serious about studies and life. They worked hard, played hard, and thought about their goals. Women adapted quickly and expected their younger dates to act maturely. Greenhorns like me, who had been high school cadets with wooden rifles, had some growing up to do. Veterans enriched the tone of campus life and deepened seminar discussions by drawing on the intellectual and emotional residues of their wartime experiences. Their influence on academia in the late forties and early fifties was pervasive and lasting. They transformed the learning experience and became role models for many like me, leaving us grateful for having spent college and graduate school years in their company. Challenged, I began to build self-confidence. With my parents living in Egypt, Bard became my home. I was happy there.

While at Bard, Sam and I soaked up the excitement of a postwar explosion in the arts. As roommates earning money by waiting on tables and sorting students' mail, we explored the galleries along Fifty-seventh Street in New York, bought cheap standing-room-only tickets behind the orchestra seats of Broadway's theaters, went to the movies to be transported by Fred Astaire and Ginger Rogers, and discovered gin and Dixieland bands in the bars of a gentler Greenwich Village. Cole Porter's lyrics celebrated romantic love and happy endings, and we sought to make them come true. What could promise more of an evening than the lights of Manhattan, its slender buildings standing apart like blades of grass on which dewdrops sparkled in luminous splendor? The end of the forties was a time of optimism, of having the world on a string, and what a giddy lift such fare provided. Yet in the daylight outside, over that city of litter and infinite angles of architecture, clouds of a cold war gathered while few paid attention.

No place exerts a stronger pull on my love of countryside, a wide river, and a feeling of belonging to the earth than Duchess County, New York. The areas around Red Hook and Rhinebeck are changing with the times and urban sprawl, but I find the remaining open spaces, apple orchards and woods, white frame homes and red barns, and the banks of the Hudson River at Barrytown much as they were at midcentury and as exuberantly American as the music of Aaron Copland. The bell in Bard's chapel tolls melancholy notes as it has for a hundred fifty years and more. In the valley below, the wail of a loco-motive running along its tracks beside the Hudson echoes through the nights. For me, there is nowhere a more wondrous sense of the moods, colors, smells, and wetness of changing seasons than at Bard.

McCarthy

Two months before our graduation, on February 9, 1950, an obscure Re-publican senator made a breathtakingly false statement before an audience of women in Wheeling, West Virginia. "I have in my hand," said Joseph R. McCarthy, of Wisconsin, "a list of 205 Communists that were made known to the Secretary of State and who nevertheless are still working and shaping the policy of the State Department." One of the first but few Republican sen-ators to challenge him was John Sherman Cooper, of Kentucky. "You have to prove that," he told McCarthy, but the senator from Wisconsin disagreed.

Such a list did not exist, there were no names at all, and McCarthy had no idea what he was talking about. But at a time when I was preparing for a diplomatic career this was far from obvious. Alger Hiss in the State Depart-ment, Harry Dexter White at Treasury, and Julius and Ethel Rosenberg with the Manhattan Project developing the atomic bomb had by 1946 been uncov-ered as Soviet spies. After the New Deal and World War II the worst seemed over. As I read more concerning McCarthy's charges I became uneasy for a time about joining the Foreign Service and was disturbed to see what a hounded organization it had become. A profession I thought of as worthwhile—even noble in some aspects—was under assault by an unprincipled politician re-strained by no one. For decades to come, people in government service would live with the damage McCarthy caused, which was compounded by the manner in which he was tolerated before self-immolating.

Joan Williams and Faulkner

Through Joan Williams, a classmate from Memphis majoring in literature, I came to know William Faulkner for a brief but intense time. Joan's writing career took flight in her junior year at Bard when she won the first prize in a college fiction contest sponsored by *Mademoiselle*. Her short story, "Rain Later," was published in the magazine's August 1949 issue. In her writing Joan was drawn to problems within her family that burdened her, to relations between blacks and whites living in ambiguous proximity, and to incompatible people with incompatible goals and appetites bound to each other by nearness and fate. The setting for these unhappy lives was her part of a hot and airless South as passionate and despairing as Faulkner's Yoknapatawpha County.

At Bard both of us felt distanced from our families, Joan because of parental drinking at home, and I because my parents were living abroad. Early in our friendship, when I had been away over a weekend, I came back to Bard to find a note from her in my mailbox. Welcome home, it said, and I realized we were falling in love. We were inner-directed people of emotional depth and sensitivity and by nature both close observers of what was happening around us: easily slighted, but easily amused, too. Joan, with social and personal insecurities, was good-natured and popular with everyone. She was more open about herself than I who became class president. She had been married in an impetuous relationship her father caused to be annulled.

Joan's mother, Maude, had been a Mississippi hill-country music teacher before marrying, and her father, "P. H." Williams, was a prosperous Tennessee dynamite salesman at a time of regional dam projects. Joan wore saddle shoes and bobby socks, skirts reaching well below the knee, sweater sets with necklaces, and garter belts like harnesses beneath dressier clothes. She had short and wavy chestnut hair, freckles under greenish eyes, and a beguiling girlish jauntiness that matched her southern accent. She said "srimp," rather than "shrimp," and this was what I called her when I wasn't calling her Myrna because she looked like the actress Myrna Loy.

Joan admired Faulkner's *The Sound and the Fury*. During the summer of 1949, while staying with her parents in Memphis, she and a cousin tried to see him at Rowan Oak. Their visit was brief and not warm, so Joan later wrote to Faulkner explaining how she felt about herself and her writing. He did not respond. When she returned to Bard in the fall, she wrote again with questions about writing, not expecting a reply. I was with her when his letter came. Ecstatic, she took it to her room to read privately before showing it to me. I felt threatened by Faulkner's words: "These are the wrong questions. A woman must ask these of a man while they are lying in bed together...when they are lying at peace or at least quiet or maybe on the edge of sleep so you'll have to wait, even to ask them."

I first met Faulkner with Joan in the fall of 1949 in the cocktail lounge of One Fifth Avenue, the apartment hotel in Manhattan where he was staying. Surely he recognized me as her boyfriend, yet his greeting seemed warm to the point of tenderness. Faulkner liked to drink, puff on his pipe, tell stories, laugh his quiet chuckle, and talk about the South. He was short and powerful, calm, courtly, reserved. A soft-spoken, silver-haired, and handsome man in a patrician way, he sported a guardsman's trimmed mustache and dressed nattily while in New York, looking in his tweeds like a country squire. His voice was measured and husky, sensuous and intimate in its Mississippi sounds. Listening to him I came under his spell, squinting slightly and leaning forward to hear him clearly. He was comfortable with long pauses in conversation and easily retreated within himself. Faulkner's eyes appeared sad to me, his gaze barely masking pain. He seemed weighed down, defeated maybe, by some undiscardable burden forced upon him by his southern heritage.

Faulkner, in his early fifties, told us it was a shame so little had been written about people in the later years of life. Their stories were rich and interesting but ignored by writers of fiction, a reflection of our society and values. I could only guess at the extent to which he recognized himself, at more than twice Joan's age, as driven by a longing for her that collided with Joan's view of him as literary mentor. I thought of Joan and Faulkner as kindred voices, thirty-one years apart, supporting each other in shared feelings stemming from their southern backgrounds and the gentleness of them both.

When I visited Joan in Memphis in 1950 as we explored our relationship further, we spent a day in Oxford, Mississippi, at Faulkner's Rowan Oak, where he showed us the typewriter on which he wrote in his high-ceilinged, sparsely furnished library. We later drove to his boat at Sardis Dam for a picnic. On the way he pulled off the road and got ice out of the car, chipped it to break it open, and made drinks. Joan remembered my saying to her, "Can you imagine being on a back road with Faulkner breaking ice to fix a drink?" His wife, Estelle, arrived before us. The atmosphere was strained because of Faulkner's interest in Joan.

That year Faulkner received the Nobel Prize for Literature. In his acceptance speech in Stockholm he said, "Our tragedy today is a general and universal physical fear so long sustained by now that we can even bear it. There are no longer problems of the spirit. There is only the question: When will I be blown up?" I asked him later to inscribe a reprint of his first novel, *Soldiers Pay*, a request that annoyed Joan. He thought for a moment and wrote: "To Brandon Grove with tenderest regards. William Faulkner at Joan Williams' 16 May 1953." I liked him very much even while he, too, was in love with Joan.

After we graduated from Bard, our lives took different paths, Joan moving eventually to Greenwich Village to learn her craft, and I to Princeton to learn mine. For the first time I felt the pain of breaking up. Joan's quixotic friendship with Faulkner blossomed as he introduced her to others in the publishing circles of New York and wrote impassioned letters to her from Oxford. I don't know whether their relationship came to more than that, as he wanted it to, but doubt that it did. She said of him later, "I never thought of myself as Faulkner's girlfriend. He was a lonesome man when we met. He knew his best writing was over and he said he wished it could be fun again." Joan soon began dating Ezra Bowen, a sportswriter and son of the historian Katherine Drinker Bowen. She married him in 1954.

Glimpses of the State Department

Two six-week internships in Washington, in 1948 and one year later, returned me to a city I had not lived in since the end of the war. Some of the provincialism was gone, but the place had not yet experienced the eruption of law firms, nongovernmental organizations, think tanks, decent restaurants, and centers of culture that would cause rapid growth from the 1960s of the Kennedy years onward. Washington continued to function on a human scale. The mansion of the nation's chief executive remained modest.

When I first walked into the State Department building on Twenty-first Street as a student intern, I was thrilled to be there. From these offices—I disregarded their drab and cramped appearances—the most powerful nation on earth was in constant communication with its diplomatic posts across the globe. In a struggle against international communism, decisions made there affected the future of mankind. Secretary of State Dean Acheson had photogenic panache with his well-cut suits, British mustache, and aristocratic bearing—an ideal statesman for Eurocentric times and a role model for American diplomats in Truman's day.

During my first internship I worked in a dreary office outside the mainstream called the Division of Foreign Reporting Services, where my job was to type up comments on dispatches from abroad made by the reviewers in

Washington who were their primary readers. For the most part favorable, anodyne, and all but meaningless, these assessments would be sent back to their originators overseas to form part of their performance files. The practice has long since been abandoned, but I found out how a State Department office functioned, where our posts were located, and the subject matter of routine, bread-and-butter reporting in the Foreign Service on economic and commercial issues and on political developments that were not particularly urgent.

In my second internship I was a clerk-typist in the geographic office dealing with Andean affairs in Latin America, where I learned what embassies did and how they meshed with the State Department. The Foreign Service officers I met spoke Spanish, knew the region from serving there, and strove each day to advance our objectives in relations. They were hardworking, informal, intellectually oriented, and mostly cheerful people. One of them, Louis J. Halle, had just completed *Spring in Washington,* a Jeffersonian sort of book that said something about its author's qualities of mind and spirit.

Security within the State Department early in the Cold War was all but nonexistent. People came and went at will without passing through checkpoints at the entrances and roamed the halls without being identified as visitors. Security awareness among people at the State Department seemed focused on closing one's safe with a bar and padlock at the end of the day, and trying to remember to do so during lunch breaks as well.

On discovering one morning that Acheson would be holding a press conference in the State Department's small second-floor auditorium, I decided to attend and found no difficulty in joining twenty or so polite and respectful members of the press, men dressed in suits with their hats placed on seats beside them. Acheson, perched on the corner of a table with one foot on the floor, hands clasped in his lap, held forth with exactitude and eloquence. There were no cameras or microphones. My strongest memory, beyond the force of his appearance, is of a confident mastery of issues ranging across the globe, his observations delivered in a straightforward manner.

After my internships and as the end of undergraduate days at Bard approached, I faced a decision about roads not to be taken. Should I become a lawyer or a diplomat? Both professions required verbal and negotiating skills, discipline, and powers of persuasion, and both valued precedents and the binding nature of agreements. But diplomacy differed from law by calling for leadership, management, and policy implementation skills, and also in the nature of the then poorly paid government service, not to mention the challenges to oneself and one's family of living overseas.

My childhood years in Europe, my schooling in German and French, and my interest in an evolving American role abroad and in new instruments of diplomacy such as the United Nations and the Marshall Plan made government service a logical choice. There were other pulls as well, not least a love of travel to exotic places fueled by Richard Halliburton, whose books of adventuresome derring-do I devoured as a boy, along with a youthful ambition to become an archaeologist in Egypt digging away with my boyhood chum Sam Allen.

Princeton

Before the outbreak of the Korean War in June 1950, I was admitted into Princeton's recently established graduate program at the Woodrow Wilson School of Public and International Affairs, where I continued my studies under draft deferments. Twenty-six of us in the school's two-year program, half from other nations, met for our seminars in a former eating club on Prospect Street. Princeton's stately campus dominated the bucolic village surrounding it, and town and gown usually got along well.

On Mercer Street, I might encounter a casually dressed Albert Einstein taking a stroll, his white hair going off in all directions from a deeply lined face. Bundled up in winter he looked more like an old woman than a man. Traffic on Nassau Street, the main thoroughfare, was light except during football weekends, when young women descending from trains at Princeton Junction brightened our existence like a sunburst after rain. I was fortunate to come to know several families and their daughters who had lived in Princeton for a long time. Through their hospitality I felt myself a part of the township as well as of the university.

The architect Ralph Adams Cram had modeled Princeton's graduate college on Oxford and Cambridge. Under the influence of Woodrow Wilson's presidency of the university, graduate dean Andrew Fleming West imitated in elitist and anachronistic ways some of the high-table traditions of those ancient institutions. Undergraduates called the place "Goon Castle." At dinner, we were required to wear black and flowing academic gowns that in no time acquired food stains by which their owners could recognize them instantly. Clad in mine as the student-elected Master in Residence, I regularly spoke an evening grace in Latin and lived in an oak-paneled Master's Suite two floors high with its own library, a stone fireplace, spiral stairs, and a striking view from the balcony of the golf links below. To welcome a weekly dinner

speaker and a small group of students in his field—for this was always a man—
I served inexpensive Christian Brothers Sherry before a fireplace fronted by a
lion's skin with its head attached.

A revolt against gowns fueled by radical elements among the engineering
and math students erupted in the fall of 1952, and a great debate was set to
take place in the Common Room one evening after dinner. World War II was
not that far behind, and some of the veterans found the custom of gowns out-
dated and silly. I presided in my gown over a rowdy session during which
scholars with improvised robes and weirdly painted faces climbed in and out
of windows fronting the golf links. But "gownies" won the vote handily, to
the relief of the graduate school's apprehensive dean. The New Yorker devoted
a couple of paragraphs to this odd event, providing it a place in American
cultural history.

I invited Joan Williams and Faulkner to visit Princeton and meet in the
Master's Suite with some of the English majors. About forty students sat on
the floor around Faulkner's chair. The event did not turn out as I had hoped.
Faulkner disliked encounters like these and was not a speaker by inclination.
I introduced him and invited discussion. He was moody and had little to say,
brief in his responses to questions and comments. But that, too, was Faulkner.
While the students were pleased to meet a writer of his renown and I was
honored to have him visit, I felt Faulkner had come only as a favor to Joan.

Norval Crawford White, who would become an architect and write guidebooks about the neighborhoods and buildings of New York and Paris, was my
roommate. Six feet six and sturdier than I, balding and funny, he was a strong-
willed, committed student, a graduate of M.I.T. Through him and his extro-
verted friends, and frequent visitors like social philosopher Buckminster
"Bucky" Fuller, creator of the geodesic dome, I gained an appreciation of architecture. Norval taught me how to look at a building to understand its components, how to see it in its surroundings. I learned how architects fashioned
their designs based on the intended use of a site and the functions and forms
of the structures to be built—knowledge I would draw upon forty years later.
Gordon Bunshaft's graceful Lever House on Park Avenue at Fifty-third Street
in New York had just been completed and stood in contrast to other buildings
as a beacon of corporate modernism. Norval and I often went to look at it. I
learned, at risk to myself and others, to enjoy walking along a city's streets
while examining the façades of buildings and the zigzagging lines their roof-
tops etched in the skies.

Academically, I found many of the required readings in government and
international relations excessively theoretical, burdened by self-conscious jar-

gon, and at times indigestible. A faddish emphasis on quantification in the political "sciences" was difficult to grasp and hard to accept. I earned a D in my course on international relations and almost didn't graduate. I preferred Professor Gabriel Almond's interdisciplinary approach to the policy-making process. In his seminar I examined the roles of pressure groups in the United States during the period leading to our recognition of Israel in 1948, and got an A.

The poems and plays of T. S. Eliot influenced many of us at the time. His voice resonated with students in the fifties, young people beginning to experience an unfamiliar Cold War and its offshoot in Korea. Like others I turned to Eliot's erudition, self-assurance, and calm, the cadence of his words and his whimsy about cats, the better to understand myself. He bridged times for which I felt nostalgia—prewar Europe in a youthful life—with a harsher world in which I now was obliged to seek my fortune.

During Bard and Princeton weekends, social life for those so inclined centered on cocktail parties in students' dorms, occasions for which one dressed in jacket and tie and often brought a date. People reached for sophistication: the quip, the pun, a bon mot. These gatherings formed part of the culture of the fifties. We may not have known of the Algonquin Round Table of the twenties, but we were emulating it. Music, whether classical, Dixieland, or the songs of Cole Porter sung by Ella Fitzgerald, set the mood. So did habit-forming alcohol, to which we turned, men and women alike, for relaxation, self-confidence, and loquacity. People like me learned to drink as students and ever after would as a matter of course have cocktails or wine at the end of a day, still reaching for the bon mot. Gin martinis were preferred at the time and were made strong, inspiring behavior that could lead to remorse when more than two drinks were imbibed. My father acquired the taste during Prohibition.

Egypt

By then my father was in charge of Socony-Vacuum Oil of Egypt, and I spent the summer of 1951 with my parents in Cairo. The scent of jasmine on the breezes after sunset and a softness in the air along the Nile were new and beguiling experiences. Except for the commanding and conspicuously modern Semiramis, great hotels and skyscrapers did not yet line the river's banks. Men wore tarbooshes on their heads, and some bore the titles *bey* or *pasha* after their names. A young, corrupt, and immensely fat King Farouk, the prototypical playboy, sat on his throne. This was the aristocratic Anglo-Egyptian world of the original Shepherd's Hotel, before it burned down in rioting, and of the Gezira Sporting Club, where *pok-pok* sounds of tennis balls spoke of status and leisure. Cairo was a city with social and political tensions bubbling below the surface, discontent fanned by Soviet ambitions in the Middle East.

Dad was one of the midcentury's business diplomats, alert and tough negotiators who lived abroad and represented their companies to princes, sheiks, and cabinet ministers, carrying the flag for American investors as ambassadors did for sovereign states. Understanding of others and tolerant of their views, my father acquired a reputation in the oil business for being a thoughtful person knowledgeable about the region. A strategic thinker, he was attuned to cultures and players on all sides. Through his gift for courtesy he knew how to be friendly toward people of differing backgrounds. He listened patiently to what was said and left unsaid and came to his own conclusions about what was going on and what it meant for the oil companies. From some of his telephone conversations with the home office in New York, I unavoidably gleaned that he was a relentlessly honest man who called the shots as he saw them, even while irritating colleagues at headquarters who had preconceived ideas of their own. He was persistent and believed that what one learned on the scene and by being well traveled elsewhere mattered. From him, a businessman, I learned about diplomacy that worked.

It wasn't always business with Dad, however. While living in London, he enjoyed entertaining on Mobil's expense account at the finest restaurants, dancing afterward, and poking around in museums on weekends. Reading thrillers, going with mother to the opera at Glyndebourne in black tie, or driving alone through Spain were some of his pleasures. He valued time by himself and had a moody side brought on by a weakness for scotch and a belief that life, all in all, was a disappointing proposition—but against what standards of fulfillment he never said. A clue to his values lay in his strongest epithet: *phony*. When I listen to Beethoven's "Moonlight Sonata" I think of him. This was the one piece of music he played on the piano. His calling as a geologist led him to a world of fossils and rock formations and inspired him to contemplate the meaning and the effects of time and its passage. With a geologist's hammer he cracked time open as he studied the inside of a rock. This could be unsettling because of questions about nature and humanity to which such probing gave rise, questions he liked to turn over in his mind.

My father and I had a close and affectionate relationship, if inherently a bit reserved on both sides. We tended in a misguided sense of manliness to prevent our deeper emotions from showing, although we knew when they were tapped. My father dreaded crying in a movie theater, and when he could no longer contain his feelings they erupted in a great sob that undid me. During stopovers in London to visit him while I was in the Foreign Service, dusk would find us leaning against a kitchen counter, ankles crossed, sipping drinks and talking. We spoke in the shorthand of people who thought alike, sharing in mother's despair during her many years of suffering from Alzheimer's, then a poorly diagnosed and tragically misunderstood disease. For a long time I had difficulty in being patient with her fading memory, in understanding how a woman who had once been so vivacious could lose her way navigating in her own apartment and need to ask for directions to her bathroom.

In the days of my first visit to Egypt the pyramids of Giza sat alone in the desert beyond Cairo. Dad insisted I first see them in moonlight, and I remain grateful for that. Near the end of summer three newfound friends and I, Carter Hills from Princeton and the Baltazzi sisters, Emma and Eileen, daughters of the naval attaché at our embassy, decided to climb the Great Cheops Pyramid. We did not expect anyone there to object but kept our intentions from overly protective parents.

Driving from Cairo before dawn we arrived at sunrise and paid baksheesh to a young Bedouin at the base to point out the safest route he alone could see. Our new friend cheerfully told us that climbers sometimes were killed while descending as they lost their footing and somersaulted down. This was the moment at which rational people would have called it quits. Mounting those steep and treacherous blocks of granite, each three feet high, we carefully zigged and zagged up the "easy" side, human sails on vertical tacks, concentrating on the next perch and always looking up. Hoisting ourselves to the summit we found a large, flat surface of stones with gaps between them, the very last of them having been dragged to the top by bone-tired workmen forty-five hundred years before. Windblown sands through millennia had smoothed the faces on which we enjoyed a picnic breakfast, exulting in our accomplishment. We felt on top of the entire world.

The view was of empty desert nearly all around us, with two smaller pyramids ranged ahead and the Sphinx nearby, its mysterious features mutilated by Mamluks who used it for target practice. Defining the Cairo side along the Nile and its canals was a broad, fertile swath of vegetation looking as if an artist had taken a brush and painted a green streak across the desert sands. Four hundred fifty feet below, gathered in a circle to sip muddy coffee and smoke, sat a handful of hawkers and camel drivers awaiting the day's few summer tourists. Only yards away, without our knowing of it and buried deep in concealing sands, lay a grand solarboat for transporting the soul of a pharaoh.

As the sun burned hotter in its summer rage we prepared to descend, and panicked. The drop looked sheer. We went pale and giddy staring at it and swallowed hard, understanding we were in one of life's situations without a choice: there was only one way back, vertiginous or not. Cautiously we low-ered ourselves over the edge and crept down, side by side, facing the pyramid and leaning into it, grasping irregular and slippery surfaces, not speaking or looking beyond the next ledge below, gingerly testing each downward step as if one of those huge stones could have come loose. We were terrified, every move of hand and foot an opportunity for tragedy. I don't know how long the descent took us—a very long time it seemed—but with our feet safely on the ground once more tensions broke. We hugged and wept and laughed exuber-antly: *we did it*, and here was a tale to tell.

Leaving Cairo on an overnight train from prewar times with powdery sand seeping into everything, I made my way alone up the Nile through its noisy villages to Luxor to visit the tomb of Tutankhamen, around which Sam Allen and I had spun our boyhood fantasies. This was August in dead, dry air—a ferocious 113 degrees in the shade. There were five other guests at the great Luxor Hotel. With difficulty I found a guide willing to cross the Nile to the Valley of the Kings and take me to my destination. Only a few handfuls of motivated visitors were in the area.

The tomb we reached in solitude appeared to have changed little on the ex-terior from when it was first opened to visitors more than twenty years before. Sixteen narrow steps, I remembered, led to a low entrance and an antecham-ber beyond which lay the sepulchral hall and a storeroom. I felt awed standing in the overwhelming silence and desert emptiness of thirty-three centuries of history. With my heart beating faster and my mouth parched from the heat, I slowly descended, at last, these sixteen steps to the entrance of King Tut's tomb. "It was locked for the summer," I wrote back to Sam rather sheepishly. "I tried big-time bribery, but couldn't get in."

Through my father's intervention I managed to hitch a ride in an Egyptian Army convoy of Jeeps and trucks bound for Gaza, where I visited a large United Nations refugee camp under Egyptian control. Facilities for Palestinians flee-ing their homes and villages in what had newly become Israel were tragically inadequate. I spent two nights in Gaza's only guest home, where my windows opened to the sea, blue in the morning and cool and dark at night. I prom-ised myself to visit Israel and more of the Middle East.

My Formal Education Ends

With the summer over and back in Princeton again, I found that the pub-lic dialogue in the United States in the wake of our recognition of Israel was largely one-sided and wrote my summer paper, "Dimensions of the Arab Case," to articulate a more balanced view of the issues and their likely consequences. I noted in 1951, three years after Israel's birth, "The essential step for Arabs is to accept Israel, with conditions about immigration and refugees if advisable, but to accept the state as a *fait accompli,* and begin to work out a way of life with her."

After receiving a master's degree from Princeton, I pursued doctoral studies in the politics department without resolve, seeking credentials that would offer a career in academia should I want one. Professor Alpheus T. Mason, a constitutional scholar of note, was teaching an undergraduate course in American political thought and asked me to become one of his preceptors, or seminar leaders. This I did with enthusiasm and found I enjoyed teaching, but my interest in further studies flagged. My eligibility for draft deferments was running out. The Korean War was unresolved, and I felt drawn to the waters I had come to know in trans-Atlantic crossings with my parents.

Many largely wasted months later, I abandoned thoughts of a Ph.D. and boarded a train to Philadelphia, one February day in 1954, to volunteer for service at the navy's recruiting office at 13 South Thirteenth Street, an address I hoped would be propitious. I was headed for spring training at the Officer Candidate School in Newport, Rhode Island, and then, if I passed my courses, to a three-year stint in the navy. I was twenty-four.

3

JOIN THE NAVY, SEE THE WORLD

1954 to 1957

A Korean truce was signed at Panmunjom in July 1953, and as a result I was not engaged in combat during my navy years. Military service was a major learning experience for me. During three years of living aboard ships in the Caribbean and Pacific, I came to understand how the military functioned, admired much of what I saw, and began finding my way in a new part of the world, East Asia.

The four months of officer candidate training in Newport were even harder than I expected. Wearing sailors' uniforms, we lived in rows of spartan white barracks, drilled each afternoon in all weather, became compulsive polishers of boots called "boondocks," and were marched everywhere we went. We took turns at cleaning the toilet areas, called "heads," to the point at which our inspecting chief petty officer might announce to those of us eagerly awaiting praise that he was ready, if need be, to eat his breakfast off the deck beside a urinal. "Your biggest problem," said the man whose place I took apprehensively on head detail, "will be hair." During the first month we were not permitted to leave the naval station.

Competence in gunnery, engineering, and navigation, math-based subjects for which I lacked aptitude, eluded me, and my grades deteriorated. My name was on posted lists of those failing their courses, and I appeared twice before disenrollment boards. I felt weak and lost. Only when my urine turned dark did I understand something was wrong with me. I had hepatitis and was hospitalized for six weeks, moving me into the next class of officer training. My illness gave me a second chance to grapple with difficult subjects. Remembering answers to many of the quizzes, I sailed through. I was made commander of Able Company, numbering about one hundred officer candidates, and in time we were a sharp-looking bunch. Pleasant memories of two perquisites of command remain with me: no more head-cleaning assignments, and access to the facilities fifteen minutes before reveille sounded and hordes of officer candidates began lining up at sinks and shower stalls.

Captain Baltazzi had been transferred from his naval attaché position in Cairo to Newport, and one day while I was still hospitalized his daughter Emma, of our pyramid-climbing quartet, walked into my ward. She was a delightful person, and following my release we went to formal Saturday night dances at Bailey's Beach Club to the music of Lester Lanin. But where to stow my tux? Our barracks was not an option, so I rented a locker in the basement of the YMCA downtown. Another sailor putting away his own uniform and watching me loop a black tie asked whether I played in a band. "Yeah," I replied, "drums."

My service was in the amphibious force, accurately regarded in the fighting navy as grimy, greasy, workhorse duty. None of the glamour of sleek destroyers, no wheeling on a dime, but I wasn't too disappointed. My first ship was the USS *Cambria* (APA-36) out of Norfolk, Virginia. In less than a decade following World War II public regard for the uniform had evaporated, there as elsewhere in the nation, except when it came to separating a sailor from his pay. *Cambria*'s function was to transport a marine battalion across the seas and deliver it safely onto a beach using her nearly twenty landing craft nested on board. She was named for Cambria County, in Pennsylvania.

In what felt like a blind date I visited *Cambria* for the first time at night, walking from my Bachelor Officers' Quarters to size her up at rest, blemishes concealed. Would I sense a welcome? Naval bases such as Newport, bustling and noisy during work hours, their finger piers pointing far into the water, at night were deserted places where footfalls echoed and rats danced. Even on a bright Sunday afternoon, those great, silent spaces with their cranes abandoned and sheds locked up were intimidating. Somehow, the walk to one's ship was always long. From a majestic height *Cambria*'s cargo lights shone down on her mooring lines, with rat guards fastened part way up. Her generators whined. There were softer sounds of water lapping on camels, wooden floats that kept her from scraping against the pier. At the top of the gangway, in a cone of light on the quarterdeck, an officer in his khaki uniform stood watch. I raised my hand in greeting. Tomorrow I will meet that man, I thought, and soon will take his place. All too quickly I would learn what a mind-numbing experience it was to stand watch at night in port.

Cambria, in fact and daylight, was what the navy called a rust bucket, an aging, oddly dignified survivor of some of the bloodiest amphibious landings during World War II: Kwajalein, Majuro, Eniwetok, Saipan, Tinian, Moratai, Leyte Gulf, and Okinawa, hallowed names of Pacific island warfare. Now she was a portly dowager in a flowerpot hat with a daisy sticking up. Rundown, rat and roach infested, she lagged behind prevailing marine and battle technology because Cold War budgets were inadequate to maintain two-ocean fleets and modernizing the amphibious force was not of great concern to Congress. I fell for her immediately and began making a home of the noisy, hot, inside state-room to which I was assigned—the worst in "Officers' Country"—by placing my Olivetti typewriter and some books, along with a photograph of my parents, on the steel desk beside my bunk. Among authors to read was Proust, in whose world of madeleines far removed from shipboard life I would find distraction.

I discovered watch-standing at sea to be one of life's unsung pleasures, especially during the hours leading to a biblical first light as time crumpled and discarded another night. There was a surge of energy and renewal, of optimism, in that faint morning light heralding, like the early stirring of a woman beside, a sun that soon would rise. Melville wrote that meditation and water were wedded forever. I learned this as we steamed in the dark and I was on a wing of the bridge listening to the wind and examining the undisturbed sea before us. With the gray hull heaving beneath me, I swayed against the motion of the ship, making small circles of my own as our bow cut through swells and troughs in the same corkscrew way—rising and sighing, listing and plunging—while receding bow waves of churned phosphorescence hissed along our sides.

Shipboard Life

The wardroom mess in *Cambria* had a president and a mess caterer; the latter's duties were to plan meals with the head cook and listen to feckless suggestions and complaints from fellow officers. Our mess president was the chief engineer, a small, wiry, humorless man named Lichtenberger. Lieutenant Commander Lichtenberger seemed to do little else than play bridge. He was widely believed, and in my view understandably, to hate going down to the engine rooms. Mess catering duties rotated among officers. One day at sea, Lichtenberger told me it was my turn. After a week on the job, and having studied the navy's printed and numbered recipes, I decided to improve the whole concept of our fare. We were in the Caribbean and it was hot. Our meals had been greasy and heavy. One fateful lunch, I arranged to have served a menu of cold cream of potato soup (having a vichyssoise in mind), cheese soufflé with

a tossed green salad, and a nice, light dessert. I heard several officers muttering "Jesus!" while poking at their food. "Is this all there is?" Lichtenberger
snarled at me. "Yes, sir," I replied. "Grove," he said, "you're FIRED!"

We steamed in the Caribbean on amphibious landing exercises, calling at
Havana, a wide-open city with a scent of sin in the air. At the Tropicana Nightclub, where several of us were standing at the bar on a sultry evening, we spotted Groucho Marx at one of the larger tables. On a dare I walked over to him
and, in an overused phrase of the time popularized on his quiz show, said,
"Good evening, Mr. Marx. What's the word for tonight?" He gave me a raffish
sidelong look, wiggled his famous eyebrows, and answered, "Son, it's so dirty
I can't tell you." At the same time, in the summer of 1955, a firebrand reformer
and budding communist, a clean-shaven student leader twenty-eight years old
who had attempted a coup against Fulgencio Batista's regime, was released
from a Havana prison. For a while, Fidel Castro chose a life of exile in Mexico
City. Soon this enigmatic Cold War revolutionary and future dictator would
take his place on the world stage and remain there longer than any other
head of government.

Some experiences come one's way uniquely through military service. In
Haiti, I was assigned as senior shore patrol officer during our ship's liberty
weekend in Port-au-Prince and had reason, in carrying out my responsibilities,
to stroll through nearly every bar and brothel in that wicked, poverty-stricken
town. The navy believed such display of authority would have a calming effect
on patrons from the *Cambria*. In practice I did not find this to be the case,
although I was six feet five and made a series of notable entrances followed by
my rugged team in shore patrol regalia.

Few ways of living stood in sharper contrast than a sedate and bookish life
in the Master's Suite at Princeton, with its lion skin rug and academic gowns,
and the endless days and nights spent in hard work aboard *Cambria*, where
boatswain's pipes and winches were constant sounds while we engaged in the
processes of loading and landing. During amphibious operations we draped
cargo nets over the ship's sides. Carrying our gear we scrambled up and down
these nets to get into, and out of, the boats bobbing below. The nets swayed
from the ship's sides as she rolled with the waves. One moment you were over
an open sea, and the next you were colliding with the side on the counterroll.
The trick was to let go with the boat safely beneath. It was a harrowing experience every time. Some of our marines became seasick before they reached
the boats; nearly all of the others got sick in them. In this condition we delivered them to the beach ready to engage in combat.

In the navy I was learning how to organize and motivate people. I came to understand the importance of morale, discipline, and leadership and of explaining to others what was about to happen and what would be expected of them. When you had something to do you did it. You checked and rechecked everything. I learned how to prepare an OpPlan for landing a marine battalion on hostile shores. I acquired a seaman's eye, the ability to recognize offending lines on a deck or anything misplaced over the sides and, later in life unfortunately, pictures hanging crookedly on a wall. I learned to respect and fear the sea, to know in my bones that the unexpected lay only an inch ahead.

The navy's emphasis on practical, physically demanding work may well have saved me from the temptations of a certain intellectual priggishness, of thinking myself a bit better than, as opposed to different from, others. The navy was guiding me through one of life's passages, a period of self-discovery and accomplishment beyond the academic world of previous years. I broke out of my shell and assumed responsibilities requiring fresh knowledge, such as understanding the glowing blips revealed by the cursor on a radarscope and how to handle a ship. I was maturing.

The Western Pacific

Efforts to secure a transfer to the West Coast after a year and a half on the *Cambria* bore fruit. I had not been west of Oklahoma City and wanted to see more of the United States and the world beyond. Driving to San Diego in the early summer of 1957, I made my way alone for two weeks on smaller, cooler, emptier northern roads, becoming fascinated by the immensity of the American West, its scenery, the history of pioneers and Indians, and the openness of its landscape and people. I liked the little town of Medora, North Dakota, so much I spent two days there and on the rugged terrain of the Theodore Roosevelt National Park nearby.

Tied up at the pier in San Diego, USS *Tulare* (AKA-112), named after Tulare County in California, was a newly commissioned amphibious cargo ship of eighteen thousand tons. She could steam in excess of twenty-two knots (about a third faster than *Cambria*) and was, in many ways, the opposite of my former ship. Her living spaces were large, clean, and cool, and her equipment was up to date. The romance of my first encounter with *Cambria* that night in Norfolk simply wasn't there. By this time I was looking at ships the way a mechanic sizes up automobiles. I reported on board as a lieutenant (junior grade), a qualified officer of the deck underway, and the new boat group commander, the person responsible for taking amphibious landing craft from the ship's sides to the beach.

At sea again, I welcomed the clean headwinds once land had dropped from view and felt at ease and restored in unbreathed air where our reference points were in the skies above. Stretching my vision to the horizon, I left it there. I was content and calm and ready for shipboard duties; every sailor knows this epiphany. We were alone, free, and self-reliant. If there was no butter on board we would do without butter. Our voyage begun, we became a speck on the water's surface indentured to the winds and heave of the sea.

Tulare in the fall of 1957 was deployed for nine months in the Western Pacific. We would be based in Yokosuka, a busy port near Tokyo. The U.S. occupation was leaving its mark in the modernization and partial Westernization of Japan but above all in Japan's progress toward democracy. Here, as I had seen in postwar Germany and Austria, Americans were the occupiers. Now I myself was in uniform, treated courteously but without warmth. Memories of atomic bombs ran deep, as I found during our ship's call at Hiroshima.

I saw as much of Japan as possible, usually traveling by train with a fellow officer, Mike McNevin, adopting the rituals of baths and cleanliness and sleeping on futons at inns. I enjoyed massages administered by the blind, who at the end walked with bare feet up my spine. In a land where most women still dressed in kimonos, and where homes had such apparent simplicity that a single vase stood out in a nearly bare room, I discovered that less could be better. I recognized aesthetic complexity in arrangements of mere handfuls of pebbles and flowers. In geisha houses Mike and I found stylized entertaining pleasing for its devotion to serving and amusing men. Western life, with tall buildings, raised beds, tables and chairs on legs, felt vertical. In Japan the lines of living tended to be horizontal and closer to the ground, and somehow they seemed more soothing and pure. Riding Tokyo's subways, I often visited the Ueno Museum. I began collecting *hanga* wood prints that were hand-pressed on rice paper by artists such as Sekino Yun-ichiro, Saito Kiyoshi, and Azechi Umetaro, forceful contemporary works influenced by French painters such as Pablo Picasso, who in turn were under the spell of African mask carvers.

We were underway much of the time, sailing one night through the Inland Sea of Japan at its narrowest passage. I drew the watch from midnight until four in the morning, identifying lighthouses and buoys and ordering course changes as we kept ourselves in midchannel. The captain was asleep in his sea cabin, and the navigator was with me on the bridge following our progress on his charts. Our conversations were low and brief, and only our voices in the dark, the ship's bell, the sightings of the lookouts, my orders to the helm, and their acknowledgment broke the stillness. We were living in every pore. The feeling of teamwork among professionals was inspiring. All went smoothly during one of the most satisfying accomplishments of my life.

Our ship visited ports such as Hong Kong, a city in 1958 with a British colonial ambience and a mere handful of tall buildings. High on a hill, the fabled Foreign Correspondents' Club overlooked the bay. Scenes for the movie *Love Is a Many Splendored Thing* had recently been filmed there. From its terrace I gazed in awe at one of the most spectacular harbors in the world. Sampans and trading ships moved slowly below, and once in a while the muffled, far-off tooting of a ship's horn could be heard. For a moment, standing there, I felt the sailor's stab of homesickness, recognizing how removed I was from accustomed bearings. In Singapore at the old Raffles Hotel, at the long bar with its rattan furniture, Mike and I grandly ordered our first and positively last Singapore Slings.

Tulare tied up for a week in Sydney to show the flag. Here was a port where Americans, having helped defend Australia from the Japanese, were treated as heroes twelve years later. Men in uniform, sailors sightseeing or merely chasing drinks and skirts, rode free on public transportation. Strong Australian beer was usually on the Aussies. Those we met bore versions of American characteristics Henry James celebrated: outspoken and unguarded; hospitable, optimistic, energetic, earthy, and ambitious; quick to anger; a bit naive; and refreshingly open.

Our executive officer designated me to represent *Tulare* at a ladies' tea where the wife of the governor-general of New South Wales would preside in honoring our ship's visit. I was to participate in cutting an Australian-American Friendship Cake. This wasn't what I had in mind for shore leave, but I understood an order when I heard one. I borrowed our gunnery officer's sword (as an Annapolis graduate he had a sword) and went to a tea party where I was the only man in a large gathering of women, all in hats and carrying white gloves. One of the hostesses, young, appealing, and unattached Mary Tancred, took me in tow, and in due course, following an exchange of inspirational toasts, the governor-general's wife and I attacked the Friendship Cake with my sword. Afterward, Mary and I made our way to Bondi Beach.

Not unjustly known among his crew as "Whisky" Jack Mackenzie, our captain was a scrappy submariner from landlocked Wyoming whose caps were a size too big and rested on his ears. His experience in Sydney differed from mine at the tea. Much caught up in the spirit of our welcome, he fell in with a striking European woman, deep throated with a come-hither aura to her, whom he also had met at a social function. Soon and to his discomfort, however, a security officer from the American consulate came on board to warn him that she was suspected of being a Soviet agent. For him there was no getting away from the Cold War.

We trained in large and small landing exercises, one of them held on South Korea's then peaceful shores. Operation Beacon Hill off the Philippine island of Luzon, in which we participated, was the largest peacetime amphibious landing in the Pacific since World War II, involving more than one hundred ships and tens of thousands of sailors and marines. On leaving these waters, *Tulare* received the Pacific Fleet's award of excellence in recognition of the performance of my boat group. We proudly painted the white crossed anchors of the Assault Boat Insignia on the sides of our bridge.

Sailing homeward, my military service nearly over, I felt honored to receive a message from the Bureau of Personnel offering as a next assignment the lure of a teaching position at the Naval Academy in Annapolis. I could probably obtain command of a small vessel afterward, Captain Mackenzie told me. But I knew my fortunes and skills lay outside a naval career, and I did not, in any case, wear the ring of an academy graduate.

My remaining weeks aboard ship as we underwent repairs in San Diego and sailed out on sea trials seemed less demanding and less interesting. I stood bridge watches while dreaming of a different life. On the appointed day I said good-bye to the proven men in my division and saluted *Tulare*'s officer of the deck, Ensign Mike McNevin, for the last time, requesting his permission to go ashore. "Permission granted, sir," he replied with a wink. After a final salute to the flag, the firm ground beneath my feet felt right.

I decided to return to Washington that winter by driving for two weeks along a southerly route, just as I had headed north on my way from Norfolk to San Diego to avoid hot weather. In Texas and New Orleans I saw a different and appealing side of America. The fifties found much of our country unscarred and open as far as the eye could see. I exulted in food, rhythms, accents, and architecture that spoke of French and Spanish heritages. Crossing the wide expanses of the Southwest in my secondhand Chevy and musing for hours along ruler-straight highways, I thought about an America I hoped to serve once more, but in civilian clothes and on the basis of still different knowledge, training, and obligations. My no longer useful uniforms and my collection of *hanga* prints were safely stowed in the trunk of the car. Proust had finally been read.

Taking the Crucial Exam

I had taken the Foreign Service examination before leaving San Diego on our Pacific cruise. On a warm December day in 1956 I had driven to Los Angeles for the written part, a first step that with luck would be followed by a successful interview and a career in diplomacy that could last a professional lifetime. I had left Princeton three years before. One didn't get much news of the world at sea, and I worried about my preparedness.

Not familiar with Los Angeles and unable to find a center to the city, I finally located the municipal building where the examination would be given on the following day. Up since five in the morning, my stomach knotted, I arrived well in advance of the appointed hour to find nearly everyone else already waiting. We eyed each other warily but did not speak and eventually were seated in a large and sunny room, our machine-readable pencils in hand for a day of multiple choice questions and an essay topic. Thanks to a five-point veterans' preference I passed the written examination, as I learned through the ship's mail awaiting *Tulare* at a Pacific port of call.

In Washington nearly a year later, three white middle-aged men sitting around a table administered my oral examination. For an hour or so they tested my knowledge and asked about my background and motivation in a clubby sort of way. Why did I want to join the Foreign Service? What had I learned about the Arab world in Cairo? I was flummoxed at the end, however, by a question seemingly off the top of an examiner's head. "Mr. Grove, what is Algeria known for in its exports?" I thought for a moment and replied, "Oil and gas." "Oh, no," he said, "they make a really drinkable red wine! I've enjoyed it often in France." I passed anyway.

Another sixteen months would go by before I could enter the Foreign Service. No one had told me such delays were normal. Where else would a serious organization be run in this manner? Security checks that slowed the clearance process were legitimate and necessary requirements for people working with sensitive information. The navy kept my clearances current, but the State Department wasn't talking to the navy. The FBI and State Department did not have enough investigators to efficiently run the process during which friends and acquaintances, associates, and especially detractors were interrogated about one's actions and attributes in search of signs of disloyalty, homosexuality, alcoholism, adultery, drug use, unmanageable debts, and more. Every rumor, scrap of gossip, or malicious remark went into a government file. At the end, a private life would be left anything but private.

With John Foster Dulles at its helm, the State Department, still relatively small and under a cloud after the McCarthy years and Alger Hiss, was replenishing its ranks cautiously. On assuming office, Dulles told his State Department team he expected "positive loyalty," whatever that meant. Large numbers of its members had been in the heaviest fighting during World War II, their loyalties never questioned then. A colleague on Dulles's personal staff, Bob Fearey, told me after consulting his private files that the secretary had said to him: "With the responsibilities I now have, I need broad support in Congress. I regret if injustice must sometimes be done to a few Foreign Service officers, but as secretary I must be guided by the larger national interest." People at the State Department soldiered on.

4

EXCURSIONS

1958

My parents lived in London during the many years my father represented Mobil's interests in the Middle East. Each passing day of staying with them after serving in the navy and while waiting for my Foreign Service appointment to materialize left me feeling increasingly frustrated. Telephone calls to the State Department yielded no beginning date, and I considered other careers, journalism in particular. In the end I decided to take advantage of an unavoidable delay, continuing my education in life by doing things I would be unable to do in government service later on. A liability would be refashioned into an asset.

Paris

For the first three months of 1958 I lived on the left bank of Paris in the rundown Hotel Soufflot on the rue Toulliers. Between each landing, halfway up, was a dank and drafty bathroom with a gritty tub and a toilet with a wooden seat and a pull chain connected to the water tank above. Toilet tissue seemed made of folded brown wax paper. *Tout Confort* the plaque outside insisted. The concierge's wife, a stout, pince-nezed, shawl-draped Madame Gersbacher, trained her gaze from the region of her counter on to those few passing through for the stairs, including my French teacher, the dark-eyed Yolande, who managed a small gallery of abstract prints in the rue de Seine.

My room on the top floor was large. Through dormer windows opening inward I could see other tiled and sloping roofs with their chimney pots and skylights and drainpipes running down the walls to the street. Wooden shutters that were everywhere in Paris bracketed the windows. Day and night, church bells tolled the quarter hours in echoes of the past, validating the present and promising time to come. I was living under the spell of a part of Paris not far removed from Eugène Atget's photographs of the turn of the century. The moods of my *quartier* covered the gamut from Charles Trenet's joyful songs when the sun shone to the mournful Edith Piaf in dismal weather. Walking the streets for hours, or reading in my room, or studying French with the dark-eyed Yolande, I felt myself on a ceaseless voyage of exploration.

Existing frugally and pinching my savings from the navy, I learned to fill up on beer and baguettes spread with mustard. I fell in with a group of artists impervious to foreign affairs, gifts of raw, unlabeled Bordeaux my admission tickets to their lively evenings. I found the building where Proust had lived in his cork-lined room. The caretaker who opened the courtyard door, on learning of my interest in stepping inside, slapped her forehead with the palm of her hand and exclaimed to no one in particular, "Encore quelqu'un pour Proust!" I didn't linger. I became an *auditeur libre* at the École des Sciences Politiques of the University of Paris, attending courses on international topics such as French colonial policy in Africa. When I was assigned to West Africa at the beginning of my Foreign Service career, I recalled the crowded lectures at the "Sciences Po" on the benefits of French rule, and the pride and sometimes condescension in the professors' depictions of what were soon to become France's former colonies there.

The USSR with a *Baedeker*

During late April and early May 1958 I visited the Soviet Union for the first time. Nikita Khrushchev had opened the door to Russia a crack for Westerners. I joined a small group of British and American journalists under the false claim of being a reporter for the *Rhinebeck Gazette* in Duchess County, New York. True, I had written some pieces for the *Gazette* while at Bard, but that was eight years before. We would spend two weeks in the Soviet Union, learning mainly by observation because few behind the Iron Curtain dared talk with us. Well advised in London about the adventures of travel there, we brought along soap, toilet paper, flat rubber bathtub stoppers (deprived guests took the hotels' plugs home), and drip-dry nylon shirts that developed incurable ring-around-the-collar, just as the insides of Russian bathtubs acquired their own sets of dark rings.

Ours was the first Russian tour for Western journalists organized in London. In the USSR we were shepherded day and night by a young Intourist guide, Irena, a red-haired Stalinist disciplinarian who did not let us out of her sight. Ernie Hill, of the *Chicago Tribune*, dubbed her "Miss Tightass." Utterly humorless, Irena treated us as miscreants on a school outing, not passing up chances to make cracks about the West and its "corruption." Despite Irena's focus on the achievements of communism, we managed to see quite a few historical landmarks that became more intriguing when examined with a 1914 *Baedeker* on Russia in hand.

Before leaving London on this journey I called on George F. Kennan, the American diplomat and intellectual father of the policy of containment, then spending a year lecturing and writing at Oxford. Although Kennan agreed to see me when I telephoned, I found him aloof and felt I was distracting him. Mrs. Kennan jollied us up with coffee and cake in her kitchen. I sought Kennan's advice on what I might do in preparing to join the Foreign Service, and what practical steps I could take to get the most out of my trip to the Soviet Union. He was not encouraging about a career in the Foreign Service, having weathered the McCarthy era and then, in 1952, been invited by Dulles to leave the State Department.

He suggested that I try to find a prewar *Baedeker* guidebook in order to examine the old maps, particularly of Leningrad. I should count the canals as we crossed them in that city and identify old buildings by checking their locations and descriptions in the *Baedeker*. Kennan said this would give me an appreciation that Soviet tour guides could not provide, since they would be unfamiliar with, or not want to discuss, specific aspects of czarist rule. I advertised in the *Times of London* for a *Baedeker* on Russia, and on the eve of my departure an American journalist called and sold his 1914 edition to me for a stiff ten pounds. I found my *Baedeker* indispensable on every trip I later made to the Soviet Union.

In the closing of a circle, I lent the *Baedeker* to George Kennan when he returned to the Soviet Union in 1976, twenty-three years after Stalin expelled him as ambassador to the USSR. We were dinner guests of the Matlocks in Moscow, where Jack Matlock was the deputy chief of mission at our embassy. Kennan, who had just arrived from the airport, shared his first impressions. He was astonished at how little change there was on the surface, except for more widespread dilapidation of Moscow's buildings. "Even the theater schedules on the kiosks look the same!" he exclaimed. I reminded Kennan of our conversation at Oxford, and he was as delighted to borrow my *Baedeker* as I was to lend it to him.

I did, in fact, write eleven articles in London following my trip, which the *Rhinebeck Gazette* published in the fall of 1958, paying $1.50 for each. "Normally, all of the columns in the *Gazette* run between 75 cents and $1.00 per week," the editor, Michael Strong, wrote to me. "However, in this case I feel they are worth the $1.50." Warm praise, indeed. Five years after Stalin's death Russian travel pieces were still a novelty. Little was known in the United States about ordinary Russians and their daily lives.

In those articles I described stores with empty shelves in Leningrad and Moscow's GUM, and how Russians in the street stared at the well-made shoes of Westerners. Living standards were appallingly low, luxuries nonexistent. Shabbiness everywhere, and nets strung above sidewalks to catch debris from crumbling façades, set a defeatist tone, except on days when the sun shone down on the river and on Moscow's parks. With the suffering of World War II only thirteen years behind them, and living under a regime that mocked its citizens with communist slogans devoid of meaning, the people I saw in the streets seemed to have had their spirits broken. Nowhere had I seen so much public drunkenness. For them happiness must have been a private matter for one's home, yet home likely was a cramped apartment shared with other families. Young and old alike had no privacy. In well-stocked restaurants for foreigners, off-limits to the public but not to Soviet elites and agents of the KGB, we might be greeted with calls and toasts of *Mir y Druzhba!* Peace and Friendship! I recalled reading Orwell.

Counting Leningrad's canals in my *Baedeker*, I saw that a mansion with grocery shops on the ground floor and crowded apartments above was formerly the Club of the Noblesse. In this city's once elegant Astoria Hotel, a marble plaque advertising manicures and pedicures in gold letters had not been taken down. In the restaurant off the lobby, a Russian beauty's low-pitched voice with the accents of her native land sang "I Love Paris in the Springtime," but she would have to love it from afar because few Soviet citizens were allowed to travel abroad. In Leningrad I was doubled up at the Astoria with an amusing Englishman in our group. On our last night, in an obvious homosexual advance, he sat on the edge of my bed while I was lying in it. Politely rebuffed, he backed off. I wondered what had motivated him to make his move.

In one article I recounted the visit of our group to an unintentionally humorous fashion show staged by Dom Modeliy, and the Soviet practice of proposing dress patterns first to a council of manufacturers and designers, and after that to a committee of light industry, planning, and trade. Balenciaga would not have made the cut. At a soccer match, I cheered as the Spartaks from light industry tied the Torpedo autoworkers 3–3. At a primary school we found impressive training in the English language and sciences, although I did not doubt that Intourist had carefully chosen a showpiece school.

In Red Square one bitterly cold morning we watched a May Day parade and its dispiriting assertions of Soviet might: tanks, artillery, and rocket carriers rumbling on and on. From the precision drill of goose-stepping soldiers and sailors, to the regimented units of Young Pioneers, this was a robotic performance to martial music and patriotic songs on scratchy recordings reminding me of what I had seen, as a boy, in Hitler's Germany. Khrushchev, his top aides, and his guest, Egypt's coup leader General Gamal Abdel Nasser, stood bundled in fur atop the Kremlin's mausoleum. Before me was the lineup of Soviet officials, so painstakingly analyzed by Kremlinologists, meant to display through proximity to a stone-faced chieftain who was in or out of favor. Thousands of bright red flags, giant posters of Lenin, and the ubiquitous banners with party slogans left me feeling joyless and intimidated.

At the entrance to the mausoleum on the following day, foreign visitors were put at the head of an incredibly long line of Russians standing for hours in the chill air. No one grumbled; we were considered capitalist pilgrims receiving a needed education in communism. On entering, I saw at the bottom of a flight of steps two glass-covered caskets on display in a hushed and softly lit marble room. The scene felt religious. An honor guard of two Russian soldiers stood motionless. The first thing I noticed was Stalin's profile reflected on the wall opposite his bier. We filed past the waxy but well-preserved remains of Lenin, a lean man with pointed features, high forehead, beard, and mustache. Lenin seemed to be peering out from beneath his right eyelid, but that was probably my imagination. Passing Lenin's casket, I stood at the feet of Stalin. Viewed from this perspective with an accent on his chin, Stalin's features were hard and unmistakably cruel. In profile, however, the dictator assumed a fatherly, almost benign appearance. He was dressed in the familiar tunic of his wartime days with more medals on his chest than Lenin.

I concluded my series of articles with a quotation from the novelist Nikolai Gogol. "The Russian possesses a multitude of good qualities and a multitude of defects. As is usual with Russians, both are mingled within him in a sort of picturesque disorder." In other words, I added for my readers in Rhinebeck, "He's a bit like you and me." Could I have guessed that in 1999 Khrushchev's son, Sergei, living and teaching in Rhode Island, would choose to become an American citizen? Or that he would write an endorsement for my daughter Catherine Jones's cookbook, *A Year of Russian Feasts?*

Mary and Washington at Last

While in London I met and fell in love with Marie (called Mary) Chereme-teff, a woman of Russian origin living there with her family. Her daunting great-aunt Sofka Dolgoruka, into her sixties and a regal, formidable figure out of a Chekov play, introduced us. With her melodic voice and accents of the British upper classes, Sofka was widely read in Russian literature and Shake-speare, chronically short of money, flabbily overweight, and dressed in the clothes of decades past. She had warmth, a tear-welling passion just below the surface, and, in the Russian way, a raucous laugh never more enjoyed than over a glass of soothing vodka at room temperature. Throughout our trip to the Soviet Union she was the London escort of our band of journalists, a sparring partner for Irena the Tightass. This was unusual work for a Russian princess, but Sofka's views on communism were ambivalent, and she was a great propaganda catch for Intourist. Her ancestor's equestrian statue, that of Yuri Dolgoruki, who founded Moscow in 1147, stood at the heart of that city.

Recounting to her the incident in Leningrad of the amusing Englishman's failed homosexual pass, I asked Sofka about him. She seemed unsurprised by my question. He may have been a KGB informant, she speculated. If so, he would have known about my intention to join the Foreign Service, which I made no effort to hide. As a way of blackmailing me down the road of a diplomatic career, sexual entrapment could have proved useful to the KGB.

One afternoon I invited Sofka to an acclaimed Soviet film at the Curzon Cinema, *The Cranes Are Flying*. Afterward, she proposed we visit the Chereme-teff family living in Hampstead, saying there was someone I should meet. Mary was a striking woman of twenty-two with large dark eyes, sometimes asked whether she wasn't the actress Natalie Wood, also of Russian origin. Her birth-place was Athens, and she had grown up in Limassol, Cyprus. Both her par-ents were born in Russia. Her father, Nikita, was a captain in the merchant fleet who became an engineering specialist for the Italian Sitmar Lines. Her mother, Katherine, was a generous and uncomplicated woman, a skilled cook of Russian dishes, especially those to be enjoyed on holidays. As children, Nikita and his cousin Sofka had played together in the czarist court.

Soon Mary and I were attending the Royal Ballet in Covent Garden, visit-ing art museums, strolling in Hyde Park, and finding our way to cozy dinners through London's foggy nights. One afternoon we stood together in the shelter of a doorway, caught suddenly in a shower splashing down like a scrim before us and closing us in. Perhaps falling in love has for each person an indelible moment: if so, mine was then. Tentatively—I was still unemployed—we became engaged. Mary had not been to the United States. I felt fortunate as a budding young diplomat to be having such a wife.

I was also tired of inventing things to do. Wanting to get on with my life, I returned to Washington, early in 1959, to learn where matters stood at the State Department. There I was assured of a place in a junior officers' class to be convened in April. I rented a one-room apartment on N Street in the heart of Georgetown. My plans were to find a job that would teach me something new before I entered the Foreign Service and also generate a modicum of income.

And so, having prepared an unavoidably slim résumé, I walked the halls of Capitol Hill offering to work for a pittance, while forgetting that taxes would be withheld even from pittances. No one in the Senate was interested, but Representative Chester Bowles's staff was. Bowles represented the Second District of Connecticut. At the start of his career after Yale, he cofounded one of the most successful advertising agencies in New York, Benton and Bowles. During World War II, President Roosevelt called him to Washington to head the Office of Price Administration. President Truman subsequently appointed him director of the Office of Economic Stabilization. Bowles was elected governor of Connecticut in 1948 but, overconfident about his prospects, failed in his bid for a second term. Truman appointed Bowles ambassador to India and Nepal in 1951. After Dwight Eisenhower defeated Adlai Stevenson in their race for the White House, Bowles returned to a life of speaking and writing until, in 1957, he decided to run for Congress and won his seat.

Bowles's administrative aide, Thomas L. Hughes, hired me on the spot. During the next three months I worked for Bowles, excited to be back in Washington with formal studies and military service behind me and a diplomatic career and marriage in the offing. I sat at a typewriter table with collapsible wings—my work space in Chester Bowles's churned-up office—answering mail, writing early drafts of speeches, talking to constituents, and meeting with lobbyists no one else cared to see. A man of expansive horizons, Bowles related the day's issues to their larger contexts. He had energy, an ability to set off simultaneously in several directions, and an agenda of populist and foreign policy goals to accomplish. An extra hand at low wages was always welcome.

Although a first-term congressman, Bowles had a seat on the House Foreign Affairs Committee. This reflected his standing in the Democratic Party, his experience as an ambassador, and his many speeches and articles advocating policies for a world beyond Europe that Americans were largely ignoring. Starting to work for Bowles, I already felt myself a minor player in a grand scene. I could not have anticipated that twice again I would be at his side as a junior Foreign Service officer, or that our brief but serendipitous association on Capitol Hill would shape my diplomatic career and life to follow.

A placid-seeming Eisenhower presidency was ending, a period of consolidation in postwar, early Cold War America. Along N Street bloomed daffodils and forsythia. For me there was nothing dull about the fifties.

5

THE A-100 COURSE

1959

I turned thirty on entering the Foreign Service. The first hurdle would be twelve weeks of training in the A-100 course. On an April morning, wearing a dark and freshly pressed suit, I left my room on N Street with a spring in my stride as I crossed the Francis Scott Key Bridge to Rosslyn on the far side of the Potomac. What would it be like, I wondered, to step behind the curtains of American diplomacy as an about-to-be-initiated insider?

Long before my walk, A-100 had been the corridor address of a spacious, comfortable room in the Executive Office Building in which a small State Department was housed. Tall windows overlooked well-tended White House gardens. After the Rogers Act of 1924 created a modern Foreign Service that unified its consular and diplomatic components, George Kennan became a member of the second class of junior officers convened for training in Room A-100. There was only one teacher, a seasoned consul general named William Dawson who was reputed to be a fine linguist. During an interview in 2004 conducted in celebration of his hundredth birthday, Kennan remembered "Calvin Coolidge coming out and putting on Indian feathers to be photographed for some reason of his own."

In 1959, training at the State Department's Foreign Service Institute took place in a reconfigured garage beneath the Arlington Towers Apartments in Rosslyn. The many classrooms were low-ceilinged, cramped, and windowless, thin green walls doing little to muffle noises from adjacent rooms in which students might be practicing the guttural sounds of Japanese. These conditions reflected the low priority accorded training, other than in languages, and the paucity of resources the State Department was willing to commit to this function twelve years into the Cold War.

We were a class of twenty-five, including four future ambassadors. Two of our members were women, one was Hispanic, and most of us were easterners. With a graduate degree and service in the navy, I was among the older ones. For the first several days we sat up straight and took notes. Quickly, however, we came together and formed friendships lasting through the years. Three or four would resign early. The rest of us remained in the Foreign Service for full careers.

Bondings like these occurred in every A-100 class and were among the rewards of Foreign Service life. Many in my class were recently married, fresh from studies, military service, or other work. They had settled into homes in the Washington area to be rented out as they were posted overseas. The marrieds invited single people like me to dinners where we discussed over wine and candle stubs our hopes for first assignments and which continents we might want to become experts on during our careers. "World enough, and time" wrote the poet Andrew Marvell, and this is what we had before us. We had waited long and kept faith to be where we were. Now we swapped ideas in our budding friendships, exulting in the wide-open possibilities the assignment process would whittle down as most of us became increasingly specialized. As yet no career paths had been taken. For me this was a time as guileless as my first visit to the USS *Cambria* that night among the wharf rats of Norfolk harbor. Just as in daylight on the following morning I saw my ship for what she was, so would I quickly discern some of the warts and blemishes of the Foreign Service, but not all of them quite yet.

Most of the time our A-100 training was lackluster. The course chairman, Michael Gannett, a career diplomat prematurely white-haired with pink cheeks and a sunny disposition, made us feel welcome and did his best to set the right tone. Midranking officials, some of whom seemed to have given their remarks little preparation, lectured us, and we met with few senior officers. We found no spark in much of what we heard, no induction into an ethos or tradition of public service, little attempt to excite the imagination or ignite the spirit, no serious discussion of global strategy in a threatening Cold War world. A whiff of McCarthyism lingered in a battered institution.

Contrasts to training in the navy were striking. We had little discussion of leadership, management, or tradecraft, although someone working with only one assistant needed these skills. Tradecraft in diplomacy was like seamanship in the navy. It was the exercise of skills in the art of diplomacy, the ability to observe, analyze, represent, advocate, negotiate, and get on with the day's business successfully. Tradecraft concerned the *how* of getting work accomplished. Our heads were crammed with organizational charts, acronyms, and neatly drawn lines of authority. We were provided useful information about other government agencies involved in foreign affairs without being let in on the realities of the competing interests, compromises, fights, jealousies, inspirations, posturing, turf battles, moments of nobility, and impugning of character that were, in combinations that varied, part of those relationships and of the process of setting policy.

Along with two or three others of my class, my mind now made up, I asked to be assigned to sub-Saharan Africa. I was intrigued by the prospect of serving outside Europe on a continent gradually becoming of deeper interest to the United States as colonial powers retreated and "winds of change" began blowing. Within the State Department, sub-Saharan Africa, unlike countries along the Mediterranean littoral, was largely ignored except for its southern cone. In search of insights and adventure, I was influenced by Chester Bowles's conviction that colonies destined for independence were becoming important to us.

Near the end of the course our first assignments were read aloud by Mike Gannett in one of the most gripping moments of a Foreign Service career. I felt the world lay at my feet. When my name was due, I leaned forward and stopped breathing. "Grove," a genial Gannett said, and then paused teasingly as he had with everyone: "Abidjan!" *Thump.* Nothing precise came to mind. The American Consulate had been established only eighteen months before in that city along the Atlantic shore of French West Africa's Ivory Coast. The name spoke of trade in elephant tusks. My reaction was not unique; others of my colleagues were as baffled about their newly opened African posts. After a bit of investigating, Abidjan appeared to be what I wanted. Mary shared my enthusiasm.

Without fanfare our class took its oath of office in the "gritty green garage," as Bill Miller, the poet among us, called it. We felt the thrill and uplift, a rush of pride in country. Repeating Thomas Jefferson's oath to a constitution, not to a monarch, was a turning point in my life. My boyhood had exposed me to the larger world. I had engaged in studies that focused on foreign relations and how we conducted them and had experienced wartime service in the navy. Now I was awed to be saying these words at last, to be doing what I claimed I wanted to do. I thought of Mary and the family we hoped to raise. We would be starting off on a remote shore of Africa and afterward might find ourselves anyplace else in the world. Could we be happy in such a life?

My Offer to Resign

I said my good-byes and wished good luck to Mike Gannett and our congenial A-100 group: assignments made, paths revealed. Leaving my colleagues I boarded a shuttle bus to the State Department across the river. What a short career, I mused, less than an hour. The first time I walked into the State Department as a full-fledged diplomat I was there to submit my resignation to the secretary of state. Christian A. Herter succeeded John Foster Dulles, who had died of cancer. In a one-paragraph memorandum to Herter, written and rewritten to make it exactly right, I cited a Foreign Service regulation obliging anyone intending to marry a foreign national to submit his resignation pending a satisfactory background investigation of the prospective bride. Mary was a British subject.

Resignations such as mine were rarely accepted, but there it was. In October 1959 the acting chief of personnel, Joseph J. Jova, wrote to me in Abidjan: "It is a pleasure to inform you that your request for permission to marry Miss Marie Cheremeteff has been approved and that your resignation from the Foreign Service has not been accepted."

6

ABIDJAN

1959 to 1961

My annual salary as a vice consul in 1959, a notch above entry level thanks to a graduate degree and service in the navy, was $3,200, supplemented by a 10 percent allowance for serving at a "hardship" post. At a post where prices were higher than in the United States, as in Abidjan, a carefully calibrated cost-of-living allowance was also provided. Talented people doing well in their careers were leaving the Foreign Service because they could no longer make ends meet during Washington assignments. Others schemed like mandarins to stay abroad, where life often was cheaper.

A subpost of Dakar, Abidjan fell under the jurisdiction of Consul General Donald A. Dumont, one of the few seasoned Africa hands in the State Department. Dumont, in turn, was accountable to our ambassador in Paris, Amory Houghton, following the colonial administrative pattern. None of the French African colonies had yet become independent as I arrived in the Ivory Coast, which achieved its independence on August 7, 1960, while I was there.

Before I left Washington, the country desk officer in the State Department who managed our relationships with all of West Africa briefed me. He had not visited Abidjan and therefore could tell me little about the place. Early in the Cold War, diplomatic coverage of Africa was spotty, in part because our interests were almost entirely commercial and managed by businessmen. The United States traditionally avoided ruffling the feathers of British, Belgian, and French colonial powers either in their capitals or on the continent. South Africa, under apartheid, was emerging as a different sort of problem for us.

While in the navy I had read John Gunther's *Inside Africa*, published in 1955 as the first popular survey of its kind for the general reader. Maps printed on the endpapers described large portions of the continent as French West Africa, French Equatorial Africa, Anglo-Egyptian Sudan, and Belgian Congo. Returning to its pages, I found little about the Ivory Coast. But there were also these words of Gunther's that I had read before without lingering: "Abidjan bounces with vitality, and potentially the Ivory Coast is the richest colony in French Africa."

No State Department Post Report describing our consulate and local conditions in Abidjan existed (I would write one), nor were there yet colleagues to consult who had lived there. I was poorly prepared. I didn't know whether many of Abidjan's streets were paved; the desk officer thought they were. He told me my personal belongings in Washington, and Mary's in London, would take a long time to reach us. They say in the Foreign Service that if you are sitting on a beach and a large crate with your name on it washes up, your household effects have arrived.

In the summer of 1959 I flew to Abidjan, stopping in Paris and Dakar to be briefed by Foreign Service officers who followed developments in the region. In Paris our embassy tracked African affairs closely because of de Gaulle's attention to France's colonies and their imminent independence. I called on an African expert at the Quay d'Orsay to introduce myself, such was the edginess of an American presence in French West Africa. An usher in formal attire, his nose a bit in the air, escorted me along the corridors of this palatial nineteenth-century foreign ministry. I thought of Benjamin Franklin in Paris during a different colonial era. His informality and plain dress reflected American values, and for a fanciful moment in my usher's wake I felt myself following in Franklin's footsteps.

A flight from Paris to Dakar on Air France brought me to that sub-Saharan capital, known to Americans for its World War II importance as an Allied base. Installed in a plain hotel room with a slowly turning ceiling fan where I would have my first encounter with bedbugs, I walked at dusk along avenues and side streets teeming with tall and aristocratic-looking Senegalese, the women wearing colorful, flowing dresses and billowing head scarves. I was in a world new to me. There, as in Cairo, music blared from radios, now to the relaxed, happy-go-lucky beat of African songs and drums. On the following day, having tossed and scratched all night, I sought out people at our consulate general with whom I would be working in the future, especially on Abidjan's consular and administrative concerns. Then I boarded Air France once more to be taken through African skies to my first Foreign Service post.

An Embassy in Waiting

The American consul in Abidjan was Donald R. Norland, and our sole Foreign Service secretary was Marion Markle. Don greeted me at the airport, and I liked him immediately. Over six feet tall, blond and energetic, Norland was a powerhouse tennis player from Laurens, Iowa. I would find him a good man to work for: informed about Africa, principled, focused, trusting, high-spirited, and open—ready to show the ropes to a newcomer like me. We resembled an embassy in microcosm, and there was much to learn.

Marion was a pioneer in the full sense of the word. Born in the small town of Harbor Beach, on Lake Huron in Michigan, she wanted to see the world. Her first assignment was to Paris, and she hoped to go to Moscow next. Instead, she received orders to what she thought was Azerbaijan (where we had no diplomatic presence during the Cold War) but turned out, instead, to be newly opened Abidjan. "I was not disappointed," Marion wrote to me later, "I just felt stupid. I had always wanted to go to Africa, having in mind missionary work or a safari. I thought if one could survive there, one could survive anywhere."

The American consulate, reached by a small and temperamental elevator, was located in the only high-rise building near the main square. Close by was the Hotel du Parc, a colonial haunt formerly the legendary Bardon. In the global reach of French colonial rule, the Bardon had been to Abidjan on a more modest scale what the Continental was to Saigon. The square below us with its open-air market was crowded on one side with vendors of African wood carvings, furtive when displaying stolen artifacts hidden in burlap sacks. In these carvings I would find what had stirred Modigliani and Picasso. The chirping of thousands of bats hanging upside down in the trees animated the nights. Somehow we were never able to get rid of the smell of wet plaster in our otherwise adequate, air-conditioned offices.

Two invaluable local employees assisted us. One was Ghanaian, Mr. Adams, a dignified and portly gentleman who dealt with consular matters. The other was Lebanese, the shrewd and quick Mr. Merheb, who handled our administrative concerns. Both spoke fluent English and French. Mr. Adams, well into his sixties, could be refreshingly direct. During the day, when I was not available, he would tell callers on the telephone, "Mr. Grove is in the toilet." No ambiguous "away from his desk" for him! My responsibilities amounted to things Norland was not concentrating on himself. These included consular, administrative, and commercial matters, although like him I became involved in everything else. Abidjan was an ideal post for someone learning the trade.

The CIA had placed one of its agents in our consulate, William Dunbar, a lanky, quiet-spoken Africa hand with rimless glasses who, nominally a vice consul like me, was forty-five and more weathered looking than Don. Dunbar was joined by a flamingly red-haired, freckled, and eye-catching secretary, Margaret Woolls, as part of the agency's effort to establish a presence in African countries about to shed colonial rule. Lively Margaret was not someone who blended easily into the African scene.

This was my first experience with intelligence operatives, or "spooks," as insiders and journalists lightheartedly called them. Evident in their behavior was an air of detachment from other work at the consulate. They had separate agendas and contacts and special, isolating physical requirements for their base at our post. They locked and unlocked their office doors (we didn't), and the rare peek inside revealed desks either bare or with a few papers turned facedown. Despite the affable personalities of these two operatives soon to become four, they did little to dispel an aura of difference and surreptitiousness surrounding their work, noticed by Mr. Adams and especially by the ever-curious Mr. Merheb. Yes, they made an effort to shroud themselves in diplomatic cover, but the mysterious character of their activities was apparent. Dunbar was declared to the French, a practice of liaison at senior levels usually followed among the Western Allies. Encountering the smashing Margaret in a hall with her office key on a band around her wrist, I sometimes got a knowing little wink.

Ground rules for relations between the State Department and U.S. intelligence agencies were poorly defined in 1959. Finally spelled out, they read like treaties signed by sovereign and not altogether friendly powers. Usually Norland and I had little idea of what our colleagues were up to. A large part of the consulate's intelligence work, recruiting and running a few local sources, was in any case beyond our purview.

One day soon after my arrival, Bill mentioned to me that in a Baolé village not far away a ceremony would be held that very afternoon to honor a new chieftain. I should consider attending. Good idea, I thought—grassroots material for a report to Washington from its man on the scene. Arriving by Jeep in my bush hat, short pants, and socks up to knobby knees, I found circles of dancing villagers in the early stages of palm wine exuberance weaving through dust stamped up by bare feet, sweat sparkling on black faces under the sun. The whole village was out, clapping, swaying, singing. Their new chieftain was hard to spot, but to show American solidarity I got into the spirit of what was going on, sampling the local brew. Encouraged to join in the shuffling to a background of repetitive drumbeats, I soon was having a wonderful time. Nothing happening was in French.

The following morning at the consulate, I sensed in Bill's smile that I had passed a rite of initiation. I had learned nothing significant about Baolé life below the surface, and would be unlikely to do much better in two years' time. Even at the softer edges of their curiosity, strangers to Africa were discouraged from intimacy with Africans by cultural barriers guarding a different world. What appeared simple on the surface seldom was. My contacts during work, while always pleasant, would turn out be more formal, more institutionally channeled, and, in unexpected ways, more distant than I had hoped. Some of the missionaries, and later Peace Corps volunteers, would understand Africans better because they lived a rural life. The villagers welcoming me functioned within an intricate culture of their own inaccessible to me, and they didn't give a hoot about the United States. To them I must have seemed a harmless visitor, if also a rather odd and forgettable one.

Sending Down Roots

Three months after reaching Abidjan, I returned to London to be married and bring Mary to our first home. We were wed in a Russian Orthodox Church during an elaborate ceremony with crowns held above our heads by three best men and music from a male choir so solemn and empowered I dared not have a lighthearted thought.

Filled with a youthful and uncomplicated sense of adventure, we set up our household in a modest white stucco villa outside the Treichville quarter, overlooking a lagoon. There was one air-conditioner for each of two small bedrooms, all the Foreign Service would provide. The rest of the house was hot and steamy, with pink lizards running along the walls and across the ceilings. I no sooner would step out of the shower to dry off than sweat would dribble down again.

We fought battles with our pseudo-parents at the consulate general in Dakar over funding for necessities such as curtains, furniture, and replacing inadequate kitchen equipment. Our CIA colleagues and eventually those from our aid mission faced no such problems. We endured the predictable arguments with the State Department's budget people that emerged when something out of the ordinary was afoot, such as setting up a new post. This was frustrating at first, but eventually we not only endured, we prevailed.

A verdant garden surrounding our home had big, old trees with thick vines growing into them. We learned not to decorate our dinner table with hibiscus, those large rose-colored blossoms that bloomed for a day and at nightfall folded up and collapsed. One of the most flea-bitten mongrels I ever came across, Noga, guarded our gate with his Senoufo master, the *guardien* Mamadou, a nearly toothless old man with a great capacity for sleep. The threat to us in Abidjan was from thieves, not terrorists.

I had hired a houseboy named Oumar who wanted to learn English. One evening I explained to him what "good night" meant, and he practiced saying it for a while. After he had finished the dishes, he came in and said, "Good night." Then he went into the garden and taught Mamadou to say "good night." As he left he said to Mamadou, "Good night," and Mamadou replied, "Good night."

The branch line of a rickety railroad ran in back. Several times a day, a wildly tooting but slow-moving train crept behind our home with people of all ages sitting on the carriage roofs and hanging from the sides. In the garden we had a chicken coop and a collection of shrubs and trees that harbored poisonous snakes. The local gardeners' network had a scam in which one of their number would kill a particularly horrible looking snake and then show it off from household to household, usually at breakfast time so the lady of the manse could scream, collecting the customary bounty after each visit. By noon the snake seemed a bit tired and the day's game was over.

Treichville itself was an overcrowded African subdivision of Abidjan, where mainly one-room shacks along dirt roads were covered by corrugated tin roofs and young children clad only in frayed little shirts ran everywhere. When rain clattered on those roofs the wailing sounds of "Tin Roof Blues" coursed through my mind. Lebanese merchants sold many goods but mostly, it seemed, bicycle tires. Women offering *manioc*, or cassava, sat on solid wooden stools their men had carved for them. Men of all ages made morning rounds balancing on their heads large glass jugs of *bangi*, a milky, frothy palm wine, offering the same tin cup to anyone who would buy. *Bangi* got stronger as the day wore on. At night, mainly kerosene lamps lit Treichville, and music was everywhere, blasting from radios or resonating from drummers and singers in its outdoor bars where local beer and Coca-Cola were sold. From our home on still evenings, we could hear those muffled sounds as we sat on our terrace at the end of the day enjoying a cool drink.

Abidjan in 1959 was a modern city by African standards. It had one congested artery across the main lagoon, the four-lane Félix Houphouët-Boigny Bridge, named for the leader who would become the Ivory Coast's future president. We found the city inviting for its African culture and stubbornly French veneer, its good French and many Vietnamese restaurants, and the food in its stores and markets, either arriving daily by air from Paris or locally produced. Mary and I became interested in wood carvings and began studying and collecting them. They could be works of rigid simplicity and astonishing force, especially those intimidating, open-mouthed masks about to shriek that seemed unwilling to release you from the stare of their hollow eyes.

Beyond the heat and frequent rains (Abidjan was said to have two seasons repeating themselves—the Big Rainy and the Little Rainy) were hardships we could not avoid: feeling homesick, for example, when our isolation closed in on us. We had neither television nor American movies. Mail from the United States was slow and arrived in diplomatic pouches; jet planes were only beginning to serve West Africa in the late fifties. Wholly inadequate medical facilities existed in a country where road accidents, malaria, and heart attacks were commonplace. There were a mere handful of other Americans in Abidjan, apart from consulate staff, with whom we could socialize. For us the personal satisfactions of life in West Africa lay in living with people of different cultures and the excitement of being transplanted into exotic surroundings.

Travels in the Bush

Small-boat experience in the navy helped me refit the consulate's Jeep with a towrope, two spare tires, an ice chest, a medical kit, and other essentials for driving in thinly populated areas. Once we settled into our home, Mary and I went on weeklong trips visiting American missionaries, who usually lived comfortably, if in isolated communities. I took along various government forms and a consular hand-press seal to notarize documents, register births, and so on. We met with groups of missionary families to tell them about our progress in Abidjan and what an invigorated U.S. policy was seeking to accomplish in their part of Africa, as well as to listen to their needs and accounts of missionary life. I sought to reassure them in the knowledge that the U.S. government had an official presence serving them in Abidjan and at each stop offered to take back letters to be sent home from the consulate, against the rules, in our diplomatic pouch.

Beyond the rain forests, much of West Africa upcountry through which we drove was primeval, exempted, it seemed, from time itself. Dense vegetation receded as the coast fell behind. Shaped by gentle rises, the savanna appeared a reddish brown. The air was hot, dry, motionless. We might stop in the shade of a baobab tree and shut off the engine, waiting for sounds of our arrival to fade and listening in suspense. Seconds later, after a few inquiring exchanges, birds and insects from everywhere and nowhere resumed their courtships and conversations until they reached a frenzied pitch. Overwhelmed by the cacophony, heat, and emptiness, I felt irrelevant at such moments, bereft of orientation, an intruder on a buzzing landscape without a past or future.

We stayed at local French-run inns, simple places with cold showers to wash away dirt caked on our hair and bodies after a day's drive along laterite roads. The usual clattering air-conditioner built into a bug-splattered wall thumped and rattled as it cooled, sounding in our state as soothing as a Bach fugue. A bed too short for me still looked inviting. During these trips we called on local French officials, hospitable in their colonial trappings, who offered visitors banquets of local game and fish along with good wines. Disrespect for Africans was prevalent among them, with a condescending "tu!" or "toi!" yelled at houseboys, laborers, and other Ivorians at hand. Some French women wore shorts so brief they revealed the teasing start of a fleshy upward curve to their derrières. I wondered what the Africans thought.

Wild animals turned up anywhere. When Mary and I decided to ride the main line from Ouagadougou to Bobo-Dioulasso in Upper Volta, we were disconcerted to find a young chimpanzee sulking in the lavatory. The bewildered beast, who presumably belonged to someone on the train, was chained to the shower pipe, and our visits were as infrequent as possible.

On returning to Abidjan from circuit riding I sent back to the State Department typewritten airgrams duly approved by Norland. They were expansive in color and detail and addressed local conditions and ways in which future aid programs might begin tackling the most immediate of development needs. I sensed that color and detail were more warmly received at the CIA than at State. I maintained a work in progress in the form of a large road map of the Ivory Coast on which I noted places where one could find cold beer; few road shacks offered a visitor ice or beer. Such information became much sought after by prospective travelers.

There was tension between the French and ourselves. They were wary to near-paranoia of anything that might appear as U.S. efforts to undermine their interests or francophone culture in these colonies about to become independent. French intelligence followed our activities with more than idle curiosity, an impression confirmed by Bill Dunbar. Their man above the surface appeared to be the local Agence France Presse representative, someone who could show up at places we would be and legitimately ask us questions. He was a likable man with a good fund of stories, and occasionally he gave as well as received.

Independence

In Abidjan we became accredited to four colonial entities then known as the Ivory Coast, Upper Volta, Niger, and Dahomey. In an effort toward integration, their leaders had formed a customs union, the Conseil de l'Entente. As a part of French West Africa, they were combined by the State Department into a single consular district three times the size of Texas that was served by us in Abidjan. The French had agreed to this arrangement, pleased, no doubt, by the low-key nature of our involvement. When these colonies achieved independence, we in Abidjan became U.S. diplomatic representatives to the four capitals: Abidjan; Ouagadougou (Upper Volta, now Burkina Faso); Cotonou (Dahomey, now Benin); and Niamey in landlocked Niger, not to be confused with Nigeria to its south. Colonizers had drawn arbitrary boundaries ignoring tribal and cultural lines, thereby yielding a legacy of increasingly ferocious internecine strife.

Why were we Americans there? Sub-Saharan Africa was of peripheral strategic importance to us during the Cold War for its resources, geographical position, and the need to counter Soviet and Chinese influences. It was becoming of increasing interest, however, to African Americans, to academics, and to foreign policy experts. Most African colonies were soon to become independent, altering the roles and relationships of the metropoles in Paris, London, and Brussels from which they were governed. Our nation's political leaders could no longer afford to ignore such large populations and empowering shifts in sovereignty, as President Eisenhower belatedly recognized.

American consulates and, later, our embassies in sub-Saharan Africa reflected U.S. objectives in being on the scene to wield what influence we had through "soft power," a sort of toe-dipping on our part into new and unpredictable waters. We wanted to know Africa better and to gain African support in international forums such as the United Nations. We sought to make friends of African leaders and their peoples, to understand their political origins and ambitions, and we wanted them to achieve the same in regard to us. Our interests also were consular and commercial. We intended to provide modest economic development assistance and, later, a Peace Corps presence. In a Cold War context, we sought to improve our almost nonexistent intelligence capabilities and to provide military assistance to leaders on our side prepared, in the first instance, to thwart Soviet ambitions in the region. It was not our objective—nor would it have been possible—to supplant in influence, cultural affinity, or presence the French, British, and Belgian governments, which already were deeply rooted in Africa and aligned with us in NATO.

Elevated to an Embassy

When the day of independence for our four countries arrived, Norland climbed on a chair outside the consulate's door, screwdriver in hand. He removed the round tin shield with the great seal of the United States upon it, replacing the consular emblem with one received barely in time through the pouch that identified us as "Embassy of the United States of America." Eventually the State Department sent us stationery with an embassy letterhead, but little else was different. Now that we were an embassy, Norland announced, our diplomatic titles would change. He became chargé d'affaires, and the graying Dunbar and I morphed into third secretaries. We sipped champagne. We ourselves, not Paris or Dakar, were now responsible for four independent countries but without representation in three, leaving coverage of them to our circuit-riding efforts. Norland retained the title *chargé d'affaires* pending accreditation of the first American ambassador to the governments of the region, which happened soon thereafter.

Accession to independence in our part of French West Africa was not disruptive to local populations, who would have been hard-pressed to say what the difference was. Life for everyone went on as usual. In Abidjan there was little jubilation about freedom won; the gain in any case was at first slight. Hatred of France had not been whipped up, and her citizens were not scrambling to leave. Threatening local pressures were absent in the countryside. Houphouët's government remained essentially the same, and key French advisers stayed in place. In the end, Houphouët overcame his reservations about independence. He was telling Norland during their breakfasts together that before he could run a railroad he needed railroad engineers. France would be teamed with Houphouët for another thirty-three years. She would retain a proprietary interest in how his railroad functioned until, during a long post-Houphouët civil war, the country all but fell apart.

More diplomats arrived in Abidjan. A German chargé who joined us was young Claus von Amsberg of movie star features and drawing room manners, who would marry Princess Beatrix of the Netherlands, later its queen. He remained a passive observer of the African scene, a disinterested and displaced European. Adam Watson, then the British consul general and later the British ambassador at Dakar, had even broader territory to cover. He was at his

amusing best describing to Mary and me his attendance at the Togolese independence celebration and the temptation he felt to join revelers in the streets
of Lomé singing, "Isn't it grand! Isn't it grand! In-de-*pen*-dent Togoland!" So
caught up was he in recalling these scenes that Adam did a little dance for us
on our terrace, gin and tonic in hand.

Félix Houphouët-Boigny governed as president of the Ivory Coast without
significant opposition. He sought to make his nation one of the leading states
in postcolonial Africa. Houphouët was short and lithe with a high forehead,
and he favored double-breasted French suits. He spoke in a calm voice and was
courteous but formal, ever conscious of status and protocol. At receptions he
moved in stately ways through the crowd, smiling broadly with his elegant,
flirtatious, and taller wife, Marie Thérèse, on his arm, his eyes blinking and
his forehead glistening under camera lights. She ran a chic Parisian dress shop
in Abidjan. Norland found Houphouët perceptive, astute, and a clever judge
of political realities at home, in the region, and in France. While punctilious
in his dealings with French officials, Houphouët maintained maneuvering
room in all of his relationships. As a statesman he stood in favorable contrast
to the three other leaders of the Conseil de l'Entente. He differed strikingly
from such maverick, marxist-influenced neighbors as Kwame Nkrumah in
Ghana and Sékou Touré in Guinea, although he had a fondness for the charismatic Touré, whom he called "my little brother."

In governing the Ivory Coast, Houphouët was a politician through and
through, managing to keep the question of a successor churning in the pot for
decades. Under the banner *Fraternité,* he exercised authority and mediating
skills with African statesmen that eventually made him the dean of surviving,
staunchly pro-Western, and rational leaders to whom stability, unchallenged
political power, and acquisition of wealth were among life's main goals. Unlike
more rapacious leaders, however, Houphouët sought genuinely to develop the
Ivory Coast's economic potential.

The last French high commissioner, Yves Guéna, aloof and haughty, had
difficulty letting go and accepting new conditions in West Africa. He derived
no pleasure from the American presence in Abidjan. At each of his arrivals
and departures from the airport before independence, heads of consulates
and senior government officials were obliged to assemble for handshakes and
the opportunity to observe him stride to his plane through a row of honor
guards. Several dozen African women of the Rassemblement Démocratique
Africaine, clad in the yellow blouses and sarongs of Houphouët's political
party, were always to one side clapping, swaying their bottoms, and chanting

gaily to the drummers' beats. A large face of Houphouët was imprinted, dead center, on the backs of their skirts, giving rise to impolite remarks among consular colleagues. This entire display was an irritating piece of theater to just about everyone, and to Africans especially. Diplomats wilting under a tropical sun quickly ran out of topics for conversation and ceased caring. Sullenly they stood and sweated.

By 1960, policy objectives and the extent of our diplomatic representation in Africa were matters of greater scrutiny in Washington. Our African efforts, or the lack of them, had become an issue in the domestic strategy of Kennedy's campaign, in which black voters played a major role. Both parties decided to give the continent a higher profile. Ambassador Loy W. Henderson, deputy under secretary for administration in the State Department, led a small team to the region that included State's top personnel manager and chief medical officer. His visit was Eisenhower's response to Kennedy's decision to send his own adviser, Averell Harriman, to West and Central Africa to highlight Eisenhower's neglect of Africa. Harriman came to Abidjan in August 1960; Henderson, a few weeks later. Both wanted to find out what was going on and made serious efforts to understand an evolving scene. In Abidjan, Houphouët, in a reference to Cold War struggles in which his ties were to the West, told Harriman, not altogether facetiously, "When I send our students to Moscow, they come back capitalists. When I send them to Paris, they return marxists!" Houphouët was disappointed that the West was not more aggressive in reaching out to young people in developing countries and training them.

Following independence, our official visitors increased apace. First came an economic assistance team of development experts, dispatched at President Eisenhower's behest, to survey the scene in West Africa. The team arrived within days after independence, and soon a small but permanent cadre of aid officials joined our fledgling embassy. Bureaucracy loathes a vacuum. We began looking for larger office space and more homes. A Foreign Service inspection team descended on us, providing advice on how to manage expansion while staying, more or less, within the regulations.

In short order we were greeting our first congressional delegation, or CODEL, led by Senator Frank Church of Idaho, including a young and assertive Edward M. Kennedy, then a practicing Washington lawyer, as well as the energetic Oregon maverick Senator Wayne Morse, whose eventual departure was hilarious. To the music of the customary drummers and dancers at the airport, this sixty-year-old from the Far West offered his own—yet in a way graceful—interpretation of African dancing. Kennedy represented his brother, the president-elect, underscoring the New Frontier's interest in Africa. I began to understand the importance of congressional travel as a means of informing one's visitors and making the case for congressional support of U.S. policies.

I never had the experience of a senior colleague in Rome, however, who was startled by the request of a traveling congressman for the companionship of an Italian woman during the evening ahead. With Foreign Service resourcefulness, my friend passed this wish to one of the embassy's intelligence attachés, who knew without hesitation how to have it fulfilled.

Former Michigan governor G. Mennen "Soapy" Williams, of men's toiletries fame, visited his new domain as Kennedy's assistant secretary of state for Africa, the first foreign affairs appointment Kennedy announced. He stirred up a fuss along his route by proclaiming that Africa was for Africans, which made sense to me but disturbed the colonials, especially in their capitals. All our visitors and delegations required briefings and logistical support, and all wanted to shop for African artifacts. Professors and journalists appeared in growing numbers, and occasionally we invited them to our homes, interested in hearing their tales. Seeking knowledge and understanding, we were swept up in a common pursuit we found engrossing.

Agricultural commodity reporting, particularly on the coffee and cocoa crops of the Ivory Coast, became an obsession with me. One of my principal sources was a Greek businessman, Basil Kokkinakis, whose crop forecasts were remarkably accurate. He was a fat man, a colonial trader out of a Sydney Greenstreet movie. I gained his confidence—Mary spoke Greek and prepared delicious Greek dishes—and Basil shared with me his personal assessments of the progress of those crops. His predictions proved useful to U.S. importers kept informed by the Department of Agriculture in Washington. During my navy days in the Pacific, while boning up for the Foreign Service examination, it did not occur to me that reporting on coffee and cocoa would be something I would do as a diplomat, or that work like this could be so engrossing. During harvesting I thought of little else but coffee and cocoa, even dreamed about them, and planned my next assault on Kokkinakis with care, beginning mentally to compose my reporting cable before I reached his office door.

Service in remote and demanding places with the crudest of medical care could exact a terrible price. My colleague Bob McKinnon arrived to establish our embassy in Ouagadougou while I was in Abidjan. From Abidjan I helped him in his groundbreaking efforts as best I could. McKinnon soon died there of overwork and an undiagnosed illness. I was unable to get out of my mind a photograph I had taken in Ouagadougou of an overcrowded hospital with a line of vultures perched along its roof.

The First Ambassador

Robert Borden Reams, a Foreign Service officer of long experience, appeared in Abidjan during November 1960 as President Eisenhower's ambassador to the four countries. He was a rounded, balding man of fifty-seven who had a colonel's mustache and the habit of stroking it toward his mouth with the fingertips of his left hand. Low-key, he came from a familiar mold of traditional diplomats. His appearance was formal and his style somewhat reserved, but those who knew him discovered a man with a zest for exploring the world around him, a lively sense of humor, and a gentle manner. In his office on many a slow day, the latest news magazine read from cover to cover, he made no further effort to look busy and had his driver take him home for a nap.

A Pennsylvanian, Reams had sampled the private sector as a salesman and hotel manager before joining the Foreign Service. Both experiences were useful preparations for diplomatic work. He had been a staff assistant to Secretary of State James F. Byrnes and, among his other posts, served jointly as consul general in Calcutta and Kathmandu, responsibilities from which he had been plucked to be awarded embassies in West Africa about which he was not enthusiastic. He relished his former part of the world, telling me, "Don't plan to die until you've seen India and China." Golf was his abiding interest; bridge and travel came next. His outlook and style, as I later witnessed, would clash with the activist mind-set of President Kennedy's New Frontier.

Norland left shortly after Reams's arrival, and Rupert A. Lloyd, fifty-three, a black Foreign Service officer, became the deputy chief of mission and my new superior. Lloyd was a Virginian with a bachelor's degree from Williams and a master's from Harvard. For several years he studied French literature at the universities of Bordeaux and Paris. His French was as good as his English. The son of a physician, he was subjected to racial segregation whenever he returned home and spoke bitterly to me of these experiences.

One evening on my terrace above the lagoon, we talked over brandy about our lives and how he felt about his career. As we spoke and watched the dark shapes of logs floating downstream to the mill, any tensions between us melted. At the time, of 3,732 Foreign Service officers, 17 were "Negroes." Not until the midseventies did the State Department make sustained efforts with muscle behind them to recruit minorities and women into the Foreign Service. I understood Lloyd's feelings of uniqueness that sometimes made him prickly. He never complained about his situation as an African American, wanting to be thought of as no different from anyone else. He could be strongly critical of West Africans, however, faulting them to their faces for not making the most of opportunities for advancement and self-improvement, now that they had their precious freedom from colonial rule. On leaving Abidjan, Rupert Lloyd became consul in Lyon and died not long afterward.

The first task assigned to me by Ambassador Reams was to arrange trips to the three other countries to allow him, during November and December 1960, to present his credentials in each. I was to accompany him as his aide. Reams had a yen for adventure. He decided to visit two of the new capitals—Niamey in Niger and Cotonou in Dahomey—by overland travel and invited our wives to join him. He approved of how I had fixed up the Jeep and stocked its ice chest with beer and Aquavit. His wife, Dottie, Mary, and the embassy's driver, Pierre, were to enjoy the relative luxury of the official Chevrolet. As we set off, Reams and I followed in the Chevrolet's dust with me at the Jeep's wheel. It was a long trip, but Reams wanted to see the African countryside, and he did.

Stopping our caravan on a remote dirt road one afternoon, we decided to walk to a nearby lake through tall, yellow grass called lion grass because it matched the coats of those animals and concealed them. We were unarmed. Reams, a birder, was looking for birds. The lake was pleasant enough, but on the way back we found paw prints crossing our path. Pierre said they were spoor of a lion that had recently passed between us and our vehicles and was close by. There was nothing to do but keep on walking in a file, and in silence, choking down panic while dreading to meet a lion's gaze. Each step through the dry grass seemed to take a long time, as in a dream's imposed slow motion when you wanted to be running away, and our footfalls sounded to us like falling trees. When we finally reached the safety of our cars—lions become active in the afternoon but are primarily nocturnal animals, and this one must not have been hungry—Reams broke out the beer and Aquavit before we set off, our hearts pounding and our mouths as dry as the lion grass itself. Never had I experienced such an overwhelming fear—the elemental, helpless terror of feeling cornered by a demon in search of meat: man in his vaunted supremacy reduced to the emotions of a fleeing gazelle.

We reached an unprepossessing hotel in a town where we were to spend a night. Our rooms were faintly perfumed and seedy. An African band downstairs, in a combined bar and restaurant from a Bogart set, gave us a warm reception. The proprietor came over and asked the ambassador to say a few words to the motley gathering of Frenchmen and African women. This he did in style, expressing the pleasure of the American people in establishing friendly relations with the people of Dahomey. He sized up his audience as he spoke and on returning to our table stroked his mustache with the fingertips of his left hand for a moment. Then he said with twinkling eyes, "We seem to be staying in a brothel." As the person responsible for our travel arrangements I nearly fainted.

Presentations of credentials to the new governments by the first American ambassador were historic events. These ceremonies were well covered by African journalists and our dual-hatted friend from Agence France Presse. Africans gave us a lot of attention because we were Americans and still the only nation, aside from France, represented in the four countries. Reams held a press conference after each event. That could be a problem, because his French was not fluent. Sometimes I would have to interpret, which sometimes also was a problem. We were cautious about discussing economic assistance levels, a matter of obvious interest to the Africans and of suspicious concern to the French. Those questions had not yet been answered within our own government. The new leaders we called on welcomed Americans, but there would have been no advantage to them in pitting us against the French. Wisely, they concentrated on gaining as much as possible from both of us.

Communist Diplomats in the Early Sixties

Toward the end of my Abidjan assignment I visited an American colleague, George Lambrakis, in neighboring Conakry, Guinea. I wanted to contrast what I had experienced in Moscow and Leningrad three years before with an experiment in communism by an African dictator in a backward country thousands of miles removed. Guinea's marxist president, Sékou Touré, alone had chosen not to remain in a special relationship with France, the former colonizer, and Guinea became fully independent under his sway.

Seizing opportunities to establish their presence, the Russians, East Europeans, and Chinese opened embassies in Conakry, introducing Cold War competition into West Africa. They would also be represented in Mozambique, Ethiopia, Somalia, Angola, and the Belgian Congo, later Zaire. Every U.S. president from Eisenhower through Reagan was to become concerned about the Congo in the context of the Cold War. In West Africa, however, the Soviet threat remained minimal.

An airport provides the introduction to its surroundings. In Conakry a sullen, uniformed official leafed through my diplomatic passport, looked at me warily, and stamped it, releasing me into an unappealing hall where George was waiting. Along the road into the city, signs of economic stagnation and decaying infrastructure were obvious.

George was able to have me included in a government reception where I noticed distinctions among the communist missions. The Chinese mingled freely, if stiffly, with Africans. The Russians kept themselves apart in their own glum circle, showing little interest or rapport with Africans, Chinese, or anyone other than the obsequious representative of their East European satellites. This social pattern reflected insecurity on the part of Soviet diplomats functioning outside areas of high priority and ideological definition, as well as strains between the Soviet Union and China. Marx had little to say about the non-Western, nonindustrialized colonial world.

The Russians never understood Black Africa.

7

BOWLES AND BALL

1961 to 1962

When it became time in Abidjan for me to think about my next assignment, which would be in Washington (the practice was to bring junior officers home after an initial two-year posting abroad), I received a telegram informing me I was to be a staff aide to the recently appointed under secretary of state, Chester Bowles.

I had not given much thought to my few months with Chet Bowles on Capitol Hill while waiting to enter the Foreign Service, nor had I been in touch with him afterward beyond thanking him for taking me on board. I recalled this spirited figure and admired the man and his humanity, remembering his drive and commitment to the well-being of ordinary people.

Preparing to leave Abidjan in 1961, I was delighted at the prospect of working again for Bowles. The time had come to dry off and bid farewell to a flea-bitten Noga, his master Mamadou the *guardien,* and the crop forecaster Basil Kokkinakis. This would be Mary's opportunity to live in America and become a citizen. On our return trip we flew from Abidjan to London and stayed with my parents, quickly to be revived by oysters, Dover sole, fresh lettuce, and Stilton cheese. We drank from the tap again and brushed our teeth with unbottled water. We were starved for the stimulation of London's theaters and crowds and yielded to the temptations of nearby Harrods.

At Southampton we boarded the SS *United States,* traveling in the lowest priced first-class cabin, as was then the Foreign Service practice. Soon afterward a member of the United States Lines' public relations staff approached us to ask whether we would pose for pictures in the dining room. I saw no harm. On the contrary, I thought this would be a good way to promote our shipping industry. It turned out we would be photographed in evening dress and party hats, toasting each other while being served a baked alaska dessert. The picture session went smoothly, and we forgot about it. Four or five months later, color photos of the two of us appeared prominently in travel advertisements in the *New Yorker* and other national magazines. The caption below them read: "At a gala dinner, Mr. and Mrs. Brandon Grove, Jr. sample a fine champagne, along with some of the world's finest cuisine prepared by master chefs. He is with the State Department." A congressman from Pennsylvania (Cambria County, no less) wrote an irate letter to the State Department.

I was appalled and thought my career finished. I went to see Fred Dutton, the assistant secretary for congressional relations, who expected an avalanche of letters tearing apart striped-pants cookie pushers. I feebly told Fred that I had served on a ship named for Cambria County, and perhaps this might help. In fact, only one letter was received, but we learned later that the dreaded Congressman John J. Rooney of Brooklyn, chairman of the House appropriations subcommittee dealing with the State Department's budget, had expressed passing interest in the photograph.

Robert Kennedy Visits Abidjan

I had been working for Bowles for a short time when President Kennedy decided that his brother, the attorney general, would represent the United States at the formal celebration of the Ivory Coast's independence in 1961. The choice of Robert Kennedy was dictated in large part by domestic politics and the civil rights movement. I was the only available Foreign Service officer who had worked at the recently opened post of Abidjan. Lucius "Luke" Battle, the executive secretary of the State Department, suggested to John Seigenthaler, the attorney general's top aide, that I be made available to Kennedy's office to help plan the trip. Seigenthaler had until recently been an investigative journalist at the *Nashville Tennessean*. He was a hard-driving, savvy, courageous, and principled newspaperman blessed with a southern accent, a gentle soul, and an impish sense of humor. He was devoted to Robert Kennedy, who in turn was nurtured by Seigenthaler's advice, companionship, and disposition to see the funny side of things.

The first time I met Robert Kennedy he was sitting at his imposing Justice Department desk, on which he had placed both feet. Bright watercolors painted by his children were taped to paneled walls. His sleeves were rolled up, his tie pulled down revealing a hairy chest. An outsize dog sprawled on the carpet. Kennedy looked like an office boy hamming it up in the boss's chair. Underneath disheveled hair, his blue eyes were penetrating. He was three years older than my thirty-two. For a moment he sized me up. "Well," he said mockingly in his Massachusetts monotone, "John here tells me you're from the *State Depaaaaht*-ment!"

This would be the first official overseas trip for the new attorney general. Soon after I began planning it, he asked me to join the traveling party consisting of himself, his wife, Ethel, and Seigenthaler. We flew to Paris on a commercial airliner and then went on to Abidjan the same way. By this time I had become acquainted with Kennedy and was beginning to understand his ways of doing things.

His interest in Africa was intense and genuine. He threw himself wholeheartedly into representing the president yet was impatient with the requirements of protocol. In general, the less developed a country, the greater its infatuation with the rites of diplomatic protocol. Kennedy professed not to understand why, in receiving lines for example, he had to wait behind chiefs of state from nations far less powerful than the United States, some of them African countries of which he had never heard. He did not want to recognize that as a cabinet officer he had to yield precedence to *any* chief of state, and he made it difficult for me to explain this to him. President Houphouët-Boigny was delighted by Kennedy's presence and received him privately.

Kennedy was hard to satisfy throughout the trip. He wanted precision in his briefings, fact separated from opinion. "Why?" was his favorite question. He maintained a frantic pace, compulsively wanting to use each minute of the day. I rarely saw him relax. He was driven, tackling everything with New Frontier "vigah." RFK did not have the president's polish or charm, making no effort to conceal his annoyance and scowling instead. All that energy became a problem in Abidjan, where hours passed without scheduled events. "You've got to keep him busy," Seigenthaler warned me. Ambassador Reams did not fill the time, and I didn't always use enough imagination to keep Kennedy involved in some sort of activity. There were dead spots in the program and worse ones in the long receiving lines in which he appeared embarrassed to be standing. Houphouët's formal dinner seemed endless and pointless to him. Kennedy's fuse was short, and I took the brunt of his dissatisfaction. When he was murdered I reflected on his impatience, and the late president's as well. Both men seemed driven and fatalistic, as if they sensed that for them time would be unfairly short while so much needed to be done. *Why can't people understand this and be more helpful,* he must have thought.

We took Kennedy out of Abidjan into the real Africa. He loved being in a village in the rain forest where he was greeted by cheering crowds, even though few, if any, understood who Robert Kennedy was. Villagers knew someone important had come to them and responded in kind. They offered music, dancing, and *bangi* palm wine that Kennedy sampled. He waved, clasped hands, and passed out his brother's PT-109 tie clips, which must have seemed mysterious to Africans who never wore neckties. Kennedy was exhilarated by these experiences outside the bounds of government protocol. The Ivorians had given him a warm and boisterous welcome. He would return to Africa several times more, focusing on South Africa and the racial segregation of apartheid. This first visit was a deeper and more complex experience than he had expected.

Reams did not think well of Robert Kennedy, considering him, as he told me, an upstart. Bob and Ethel found Reams stuffy, old-fashioned, and numbingly low-key. He wanted the president's ambassadors to be actively engaged in representing the New Frontier. This was more than a clash of personalities. Reams was wedded to traditional ways and believed the Foreign Service knew best. He remained insensitive to the status of his visitor as First Brother, stayed away when he could, and failed to pick up Kennedy's signals and shift his posture. The upshot was that upon our return Kennedy told the president he needed a new ambassador in Abidjan. The episode saddened me because I liked Reams, understood the problem from both sides, and had spoken in his defense. Reams retired from the Foreign Service and was succeeded by James W. Wine, a political appointee from Connecticut then serving as ambassador to Luxembourg.

From New Deal to New Frontier

Working with Chester Bowles and Robert Kennedy early in my career, and for a while simultaneously, provided opportunities to contrast them. Here were two people from different wings of the Democratic Party, a generation apart, serving in an administration where the accent was on youth and new frontiers.

Bowles's roots were in the New Deal. He achieved national prominence in 1943 as head of the wartime Office of Price Administration, an unprecedented intrusion of government into the domestic economy. With him was a young assistant professor of economics from Princeton, John Kenneth Galbraith, whom he would, on a far-off day, succeed as ambassador to India. After

Truman's time in office, custodians of the New Deal stayed on in Washington or returned to Cambridge and New York. When John Kennedy came along, these party loyalists constituted not merely a cabinet-in-waiting but almost a government-in-waiting. Bowles, who was JFK's nominal adviser on foreign affairs during the campaign, and Adlai Stevenson, also, hoped to become secretary of state. Kennedy, however, brought none of the former New Dealers into his cabinet.

Robert Kennedy was a man of passions and causes. His public career began inauspiciously in 1952, when his scheming father persuaded Senator Joseph McCarthy to appoint Robert as assistant counsel to his subcommittee on investigations. Kennedy did not participate in witch hunts at the State Department or the Voice of America but in the six months he worked for McCarthy produced a report on worldwide shipping to mainland China during the Korean War. The taint of association with McCarthy stayed with him. At the convention nominating JFK, RFK's impact was that of a tough and disliked political manager, someone on the convention floor who bullied delegations and fence-sitters into line. While Bowles presided over the more remote Platform Committee embodying the liberals' views, Robert Kennedy reflected the take-no-prisoners Irish ways of Massachusetts. He was considered of the fray rather than above it and deliberately took political heat for his brother to keep JFK looking statesmanlike.

Tom Hughes, Bowles's longtime associate and adviser, was at the 1960 Democratic Convention and recalls that Bowles viewed JFK as a man "with no moral compass" and his brother Robert as a ruthless cohort of Senator McCarthy and J. Edgar Hoover. To the Kennedys' annoyance, Bowles did not discourage a Bowles-for-president movement at the convention; its placards were there for all to see. According to Hughes, Bowles announced a liberal Democratic platform without consulting Kennedy beforehand. Hughes describes the Bowles-RFK relationship as contemptuous on both sides. In 1961, nevertheless, a thirty-five-year-old attorney general and Bowles, at sixty an under secretary of state disappointed in occupying the number-two position, began serving in the presidency of a forty-three-year-old John Kennedy. Vision and values motivated Bowles. The Kennedys lived by nonideological pragmatism. Their approaches would clash.

A lively, all-but-fairy-tale social scene unfolded in Washington. Beginning with the first snowbound inaugural parties in Georgetown, journalists, photographers, and other predators seemed obsessed in their search for tidbits about who had been invited where and by whom. A man of inborn charm and flair, whose life and family caught the world's imagination, John Kennedy enjoyed his ties to prominent people on the social scenes of New York, Miami, and Hollywood and to the fast-living glitterati of the jet set. Few knew of his ill-nesses or sexual peccadilloes. His wife, Jacqueline, familiarly known everywhere as Jackie, became the most written about and photographed woman in the world. She was a person of accomplishment, speaking Spanish and French, the latter so fluently she once served as interpreter between her husband and Charles de Gaulle at a state dinner in the Elysée Palace. Asked what sort of music her husband liked, she responded in her feathery voice that his favorite tune was "Hail to the Chief." A dazzling aura surrounded the presidential cou-ple. They seemed to have sprung out of the imagination of F. Scott Fitzgerald.

Issues such as poverty, civil rights, and wages and prices in the steel indus-try were bringing Robert Kennedy's serious side to public notice, and not always favorably. He acquired greater depth and became more meditative and moody. Shyness in social settings and disdain for small talk inclined him to avoid the social scene at the White House. Formal dinners for visiting heads of state and their retinues, choreographed by diplomatic protocol, held no allure for him. I heard him complain more than once about being placed "between two large women" he had never met before and quickly running out of conversation. This was all, he thought, a waste of his time. Such formalities did not touch the essence of his life or the responsibilities he bore for the president. People in Washington prized their White House invitations as evi-dence of influence and status. Their names, appearing in the small print of guest lists at state dinners, were published the following day in the *Washington Post* for all to examine. For Robert Kennedy this was irrelevant.

Parties Mary and I attended at his Hickory Hill home were boisterous and fun, sometimes with a sophomoric twist or two. One evening I observed an ill-at-ease Vice President Lyndon Johnson at the edge of a large outdoor gather-ing standing almost alone by the bar and looking for someone safe and sane to talk at, or flirt with. An irrepressible Ethel, unperturbed by the finer points of entertaining, set the tone: children rioting everywhere and the unavoidable presence of Brumus, a shaggy Newfoundland, surely one of the world's biggest and least engaging dogs who, as many would discover, pooped copiously. Some-one was always on crutches, a personal badge of honor in the tribe. Ethel had the wholesomeness and fresh-air beauty—the outdoor qualities of an athlete and spontaneous laughter—of the cover girl from the upper-class preserve of Greenwich, Connecticut, that she was. At her funniest she engaged in a teasing form of understatement about people and situations around her, delivered deadpan and revealing a keen eye and sharp tongue. The swimming pool be-

came a magnet in late hours, with a prominent someone being pushed or hap-
pily jumping in fully clothed. Most people there loved it, among other reasons
for the excitement of what might happen next. After one more swimming pool
incident that made the papers, Ethel told me JFK had said "Enough."

A handsome, dapper graduate of Choate and Yale, a former governor of
Connecticut and congressional colleague of John Kennedy's, an accomplished
golfer and multimillionaire, Chester Bowles seemed at first blush to have much
in common with the president. Puritanical a bit, and conscience-driven, he
had no patience for time idly spent in banter or for swimming pool shenani-
gans. Chet was a voluble talker but a reluctant, impatient listener, adept at flattery but not inclined to show deference. His wife, "Steb," the former Dorothy
Stebbins, was a thoughtful, gentle, and perceptive woman who had no interest in Kennedy goings-on and found many of them undignified, although she
was a fun-loving person herself.

When the Bowleses entertained in their Georgetown home on N Street, or
around their garden pool, their guests were drawn from intellectual circles and
the ranks of liberal Democrats. The atmosphere was informal, but no one
would describe it as boisterous. Chet and Steb favored young people, and I
would find myself delighted to be talking with someone like the *New York
Times* journalist James "Scotty" Reston, propped against the mantel with a
drink in hand. Chet's mind clicked away on issues of Asia, Africa, and Latin
America, unable to let up for long even in family surroundings. It was always
issues with Chet: less so the immediate and narrowly defined questions of the
day, but more likely within the biggest picture he could frame. Chet liked to
"toss continents around to see how they splashed," Reston observed. His style
of advocacy, even with the president, could become insistent, overstated, and
at times unintentionally arrogant when he lectured his chief in long memos
tending to stray from the topic at hand. Bowles was an idea man by nature
and preference. He told me: "I like to think I can have ten good ideas a week.
I know seven of them aren't going anywhere, but three of them might, and
sometimes do. So, my score is three good, workable ideas a week. That's not
bad." The search for good and bold ideas, "fresh thinking" Chet called it, was
the holy grail in the advertising world of Benton and Bowles. It was also what
made a man a visionary.

The president seemed to take Bowles seriously and respected, and I think
shared, some of his foreign policy views. But Robert Kennedy felt uncomfortable with Chet, criticizing to me his erratic performance at the State Department. Fundamental differences existed between Bowles and the Kennedys involving covert actions in the Dominican Republic, as well as JFK's Bay of Pigs

adventurism in Cuba. Bowles shunned spycraft and military actions. Robert Kennedy was uncertain of Bowles's loyalties and wary of his alliances with powerful liberal friends. He saw Bowles as someone with an agenda of his own, one that would not always match the president's. A cardinal sin attributed by both Kennedys to Bowles was that he talked to the press to promote his own opinions and objectives—and he did. But when I informed Bob in June 1963 that Bowles, who had been fired as under secretary of state eighteen months earlier, had asked me to join him in India on his second tour as ambassador there, Kennedy's surprising reply was: "Do it. He's a good man."

Bob's gaze on the world was acquiring greater depth. Bowles's emphasis on Third World countries with enormous populations struggling to get on their feet while superpowers fenced with each other was more understandable and seemed wiser to him now. Their leaders, influence, and futures mattered in spheres beyond the bipolar struggles of a zero-sum game in international politics. Southeast Asia, a region about which Bowles held passionate views, was increasingly in Kennedy's troubled thoughts.

An Irrepressible Bowles at Work

After traveling with Robert Kennedy to Abidjan, I returned to my new job with Chester Bowles. His State Department office included people he had brought with him from Capitol Hill: his closest adviser, Tom Hughes, and Patricia Durand, a lively and committed young woman who was Bowles's secretary and knew nearly everything about him. But there were also Philip Merrill, later publisher of the *Washingtonian* magazine and president of the Export-Import Bank; Samuel W. Lewis, who was his senior Foreign Service assistant, although a bit green for the job; Andrew Rice, an economic and development assistance expert; James Thomson Jr., who specialized in Asian matters; and me at the bottom of the pile as factotum.

At his initiative I had joined Bowles as a former member of his Capitol Hill team, not as a junior Foreign Service officer on his first assignment to Washington duly selected by the people in personnel. Although I never thought of it, my credibility and credentials as a serious professional were on the line. I was happy to be with Bowles, eager to understand America's changing role in the world and to gain insights into my chosen field from such a remarkable vantage point.

Bowles's Foreign Service staff was thin in numbers, rank, and experience. Sam Lewis had recently been in charge of Italian affairs as a midlevel officer. I had no Washington background and only one overseas tour under my belt in a remote former colony in West Africa. Bowles liked the fact that my first post was Abidjan, and to him I probably appeared untainted by the State Department's wayward ways. He would have been wiser to have had the benefit of more senior Foreign Service people around him, skillfully involving him in the department's work and speaking more authoritatively on his behalf to its other leaders. There seemed to be no one he knew or trusted to serve him in such loyal fashion on his personal staff, and he liked the team he had.

The Executive Secretariat managed the State Department's paper flow, and Nick Veliotes was our point of contact there. So began a three-way friendship for Lewis, Veliotes, and me that flourished beyond our careers. We were nearly the same age and shared a common span of the American experience. Sam Lewis's legacy to U.S. diplomacy would come to reside in his eight years as ambassador to Israel, confronted time and again by the most vexing and delicate problems in this exceptional relationship.

In 1985, the Italian cruise ship *Achille Lauro* was hijacked in the Mediterranean Sea by terrorists of the Palestine Liberation Front led by Abu Abbas. A sixty-nine-year-old American confined to a wheelchair, Leon Klinghoffer, was shot and dumped overboard. Veliotes, our ambassador in Cairo, gained international renown when, having later boarded the ship in Alexandria to speak with the passengers, he radioed back to his deputy at the embassy, "Tell the foreign minister we insist they prosecute those sons of bitches!" Nick didn't know his conversation would be overheard by the media, or that his instruction would be repeated verbatim on American newscasts. This was exactly what an enraged public wanted to hear from its ambassador in Cairo. Nick would become the deputy chief of mission, or DCM, in our embassy in Tel Aviv before Sam Lewis's arrival, ambassador to Jordan, and assistant secretary of state in charge of our relations with the Middle East while I served in Jerusalem.

Rusk had commended Bowles to John Kennedy for the number-two position at State before his own nomination as secretary was assured. He knew Kennedy only slightly. Rusk had served in senior positions at the State Department under Acheson during Truman's administration and was acquainted with Bowles from his days as president of the Ford Foundation, where Bowles had been a trustee, and from a trip they took together in India. When people travel together they develop feelings about their compatibility. Rusk presumably would not have mentioned Bowles's name to Kennedy if he did not believe he could work with him. Or perhaps Rusk was signaling that he believed Bowles should be thought of as a deputy, not a potential secretary of state. Both at the time were vying with others for the top job. In any case, this was a recommendation Rusk would quickly regret.

Bowles was a national figure and remained involved in the civil rights movement. He stayed in touch with his network of liberal Democratic friends and officeholders in Kennedy's administration, lowering his profile only somewhat when he left Capitol Hill and moved to the State Department. His independent behavior and eccentric work habits were those of an advertising mogul, governor, and congressman, an optimist and free spirit accustomed to success who churned with energy, intellectual drive, and creative juices.

Working for Bowles at the State Department, I sat with Sam in a glassed-in office facing the double doors opening onto Bowles's dark-paneled and grand seventh-floor executive suite. Our surroundings were comfortable and dignified in a muted 1950s way. Government-provided furnishings in Bowles's office consisted of blue leather chairs and couches with small tables and lamps before and beside them, as well as a large, symbolic globe. On the walls hung fine examples of nineteenth-century American paintings. The under secretary's glass-topped desk was the focal point. Across the hall was a conference room with a long table and additional chairs lined up against the walls. Staff aides like me, wearing narrow ties, white shirts, and charcoal gray suits, sat in these chairs, taking notes to follow up on the discussions of our superiors at the table. Early in his tenure as under secretary, Elliot Richardson turned to a colleague at his side to ask, "Who are all those black crows along the wall?"

On the walls of the formal corridor leading to the executive suites hung large, solemn portraits of former secretaries of state. In Bowles's outer office black-framed photographs of his predecessors were neatly arrayed in several rows. I recognized their signatures: Sumner Welles, Joseph Grew, Dean Acheson, Robert Lovett, David Bruce, and Douglas Dillon, among others. In the rarefied atmosphere of the seventh floor, I wondered, would I be able to make myself useful to a whirlwind Bowles?

Our office was noisy and disorderly, with people walking in and out at will. Pat Durand, sitting at her messy desk, let out shrieks of laughter as she joked and addressed many of our visitors by their first names. Our suite had an engaging, happy, and politically charged atmosphere that did not translate into an effective or smooth operation for Bowles and contrasted oddly with the decorum and low murmurs in Dean Rusk's bank of offices down the hall, where business was done in traditional ways and the machinery was well oiled. We seemed, I thought, part campaign headquarters and part congressional zoo. Bowles viewed himself as a policy maker, not a manager of policies or an administrator of the State Department beyond his recommendations of people for top positions. He was unwilling to think his visions through to the con-

crete steps, time lines, and predictable conflicts and compromises that fuel decision making in a bureaucracy. All of this made him difficult to work for.

I soon recognized, for example, how hard it was to get Bowles to focus on
the regular flow of decision papers about policy issues, often tightly framed
but important enough to reach his desk. Their numbers increased while the
secretary of state was away and Bowles also was acting for Rusk. Policy is shaped
incrementally. The drift of day-to-day choices and narrowly based decisions
needs to be monitored lest in time it create an unintended change of course,
something Bowles chose not to acknowledge. He was a big-idea person who
didn't do implementation. Not only did the papers piling up on my desk concern me when they were ignored, but Bowles's failure to act also frustrated
people down the line who needed decisions and were pressing me to get things
moving.

One morning I told Pat Durand I wanted an uninterrupted hour with her
boss and asked her to make certain he would see me. When Bowles gave me the
time, I walked into his office with an accumulation of papers, ratcheted up my
courage, and said to him, "Chet (astonishingly, in the State Department culture
of the day we all called him that), there are some things you really must do as
under secretary of this department, and I have a stack of them here, sir." He
sighed, but did not complain. We sat together and went through the pile, document by document. I summarized the content of each, and he reached his decisions and put his initials in the proper places, or sent his comments back.

To help those of us on his staff keep track of what concerned Bowles, we
monitored his telephone conversations by depressing a plastic button that
allowed us to listen in without making a clicking sound as we picked up the
receiver. This was standard practice on the seventh floor, and sometimes as
many as three or four of us tuned in from our desks. Pat Durand, or one of
his other assistants, was expected to write summaries of these conversations
called "telcons," which were tightly held and distributed only to the people on
Bowles's immediate staff needing to act on them.

In a further complication of our work, Bowles was uncomfortable with the
Foreign Service and its ways, believing it to be tradition-bound and conservative, narrowly Eurocentric, insensitive to younger generations of leaders abroad,
wrong on China policy, and driven by a sterile bipolar Cold War agenda.
Worse, he believed there were few, if any, "fresh thinkers." Nor was everyone
in the Foreign Service pleased with him. To his critics he seemed an ideologue,
a glib, disorganized, and opinionated politician with a liberal agenda who
tended to use meetings over which he presided to lecture on larger but not

directly relevant issues. They would have preferred a steely eyed bureaucratic warrior with clout, someone to fight the interagency battles on State's behalf, speaking recognizably for Rusk. Several old-time ambassadors of the Dulles era took his advent, correctly, as a sign that it was time for them to leave.

Choosing Ambassadors

The modern Foreign Service came into its days of glory at the onset of the Cold War. The most talented body of diplomats since Benjamin Franklin's time emerged during the forties and fifties. They shaped alliance diplomacy and set the stage for an internationalist twenty-first century. In its greatest crisis, America found it had men and women equal to the challenge. Their names resonated in the corridors as warriors on the diplomatic edge struggling to create a durable peace between superpowers armed with nuclear weapons. They focused on Russia, Japan, and Germany, but not soon enough on China. For my generation they were people to emulate.

Bowles deeply involved himself in the selection of an extraordinarily able group of noncareer ambassadors, many his friends. He paid less attention to highfliers in the Foreign Service. Overall, his choices may have been the most qualified and intellectually forceful group of ambassadors from private life to serve the nation together in the twentieth century. Among them: Harvard's Edwin O. Reischauer, to Japan; George Kennan, then at Princeton, to Yugoslavia; William Attwood, foreign affairs editor of *Look* magazine, to Guinea; Amherst's president, Charles W. Cole, to Chile; Lincoln Gordon, a Harvard economist, to Brazil; Oberlin's president, William E. Stevenson, to the Philippines; the president of the American University in Cairo, John S. Badeau, to the United Arab Republic; Philip M. Kaiser, with a background in labor affairs, to Senegal; and in an outreach to Hispanics, Teodoro Moscoso, from the office of the governor of Puerto Rico, to Venezuela.

Ambassadors reflect the United States and radiate our values. They are personal representatives of a president and should be the most qualified among our citizens. They have serious work to do. The best come from private life and the Foreign Service alike, as career diplomats have no lock on what it takes to succeed. Some are close friends of a president and chosen by him, or are people in whom he has confidence and whom he wants to engage in his administration. Others from private life are put forward by the political staff in the White House on the basis of their campaign contributions, and therein lies a problem.

Historically, about one-third of our embassies, usually in European capitals and other agreeable places in which to entertain one's friends, have been awarded to political appointees. But this is not a matter of proportion. When unqualified ambassadors get their posts as political payoffs in one of the last vestiges of a spoils system, the American people are poorly served and the governments to which they are sent are not always flattered. Such governments are inclined to shift their weightiest conversations with us to Washington, where their own representatives can carry the burden of relations. Foreign leaders tend to doubt that presidential ties to an erstwhile political fund-raiser from a key state will do them much good when it comes to the specifics. Many prefer to deal with an American ambassador more professional and knowing in the ways of Washington, someone skilled in their language and culture, a person of both passion and precision. And sometimes they tell us so.

Few issues tap into Foreign Service emotions more deeply than the question of political versus career ambassadorial appointments. Would you put a neophyte in charge of an aircraft carrier? But asking that begs the question of competence. Many people in public and corporate life have had broad experience overseas and bear solid international credentials and reputations. They can be well attuned to a president's intentions and the economic underpinnings of his foreign policies. True, some political appointees have been embarrassing public failures and others only marginally competent. But it also is a fact that some Foreign Service officers have been called home from their posts, and others scraped through with barely a passing grade. Neither circumstance fits our times. There is no rational argument for having our nation represented by mediocre talent, no matter what its origin. The problem for the Foreign Service often enough is that a secretary of state is not willing to push the best career people forward and fight for them in the Oval Office, if need be. I served with six politically appointed ambassadors and two from the Foreign Service. The best and worst were Foreign Service officers.

Dean Rusk approved most of Bowles's ambassadorial proposals, reserving to himself key personnel choices for Asian and European posts, in particular. The director general of the Foreign Service, Ambassador Tyler Thompson, kept track of vacancies nine months ahead and put forward the names of Foreign Service professionals qualified to fill each of them. His choices reflected competence and experience over many years, knowledge of a country and its region, and the best language training available in the United States.

Bowles asked Thompson to reach down into the organization to find younger officers for some of the smaller embassies and to dispatch European specialists to Latin America, and vice versa, to stretch their minds. Years later Henry Kissinger, a very different player in the game of diplomacy, acted on the same instinct. The personnel policy of global assignments he imposed bore the arresting acronym GLOP.

Troubled Waters

All of us working within the seventh floor's executive cocoon noticed a growing coolness between Rusk and Bowles. Luke Battle, as the State Department's executive secretary and a discerning diplomat of tact and insight, sought to reduce the tensions, steadfastly trying to bring about reconciliation. Walter Cutler, my counterpart in Rusk's office, and I, both of us serving at staff levels where good work of this kind can be done, tried with minimal success to smooth things over. As they drifted further apart, we recognized that we needed to strengthen the fraying ties between these leaders of the State Department, but we no longer knew how to do so. Their differences stemmed from personality clashes, failures in communication, competing agendas, conflicting management styles, and Rusk's disappointment that Bowles was not the supportive under secretary he wanted.

In May 2004, Cutler and I reminisced about relations between Rusk and Bowles forty-three years earlier. "The first two years of the Kennedy administration were extraordinarily filled with high-pressure foreign policy challenges," Walt recalled. "The demands of the president and his White House staff on the State Department and on the new secretary of state in particular were relentless. Adding to those pressures was the fact that Rusk was an outsider, a new boy on the block feeling his way among many who had known Kennedy personally for many years. Rusk always addressed Kennedy as 'Mr. President,' in contrast to some of the others serving on Rusk's senior staff who did not hesitate to pick up the phone and call 'Jack' directly.

"If Rusk was by nature a workaholic, he was doubly so during those initial, hectic days," Walt continued. "He arrived early and seldom left the office until well into the evening, carrying a briefcase packed with papers on which he would work for hours into the early morning. He desperately needed a competent deputy to share the overwhelming burdens on his time. This, sadly, was not what he found in Bowles. Whereas Rusk would seek to make every minute count in trying to manage multiple crises, Bowles seemed quite oblivious to the exigencies of the workday. Whereas Rusk was a man of restraint and few words, all too often Bowles sought to 'rap' at length with his boss. Bowles's appearance at Rusk's office door and the phone calls from an equally loquacious Adlai Stevenson at the United Nations—both often coming toward the end of an exhausting day—elicited the few words of irritation I ever heard the secretary mutter to his immediate staff. He was too much the southern gentleman to say more."

Dean Rusk, as I saw him and heard about him from my end of the hall, was further uncomfortable with Bowles as his alter ego. He was annoyed by Bowles's lack of interest in matters vital to carrying out policy and to the smooth functioning of the State Department on substantive issues. He was dismayed by Bowles's holistic but disorganized approach to the developing world. Rusk wanted a focused deputy who would help him manage the global consequences during the Cold War of the full array of our foreign policies. Bowles was by temperament unsuited to the role of a number two anywhere, and that was the core of his problem. Face-to-face communication between Rusk and Bowles dried up, with Bowles writing increasingly wordy memos to Rusk down the corridor. Bowles, too, had fallen from whatever favor he enjoyed in the White House by criticizing Kennedy's Bay of Pigs decision to journalist friends who only lightly masked their source. Others in the building, ever sensitive to shifting breezes, noted all of this.

Rusk endured stoically the strains of working for Kennedy in a relationship that never became close. McGeorge Bundy, heading the National Security Council (NSC) staff, was from the outset the president's principal foreign policy adviser. Rusk was losing confidence in Bowles while he was obliged to deal with an ever more fractious Soviet Union following Kennedy's unsuccessful first encounter with Khrushchev in Vienna. Then, too, Rusk was helping to shape presidential decisions during the early stages of U.S. involvement in Vietnam, when the extent and nature of that engagement hung in the balance. It must have been a joyless time for him. I saw little of Secretary Rusk, and as those of us on Bowles's staff dealt with his immediate staff we occasionally felt some of the tensions between our principals reflected back at us.

Many years after Rusk left the State Department, I found myself sitting with him at the long table in the eighth-floor executive dining room that had open seating. We were three or four people enjoying a late lunch when, having concluded whatever business brought him back to the building, Rusk wandered in and joined us. For an hour or so, he regaled us in his husky-voiced southern accents with tales of his stewardship and his current academic concerns at the University of Georgia. Rusk's warmth and humor, and an earthiness and modesty to his manner, were engaging. He seemed at peace with himself, and I felt privileged to see this side of him. Then, twelve years after Bowles left the State Department, I came upon Dean Rusk at a cocktail party in Georgetown and afterward made a note of our conversation. Bowles, he told me in answering my question, was an admirable man with "great, great ideas, but he made two mistakes. He was on the wrong side of the Bay of Pigs, and let people know that. And he let papers pile up on his desk."

My tour with Bowles ended abruptly. Despite everything, I was startled to hear on the radio, during Thanksgiving weekend of 1961, that the president had fired Bowles. He had become part of the "Thanksgiving Massacre," as other changes were made in the administration that day. George W. Ball, then in charge of economic affairs at State, would become the new under secretary. I felt pained and embarrassed by the abrupt manner in which Bowles's belongings were moved to a much smaller office outside the executive suites, but above all by the humiliation in Chet's face. Bowles had been kicked sideways rather than out to avoid uproar in the liberal wing of the Democratic Party. Soon his black-framed photograph joined the pantheon of his predecessors, the fine features of a civilized man whose composed expression offered no insight into the reality of his ten-month tenure as Dean Rusk's deputy.

President Kennedy had fired two of my superiors at the outset of my career: Reams in Abidjan and Bowles in Washington. These were lessons in the politics of life at the top, giving me an appreciation of what could happen to people functioning behind grand titles.

George Ball, Cerebral and Passionate

When George Ball became under secretary, he kept me on to carry out tasks I had learned to handle under Bowles. I remained at my desk outside the great doors, but my role changed to performing the many functions of a junior staff assistant in a more formal relationship to my chief, with whom I rarely spoke beyond the day's greetings. I attended meetings in Ball's office as a note taker and recorder of decisions. Afterward, I followed up. I was not among those who monitored his phone calls, and it never occurred to me to call him "George."

A forbidding woman who demanded deference and managed to intimidate all who approached her took Pat Durand's chair. The same senior people in the building who had bounded in to see Bowles now were straightening their neckties and standing silently, or murmuring together, as they waited for their appointments with Ball. Not all of the new crispness was bad.

George Ball was a great contrast to Bowles in personal and managerial styles. He was a tall, heavyset midwesterner with curly, graying hair and a strongly featured face. He looked and dressed like the international lawyer from a prominent New York firm he was. He conveyed an impression of authority. Ball was a man of forceful intellect, affable toward friends and colleagues but otherwise cool and aloof. He functioned with a small, tightly knit, and extremely competent staff skilled in his issues and the ways of bureaucracy. He liked to hold meetings, but small ones. He exercised seasoned political judgment, having been involved in the political campaigns of Adlai Stevenson and John Kennedy. In taking up new responsibilities, Ball saw to it that his relationship with Rusk, a friend of long standing, remained supportive; he was often to be found in the secretary's office down the hall. I sensed, almost physically, a return flow of power to the under secretary's suite.

Lawyers serving in the State Department's top policy jobs tend to keep their law firm ways. They like to function with only a few trusted people around them, clerks and partners in a sense, with whom they huddle and debate in secrecy. Advocates and negotiators, they are not by inclination managers of large organizations. Lawyers are accustomed to having clients approach *them* with their problems. They tend to think on a case-by-case basis, valuing principle, precedent, and procedure, rules and logic, and they shy away from bold or new initiatives. They seek to win an argument before a deciding judge or jury, usually on narrow aspects.

Intractable foreign policy issues do not present themselves that way. When diplomacy fails, governments can resort to force, a prospect lawyers do not ordinarily contemplate. This doesn't mean lawyers are unable to succeed in the sausage factory ambience of foreign policy making, or lack passion when it is needed. For many this becomes a matter of having to adjust to a different professional environment, obliging them to change their accustomed roles and behavior. As they settle into the comforts and pleasures of their suites on the seventh floor of the State Department, lawyers must prepare, in short order, to become generals of bureaucratic armies and articulators of policy to audiences across the world. Ball settled in effortlessly.

He opposed our military buildup in Vietnam and questioned the capabilities of various leaders in Saigon. James Reston wrote in his memoir that he asked Ball how Kennedy and Johnson became ever more deeply enmeshed in Vietnam. "[They] just didn't ask the giraffe question, he observed mysteriously, and then clarified this with a story. A man took his little boy one day to the zoo and, pointing to a long-necked spotted creature, said, 'That's a giraffe.' And the little boy said, 'Why?' That was the problem, concluded Ball. 'We didn't ask the little boy's simple question: Why, *why*, WHY did we get into that mess in the first place?'" Ball found himself isolated on this issue even in the State Department, where Rusk and William Bundy, the assistant secretary for the Far East, professed to believe in a successful military outcome.

In 1966, Ball returned to private life. Later, he would write about Bowles as under secretary that he was "too noble for life in the bureaucratic jungle." The same observation would apply in the end to George Ball himself.

8

AROUND THE WORLD WITH RFK

1962

After our Abidjan trip, as I began working for Chester Bowles, Bob and Ethel Kennedy often invited Mary and me to Hickory Hill. There we met people attracted to Washington by the excitement of serving in the new administration and at Bob's Justice Department, as well as journalists, film stars, athletes, the astronaut John Glenn, and pretty much anyone else who was famous. The Kennedys tended to be starstruck. Bob's division heads were perhaps the most talented lawyers ever to work together at Justice. Many felt it was like the early days of the New Deal to be serving in an administration aggressively seeking social change and progress.

On a bright April Sunday in 1962, Bob and Ethel invited the new Soviet ambassador, Anatoly Dobrynin, and his wife to Hickory Hill for a family get-acquainted luncheon. We gathered with a few other guests on the stone terrace overlooking the rolling lawn with its old trees and the blue swimming pool beyond, where Kennedy children and the pony-sized Brumus cavorted. I was amused to see Dobrynin blink at this scene, unsure of how to behave amid such chaos. Despite his stiff Soviet manner, he soon relaxed and began to enjoy himself in this family free-for-all. Although I was sitting at his table, I do not remember a serious subject being discussed. Six months later, Robert Kennedy and Dobrynin would play critical roles in secret negotiations defusing the Cuban missile crisis and avoiding nuclear strikes, both becoming indispensable voices of their governments at a time of greatest tension. By then they knew each other, and each had judged the trustworthiness of the other. People, after all, conduct diplomacy.

While I was still working as staff aide to George Ball, Robert Kennedy asked me to join John Seigenthaler in planning his trip around the world scheduled for February 1962. "Things don't happen," Bob liked to observe, "they are made to happen." This would be a high-profile tour to spread the message of new energy in America's leadership. Ball, who neither liked nor trusted RFK, was happy to have just one person at the State Department responsible for the detailed planning that would go into this trip. As I was on his immediate staff, he could keep an eye on progress. When Ball encountered me in his private elevator, knowing what it could be like to deal with Robert Kennedy, he would shake his head and ask with a chuckle, "Are you all right?" I always was. I moved into a small, windowless back room along the seventh-floor corridor, until then assigned to our messengers, and turned it into a command center of sorts.

The traveling party would consist of Robert and Ethel Kennedy; John Seigenthaler; Susie Wilson, the wife of Donald Wilson, deputy director of the U.S. Information Agency; and myself. Susie was a close and high-spirited friend of Ethel's and had been assigned to the trip by the *Ladies' Home Journal* to write an article about her. We had no security people and were accompanied throughout by four American reporters and one photographer, all of us traveling on commercial airlines. John Seigenthaler and I "advanced" the Asian portion of the trip before the Kennedys left. Our task was to set the agenda and schedule for each stop. This gave us an opportunity to meet with key actors to discuss the attorney general's wishes and the problems these could cause our embassies. We were planning a globe-circling trip of thirty thousand miles with fourteen stops in twenty-eight days.

On the Road

Kennedy made youth a major theme of his trip and was scheduled to meet young people in different settings along the way. He saw them as future leaders and natural recruits to the vision and dynamism of the New Frontier. One of his criteria for judging an embassy was how well its officers were acquainted with new generations who would be taking over. In Tokyo, our Japanese hosts created an "RFK Youth Committee," whose leaders were hovering around their forties. Our traveling press loved it and never stopped making "youth" jokes. By now, RFK was recognized nearly everywhere and known to be the president's closest confidant. Kennedy was cautious, however, when his briefs took him into foreign policy questions, sometimes consulting Rusk along the way. Among other concerns, he did not intend to annoy the president with squabbles in his cabinet, and he was on Rusk's turf. He did not trample on many toes and took care to heed most of the advice our embassies proffered.

Separate schedules were planned for Ethel and Susie, but Mrs. Kennedy wanted to be with her husband, and we had their schedules coincide as much as possible. Ethel did not take to the standard fare of spousal programming—visits to children's hospitals, local museums, and ladies gathered for tea—but was prepared to be a good sport about it. She found her own ways to accomplish major shopping and otherwise chose to be with the group around Bob as he moved through crowds sometimes numbering in the thousands. As in any political campaign, this is where the excitement was. Ethel adored her husband, managing to sidestep his tight-lipped exasperation over the time it took her to dress for dinner and put on her makeup—and occasionally a wig in the fashion of the day. I never saw them quarrel seriously. As a couple they were affectionate and confiding, read each other's thoughts and moods, and laughed at the same things. Bob loved her and was proud of her. He listened closely to her advice and assessments of people. He drew on his wife the way a plant draws on sunlight.

The trip succeeded due to the amount of work Bob put into it. He cared with single-minded passion about what he was doing and about furthering an agenda each capital and Washington had agreed upon. Robert Kennedy was a shy and private man. Constant public exposure was not easy for him. Yet he radiated his broad-grinned, tousle-haired charm to enormous crowds in Tokyo and Berlin who literally turned him on, as he did them. When he remarked about the size of crowds afterward, sometimes in awe because he was not yet the family politician and still in JFK's shadow, it was in wonderment, not vainglory. At each stop he saw himself as representing his brother, the president.

We had an awkward moment in an elevator at Tokyo's Okura Hotel one morning, when its manager assigned a slim woman in white kimono to polish Bob's shoes on our way down to the lobby. When he saw what was happening, Bob softly cried "Oh no, *please!*" and John and I lifted her gently to her feet before the doors opened on the usual crowded scene. I don't recall ever seeing Bob more rattled, thinking no doubt of what a picture that would make. I turned briefly to console the woman and found in her face a deep blush of shame and disgrace. She was staring at her feet and did not catch my smile, this frail casualty of the unpredictable "round eyes."

The most dramatic incident of the trip occurred at Waseda University in Tokyo, where Kennedy was scheduled to speak. Shortly before he was to appear we learned that a leftist youth group, Zengakuren, was organizing disruptions.

Ambassador Reischauer was concerned about Kennedy's safety. We talked the matter over, and Bob decided to stay with his schedule. In a student auditorium designed to hold fifteen hundred people, we found twice that number jammed together. A heckler in the front row interrupted Kennedy and criticized the United States along communist propaganda lines. Then the lights went out, deadening the microphone. Kennedy was given a bullhorn and spoke extemporaneously in response.

"Let me just tell you what the United States stands for. . . . We were born and raised in revolution. . . . We believe in the principle that the government exists for the individual, and that the individual is not a tool of the state. . . . We in America believe that we should have divergencies of views. We believe that everyone has the right to express himself. We believe that young people have the right to speak out and give their views and ideas. We believe that opposition is important. . . . We are the heirs of the true revolution. We are committed to progress while maintaining the rights and freedom of the individual. . . . It wasn't necessary, for instance, for the United States to erect a wall to keep our people within our society as was done in East Berlin. If it's a workers' paradise on the other side, it is strange that it has finally come to this." Here was inner-core Kennedy, controlled yet passionate. I glanced at Seigenthaler to catch his eye, and like me he was moved.

At the end, we all joined in singing the Waseda school song. Kennedy's interpreter had scribbled a phonetic version of the first two or three lines, and Ambassador Reischauer, Ethel, Susie, John, and I crowded around Bob. Each verse ended in shouts of "Waseda! Waseda! Waseda!" and there's where we excelled. The attorney general's Waseda visit was given extensive coverage, live and on the evening news programs at home, as was the turbulence of the meeting itself. This rivaled RFK's Berlin stop as the big story of the trip, displaying his outreach toward young people and his ability to cope with organized disruption eloquently, knowing that the students' applause at the end would be restrained.

When something went wrong during our travels, it was usually of our own doing, like the Vespa incident in Rome. Nearly a month into the trip and only days from our final stop in Paris, our exhausted traveling party decided to treat itself to the best of luncheons at a Tuscan restaurant recommended by our "control officer," the unflappable Robert Duemling, then a junior member of the embassy's political section. The restaurant was a delightful place, its front open to the street on a balmy spring afternoon. The owner was pleased to have us. At first.

Well into lunch and wine, recovering members of the press decided to surprise Ethel with a Vespa motorcycle, having noticed a store nearby selling them. Kennedy cautioned her: "Ethel, remember your brother-in-law!" A delighted Ethel revved up her new bike at the restaurant's entrance, nearly blowing away the cheeses. She flew into the middle of Rome's traffic and hit the side of a car. There was a thump, but no one was hurt. Duemling spoke with the driver and settled the matter on the spot. We continued with lunch, the press pleased with an occasion it never reported. Kennedy later asked Duemling to have the Vespa repaired and shipped to his home, implying without cost to himself, something the astonished Duemling was able to do by painting for Vespa's public relations people a seductive picture of their product in the country setting of Hickory Hill.

I was the man behind the scenes throughout this trip, making sure at each stop that our embassies did what they were supposed to do in terms of the brokered contract between their capabilities and wishes and Bob's intentions. "Bad News Brandon," Ethel called me, not jokingly, when I brought problems to Bob's attention or argued for changes. John Seigenthaler and I accompanied Kennedy on virtually every appearance. There were long days and short nights. Kennedy was pleased with the trip as it progressed. There were a few minor messes, but in general the media were giving him high marks. This was a plus of sorts for the president, as well, demonstrating his concern for East Asia and Berlin, in particular. Kennedy held press conferences at all stops, during which he was asked questions about the American political scene, especially the civil rights movement. He was becoming more sure-footed abroad.

As I learned in Africa, conventional protocol annoyed RFK; he did not like to do things for form's sake. We kept the ceremonial aspects of the trip to a minimum, but this was still too much for Kennedy. He tried to leave an elaborate and seemingly perpetual dinner in Jakarta offered by Indonesia's attorney general, Dr. Gunawan, who customarily wore a military uniform. The spectacle of an attorney general in uniform irritated Kennedy. He kept sending me obvious signals that he wanted to leave, which would have been impossible without offending his host. I signaled back that he couldn't go. RFK's solution to boredom took a drastic turn. After watching a long but graceful display of the Indonesian candle dance, he announced that Susie Wilson and I, in return, would perform an authentic American dance, the twist. This was inappropriate, but we danced a few steps—without music, awkwardly, and with embarrassment. "Susie obliged brilliantly," he later wrote, "while Brandon, mumbling bitterly about his Image in the [State] Department, produced a genteel and polished Charleston." The press group applauded us, as did Kennedy, and made our performance a gossip item in the *Washington Post*. The Indonesians were bewildered.

In Jakarta at the end of our third week together, all of us were frazzled. By early afternoon on the day we were to take a five o'clock flight to Saigon, Ethel and Bob still had not returned to their suite in President Sukarno's guesthouse. Little of Ethel's wide-ranging wardrobe had been packed, and there was not sufficient time for her to do this herself. I thought of what would happen if we missed our plane and torpedoed the schedules along our route. In discouragement and trepidation, and with the daring of the desperate, I began to pack her varied and sometimes dainty belongings and had nearly finished when she burst on the scene and asked what I was doing. "Ethel," I said slowly and I hoped politely, "this is a real world with real people and real airplanes. Pan Am isn't going to hold the plane for us!" She wasn't pleased but said nothing more about it. During a reunion of our travel group at Hickory Hill soon after we got back, Ethel, with a sweet smile, slipped a small leather box into my hand and said, "Bobby and I want you to have this." Inside were two gold cuff links, one inscribed "Real World," the other "Real People." On their backs were the initials BHG and RFK.

John Glenn orbited the earth while we were in Rome, rivaling the Soviet Union's Yuri Gagarin in this accomplishment. Glenn's youth and daring, his wholesome Ohio optimism, fit neatly into the Kennedy image of vigor and new frontiers to conquer. Emotional Italians were stopping Americans on the street to shout their bravos. Pope John XXIII blessed our group—including journalists—promising that his few words "will not do harm to those of you who are not Catholic." On greeting me he said in French: "You are a big man. I am a small man who seeks to do big things in the hearts of men."

We moved on to Berlin and looked at the wall built just five months earlier, in August 1961. It wasn't yet anything like the naked triumph of prison technology, with dogs and killing fields, it soon would become. Shabby gray buildings along Bernauer Strasse, pockmarked and ravaged by World War II, had their doors and windows bricked up by East Germans on their side of the wall. We walked along that cold and cobbled street where wreaths, flowers, crosses, and pictures of the dead, some of whom had jumped from windows to escape, were propped against this makeshift barrier. Instinctively we touched a battered façade the way one strokes the coffin of a friend. Those doors and windows were forbidding, their casements and pediments serving as frames for the bricks and mortar slapped together to seal them. Through those closed doorways shouting youngsters had left for school. From the now bricked-up windows, mothers had leaned out to follow their children's hops and skips down Bernauer Strasse. The windows we saw along this street were like the dried-up eye sockets of a blind person.

RFK on the Foreign Service and State Department

As he became better acquainted with it, Kennedy's opinion of the Foreign Service rose. He was struck by the expert knowledge and language skills of our diplomats. They knew potential future leaders and many others in different walks of life. He was impressed by how hard people at our embassies worked to advance U.S. interests and how attuned they were to the moods and concerns of the local populations as well as to their leaders. In his eyes, people at our embassies became likable Americans choosing to live abroad to serve their country. This was a different world from his father's embassy in prewar London, where Ambassador Joseph P. Kennedy became isolated and disliked for his accommodationist views toward Nazi Germany.

Bob assessed each American ambassador he met and shared his opinions with me. There were pluses and minuses, career and noncareer people, and he came away from his trip favorably impressed by the chiefs of mission he had seen at work. Ambassador and Mrs. Reischauer, in Japan, topped his list. Kennedy did not like to sit with "Country Teams," a new management tool of formal interagency meetings led by the ambassador. He preferred one-on-one conversations, believing he would get more honest and targeted briefings and avoid the posturing in structured meetings. He usually declined separate briefings by the CIA's station chiefs. He did not like being lectured to and probably harbored resentment toward the agency over the Bay of Pigs, still fresh in our minds.

Never talking to me about the State Department in any systematic way, Kennedy nevertheless gave vent to his frustrations as presidential brother. He made little connection between the Foreign Service people he met overseas, whom he by and large admired, and those working in a State Department he disparaged who were Foreign Service officers assigned to Washington. He believed State lacked the energy and creativity required to address the larger challenges faced by the president. He found it slow to respond to presidential guidance and considered its careerists to be pursuing their own objectives in their own fashion. In his eyes the State Department, personified by a phlegmatic Dean Rusk and a disorganized Chester Bowles, was a stultified bureaucracy constantly clearing and coordinating unnecessary papers rather than thinking in new directions on the president's behalf. RFK was comparing a poorly led agency to his own energized, responsive, and politically attuned Department of Justice with himself at its head. I suspected his opinions mirrored the president's.

What Did Kennedy Learn?

His month of travel around the globe was a transforming and intellectually nurturing experience for Robert Kennedy. I have not seen someone grow as much, at any age. He stuffed his mind with knowledge and comprehension. During a trip like ours, impressions occurred at the edges and worked their ways in. Kennedy was occupied by little else beyond the people he met and what he was absorbing in tightly scheduled days. On a Pan Am flight, sleeves rolled up, shoes off, and tie loosened, he might lean back in his seat and marvel at what we had experienced, ready to laugh with our press group at what was funny, or to shake his head and mutter about the tragedies we had come across.

He had not before looked at America's place in the world in that way, nor had there been similar opportunities for him to make conceptual sense of the global purposes and consequences of our foreign policies, or of their relationships to what we were doing at home. He found himself, in Tokyo and Berlin, gazing into the Cold War's different faces as he encountered university students befuddled by Soviet propaganda and then days later glided his fingers along the Berlin Wall. Beyond the satisfactions of finding so much enthusiasm for President Kennedy and himself, he had acquired a firsthand appreciation, in raw and troubling forms, of the breadth and purposefulness of Moscow's influence. Kennedy would come to learn more about Soviet cold-bloodedness during a harrowing Cuban missile crisis only months away.

He believed America to be the strongest hope for the free world. Beyond assuring military preparedness, we were right, he thought, to reach out to younger generations everywhere, broadcasting our ideals as he had done in his rebuttal through a bullhorn at Waseda University. Home once more, he stressed in his speeches the importance of making progress in civil rights and on other social issues. This would demonstrate the strength of our democracy, he argued, first to ourselves and then to others, and nourish the "tremendous reservoir of goodwill toward the United States" he had found abroad, steadily to be siphoned off by the war in Vietnam.

Kennedy was a committed man in much that he did. His detractors charged him with ruthlessness. Occasionally, because he felt the sting, he joked about the word in self-mockery. There was mean-spiritedness and disrespect for Indonesian culture and his host in his command to Susie and me to make fools of ourselves dancing in Jakarta. His actions could be self-centered and petty, as in his carping about diplomatic receiving lines and his cavalier treatment of Ambassador Reams in Abidjan. At such times the charge of ruthlessness was on target. But it did not describe the fundamental nature of the man, the maturing of his values. During my public service I have found no one more caught up in the misery of others, whether they lived in Appalachia or Capetown. Kennedy's pain over their plight was deep, and he sought the means to ease injustice any way and anywhere he could. His feelings had a moral base as humanistic as it was Catholic. This side of his nature was more broadly understood in the later years of his life during his campaign for national office. It did much to explain the fervor of crowds who believed that here was a moral leader who might make the world a better place.

On his return to Washington, Kennedy wrote a book about his trip, *Just Friends and Brave Enemies*, taking the title from a letter written by Thomas Jefferson to Andrew Jackson in 1806, in which Jefferson said, "We must meet our duty and convince the world that we are just friends and brave enemies." While I was going over the galley proofs with him one afternoon at Justice, he was writing his acknowledgments. After some words about me, he added: "What is so important on a trip like this, [Brandon Grove] always kept his perspective and sense of humor." That was saying quite a lot.

Our Home on Prospect Street

I usually felt I was leaving the scene of battle when I walked home, sometimes guiltily, from the State Department. Mary and I loved Georgetown and our small ground-floor apartment on Prospect Street with its fireplace, a tiny garden hidden away in back, and a prized garage. Wisconsin Avenue and M Street, in the early sixties, were quiet thoroughfares with small shops and only a few restaurants. Our budget took us to Chez Odette and Martin's, rather than the tony Rive Gauche nearby frequented by Jacqueline Kennedy and the Beautiful People. We lived on Prospect Street for two happy years.

This was an exhilarating time to be young and in government, where many of us believed, in Robert Kennedy's phrase, we could "make a difference." "Especially in the beginning, we were electrified by the prospects of this administration," Katharine Graham, publisher of the *Washington Post*, recalled in her memoir. Life was good and purposeful; at a turning point in history so many worthwhile goals seemed attainable. People like Mary and me were innocents, perhaps, but I would not trade the spirit of the Kennedy years for the cynicism and negativism of much that followed.

Jack

Visiting Rio de Janeiro in 1963 with the State Department's top manager, William H. Orrick Jr., I had a brush with death. At dawn Bill and I went for a swim in the ocean, paying little heed to a deserted beach and failing to notice red warning flags. As the surf rolled in I dived into the bottom of a wave, thrilled to feel its weight passing over me. When I rose on the surface of an undertow I had lost my bearings, unable to see the beach. I swam toward it moments later but was pulled back out to sea during several more tries as the wave under me receded from the shore, sucking up sand and pebbles in its seaward rush. Eventually, striving not to panic, I gained footing, clawing forward and resisting an ever weaker undertow now tugging at my ankles but still wanting me back. Standing in dread, I thought of Mary and the baby she was carrying and of what had nearly happened to me.

Our first child, John, or Jack as we called him, was born in March 1963. Jack had the genes of his great-grandfathers, one a furniture craftsman and the other a civil engineer, and subsequently founded his own architectural renovation company in Boston. He married Hannah Hero Wood, a British-born public relations executive in the international banking world. Perhaps Jack had seen enough of the toll bureaucratic warfare could take on diplomatic warriors that he never gave a moment's thought to following in my footsteps — not that I would have urged him to.

9

INDIA

★ ★ ★ ★

1963 to 1965

After the Cuban missile crisis, Chester Bowles left his position as under secretary of state to assume, at President Kennedy's request, the newly created duties of presidential special representative and adviser on Asia, Africa, and Latin American affairs. This was intended as little more than a sinecure, and Bowles felt frustrated and sidelined. The president and Rusk were not pleased about the arrangement, either. There were squabbles over such matters as the use of a White House car.

Kennedy proposed to Bowles that he return to India, where he had served under President Truman twelve years before as the ambassador in New Delhi. Bowles's first appointment lasted little more than a year, brought to an end by Eisenhower's victory over Adlai Stevenson in 1952. During that short time he had made himself famous. Bowles had traveled throughout India with a populist message and words of understanding for Indians. He was widely known to have advocated comprehensive bilateral aid. Ordinary Indians were persuaded that he, and therefore the United States, cared about them. He had enjoyed his successful first tour in Delhi, and so had his wife, Steb. Her happiness was important to Chet. But should they go back? They took the plunge after much hesitation. For Bowles this would prove an ill-fated venture.

While Bowles was going through the process of being confirmed by the Senate, he asked me to join him in India. He saw my task as helping him "pull things together" in the ambassador's office. I was to become a "special assistant" who, Bowles told me, would help make sure that people working in a large and convoluted embassy could get their thoughts to him when they needed to and that, in turn, his decisions would be carried out as he wanted them to be. Bowles asked me to become involved in working on his policy recommendations with an eye to clarity, brevity, and impact. That sounded like a new Chet, and I had my doubts, but the prospect of serving in India with the Bowleses overcame them.

Bowles discussed his priorities: nourishing the relationship with Prime Minister Nehru, founding father of an independent India; fostering India's economic development; increasing the levels of long-term U.S. military assistance; and easing India's hostile relations with Pakistan over Kashmir. Since Bowles's previous tenure as ambassador, Nehru had distanced himself from the United States, staking out his own ideological territory in the Cold War as leader of a "nonaligned" movement that saw U.S. fears of communism as exaggerated. Bowles also intended his voice to remain heard in Washington on the dangers of our deepening involvement in Southeast Asia.

He would be obliged, he knew, to adjust to a changed India, one in which his relations with Nehru would be marked by less ease and by estrangement on many issues. Indian officials in the midsixties were resisting advice from Americans about how to manage their country and its economic development. Such prescriptions from eager, self-assured hordes of U.S. aid officials sounded presumptuous and condescending if not offered sensitively, and Indians were quick to feel offended. Bowles understood their lack of self-confidence, which they sometimes obscured by arrogant attitudes of their own.

Bowles Takes Charge

Two people could hardly have been more contrasting in personal styles than Bowles and his predecessor, John Kenneth Galbraith, the lanky economist of world renown, although both were liberal Democrats and liked each other. Rarely do people of such intrusive public profiles succeed one another as ambassadors; both men enthralled Indian elites, who liked to discuss personalities and gossip. To get things ready for Bowles, I arrived in New Delhi several weeks before him, providing me an opportunity to observe Galbraith in action.

Bowles and Galbraith were fond of being in the public eye. Galbraith towered over Indians like a Giacometti figure. He enjoyed traveling by train in a special coach with his wife, Kitty, and the film star Angie Dickinson when she visited them. He had his picture taken in rice paddies into which he waded barefoot, khaki pants rolled up to bony knees à la New Frontier. This was good public diplomacy, accenting his interest in agriculture and the peasant families at the core of Indian life who were the focus of our aid programs.

Galbraith savored the splendors of India's palaces and the opulent homes of maharajas, delighted to find himself at lavish candle-lit dinners gliding like a sloop among guests wearing turbans and beautifully bordered saris. He conceived and staged Jacqueline Kennedy's photogenic, fairy-tale visit to India, an occasion of such moment he had the embassy's staff rehearse the dinner in her honor beforehand. Her code name in cable traffic between Delhi and Washington was "girlfriend." Indians enjoyed Galbraith's cerebral humor and respected an intellect that matched his height. Galbraith displayed energy, ego, and a regal aloofness they admired. Fortuitously for him, he ended his assignment to India on a high note, turning over to Bowles problems in the U.S. relationship that would prove impossible to resolve.

Uncomfortable in palaces, Bowles headed for the common man instead. He liked nothing better than traveling by car through the countryside, once the embassy's aircraft had deposited him in a far-off province where he could meet with villagers and young people in their schools. A powerful voice not least because he spoke from his conscience, Bowles talked extemporaneously about democracy, social justice, and hope; about the need for social programs that worked; about his empathy for villagers in whom he encouraged feelings of self-worth; and about the inspiration of Mahatma Gandhi in American life, particularly among civil rights leaders such as Dr. Martin Luther King Jr. Many saw Bowles as a father figure. To me he sounded like someone waging a political campaign for the United States and its values. This too was good public diplomacy. In battles of ideology during the Cold War, the West relied greatly on its human voices, while the Soviets worked clandestinely through their global party apparatus and the media they influenced or controlled.

Once installed in New Delhi, I remained troubled by the prospects for my relationship with Bowles's soon-to-be-appointed deputy chief of mission, whoever that might turn out to be. The deputy to an ambassador, a senior Foreign Service officer, normally does many of the things Chet wanted me to do for him on a personal basis. I feared that a new DCM and I were bound to clash. A successor to Benson E. L. Timmons III, Galbraith's DCM with a splendid Foreign Service name, surely would have concerns not only about me but also about the other young, handpicked, and relatively inexperienced members of the coterie around Bowles. Characteristically, Bowles chose young and loyal assistants in whom he had confidence, people he thought would do well in their careers afterward and, sharing his outlook, would remain allies in his ever-expanding network of friends and supporters.

An ambassador's Foreign Service deputy is the embassy's day-to-day manager, someone who makes sure that people work together as efficiently and

harmoniously as possible. He or she integrates the embassy's reporting; serves
as the ambassador's alter ego; and becomes the chargé d'affaires ad interim,
the person temporarily in charge of the embassy during an ambassador's ab-
sences from the country on leave, illness, or consultations in Washington. In
the business world, the DCM is analogous to a COO, or chief operating officer
of a corporation. In short, the DCM "pulls things together," Chet's phrase for
much of what he expected from me. Bowles chose Joseph (Jerry) N. Greene Jr.
as his deputy, and the two of us, finding ourselves compatible, worked out a
division of responsibilities that did not detract from my access to Bowles or
Jerry's more formal duties. Chet was the consummate political ambassador,
Jerry the seasoned Foreign Service professional, and I, with my notepad and
broom, would occupy space somewhere in the middle.

Greene had grown up in New York City, a product of Hotchkiss and Yale.
He was tall and wiry, balding, wry, and a fine tennis player. The first impression was of someone intense and finicky. At forty-three, he had previously
served in Montreal, Ottawa, Trieste, Rome, Singapore, and Bonn, and he had
been a Foreign Service assistant to Secretary of State Dulles, which gave him
an intimate appreciation of how the State Department's seventh floor functioned. This would prove useful in staffing Bowles, who had recently come
from that setting. It was not unusual for a Foreign Service professional, expected to be without partisan views, to work for such opposites as Dulles and
Bowles. Jerry came fresh from punishing responsibilities as DCM at our
embassy in Lagos. His diplomatic skills and smooth but firm management style,
his exacting speech and green-ink pen, were well paired with Chet's abhor-
rence of structure and inattention to detail. The hardest thing for Jerry with
Bowles would be to plead the case for precision in what he wrote. Soon Jerry
was drawn into the inner circle, the "Chet Set" around Bowles, and enjoyed
warm relationships with him and Steb, as did his new British-born wife, Kitty,
whom he had met in Lagos.

Our front office in New Delhi consisted of the ambassador and two Foreign Service secretaries who keenly felt the challenge his energetic pace posed
to their composure and professional skills; Jerry Greene and his secretary;
and three special assistants, Richard F. Celeste, Douglas J. Bennet Jr., and me,
along with *our* secretary. Celeste handled Bowles's U.S. political affairs and
answered his voluminous Indian mail, most of which asked for money. Bennet concentrated on economic issues, worked on Chet's speeches, and wrote a
book for him on development. This team met Chet's needs about as well as
possible.

With a background in Democratic politics, Celeste later became director of the Peace Corps and governor of Ohio. In 1997, President Clinton appointed him ambassador to India and thus a successor, many times removed, to Chet. Bennet, after several jobs in government, including director of the Agency for International Development, headed National Public Radio and then became president of Wesleyan University.

Roosevelt House: Big and Banal

On arriving, the Bowleses briefly moved into Roosevelt House, the newly built ambassador's residence conceived by Edward Durrell Stone, who later designed the similar looking Kennedy Center for the Performing Arts in Washington. Roosevelt House was not a building that projected domestic warmth.

Rectangular on the outside, the building had an overhanging flat roof that was supported by slim concrete pillars placed at some distance from its outer walls. Domesticated peacocks screamed unpleasantly from the nearly treeless, shrubless lawns. The interior walls, for the most part, were a see-through filigree of carved stone. Robin Duke, a friend from New York visiting the Bowleses, felt she could be watched as she undressed for bed. Sound traveled easily. When Averell Harriman came to visit, Chet told me his snoring had kept Steb and him awake. We subsequently referred to the visitors' bedroom as the Harriman Room. Huge glass chandeliers hung from the ceiling of a barnlike and coldly formal reception hall. An enormous Indian rug covered the floor. Visitors felt themselves in a diplomatic version of the Taj Mahal, a seventeenth-century Muslim memorial not far away.

A shallow fountain at floor level lay near the entrance by Jo Davidson's head of Franklin Roosevelt, for whom the residence was named. A stream squirting upward from the middle of this pool was no more than eight inches high. It was easy to miss. I watched our assistant air attaché step directly into it while making his way to the ambassador's receiving line, his wife narrowly avoiding a similar mishap. With military aplomb, the hero of this tale continued straight ahead, wet above his ankles and dripping, to pay his respects to a startled Bowles. Celeste and I afterward surrounded this threat to decorum with a barrier of highly visible potted plants.

Chet and Steb felt uncomfortable in Roosevelt House; it did not suit the American message or the image they wanted to project. So they decided, over hysterical protests from the State Department, to move back into the house where they had lived during their previous time in India. That showed what a powerful, politically appointed ambassador could get away with, as opposed to a more beholden career diplomat, who would have been swatted down for proposing such a change. The Bowleses were happy in their old three-bedroom bungalow on Ratendone Road, a relic of British rule with a lush garden and comfortable, homelike charm. Roosevelt House became an appropriate setting for large-scale entertaining and was used by the U.S. Information Service in imaginative ways for public affairs programs of American music, dance, art exhibits, films, poetry readings, and lectures.

On one of her village visits Steb had come across a dozen scruffy-looking American hippies. They were embarked on a spiritual journey of some kind, with backpacks and guitars, jeans, and long, unkempt hair. "Look me up in New Delhi," she lightly said on parting. During one of Chet's rare formal receptions for Indian guests, prominent members of the American community, and other ambassadors (he felt uncomfortable at such "useless" functions), in came Steb's new friends. "How did *they* get here?" Chet must have wondered, as Steb, probably welcoming fresh energy in her diplomatic do, remembered she had invited them. In the early sixties, security measures protecting ambassadors were lax, allowing greater freedom and openness in meeting people and traveling about, and in this case having them come to visit you.

Steb frequently wore saris; she identified strongly with Indian culture. In those settled times, however, American women had not yet discovered the delights of saris. Her decision to wear them caused a flurry, more in the American community than among Indians, who were flattered by her choice. Some Americans wondered whether the wife of their ambassador hadn't gone native. Steb simply found saris more comfortable and looked good in them.

Delhi Life

Then in its sixteenth year of independence, New Delhi was a bustling, dusty place with a strong aftertaste of the British raj. Cattle freely roamed the main thoroughfares. The large hotel used by Europeans and Americans, the mismanaged Ashoka, bore the flavor of Mogul times. There were few good restaurants, our favorite being a cramped place in Old Delhi serving spicy chicken tandoori from an open hearth. It was not city life that attracted me to India in any case, but rather the rural areas and the men, women, and children who worked the soil. The downtrodden Indian farmer and his family were people to admire and respect, living out their hardscrabble lives in nearly half a million villages. In India, people seemed to exist in several centuries simultaneously: peasants working by buffalo-driven waterwheels in proximity to nuclear physicists of the first rank engrossed in their calculations.

Our household was never a dull place. Those who worked for us were constantly asking for salary advances, and soon I opened a ledger to keep track of these transactions. Our quarrelsome, incompetent cook replaced his generous samplings of gin by pouring water back into the bottle. Alcohol was banned in New Delhi, and the government tightly controlled its prohibition. A few restaurants allowed their regular customers to bring "grape juice" and looked the other way when wine was poured, a consideration acknowledged in the tip. There was another option of which few, if any, of us availed ourselves: to have a physician declare one an alcoholic and provide a medical permit authorizing the intake of alcohol in hotel bars and dining rooms.

I offered to promote one of our young houseboys, a bearer, to cook. He had turned out to be an adequate part-time chef after we had fired his gin-guzzling predecessor. I proposed a tempting raise, but Piara Lal turned me down, saying he was born a bearer and would remain a bearer. His view of life intrigued me, because it represented one of India's great problems, acceptance of caste to the detriment of making something more of oneself. Working in the small garden outside our ground-floor apartment in Malcha Marg were three underemployed, unambitious, and highly self-specialized gardeners, none of whom did much good.

There were experiences in India to relish. I spent a morning on the back of an elephant in the northeast, sitting sideways at unaccustomed height behind a driver facing ahead with his rifle, as the elephant picked its path through marshlands by testing each step with the grace of a ballerina. We came upon a herd of other elephants, one standing conspicuously apart whether by choice or through ostracism, and were able to see for ourselves what the word *rogue* meant.

With Chet and several other members of the embassy's staff, I flew in a military aircraft to the remote town of Leh, in the Ladakh range of eastern Kashmir. At nearly twelve thousand feet in the snow-covered Himalayan mountains, Leh was one of the highest permanently inhabited communities anywhere and had been described as "the roof of the world." The air was thin and fragile. Our party tired as we walked toward an ancient monastery rising up against a mountainside where nearly one hundred monks lived, their seniors receiving us formally for tea. We lunched with Indian officers in their mess, having brought the latest books and magazines from Delhi. The remoteness and beauty, the spirituality of this otherworldly place, defied description.

Working in a "Crazy" Embassy

As with his design of Roosevelt House, Edward Durrell Stone seemed to have conceived the chancery for effect rather than efficiency. Galbraith decried its lack of functionality but noted also that "to be nonfunctional is greatly appropriate for an embassy, for so are many of its functions." It had two floors of cramped offices—few connected to each other—with an open, rectangular pool in the middle from which splashing fountains rose, showering the ducks. Trees planted in stone pots were asymmetrically placed in the water, and a walkway of slate with a Japanese feeling offered a stroll across the pool itself. Bennet, Celeste, our secretary, and I, our desks jammed together in two small offices adjacent to the ambassador's suite, had no way of getting to him without walking around the pool outside. In summer's heat we wilted, and during the monsoon season we nearly got blown away.

I worked directly with Bowles, and my role was more substantive than it had been in Washington. Chet was interested in the results of work, not its process. Nevertheless, he urged Jerry and me to think of better ways to integrate the efforts of our numerous American staff members. He believed, for example, that our political and economic officers were not talking enough to each other, a common failing in the Foreign Service. He wanted a cohesive picture of the Indian scene to emerge from his embassy's reporting, and so, in a Foreign Service breakthrough, Jerry and I devised and implemented a plan to meld those two large sections. It proved awkward to administer and did not have the State Department's blessing. Egos clashed over the division of responsibilities at the top, and the arrangement did not survive Bowles's tenure as ambassador.

More difficult still was the need for Greene to coordinate the work of more than three hundred Americans, most of them in the economic and military assistance missions, and more than seven hundred Indian employees. Bowles's Country Team, which functioned somewhat like a cabinet, had more members than President Kennedy's cabinet in Washington. The embassy had its own carpentry and upholstery shops, painters and electricians, and hordes of gardeners and watchmen. Teams of people cut and hung the curtains in our homes. The medical office had a State Department doctor and two nurses, and the embassy ran a housing compound built for junior staff that had a swimming pool and an American-style snack bar. These services and facilities, designed for a hardship post, were unavailable elsewhere in New Delhi.

A large consular section looked after Americans in the country, from missionaries living in India to sightseeing tourists, providing new passports when old ones were lost, visiting them in jails, and holding their Social Security checks for them to pick up. When an American died, Foreign Service consular officers were prepared to help with notification of family members and shipping of remains; to deal with funeral homes in the United States and inventory the deceased's effects; and to provide legally valid death certificates—in short, to offer as much help as possible without spending money. We also did a land-office business with Indians wanting to come to the United States seeking various kinds of visas, and not particularly concerned about making fraudulent claims to support their applications.

Our embassy supervised American consulates general in Calcutta, Bombay, and Madras that were part of far-flung efforts, in these vast consular districts, to help India develop economically and allow us to stay closer to its people and their lives. They were mini-embassies themselves. India was a stimulating place in which to be working, and Bowles persuaded some exceptional people to join him there.

The U.S. Information Service, under William H. Weathersby, was among the most elaborate and sophisticated anywhere. Chet had enticed his friend Robert Brooks, the dean of Williams College, to join Weathersby and shape the cultural affairs program. Bob, in a sweltering India, would have to forgo for a while carving the prizewinning ice sculptures he had a passion for creating at Williams. A Peace Corps contingent of about fifty volunteers, among the first young and idealistic Americans to sign up for service in this inspiration of Kennedy's, was working on agricultural projects in the villages of Punjab. Our military attachés, carefully picked at the Pentagon, managed weapons procurement issues and the military assistance programs.

We accommodated under State Department cover one of the largest and most capable CIA operations anywhere, case officers interested not only in India and Kashmir but also in neighboring China, still closed to Americans. David Blee, the station chief, saw to it that his people had cooperative relations with their Foreign Service colleagues. Many of Blee's staff, however, were not much better at concealing the nature of their work from our Indian employees than Bill Dunbar and Margaret Woolls had been in Abidjan. When Stalin's daughter Svetlana Alliluyeva decided to defect in New Delhi in 1966, she announced herself to a marine guard on duty at the embassy and was placed in Blee's care to be spirited to the West.

Bowles saw his greatest challenge in being able to contribute in lasting ways to India's economic and social development. With the help of John P. Lewis, formerly on the President's Council of Economic Advisers, and Yale economist John Lindblom, Chet's efforts helped bring about a Green Revolution in

India. That he had been able to persuade such people, and others from private life, to join him in a remote India said something about his reputation outside government and the force of his personality and ideas. As with his selection of ambassadors at the State Department, Bowles showed himself to be the sort of public figure whose view of public service was that only the best and brightest were adequate. Bowles's embassy sparkled with talent, intellectual curiosity, and drive. His work habits, however, would again cause him problems and disappoint his closest advisers.

As a leader Chet became more erratic, now that he was running his own show and could adopt the managerial style he wanted. In no other aspect of their work do ambassadors differ more than in how they lead their missions. Feeling accountable only to himself—presidents and secretaries of state existed in his mind to be persuaded of his views and then to support them—Bowles sheltered himself in his daily routine from all but a handful of aides and key people in the embassy. In his impatience Bowles often moved too quickly on issues that required deliberation, not seeing how much he needed the expert knowledge and guidance of others in his embassy to bolster his views. He could fire off cables to Washington that landed as ill-considered duds. He might, on a good day, proffer a draft telegram to someone qualified to comment on it, with the admonition that he wanted it back in twenty minutes. His disinclination to hear opposing views was a costly flaw. It prevented him from seeing problems as a whole and from strengthening his argument by taking into account the legitimate concerns of others and learning from them. He had little talent for anticipating criticism and defusing it, nor could he easily put himself in a Washington reader's place.

Bowles's unremitting depiction of a noble India was well intended but impervious to reality, costing him credibility in Washington, where he appeared to be arguing on India's behalf rather than establishing his reputation as a special pleader for U.S. interests. In his cables, Chet believed it a duty to make his case at length, in the first person, and as strenuously as he could. Had he been more dispassionate and painstaking, had he labored over his recommendations with a keener eye to their persuasiveness, he might have been able to accomplish more. A former ad man, Bowles nevertheless had little feeling for how to package and sell his product to consumers in Washington. For the selling part to work, a fine appreciation of the bureaucratic politics in play was needed. Neither Greene nor I would have much effect in reining him in.

People at the embassy considered Chet a warm and admirable person, enjoyed watching him at bat on the compound's diamond, and recognized that at heart he was a well-meaning man able to convince himself regarding India that plain meant beautiful. I heard a political officer comment on the embassy's "craziness," referring to Chet's management style. The reality was that beyond Chet's idiosyncratic ways, the machinery purred reliably and to Washington's satisfaction, with people vying for assignments to India and Bowles's team. Chet excelled at speaking before embassy groups including families, who admired his eloquence and energy and his qualities as a visionary and democrat. They saw him as a moral man passionately convinced of the soundness of his views, seeking nothing for himself beyond an honorable place in history, and they felt inspired.

After Chet's first year in New Delhi, the embassy's doctor, John Beahler, concluded that Chet had Parkinson's disease. One foot was beginning to drag. In New York's St. Barnabas Hospital, Chet underwent brain surgery after registering under a false name to avoid publicity. I visited him there, while taking advantage of his absence from Delhi to return to Washington, and found a man in good spirits with his head shaved clean, striving to remember his assumed name. He jokingly asked whether he looked like Dwight Eisenhower, and I told him he looked more like John Glenn. But it wasn't quite the same for him when he came back.

Nehru Dies and Shastri Follows

By 1963, Prime Minister Nehru appeared a very sick man. I saw him from time to time, and he was frail, vague, and not in charge any longer. Knowledgeable Indians referred to Nehru's "dead hand" on the levers of power. His government gradually became all but immobilized; nothing important seemed to happen because Nehru put off making decisions. He suffered a stroke in January 1964, eight months after Bowles's return to India, and died four months later. His passing from the scene deeply affected Chet, who had prized his close ties to Nehru since the 1950s and now wondered how he could best advance the U.S.-Indian relationship. Nehru's funeral inspired mass hysteria. As his body was borne to its pyre, all of New Delhi seemed to be in the streets in an orgy of shoving, shouting, and grieving. The void left by the death of "Panditji" was deep.

Lal Bahadur Shastri, who succeeded Nehru, was a man of promise, but less than two years later Shastri died of a heart attack during a visit to Tashkent. The diminutive Shastri, a senior Congress Party leader and uncharismatic politician from Uttar Pradesh, was his own man. He was a self-effacing and modest person, a populist identified with the interests of the working class and India's peasants. Before taking office he had never journeyed outside India. I saw him as a bit Lincolnesque, a common man in plain cloth and right for India. Had he lived longer, he might have been able to reform India's ways of governing. Even then, many of the Congress Party's adherents had clung to power too long and corruption was widespread. Shastri's potential may have been as underestimated as Harry Truman's. Who was he? What would he do? His time was too short for anyone to know.

As Shastri assumed power, Bowles struggled to forge a productive relationship with him. Bowles had not met him before and intended to make his mark quickly. He composed a "Plan for the Common Man," a bold declaration of social goals along New Deal lines that he hoped would appeal to India's inexperienced leader and serve as a beacon for the proverbial first one hundred days. He probably saw this also as a way of easing himself into the decision-making stream of a new Indian government. Shastri remained reserved toward Bowles personally and resisted U.S. blandishments generally. In his dealings with Shastri, Bowles faced an unaccustomed need to proceed like a more traditional diplomat, someone who must build trust incrementally and cannot at the outset assume its existence. At the beginning of his first ambassadorship, Bowles had found rapport with Nehru during a different era of relations in Truman's time and before nonalignment. The soaring dialogue and bonhomie about India's future and the problems of the world, conducted in the 1950s by these two men of vision and reinforcing idealism, wasn't possible with Shastri. Nor was it possible to talk with him about America's founding fathers and what they faced while emerging from British rule, as the New Englander Bowles had done with a somewhat similarly positioned Nehru in India.

Bowles stepped up his media relations, holding frequent press conferences, although Indian journalists often were unkind to him. He had a smart press attaché in Jack Stuart, a short, stout, and scrappy Scotsman, who put together a well-conceived media strategy. Stuart groused a lot and was fearless in dealing loudly with Bowles, but the two got along famously. Communists were strong in India during this time, publishing a weekly newspaper, *Blitz,* that was so outrageously anti–United States that it unintentionally provided entertainment.

Bowles did a lot of public speaking around India, and sometimes I traveled with him. He enjoyed the give-and-take, although the war in Vietnam was a painful subject for him and discomfort showed on his face when he spoke about it, caught as he was in the role of ambassador as advocate. At a podium, Indian hosts had the annoying habit of introducing a guest speaker, hearing him or her out, and then offering in the words of thanks a rebuttal of what had been said, providing the hapless speaker no opportunity to reply. Chet did not always play by these rules. He would rise again and set the record straight.

Relations between our ambassadors in New Delhi and Karachi were strained, reflecting adversarial relations between India and Pakistan. Occasionally in diplomacy, chiefs of mission and members of their staffs side with the viewpoints held in their places of accreditation, a condition known as "localitis." What suffers is the credibility, in Washington and among other posts in the region, of all concerned. Bowles in India and Walter P. McConaughy in Pakistan each, too often, supported his capital, and both were appropriately discounted. When official visitors passed through New Delhi, Bowles told me only half in jest that he was stuck with Nehru walking around in white pajamas, while McConaughy could trot out Ayub Khan, who had gone to Sandhurst and mixed a mean martini. Bowles felt himself outmatched.

President Kennedy Is Assassinated

Bowles returned to Washington in November 1963 with me along to staff him in arguing for long-term military assistance to India. In my briefcase were his memorandum to the president and supporting documents. Chet characteristically began to rewrite the Kennedy memo, meticulously crafted for him by the embassy's senior advisers, once we had taken off from Palam Airport on a grueling twenty-eight-hour flight.

Registering at my hotel, I found a message from Ethel Kennedy inviting me to Bob's birthday party at Hickory Hill on November 20. The energy and optimism of the New Frontier were palpable, especially to me, fresh from New Delhi where cows roamed the streets. Friends with outlandish gifts paid tribute to Bob, who grinned his toothy smile. All seemed right with the world, maybe too right in the self-satisfaction of that evening. How could any of us have imagined what lay only hours ahead?

Bowles met with President Kennedy. Their conversation, he told me, went well. Kennedy had decided to approve a five-year military aid program for India; Bowles was to see him once again to finalize the matter. To prepare for the concluding session with the president, Chet, one or two people from the State Department, and I met on the morning of November 22 with Robert Komer, the NSC's staff director responsible for the Indian subcontinent. While waiting for Komer, I looked at the White House from an office window, idly watching Caroline and her little brother, John, on the Truman balcony with their teacher. An appointment with the president, who was attending to Democratic politics in Texas, was scheduled for November 26. Chet was pleased.

I had invited friends at State to lunch in a Georgetown restaurant and returned to the State Department afterward to work on Chet's meeting. In the lobby I learned from a colleague in my A-100 class that President Kennedy had been shot in Dallas. "That's impossible!" I said in disbelief and denial. I took a cab to the Justice Department to see whether I could be useful. Bob's secretary, Angie Novello, told me he was at Hickory Hill. That night, alone in my hotel room, I wept. Two days after Kennedy's assassination, emotionally numbed Americans watching television saw Jack Ruby shoot and kill Lee Harvey Oswald, Kennedy's unexplained assassin, inside the Dallas County Jail. Ruby, the proprietor of two seedy nightclubs in Dallas, one a striptease bar, was also a mystery. Life had turned surreal.

It is difficult now to recall the measure of shock and grief felt throughout the world, even in communist countries. Kennedy was the postwar embodiment of a revitalized America. The world admired such a Cold Warrior. In West Berlin confetti had rained on his motorcade. Candles appeared in the windows at his death. Many stores closed, and churches filled. In chilling times he stood for hope. He had told Berliners he was one of them. When he died, so did a large part of our native optimism. I watched his funeral procession leave the White House as I had watched Franklin Roosevelt's cortege when a boy in high school. No longer young, I well understood what had been lost and that the sorrow of it would never leave me.

Chet and I flew back to New Delhi, our mission unaccomplished. He had not been close to Lyndon Johnson, considering him crassly manipulative, egocentric, and a person whose mind was often shut. "That man has no real friends," Bowles told me about Johnson on the day Kennedy died. In Delhi once more, we attended a memorial service for Kennedy organized by the American community. During our return flight, I had jotted down some thoughts for Chet to use on that occasion, but he spoke only briefly and without emotion, something noticed by all. He had been deeply wounded by the Kennedys, for whom he had no affection, and sensed correctly that his fortunes were unlikely to improve under Johnson.

Robert Kennedy remained in Johnson's cabinet as attorney general, and we stayed in touch. In response to a letter I sent from New Delhi, Kennedy's staff prepared a short, rather formal acknowledgment from him, dated May 4, 1964, nearly six months after the president was assassinated. After signing it he wrote in the left-hand margin, in an uncharacteristic confession of his emotions, anger, and frustrations under Lyndon Johnson: "Dear Brandon. I didn't write this rotten form letter—We miss you. Ethel sends her love and from me my best to you both—It is difficult here—Bob."

Star-Crossed

"I feel like someone carrying a mattress up a narrow staircase in the dark," Bowles told me. Presidential succession in the United States affected our policies toward an Indian subcontinent already viewed with indifference. Johnson was consumed by the war in Vietnam and its dimming prospects for success; by body counts and force levels; and by his efforts to stanch an erosion of public and congressional support. He caused a sweeping civil rights act to be passed in Congress, one of the finest accomplishments in our nation's history, yet his worthy plans for a Great Society were becoming sidetracked. Alienation of young Americans and violent protests against the war that met with police brutality were building to the nightmares of 1968.

To us in Delhi, Rusk seemed increasingly remote, and South Asia even further down on his agenda. He knew India well from service there in World War II, but he and Bowles could not agree on how to balance the relationship with Pakistan. Bowles had accurately predicted that our unwillingness to help the Indian air force would cause Delhi to turn to Moscow, an important shift in Cold War postures. Rusk visited India to attend Nehru's funeral, spending a night in the intimacy of Ratendone Road. This was not a cheerful experience for either man, as I could see when I joined them on the following morning. Among other irritants, none of us had been able to break Chet's self-defeating habit of sending end-run messages, skirting Rusk, to influential figures in Washington. Rusk often found out and fumed.

Yet, ever the optimist, Chet hoped he could influence Johnson on his pet issues. That was not to be. LBJ considered Bowles softheaded, especially on Vietnam, an "Indian lover," and more bother than he was worth. Somehow the president's depiction of him as an "Indian lover" reached Bowles in New Delhi.

The irony is that Chet was right on the important issues and stayed with his priorities. He did his utmost to influence Nehru—no one could have done more—but Nehru died. He tried to persuade the little-known Shastri to adopt an agenda for the common man in Shastri's own and India's interests, but he was unsuccessful, and Shastri died. He understood India's development needs as few others and pushed Lewis and Lindblom to address his ideas with all the imagination and resourcefulness at their command, and in this he succeeded. He persuaded Kennedy of India's long-term defense requirements, but too late. He made a stream of proposals about Kashmir, but Washington, spellbound by the unfolding disaster in Vietnam, paid scant attention. As for Vietnam itself, he was among the earliest of farsighted Americans to understand that warfare would not work, but his voice went unheeded.

Time to Leave

There is no better early training in diplomacy than staff work during which you, a junior person, serve directly under an official at the top helping to manage your boss's concerns. Your outlook becomes global as you screen telegrams from posts across the world, pulling out only the most important to be seen by your chief. You anticipate. You understand the qualities and operating styles of your superiors in ways that cannot be taught in a classroom. You learn about conflicting policy considerations as they tangle at the top and how business is conducted there. When things go wrong you hear about them promptly, whereas you tend to enjoy the satisfactions of success vicariously.

The leaders with whom I had worked in Washington and India were from political, not Foreign Service, backgrounds. Some of my colleagues, I suspected, thought me a career opportunist and a political horsefly. As I completed my fourth year of staff work after only six in the Foreign Service, I began to wonder who I really was.

By 1965, living in India had worn me down, its exoticism and palaces not relieving my dispiritedness at the poverty everywhere and the lack of education and ambition in so many of its people. I felt frustrated working in New Delhi without diplomatic responsibilities beyond the walls of our embassy. When Indians or diplomats from other embassies chatted with me on social occasions, their conversations usually were aimed at finding out what Bowles was thinking. In their place I would have done the same. I wasn't enjoying India. My frustrations were due to the lenses through which I was obliged to peer out. I was fixated on Bowles and embassy operations rather than on what I wanted to experience and work on in the India beyond.

On the State Department's list of available assignments in 1965, I noted several political section openings, including one as U.S. liaison officer to the city government of West Berlin, a responsibility like no other in the Foreign Service. Jerry Greene knew Elwood Williams III, a key person on the German desk, and recommended me to him. At breakfast one day in March on the shaded terrace at Ratendone Road, and in comments over which I had agonized the night before with mixed emotions, I told Chet how I felt. I feared that he might interpret my intentions as disloyal. He was disappointed and said so, but he understood I had a career to pursue. As my successor he would choose William Dean Howells III, then working on management issues at the State Department.

I was touched when, on the way to the airport to see us off, Chet invited me to ride with him, while Mary and our children rode with Steb. As we turned into Palam Airport, with his mind on work not small talk, Chet asked what I thought of a particular approach he was considering in a cable to Washington. I gave him my best answer. I recognized that my years of apprenticeship in diplomacy were over as I stared from the plane at the dusty Indian countryside receding below and held my two-year-old son, Jack, in my lap.

Soon after we left India, Chet wrote to me in Washington about the decision "apparently taken by the President and the Secretary to cancel out the Ayub Khan visit [to Washington] and the reflex action that required that Shastri be given the same treatment . . . it is by all odds the worst setback we have had in all the years I have been in India." He then offered a lament voiced by many an ambassador at one time or another. "Inevitably it gives one a sense of futility. This is particularly so because the messages from Washington offering a rationale for the switch have been almost wholly out of touch with the actual situation in India. Thus, either (a) our own cables have been wholly unclear, or (b) the people who read them had rejected them, or (c) they hadn't read them." In a postscript he made a request: "I will be grateful if you could get together the best possible evaluation of what people are thinking and likely to do—particularly in the White House. Where can I reach you by telephone from Essex on Sunday, the 16th?"

I saw Chester Bowles for the last time in 1984, two years before he died at eighty-five, at Hayden's Point, his wooded estate in Essex, Connecticut. He sat slumped in a wheelchair with a blanket covering his legs, staring without expression at sailboats tacking beneath a sun that dazzled the Connecticut River. This former venturesome sailor and man of too many words was mute. He seemed unaware of me except for a fleeting moment when I shouted, "Chet, it's Brandon!" He raised his head and shoulders almost imperceptibly at the sound of my voice, I hoped in distant recognition, and then retreated once more. I recalled how we first met when he hired me out of a congressional corridor to work in his office. I would have liked to thank him once more for his faith in me and for the experiences, good and bad, he allowed me to share with him.

I learned much from Chet, especially about the importance of principle and the long view in foreign policy. I had seen how and why he got hurt in that business. Chet's interest in young people and the ways he involved them in his life had a transforming effect on many of us. Later in my career I tried to do the same for others. When old India hands of my generation get together we talk about Chet fondly, his failings long put aside. There was something vital about the role of values to absorb from him, well expressed in Howard Schaffer's biography of Bowles in which he calls him "the standard bearer of American idealism at the height of the Cold War."

Cathy

Our daughter Catherine was born in March 1964 at Holy Family Hospital in New Delhi, where, in an uncomplicated birth, care for mother and child proved adequate. Chet offered his limousine and its turbaned driver, Jiwan Singh, for Cathy's ride home. The Cadillac in New Delhi was to be her first, but by no means only, experience with government transportation. She would marry a Foreign Service officer, Paul Wayne Jones, and write acclaimed books on cooking. Their first post together would be Skopje, Macedonia, where like Mary and me years before in Abidjan they were pioneering in a newly established American embassy.

10

WEST BERLIN

1965 to 1969

In Washington once more, after leaving New Delhi, I began, in State Department parlance, "reading into" Berlin. I sought out Elwood Williams III, one of the department's experts on German affairs. He had an encyclopedic knowledge of the U.S.-German relationship, and assignments to policy positions in Germany required his tacit approval. Rarely have I met a wiser, more thoughtful man.

I was among many colleagues in the "Berlin Mafia" who felt privileged to guide his wheelchair, to which he was contortedly confined with multiple sclerosis, into the cafeteria for lunch. There, helped to eat by his attendant, he spoke in low tones and paused for breath, his head resting on a chin support attached to his shoulders. From him I gleaned unique insights, learned recent and not so recent German history, and heard wise counsel. Later on, when Elwood sometimes made a kind remark about my work in Berlin, those were words from the headmaster.

The "Berlin Mafia" was an amorphous aggregation of the many people who had served there, spoke German, and knew German history. The redoubtable Eleanor Dulles, for example, sister of the former secretary of state, had devoted much of her life to Berlin's issues and to finding ways to support the city and its governing mayors. I remained in touch with her throughout my involvement with Germany. Our diplomatic presence in Germany was commingled with the presence of occupation forces. Service under the unique conditions prevailing in Berlin created bonds of friendship and esprit.

Following Hitler's defeat, the four victorious powers of World War II established military "zones" of occupation in Germany as a whole and carved out "sectors" for themselves in Berlin: the United States, Britain, and France occupied the western part of the city, and the Soviet Union the more industrialized eastern. Democratic ideals and institutions flourishing in West Germany and the issuance of a separate currency only widened the breach. Germany's three Western zones evolved in May 1949 into the Federal Republic of Germany. The Soviet Zone became the German Democratic Republic, or GDR, five months later. Two separate and distinct Germanies were emerging. A bifurcated Germany came to symbolize the divisions of the Cold War.

With two mayors, Berlin became a divided city, itself an enclave 110 miles inside East Germany surrounded by the GDR. The Soviet Sector of Berlin became the capital of the GDR. In practice, West Berlin came to be treated as part of the Federal Republic, East Berlin as part of the GDR. The rights and responsibilities of the four wartime allies in Berlin, however, were not relinquished. Their exercise would cause friction until the Cold War ended. Upholding them would form the basis for unification, should that prospect emerge.

The Cold War had begun on July 2, 1947, when Soviet Foreign Minister V. M. Molotov led his delegation out of the conference in Paris that launched the Marshall Plan for European Recovery. It ended in Moscow on December 25, 1991, with Mikhail Gorbachev's resignation as president of the USSR and the disintegration of the Soviet Union. Symbolically, the Cold War was laid to rest with Ronald Reagan's state funeral in June 2004.

My assignment in 1965 as U.S. liaison officer to the West Berlin city government began nearly three years after the Cuban missile crisis was defused, and four after the East Germans, with Khrushchev's blessing, built their wall. Arriving with my family at Tempelhof Airport in the American Sector on a summer afternoon of 1965, I wondered, as one does on reaching a new Foreign Service post, what the next four years would bring. No other place resembled Berlin. Nowhere else—not in Japan, Italy, or Austria—were so many consequences of a great war bequeathed as riddles.

Dominating the plaza in front of Tempelhof Airport stood a high concrete monument curved in an upward sweep like the wing of a bird pointing three tip feathers toward the sky. It commemorated Allied solidarity with Berliners during the eleven-month Berlin Airlift that began in 1948. The airlift delivered two and a half million tons of essential supplies such as coal, food, milk, medicines, ambulances, and even snowplows, to overcome a Soviet blockade of West Berlin. During that siege, seventy-eight British and American fliers lost their lives in air and ground accidents. Their names were inscribed on this soaring memorial, which Berliners, never at a loss for self-mockery, dubbed the "Hunger Rake." That sculpture was the first sight an American arriving in Berlin was likely to encounter upon exiting the terminal.

Before getting into a van that would deliver my family and me and a large pile of luggage to our future home, I gazed for a moment at the winglike monument celebrating the sacrifice and grit of Allied fliers. In one of the most harrowing episodes of the Cold War, they saved Berlin from the Russians. I would fly in and out of Tempelhof many times, and on coming back find my mood subdued by a glance at the "Hunger Rake" as I stepped outside the terminal looking for a taxi.

We would live on the Thielallee in Dahlem, part of the American Sector of Berlin, in a gemütlich prewar villa that felt like the country home it once had been. Dahlem, long a suburb for the wealthy, had been little damaged during the war. Our home had a sloping garden of fruit trees, beyond which were a park of old chestnuts and a duck pond tucked away. In winter our children went sledding in the park, returning red-faced, giggling, shouting, and alive in every pore, clumps of snow sticking to their woolen mittens. As the yellows, pinks, and greens of springtime came, Dahlem and the Grunewald forest were places for walking in the unpolluted air of West Berlin. There was a smell of pine.

Jack and Cathy, and eventually little Paul, attended the Thomas A. Roberts army school and were happy there. Unlike my childhood in Hitler's Hamburg, where another boy and I were the lone Americans at the Bertram Schule, our children were receiving an American education in Berlin, and I was glad of that. We found it almost effortless to live in comfort near the military PX and a food commissary that appeared to have everything one might want at discount prices. The Outpost Theater (now the Museum of the Allied Forces) offered hot buttered popcorn with films from home, and a U.S.-run garage stocked parts for American cars like our old Buick station wagon. Such benefits made life easier. Yet few could shed feelings of remoteness and menace. I have served at no post, including in the heart of Africa, where people felt their isolation more keenly.

Cities are street theaters where social relations play themselves out. West Berliners lived in a truncated, raw half-city that made no municipal sense. West Berlin, without a hub in its downtown area, left one feeling disoriented and dissatisfied. Missing was a sense of completion and harmony: the visual rhythms of buildings standing together along busy streets leading to a coherent center. One searched in vain for a Piccadilly Circus or a Place de la Concorde. The leading KaDeWe department store stood by itself without any particular relationship to the surrounding space. The Kurfürstendamm, West Berlin's premier street of near-elegant shops, cinemas, and cafés, became a wide ribbon of colored lights at night ending ingloriously near the wall. An architectural landmark, the Memorial Church was a bombed-out shell left standing on Kurfürstendamm to recall the suffering and devastation of World War II. It came closest to being the mile-zero point of reference from which all distances in West Berlin might be measured.

Beyond their ability to travel to other communist countries, East Germans had nowhere to go. Their borders to the West were sealed, and they faced a wall zigzagging through the city of Berlin for twenty-eight miles and around the West Berlin–GDR boundary for another seventy. For them there was no ribbon of light like the Kurfürstendamm, no tempting KaDeWe.

Playing by the Rules

Western Allies referred to themselves as occupying powers to hold the Soviets to agreements at the end of a war that gave the Four Powers an "occupation" right to be in Berlin. Maintaining that right was politically, as well as militarily, necessary. Allied practices were intended to endure, just as they were, until the four Allies could agree to change them—no matter how inefficient or senseless some of them became.

By the time I arrived in Berlin, apart from three aging Nazis convicted in the Nuremberg Trials and locked up in Spandau Prison, there had been for twenty years no one left for Allied armies to subdue. In military terms, our forces in West Berlin served as a trip wire, should the Soviets move their troops westward toward the Fulda Gap and then pour into Frankfurt. West Berlin could have been overrun in hours. Allied forces insured through NATO the immediate engagement of Western powers in any renewed Central European conflict. The symbolism and trip wire mattered, therefore, and Allied commandants held their parades and cultivated good relations with district mayors with this in mind.

But what would have happened if the Russians had overrun West Berlin *only* and then stopped without launching a general offensive against Western Europe? This possibility was explored in military war games. Would Allied troops have fought in Berlin, risking the loss of hundreds of their men in a hopeless battle? How would the Western capitals and NATO have responded to Moscow? Would we have employed, or threatened to use, nuclear weapons? My colleague Gerald Livingston recalls asking that bold question during a briefing by a U.S. general officer in Berlin "and seeing a horrified look cross his face."

Cold War politics had a chessboard feeling. Allied missions in West Berlin, mirroring each other, included legal advisers on their staffs, as did Allied embassies in Bonn, an arrangement dictated by the intricacies of the legal aspects of a Four Power presence in postwar Germany. The smallest measures affecting Allied-Soviet relations were likely to acquire legal dimensions in terms of agreements, precedents, rights, and responsibilities. Little was done impulsively. It is unlikely the world will see such arrangements again. Yet in their cumbersome ways they worked.

The State Department's lean mission in Berlin, abbreviated as USBER, was on Dahlem's Clayallee in a dreary military headquarters building that had contained elements of Göring's air force. At its head was a Foreign Service officer with the title of minister. Its large hallways, poorly lit in a yellowish light, had black strips of rubber matting running down the middle of the floors, and walls that were painted green halfway up. The halls bore a constant whiff of ammonia, laced with some sort of sweetener, emanating from a brew applied each day by the cleaning crews in mopping lavatory floors. When I returned to USBER years later to open our embassy in East Berlin, even the waft of that concoction, like so much else in the city, had been kept intact. And as smells do, it brought back swirls of memories. Our diplomatic mission comprised only a small number of the Americans working on Clayallee, most of the rest being civilian intelligence operatives and uniformed military personnel. The work environment was austere and businesslike, with everything properly squared away and desks cleared bare at the end of a day. Except in offices occupied by diplomats with sloppy habits, neatness, order, and an aura of battle readiness prevailed. All in all, our headquarters was a cheerless place in which to work, but no more cheerless than the nature of the business at hand.

Diplomats at City Hall

As U.S. liaison officer to the city government of West Berlin during 1965–1969, I represented the American commandant to the governing mayor and to Berlin's House of Representatives. For part of my stay, the governing mayor was Willy Brandt. The British and French had identical liaison functions, also staffed by their foreign services. The United Kingdom's Barbara Deavin was the most experienced. My subsequent British colleague, Christopher Mallaby, later became ambassador to Bonn and Paris.

The Western Allies had established a procedure of rotating the chairman-ship of the occupying powers among themselves. Before the Russians walked out of the Allied Kommandatura in 1948, rotation occurred among all four powers. Seniority filtered through the system, and one of the liaison officers also became the senior Allied spokesman at city hall for all three powers during the month when his or her commandant was in the chair. Rotation of se-niority, and the process of "handing off" to a successor commandant, obliged Allies at every level to consult and work together in an arrangement forcing cooperation on its participants. A practical consequence of this system was its hold over our leave schedules. Sometimes we discussed whether it would be better, vis-à-vis the Russians, to get a particular thing done in the "French month" or the "American month," a level of nuance best left to professors of international relations.

The U.S. liaison officer occupied a high-ceilinged, formal office in the prewar Rathaus Schöneberg, West Berlin's cavernous city hall on the renamed John F. Kennedy Platz. From the top of its steps in 1963, JFK had proclaimed himself a Berliner. Provided by the governing mayor, my office was meant to reflect the authority of the United States as an occupying power. It was almost as large as his own. My office had an intimidating effect on visitors; with plants and col-orful reproductions of American art, I strove to overcome an atmosphere of self-importance but never felt entirely comfortable there. I was at city hall part of the time on most days, working a political beat that gave a diplomat like me a rare look at the gears and pistons of a city's life. And what a city!

A farmers' market appeared twice a week in front of the Rathaus. Its canvas-covered carts offered fresh produce to the women and old men of Schöneberg, who carried elastic shopping nets expanding like spiderwebs around the goods they held. My windows overlooked the square, and I enjoyed watching a mar-ket scene that before leaving for home I sometimes joined with a shopping list of my own. I recall looking out those tall windows into the rain or a falling snow and giving in to depression, a Berlin affliction as catching as the common cold. In Berlin much depends on the weather. In the row of gray buildings across the square, near the mortician's window display of caskets, was a *Kneipe*, a drab workingmen's pub smelling of spilled beer and cigarette butts ground into metal ashtrays. Not to be dismissed, it offered local fare for lunch such as the delicious *Königsberger Klopse*, meatballs in a cream sauce of capers and an-chovies. My time at city hall took me out of the Allied political-military world of USBER and, to my relief and pleasure, into the heart of a Berlin middle-class neighborhood in the British Sector. More than nearly anyone else at our mission, I worked with and came to know Germans under occupation.

I met occasionally with the governing mayor but more often with members of his staff. Along with my French and British colleagues, I monitored sessions of the House of Representatives, ostensibly to insure that no laws were passed contrary to Allied responsibilities and obligations. During such meetings we entered the hall rather formally and seated ourselves behind the desks assigned to us. There were never surprises. The debates, especially on student demonstrations, could become acrimonious. Political party conventions at the Kongresshalle were attended by the Allied liaison officers and sometimes also by a personable Russian observer, fluent in German, from the Soviet embassy across the wall. The three of us watched him like nervous chaperones to observe who would become his conversation partners among the Germans. Fighting the Cold War got a bit childish at times.

The Allied liaison officers met almost daily with officials of the West Berlin government, whose executive branch was called the *Senat*. Conducted in German, our discussions ranged from economic investment in Berlin to the most sensitive and closely held developments of inner-German relations. Based on the needs of the moment, each liaison officer had bilateral issues to take up with the chancery that for me might be as weightless as programming a visit by Jimmy Stewart or Milton Berle.

The normal channel of communication was to the Senat's chief of chancery, Dietrich Spangenberg, and later his successor, Horst Grabert. Spangenberg, called "Spangers" by the British behind his back, was the gloomy ("It's almost midnight!") pessimist, and Grabert the jovial ("We'll do it!") optimist. Both were skilled interlocutors, sharply intelligent and articulate, strategically oriented, open, frank, deeply engaged, and warmly disposed toward us. They shared our values and emotions and were able to give us an idea of what it was like to be a postwar German on either side of the wall. The four of us— the liaison officers and the chief of chancery—became an intimate group committed to supporting each other, having dinner in rotation at one another's homes for long and relaxed conversations and remaining close in our social relationships within Berlin's stratified diplomatic and military communities. It was always the familiar "*Du*" among us. When our French colleague died of a heart attack, we felt his absence like a loss in the family and shared in the cost of a single funeral wreath from us all.

We spent hours at the Rathaus discussing whether to remove a tall wooden spar on the West Berlin side of one of the lakes but near the GDR's water boundary, as the Senat was proposing to do. The protruding spar was a hazard to navigation, yet the ever apprehensive Allies were concerned that such an action by West Berlin authorities might be considered provocative in the congealed state of relations with the East. Our partners in the Senat doubted this, but Allied machinery got cranked up anyway. Exchanges of telegrams involving Washington, London, Paris, Bonn, and NATO, with Moscow and our mission at the United Nations as information addressees, yielded the result that the Germans should proceed without causing "a big splash," a stipulation that inspired imitations of various splashing sounds as we considered how, exactly, to accomplish this. At our level we sometimes found irreverent humor in what we were doing, and that was good. In the event, there was only a small splash, and the GDR and the Soviet Union could not have cared less. Working in Berlin was like that when a rare and genuine crisis did not threaten. The German side generally, including Brandt, was disposed to a more relaxed and humane view of what was going on. Allied commandants and the State Department's ministers, who bore the occupiers' responsibilities, were driven by extreme caution and unremitting angst.

Our discussions with the Senat could be blunt. We pressed for details about what Brandt was up to, warned of possible missteps, delivered official letters or orders from the commandants. The Germans, equally outspoken, criticized Allied timidity and inaction or, privately to me, crossed lines involving U.S. intelligence activities. Raising an intelligence matter with me was intended to place it in a political light; separate channels were used for intelligence liaison. Such give-and-take and trading of information, duly reported by us, helped shape Allied comprehension of, and influence upon, developments in Berlin and permitted the Germans routinely to understand our positions, feelings, and constraints.

For diplomats like the three of us, what we were doing was unique and far removed from normal work, but not from diplomatic skills. Allied relations with Berlin's officials were lopsided, with ultimate responsibility and authority in the city residing with its occupiers. For a towering figure like Governing Mayor Willy Brandt, already a candidate for chancellor in 1961, this imbalance of power gave him a thin-skinned prickliness in dealing with us. Exceptional tact and attunement were needed in exchanges with Germans in Berlin, yet those considerations did not always suffice. Brandt could lose his temper during discussions with the commandants, resenting their encroachment on what he believed were his responsibilities or the dignity of the mayor's office. On at least one occasion he ended a conversation abruptly, and the three generals, who tactfully wore civilian clothes to such sessions, behaved like two-star pussycats and didn't press their point.

Only in Berlin

Life under military occupation had surreal aspects. The decades-long administration of Spandau Allied Prison by the four victors was one of them. This establishment of more than six hundred cells was in my day maintained solely
to support three Nazi prisoners: Rudolf Hess, Hitler's deputy; Albert Speer, his
anointed architect; and Baldur von Schirach, leader of the Hitler Youth. After
1966 Hess was alone, and would remain alone, until his death of a heart attack
in the prison garden at the age of ninety-three. The Soviets took their Spandau
responsibilities extremely seriously. Hess seemed to them a stand-in for the
Hitler they had never captured. In symbolic punishment for Russia's suffering
during the war, they were determined to keep Hess locked up until the end.

Guests of Allied legal advisers, like Mary and me, would occasionally be
invited to one of the formal monthly luncheons at Spandau. It was *théâtre noir*
to have a five-course meal, accompanied by French and German wines, served
elegantly in the prison commandants' paneled dining room, while Rudolf
Hess, a few yards away, read in his cell or worked in the garden. Mary and I
happened to be invited during the Russian month. The changing of the guard
in the courtyard at Spandau was an extraordinary sight, especially when Americans handed off to the Soviets in a stiff military ritual.

The Berlin Air Safety Center (BASC) monitored all flights in the Allied
corridors over the surrounding Soviet Zone, the GDR. It did not control traffic,
which was done at Tempelhof, Tegel, and Gatow Airports, but provided the
means for securing a necessary Soviet clearance for each flight through Soviet
airspace. Westerners could not enter or leave Berlin by air without flying
through narrow corridors with a ceiling of 10,000 feet. Military officers of the
Western Allies sat at their desks, routinely passing flight plans on slips of
paper to their Soviet counterpart for him to stamp. Each Pan American, Air
France, or BOAC flight coming to or from Berlin in the prescribed, tubelike
corridors required Soviet approval. Other airlines, such as Lufthansa, did not
provide service to West Berlin, and no Allied nations had flights into East
Berlin. When, for one minor reason or another, or to make a point, the Soviet
official hesitated in granting approval, alarm bells went off at Allied headquarters. Sometimes there was banter, and exchanges of American cigarettes for
Stolichnaya vodka were not unusual.

Pan American's pilots alerted passengers nearing the land frontier of the
Soviet Zone that they were "about to enter the Berlin corridor," and one felt
the plane descending below 10,000 feet. I would look up from my reading at

this announcement as if somehow to find the ground beneath us colored red. The back of my neck tingled at a matter-of-fact reminder of the Cold War, and there was the feeling of entering a combat zone. Occasionally, Soviet fighter pilots drew near for a look or were sent up if a plane strayed out of its corridor. Sometimes those pilots came too close, and the Allies protested. "We could see his face!" a Pan Am pilot angrily complained more than once.

As with the administration of Spandau Prison, BASC brought representatives of the four powers together daily in Berlin to work within institutionalized procedures devised and respected by all of the participants. Those ties might seem slender, as relatively few people were involved in carrying out either function, but they symbolized continuing forms and habits of four-power engagement and cooperation in Berlin. They were officially sanctioned, nondiplomatic means of communication in a Cold War environment of political and military stalemate. If Allied rituals in West Berlin bore an aura of unreality, what was being done kept occupation procedures intact until the victors could agree among themselves to change them.

Berlin did not lack drama. One afternoon West Berlin's police spotted an East German on the opposite shore intending to escape across one of the lakes. He was hiding in the reeds, waiting for darkness. So far, the GDR's patrol boats, crisscrossing the waters whose boundaries were marked by buoys, had not seen him. With their powerful searchlights at night, however, they might spot him in the reeds or pick up the ripples of his swimming strokes. I learned about the escape attempt in the Rathaus as it began, and about the rescue measures Berlin's authorities were preparing. They had hidden an ambulance in the woods near the shore and were staying out of sight until dark. This was an afternoon of rain clouds. The man's success would almost surely be decided by the weather. If it rained, his chances of escaping were good; if it didn't, they were slimmer. That evening, as Mary and I prepared to attend a social event, I became obsessed by the weather. *Let it rain!* When we left our front door to walk to the car, leaden skies began to sprinkle, then opened up and poured. We had never felt so happy to be under an umbrella. The man safely made it across, the ambulance unnecessary.

Checkpoint Charlie

My family and I found occasions to visit East Berlin, never suspecting that one day we would live there. At the Checkpoint Charlie barrier on Friedrichstrasse used by foreigners, we lowered the car windows a crack to be able to hear the East German guards. ("Charlie" was the military communications term for the third letter of the alphabet: this was U.S. military crossing point C.) Following rigid Allied instructions, we did not permit border guards to handle our passports, much less take possession of them. We pressed our passport covers and photo pages against the window glass and then proceeded through the checkpoint. In case of a problem, we insisted on speaking with a Soviet officer who had remained out of sight. We never knew whether the other side intended to provoke an incident. The checkpoint was an exposed nerve of the Cold War, the only place where, on October 26, 1961, American and Soviet tanks confronted each other barrel to barrel in a high-stakes test of wills. The Russians blinked.

The reasons for procedures uniformly observed by the Western Allies were at the core of the legal status of all of Berlin as occupied territory. We were prepared to deal with Soviet military authorities on questions pertaining to the four sectors of Berlin but refused to discuss such matters with East German officials because we did not recognize their authority in the Soviet sector of Berlin. We regularly asserted Allied rights to cross in the belief that a right not exercised soon ceased to be a right.

Those were the procedures, but how did it feel to make this crossing? There was always anxiety. Checkpoint Charlie was a Cold War passage across a death strip to the other side of the wall. Few more grimly businesslike places existed outside prison compounds. Your freedom was surrendered to an East German guard with a weapon strapped to his shoulder who peered at the occupants of each vehicle. Slowly he studied a passport photo, slowly he looked into the face of the traveler, his unfriendly stare compellingly met, and slowly he returned to the photograph, which by then you hoped still looked like you. For someone crossing in a hearse, the coffin lid was raised and the corpse similarly inspected; the ruse of escaping as a dead body no longer worked. Dismissively waved through, visitors were rewarded by the sorry fruits of communism that lay ahead. On returning to the West, having reversed the process through the final barrier of the checkpoint, you were greeted by the famous wooden sign on its two white posts proclaiming in English, Russian, French, and German, as if you didn't know, that you were entering the American Sector, and there, beyond our flag, were the lights and sights and sounds of freedom. *Hallelujah!* I whispered under my breath.

Understanding the Other Side

A separate political/economic section of USBER was devoted to East German and Soviet affairs. The diligent Foreign Service officers manning it, however, were unable to do the normal fieldwork of reporting. Barred from traveling outside the Soviet Sector of Berlin, they crossed to East Berlin through Checkpoint Charlie to look around and visit their East German sources—a few harmless writers, opera folk, and young dissidents. Much of what they gleaned about East Germany came from tea-leaf readings of *Neues Deutschland*, that dismal party newspaper of lies, omissions, and distortions; from talking to journalists who could travel there; and from analyzing the heavy volume of diplomatic reporting from Moscow and our other embassies behind the Iron Curtain.

The Allies sanctioned informal and unofficial contacts between designated Foreign Service officers in their Eastern Affairs Sections and certain diplomats made available by the Soviet embassy in East Berlin, whom we took to be KGB agents. Official Russians moved freely around West Berlin, usually, it seemed, trying to cultivate a single source. Our people, and Germans as well, referred to Soviet contacts like these as their "House Russians" or, less charitably, "KGB-niks." Such encounters were tiny safety valves, human contacts among remote Cold War adversaries, but hardly a substitute for the open relations between governments normally enjoyed by diplomats. We were skeptical of what we heard, intrigued by the underlying purposes of what we were being told, fascinated by the other side's agenda. Accounts of those meetings, sent to Washington and shared with NATO, our embassy in Moscow, and other posts in Eastern Europe, became pieces added to the jigsaw puzzle of the Soviet Union on which all of us were working.

Interlocutors in this diplomatic netherworld of the Cold War in Berlin met every month or so on either side of the wall in cafés and restaurants or sometimes for a private meal at an American home in Dahlem, heavy on steak, fresh salad, and chocolate ice cream. Such channels outside the system were a means of exchanging information, probing, hinting, warning, fishing, and reading the mood in relations. During the few hours of each meeting, the enemy showed himself to be as flawed and vulnerable as the rest of us. He might have been a rough-edged, ill-at-ease Russian sensitive to slights, who smoked and drank liberally, a player who had his own array of questions and superiors to inform. What he lacked in interpreting our side was a paradigm for thought and life in the West. At the core of prospects for gain by either side from tenuous efforts at interpersonal diplomacy such as these lay sensitivity and compatible chemistry and the skills of leading and listening, rather than lecturing. There was something titillating about meeting one's opponent face to face under civilized circumstances, like tasting forbidden fruit.

Experts such as Frank Meehan and Bill Woessner, men of knowledge and experience, toiled day by day in the cluttered offices of USBER's Eastern Affairs Section, where piles of *Neues Deutschland* were stacked high. This was what a communist den near the British Museum in London must have looked like in the thirties. I was impressed by what they and their colleagues were able to figure out about what was happening on the other side of the wall. Away from such research, Meehan and Woessner entertained the rest of us at some of the best parties in Dahlem, especially on the birthday of the poet and Scottish icon Robert Burns in cold January. Haggis, that dreadful combination of the hearts, livers, lungs, and I suspected testicles of a sheep, all boiled together with fatty white lamb suet, oatmeal, and onions, and then presented as some kind of sausage, was ceremoniously and irrationally carried into a packed hall by Frank and Bill wearing kilts and accompanied by the sound of bagpipes. Meehan was a Scot by heritage, Woessner through marriage.

In April 1966 our mission invited Allied colleagues to a sing-along for which we wrote a *Willy-Walter Songbook* celebrating Willy Brandt and Walter Ulbricht. Ulbricht was the East German communist who led the GDR from 1950 until 1971. A favorite offering, repeated on demand, was "Meet Me at the Checkpoint, Charlie," to the tune of "Meet Me in St. Louis, Louis."

Meet Me at the Checkpoint, Charlie

Meet me at the Checkpoint, Charlie,
Meet me there at three.
There'll be VOPOS lookin' snarlie,
Right at you and me.
We will dance the VOPO tango,
While the guns go pop and bango.
So-o-o meet me at the Checkpoint, Charlie,
Meet me there at three.

Willy Brandt: The Mayor and His Vision

Willy Brandt was a visionary, but not of the dreamy sort. In the stultified atmosphere of East-West relations in Berlin, where in the midsixties not much was presumed to be happening between the two Germanies, he was making progress in what he called "small steps" of accommodation brokered at technical levels with East Berlin's counterparts *drüben*, over there. In baby steps at first, they dealt with matters such as canal traffic, sewage flows, and the GDR's

S-Bahn subway system running through the wall. The emergence of Brandt's *Deutschlandpolitik*, or policy toward the East German regime, no matter how fragile, signaled a course adjustment on the German scene.

A few of us saw these developments as tentative first swings of a wrecking ball against the wall itself. We liaison officers described to our governments what was happening, barely discernibly, in such undertakings as the removal by West Berlin's authorities of a clock in the S-Bahn station of Steglitz. This aboveground subway station in West Berlin was scheduled for demolition, but the clock was part of a centrally run East German timing system and belonged to the GDR. Did East German officials hold a veto over the removal of their clock, and therefore the ability to impede a construction project in West Berlin? The matter was discussed with their subway authorities—once both sides had sorted out the nature and location of the intended meetings, the bureaucratic levels of participants, and their normal functions. A station clock might not have seemed important, but Brandt as governing mayor was monitoring this enterprise himself. The commandants, NATO, and Allied capitals were kept informed. In the end, the East Germans did not object to the procedure; negotiation of a practical matter had occurred, and dialogue had led to agreement. This was the American month. "Alles in Ordnung," West Berlin's chief negotiator, Dr. Gerhard Kunze, cheerfully informed me in a telephone call after midnight once the deed had been done. Of such stuff was improvement in inner-German relations made.

In a city whose people depended for their security on Allied-Soviet stability, here came the Germans themselves making ripples of progress, as they alone could do, in their ties to each other. Brandt's intellectual mentor was Egon Bahr, his closest adviser and personal agent. Bahr was a stocky man of medium height and an unprepossessing appearance. I found him a brainy, dour, and secretive person. His principal channels of communication to the Allies were through their ministers and commandants. In that setting he talked more like a professor than a politician, and officials on the Allied side tended to listen to him in an overawed way, keen to learn about the Bahr/Brandt vision for loosening constraints between the Germanies, but usually not engaging him with many hard questions.

More than anyone, Bahr was the architect of a broad inner-German policy of "change through rapprochement." He understood that the West German side alone could advance inner-German relations. A clever tactician as well, he developed close ties to one or two senior people in the CIA family in Berlin, thus providing himself a separate channel of communication bypassing Spangenberg and the State Department and engaging the agency in his activities.

He functioned as an éminence grise, and I wondered who, beyond Brandt himself, knew Bahr's innermost thoughts or the range of his activities at all points of the compass. He did not inspire trust.

The furthering of East-West relations among Germans undertaken by Brandt remained, in essence, the responsibility of the Western Allies. Both sides in the Cold War gave Brandt room to maneuver: the Allies, because they favored improving living conditions for all Berliners and a dialogue that might soften the city's division, if only slightly; the Russians because they hoped to wean Brandt from the West and thereby bring a "neutral" West Berlin more directly under their influence. Potentially, the Western Allies had more to lose. It all boiled down to how far they could trust Brandt.

Brandt's motives in his *Deutschlandpolitik* were to achieve a more healthy and humane relationship among Germans themselves, even at the cost of accepting, de facto, two German states. He was not giving in to the East, yet his moves at times caused suspicion in Western capitals as to whether he might someday trade West Germany's Western orientation for unification. Brandt navigated cleverly within the understood Allied framework for his actions. Steadily, sure-footedly, and without serious Allied objection, he expanded his parameters of accommodation. Pragmatic political steps under *Deutschland-politik* began transforming themselves into building blocks for strategic change in inner-German relations. Here was an object lesson for anyone seeking reconciliation: begin with the smaller issues and foster habits of cooperation.

Judging traits of integrity and dependability in one's discussion partners, even among those who are friendly, is one of the core tasks of a diplomat, and this can be a difficult and risky business. Cobbling together a U.S. assessment of Willy Brandt was a process that ran through the years. The snapshots that emerged reflected a blend of German views from many sides, intelligence reports, the opinions of our allies, but most of all the judgments of our diplomats in Germany and of those, like Elwood Williams, who served in Washington and were experienced in German affairs. As leaders change their policies, they sometimes do so in small increments that only people on the scene detect. *Deutschlandpolitik* originated with Brandt, an international figure and likely future chancellor. In Berlin, at the center of the Cold War, the West could not afford to misread the man. They trusted him throughout, supported him, and were right in doing so.

I became acquainted with Willy Brandt while he was governing mayor of Berlin. He was also national chairman of the Social Democratic Party, the SPD. Brandt's role in national politics enabled those of us in Berlin to observe and report on the internal workings of the SPD, whose headquarters were with

Brandt in Berlin. Appointed foreign minister in December 1966 in a boost to his nascent outward-looking *Ostpolitik* toward the Soviet Union and its satellites (initiated three years later when he became chancellor), Brandt moved to Bonn. His deputy, Heinrich Albertz, a moody Lutheran pastor and ineffective mayor, succeeded him. With Brandt gone and Albertz absorbed in the city's internal workings, the game became less stimulating for liaison officers accustomed to conversing about the scope of German relations in an uncharted future.

Brandt was a gravel-voiced, charismatic, and rhetorically powerful leader, as I observed while attending Berlin's SPD conferences. An illegitimate child, his patronymic was Frahm. During World War II he fled the reach of the Gestapo in his native Lübeck, where he had been a Social Democratic activist, slipped into the uniform of a Norwegian soldier, and eventually made his way to Sweden in 1940. He was a barrel-chested, physically intimidating, and earthy man, popular because ordinary people identified with him and thought him sincere. They wanted to hear from him. He came across as tough and dependable. Brandt was an emotional person, attractive to women, and given to bouts of depression. Tormented or brooding, he displayed a fierce temper. He drank heavily, preferring brandy, *Branntwein* in German, as political satirists liked to point out. When I brought visitors or our ambassador in Bonn to his office, we might encounter Brandt with a hangover sitting in a funk and saying almost nothing. I warned official Americans before their meetings of his moodiness and that they might find lapses in conversation. Willy Brandt enriched my appreciation of what one person with a compelling sense of purpose can accomplish. He saw himself reflected in this aspect of John and Robert Kennedy, to whom he sometimes referred.

Brandt in Berlin, with Allied approval for the opening phases of his *Deutschlandpolitik*, began talking directly to the Russians, meeting occasionally in East Berlin with Soviet ambassador Piotr Abrasimov. As it became likely that Brandt would be moving to Bonn, the Russians took great interest in him. Brandt did not intend to limit his contacts to East Berlin's subway and sewer technicians. The Western Allies asked for, and received, accounts of these sessions. I doubted, however, that anyone in Allied ranks was fully apprised of Brandt's activities, or of Bahr's, and suspected he followed a more elaborate agenda than he shared with us. The risk of leaks in telling all was high in such a delicate process. It would have been only human, would it not, to have reserved to oneself and one or two trusted partners in the intimate German circle an insight, a feeler put out, a look in the eye, or an unspoken understanding?

I would drive to the Rathaus late at night through the slumbering streets of Berlin to be debriefed by Spangenberg, along with my tripartite counterparts, on Brandt's most recent activities. "*Na*, this is what happened at the meeting with Abrasimov," Spangenberg might ponderously begin, having been present himself. We liaison officers leaned toward him and began making notes for our telegrams later that night to await a morning readership in our capitals. Mine, as usual, were jottings on folded yellow legal paper. For us, these sensitively classified cables might begin: "*Senat Chief of Chancery Spangenberg informed Allied liaison officers just before midnight on May 17 that Brandt's meeting with Soviet Ambassador to the GDR Abrasimov, conducted in an 'extremely cordial atmosphere,' proceeded as follows...*" Soon it would be not just the three of us on the Allied side, in the middle of the night, who knew what Spangenberg said had happened.

Willy Brandt was awarded the Nobel Peace Prize in 1971. Three years later, his longtime friend and confidential secretary in Bonn, Günther Guillaume, was revealed to be an East German spy. Brandt, now himself a casualty of the Cold War, resigned as chancellor.

Where Have All the Flowers Gone?

In the mid-1960s, Rudy Dutschke led a student movement of thousands in West Berlin fueled by his embrace of nihilism. An uprising in Paris had been inspired by "Dany le Rouge" Cohn-Bendit, who battled police, brought on a general strike in solidarity, and indirectly caused the resignation of President de Gaulle. Like 1848, the year 1968 was one of turmoil in Europe. Across the Atlantic, a war in Vietnam, the assassinations of Martin Luther King Jr. and Robert Kennedy, and racial unrest in Washington and Watts were reaping havoc. This was a terrifying and disorienting time.

Media coverage of demonstrations with red banners and shouting students punching their fists into the air—the police responding with powerful jets from water cannons—seemed ominous for West Berlin. The city's precarious status required stability. While the Allies were ultimately responsible for protecting Berlin, coping with this movement was a problem for German authorities. The Allies believed the Soviets would not take advantage of Berlin's seeming vulnerability (it never became destabilized, and they didn't) but would choose to exploit its social origins through propaganda. The phenomenon of unrest and its tolerance by city authorities without severe repression must have baffled the Russians. "We All Live in a Yellow Submarine," proclaimed the sensational Beatles from Liverpool. In the eyes of totalitarian regimes, these youths with new sounds and psychedelic lyrics were incomprehensible and somehow threatening to the social order. Berlin remained divided: an oppressed population existing on one side of the wall, and a vibrant, albeit unruly, democracy bubbling on the other.

West Berlin's demonstrators felt blameless for a Nazi past beyond their ken. They felt alienated from an "economic miracle" in West Germany catering to a middle class they viewed as made up of obese and depraved figures depicted by George Grosz long before. They proclaimed their parents, pastors, professors, and what they were offered in the social sciences and humanities irrelevant to their times and needs. They were revolutionaries storming the barricades of gemütlichkeit. They dedicated themselves to reshaping what they perceived as a materialistic, patriarchal, and sexist order to vaguely marxist ideals but found little to offer by way of remedy. An ideological cleavage between generations was occurring over matters such as religion and the proper functions of the state, sexual freedom, consumerism, drugs, and long hair on men. The demonstrators' yells of frustration in the end had the force and transitoriness of a passing gale.

Disaffected young people regularly interrupted theater and concert performances, leaping onto stages to shout slogans until hustled away. Their behavior was maddening to actors, musicians, and audiences alike, who shouted back and stomped their feet. But the spell of a performance remained shattered. Empowering themselves, protesters concentrated on defamation and mob action. The police, who usually controlled them with skill and restraint, were "fascist pigs." Anti-American sentiment over Vietnam erupted at the Free University—heavily subsidized by Americans—and in attacks on the Amerika Haus library and cultural center downtown. Individual Americans did not feel threatened during the unrest. Students were callously unconcerned about repressive conditions for Berliners like themselves on the other side of the wall, where there would be no protests.

I recall the movement as self-centered, a lark for many of the demonstrators, and unfocused by the leadership beyond expressing their hatred of a German bourgeoisie and creating turmoil for its own sake. At the core it was also an expression of alienation from society, an outcry in pain against the wars, materialism, and conservative thinking of the times. These young people neither fit in nor wanted to fit in but did not know where else to go. There was a hollowness at the movement's epicenter that was sad and invited transcendent understanding, with attendant risks of condescension, that eluded West Berlin's authorities.

Willy Brandt's sons, Lars and Peter, were among the marchers in Berlin, but Brandt understood that today's protesters were tomorrow's mainstream politicians, which was harder for the occupying powers to grasp. Eventually, most protestors who stayed politically active went into the SPD or helped form the Greens. Cohn-Bendit later became a Green deputy in the European Parliament.

Mary and I were guests at a performance of *The Magic Flute* one evening in June 1967 to honor the shah of Iran's visit to Berlin. Students despised him as a ruthless autocrat propped up by the United States and demonstrated rowdily against him. That night outside the opera building, a twenty-six-year-old theology student named Benno Ohnesorg, a bystander, was accidentally shot and killed by a West Berlin policeman. Before anyone else inside the theater knew what was happening, Berlin's police president had left his seat. During an intermission rumors circulated that there had been a shooting outside. Police moved expeditiously to clear the immediate area of demonstrators, and by the time the opera ended, even though tension in the streets was evident, signs of the tragedy had disappeared. This incident triggered uglier confrontations from then on and further radicalized a student movement that now had its martyr.

One of our Foreign Service officers working in the U.S. mission, Kenneth Keller, produced a flow of reporting and analysis of student upheavals throughout this period unmatched by anything coming from other Foreign Service posts. Ken was a quiet man from Bonners Ferry, Idaho, who loved the freedom and open spaces under the skies of his native state and never used more words than he needed, but they were the right ones. He was getting bald and had a shaggy mustache, slouched a bit, and felt happiest in jeans, cowboy boots, and an open flannel shirt. In soft Viennese accents, Ken knew how to elicit conversation from nearly anyone and was teargassed and watercannoned along with the demonstrators, an experience shared by no other diplomat in Berlin. Joachim Bölke of *Tagesspiegel*, whose initials "J.B." at the bottom of an always thoughtful column commanded attention, sought Keller out. Ken made a decisive contribution to the understanding in Washington and other capitals of those turbulent and perplexing times.

Assassination of Martin Luther King Jr.

On April 4, 1968, at the age of thirty-nine, the Reverend Martin Luther King Jr. was assassinated in Memphis. Klaus Schütz by then had succeeded the former pastor Albertz as governing mayor of West Berlin. Schütz, in the wake of disruptive student demonstrations that plagued the city, decided to lead a march of his own to memorialize King. The point he wanted to make, beyond expressing Berliners' admiration for King, was that not all demonstrations needed to voice protest; they could be held to express positive feelings. Schütz and I were in the front rank of this march honoring Dr. King's memory. I never before had been in the streets as a demonstrator and felt moved by the feelings Berliners displayed toward King and the American struggle for civil rights. Berliners knew what it was like to be oppressed.

Unification

German and Japanese forces surrendered unconditionally at the end of World War II, and to the victors belonged the spoils. In Berlin, I witnessed, and from a modest perch helped shape, a willingness by Allied governments to share political power—not Allied/Soviet occupation rights themselves—with Willy Brandt. The ultimate goals of the Western alliance were to see Germany united as a democracy and to end Four Power occupation through a peaceful accommodation with the Soviet Union acceptable to the Germans themselves. We wanted to depart as soon as we could on our terms but were prepared to wait, as it turned out, until the summer of 1994, when Allied forces held their last parades and left Berlin.

How the Allies behaved as victors in Germany during the Cold War changed for the better the world we now live in. The same can be said for the objectives and consequences of the U.S. occupation of Japan. Both occupations were benign and successful. Just as the outcome of World War II defined the twentieth century, so did the reconciliations that followed.

During my time in Berlin the unification of Germany appeared a fading prospect mentioned less frequently in the West. Allied powers had settled in for the long haul. West Berliners accepted the strains and comforts of their lives. They made the most of opportunities through extortionate wall passes issued by the GDR to visit relatives on the other side on holidays or during family emergencies. The city's division seemed complete except for sounds in the background, faint but persistent scratches signifying progress in Brandt's "small steps" toward normalization. The Allied diplomatic role was central to Berlin's survival, and little understood. It kept the Cold War cold.

I returned to Berlin in 1987, invited by the city government as one of its guests of honor during the celebration of Berlin's 750th anniversary. The wall was solidly up, and by then I was ambassador to Zaire. I was elated to join again the Senat's Gerhard Kunze, who had taken down the Steglitz station clock, and other friends. On behalf of the Rathaus, Kunze presided over a luncheon that included the current Allied liaison officers among his German guests. Responding to his toast, I spoke of the need to hold on to the goal of a unified Germany, recalling Brandt's early steps so well remembered by my host and me. I could sense as I did so that I sounded out of harmony with the time, a voice from the past addressing a subject no longer considered current in 1987. It was a nice thing to mention, to be sure, but like my graying hair it dated me. In everyone's calculations unification was not likely to happen soon. How wrong we all were.

I look back in near disbelief remembering decades of occupation and stand-off in Berlin. It is too easy now to forget those Allied uniforms and what they represented in terms of commitment to Berlin's survival and to overlook the suffering of Berliners in that divided city and let slip away memories of some two hundred East Germans who lost their lives attempting to overcome the wall. From 1945 onward, Berlin was the Cold War's testing ground of Allied and Soviet resolve. The Western Allies acted in concert in Berlin, Bonn, and NATO to engage Germans in governing themselves. In the end the Russians, with troubles at home and abroad beyond remedy under communism, walked away from all of Germany without a struggle. Already I have about those times the sense of remoteness and poignancy I feel when looking at a sepia print from years long gone by.

Berliners continue in their intellectual sparkle and cockiness; their love of the avant-garde and zest for living; scatological humor; meanness and maudlin sentimentality; stubbornness, courage, and rudeness; their passion for dogs, white asparagus, a summer's beer laced with raspberry syrup; and in touting the vaunted air of their city. They sum up a brassy, sassy self-confidence in the words *Schnauze mit Herz*, meaning, roughly, a big mouth coming from the heart. And this: after the wall came down, East Berliners returned books to the Amerika Haus library borrowed before the wall had suddenly appeared.

Paul

Family is at the heart of one's life, whether children grow up in a single neighborhood or travel as uprootingly around the United States and the world as people in the Foreign Service and military life, and many families in the private sector, are obliged to do. Our son Paul was born in May 1965 shortly before we left Washington for Berlin. Outgoing and engaged in the world about him, Paul would develop an interest in foreign affairs, eventually working as a senior Senate staffer on Capitol Hill. His wife, Martha Merselis, a classmate at Bates College, became an archivist at the National Archives. They lived their first two years together in Cambodia, where Paul represented the International Republican Institute and Martha created its women's programs.

LEFT: On the cusp in 1950, at twenty-one, I was between studies at Bard College and Princeton University.

BELOW: Joan Williams from Memphis, a classmate at Bard, began a friendship with William Faulkner based on her ambition to become a writer. She viewed him as a mentor, but he fell in love with Joan while I, too, was romantically involved with her. At the graduation dance for our class in 1950, Joan and I share a moment of intimacy. (Joan Williams Collection)

While spending 1946–1947 with my parents in Vienna, I began a lifelong friendship with the Polish pianist Andrzej Wasowski. We concocted a successful scheme to spirit him to freedom on a train through the Soviet Zone of Austria by bribing Russian border guards. His playing of Chopin's music, in particular, won him international acclaim. (Maria Wasowski Collection)

Climbing the Great Cheops Pyramid in Egypt was foolhardy, but at the top in 1951 are two friends and I—Emma Baltazzi, center, and her sister Eileen. Carter Hills, the fourth member of our intrepid group, took this picture. (Carter H. Hills Collection)

American servicemen were still warmly welcomed in Australia in 1957. As the amphibious boat group commander, I represented my ship at a ladies' tea in Sydney, where I stand beside hostess Mary Tancred.

This is my favorite photograph of my father, Brandon Grove Sr. At fifty-six, he is attending an international oil conference at The Hague and deliberates before sharing his thoughts. A geologist, he reflected on time and humanity and why all of us are here. He was the person who most strongly influenced my life and decision to become a diplomat.

The publicity photo taken in 1961 of my wife, Mary, and me sailing homeward aboard the SS *United States* after two years in Abidjan. I believed we were helping to promote American shipping but later worried I would be fired from the State Department for a fatuous display of elitism.

When Attorney General Robert F. Kennedy and his wife, Ethel, traveled around the world on a goodwill mission during February 1962, I was their State Department escort. The three of us are emerging from an audience with Pope John XXIII in Rome. This monthlong trip gave RFK a sobering appreciation of Soviet influence abroad.

My parents in 1963, who were then living in London where my father represented the Middle East interests of Mobil Oil. They are admiring their first
grandchild, John "Jack" Grove, at our home in Georgetown. Mother was born
in Warsaw and came to Chicago in 1923 on a YWCA scholarship to study and
teach gymnastic dance.

ABOVE: Chester Bowles and his wife, Steb, were happy in a smaller home after they decided in 1963 to move out of the newly built official residence in New Delhi designed by Edward Durrell Stone. They found the residence barnlike and unrepresentative of the American values they wanted to reflect in India. Bowles met with mixed success on his second tour as ambassador, during which I was one of his closest aides.

LEFT: At our large embassy in New Delhi people gave costume parties. Here, in 1963, my wife, Mary, and I join in a luau. Mary, with Russian origins in the Cheremeteff family, is expecting our daughter, Catherine, who was born in India.

Ambassador John Sherman Cooper, a former senator from Kentucky, insisted our relations with the German Democratic Republic be established in a "correct" manner. The East Germans were flattered in 1974 to have a man of his standing and political credentials in Berlin. Cooper left to me as his deputy the day-to-day concerns in these relations, and embassy management as well. He took an interest in developing a friendship with the veteran Soviet ambassador in Berlin, Piotr Abrasimov. Here we are discussing the day's work. (Gertrude D. Musson Collection)

Lorraine Cooper, the ambassador's wife, was a leading figure in Washington society who, in 1974, brought elegance and beauty to the official residence in drab East Berlin. "It should be like walking into a big red rose," she said of her drawing room pictured above. She pushed the State Department's procurement regulations to their limits as she sought to make her visions for this shoe-box-shaped home come true. (Gertrude D. Musson Collection)

Our nation's two-hundredth birthday in July 1976, celebrated at Foreign Service posts throughout the world, provided Lorraine Cooper in East Berlin a long-awaited opportunity to entertain in a grand style, and she rose to the occasion. *Bicentennial Smile*, a painting of me made at the time, reflects the joy and pride in our nation felt by Americans overseas everywhere. (Portrait by Ursula Wieland Lambach)

Ambassador Philip C. Habib tells the Jerusalem press corps, again, that he will
not comment on his negotiations during 1982 to oust the PLO from Lebanon.
Phil stayed with me at the renowned Ottoman residence of the American consul
general in Jerusalem, whose rose garden he dearly loved and where a plaque
commemorates him.

With his wife, Sallie, U.S. ambassador to Israel Samuel Lewis, in snorkeling gear, gave a costume party at their residence in Tel Aviv in 1982 at which I arrived from Jerusalem disguised as an Arab. In those times I would not have startled any Israelis.

When former president and Mrs. Carter came to Jerusalem in March 1983, Father Godfrey and I took them to visit holy places. Later this Franciscan friar and archaeologist
gave them books in my home. Carter's meetings with Palestinians and the Israeli settlements he saw on the West Bank dismayed him. "I never considered [during the Camp
David negotiations] that the definition of autonomy would be so narrow as has been
preferred by the Israeli Government," he told reporters on leaving.

President Reagan received each of his ambassadors at the White House before they departed on assignments abroad. His purpose was to impress upon them that they were his
personal representatives and to provide a signed photograph attesting to this connection
to be displayed on top of the piano in the official residence. My family and I met with
him in 1984, absorbing his warmth and joviality before I left for Zaire. (Official photograph, The White House)

My son Mark and I, in 1985, visiting the vast game preserve of Virunga, Zaire, withheld from commercial tourism by Mobutu. Years later I learned that Mark, then fifteen, was beginning to sense something distinguishing him from other boys his age in school and from his friends.

During the three years I served in Kinshasa as ambassador, I enjoyed none of my conversations with President Mobutu Sese Seko of Zaire, a dictator running a kleptocracy. I wish I could recall what we were discussing here in 1987. Economic reforms?

The renowned CIA operative Larry Devlin and his new wife, Mary Rountree, at my residence in Kinshasa in 1987 before we settled down to one of our Sunday luncheons together. Larry, as station chief in Léopoldville, had given Colonel Mobutu a nod in 1960 that changed the Congo's destiny. He and I became friends during trying times in Mobutu's Zaire, where Larry, by then retired, represented a New York City diamond trading company.

My wife, Mariana, feels the joy and amazement of peering through a crack in the Berlin Wall during our visit in 1990.

Dr. John T. Sprott, deputy director of the Foreign Service Institute, and I rejoice in 1991 in progress toward building a permanent center for foreign affairs training throughout the U.S. government at Arlington Hall, Virginia. My role in creating this facility was my most satisfying accomplishment during thirty-five years as a diplomat.

Mariana and I, in 1994, on a bench with Benjamin Franklin in the courtyard of the Foreign Service Institute at Arlington Hall, with newly planted cherry trees behind us.

My family gathered for daughter Cathy's wedding in Washington on June 24, 1995. In the top row, left to right, are Mark Grove, Hannah and Jack Grove, Martha and Paul Grove, Michele Parsons Shotts and David Shotts, and I, father of the bride. Below, my wife, Mariana; the groom, Paul Wayne Jones; and Catherine Cheremeteff Jones.

11

ROBERT KENNEDY

1968

During my visit to the State Department from Berlin in the winter of 1967, Robert Kennedy invited me to Hickory Hill for dinner with Ethel and the football star Roosevelt "Rosie" Grier. After the meal we sat in his study and our conversation turned to politics. Bob was wondering whether to run for president, hesitating to get into an ugly fray and far from confident that even the nomination could be his. He was a man undecided about what to do and dispirited by the options facing him. Johnson, whom he hated, was president and would run. The primary campaign would be divisive and difficult. The country was being torn apart by Vietnam, the civil rights movement, and young people feeling themselves alienated from the rest of society.

Bob believed we were bogged down in the White House and in Congress, where, as a senator, he said he felt frustrated and bored. You can't get anything done there, he told us. Being the junior senator from New York wasn't adding up to much. He believed he could make a difference in the campaign and as president, but still he hesitated. Rosie and I urged him to try to make that difference. Ethel was noncommittal, but I sensed she agreed. That evening I felt overwhelmed by America's problems and not encouraged by the presidential candidates on the scene. On my return to Berlin, in a poorly articulated attempt to put my thoughts on paper, I wrote to Bob urging him again to run. On March 16, 1968, Kennedy declared his candidacy. Teasingly, he replied to me two weeks later: "On reading your letter I decided to run." On March 31, Johnson announced at the end of a television address on Vietnam that he would not seek another term as president.

Robert Kennedy was assassinated in Los Angeles on June 5 at the age of forty-two. I found it impossible to explain to Germans or to anyone else why this had happened. Berliners blamed a deep streak of violence in American society. People felt there was something wild and ungovernable in the American psyche, a sickness in our national character. West Berliners, when Bob was killed, placed lighted candles in their windows, something they did only on deeply felt occasions, as when President Kennedy was murdered.

At the invitation of the Kennedy family, I returned to New York for Bob's funeral to be an honorary pallbearer at the ceremonies in St. Patrick's Cathedral. When the pallbearers were lined up alphabetically outside so we could enter the church as a group, I found myself once more next to Rosie Grier. Now there was nothing to say: no options, no hope for the kind of change Robert Kennedy might have brought about. Standing by his casket in the cathedral when my turn came, touching it before I left, I felt somewhere beyond reason and reality. Afterward I joined the family and funeral cortege on the train back to Washington and at the burial in Arlington Cemetery, where Mrs. Kennedy insisted no weapons be fired in tribute.

The weather was hot on Saturday, June 8. As our train emerged from the tunnel into New Jersey and proceeded slowly down the tracks toward Washington, a trip made so often before, we were amazed to find people crowding station platforms and standing in ragged rows along the roadbed, or sometimes just alone. "Look at those *people!*" I saw men from veterans' posts wearing their overseas caps and saluting; families with children lifted high; nuns dressed in their habits; people holding flags or carrying a few flowers, some waving slowly as we rolled by through the silence. Hundreds of thousands of people had come, many of them youngsters brought by parents who wanted them to remember this day. I looked into their faces and saw dignity, shock, and grief. These were ordinary Americans, many of modest means, whom Robert Kennedy had touched, and instinctively they came to the tracks. Casual summer clothing made them more immediate, briefly called away from what they had been doing on a Saturday afternoon. Some lived in homes along the tracks, and now, when I ride past the older houses and see people in their later years, I wonder if they were there on that day.

The furies were unleashed. I was horrified to see on the roadbed the bleeding body parts of two bystanders near the Elizabeth, New Jersey, platform, who had been cut in two by an oncoming train. One man was wearing a T-shirt, and its whiteness caught my eye. Rail traffic from the opposite direction was stopped, and we proceeded along empty tracks to Washington like a solitary toy train, taking more than eight hours to make the journey. The farther south we went the more African Americans were in the crowds, and the larger the crowds grew. In Baltimore, as we crawled through the station and pressed against the windows to wave back, people on the platform were singing the "Battle Hymn of the Republic." Something in many of us snapped and tears flowed. The train was a capsule in which *we* had become spectators looking out at those enormous numbers of people, hour after hour, who were there to see a casket pass and pay their respects, or just watch. We felt sweaty, thirsty, drained, and did not speak much, surrendering ourselves to the incredible scene along the tracks. Ethel Kennedy walked through the coaches and greeted each person with a quip and a smile, making some remark to me about the luggage as she might have done on our trip around the world in 1962. We hardly knew what to say. Riding those tracks today I have not been able to free myself from sadness, from a might-have-been.

There was a place, somewhere in Robert Kennedy's inmost self, to which he withdrew when he thought or listened intently. From this quiet and personal center came his deepest feelings and convictions; it was the source of daring, even noble, commitment and action. He quoted Aeschylus from memory. At the core were his Catholic faith and a capacity to endure pain and self-doubt and, ultimately, bear the weight of a tragic sense of life. When he was in that inner place of mind and heart, his hooded eyes lost focus and stared ahead as his voice trailed off. During such retreats, you could almost see him reaching a conclusion. Sensing his vulnerability in that private process, you kept silent. Acceptance of responsibilities thrust upon him that he believed he must meet drove him to the edges of endurance as few others are driven by an awareness of public purpose in their lives. He had begun his book about our trip around the world with a quotation from Emerson: "the world is a proud place, peopled with men of positive quality...who will not let us sleep."

To people of my generation who believed, as the Kennedys did, that government could do good, the shock was indescribable. Part of our world had been fractured and would never reassemble itself the same way. When Lyndon Johnson announced he would not seek the presidency because of his failing war in Vietnam, I thought Bob Kennedy had a good chance to succeed him. Perhaps then there might have been an opportunity for me to work with him again. I now wonder whether he would have found enough support in the southern states to win.

On my way from Berlin to New York to attend the funeral, I stopped in London to spend the night with my father, who was disillusioned by the war in Vietnam and the violence in his native America. No admirer of Robert Kennedy, he understood my feelings. After dinner, I walked through Hyde

Park in the warm air. The Serpentine pond was dark and quiet, and the bridle paths and trees provided a place to grieve and think about two dead brothers and what they had meant to much of the world. London's traffic flowed around the edges of the park, muffled by tall trees and shrubs so it sounded like a continuous, gentle waterfall shushing downward from some far cliff.

I waited in a long, silent line in front of our embassy in Grosvenor Square to sign the condolence book. When it came my turn, I read what the young woman in front of me had written. She asked: "Why do you Americans kill the best in you?"

Family

Our prospect of returning to Washington—of being home again from Berlin—became an opportunity for Mary and me to find a house of our own for the first time, a place in which to raise, by then, three small children. We wanted to live out the American dream of being an independent family on our own plot of land. We sought a sense of permanence and were drawn to Spring Valley, a wooded neighborhood near Massachusetts Avenue whose homes dated from the 1930s in an imaginative development of that gently hilly area.

Houses were set back along streets where uninterrupted lawns created a sense of community. The songs of crickets gave depth to the nights. Smells were of earth and mown grass or, on a weekend, the lazy fragrance of steaks sputtering on a grill. In summer a white Good Humor van made its rounds. Bells jingling ring-a-ding-*ding* summoned children to ice cream sticks as they ran across sidewalks and lawns clutching coins in their fists. In fall's chastening mood, taken unawares on a chilly day, you might catch yourself looking up uneasily on hearing the wind rattle dry leaves in a tree. Near the top of a hill on a bending road in the shade of big oaks, with the original spring threading its rocky way below, our brick house on Quebec Street was nearly perfect for us. We thought of our home as a symbol of roots for children soon to endure again the dislocations of Foreign Service life. Here would be their home for years to come of Christmastimes and birthday parties, until it broke apart.

12

PANAMA

★ ★ ★ ★

1969 to 1971

From his State Department suite of offices Findley Burns Jr., the new executive director of the department's Latin America bureau, telephoned me in the spring of 1969 as my time in Berlin was coming to an end. He wanted to discuss an assignment in Washington.

I first met this urbane and cultured Baltimorean with a wry sense of humor and the accents of Maryland while he was in charge of administering our embassy in London under one of America's great ambassadors, David K. E. Bruce. Grosvenor Square had been right for Findley, with his knowledge of antiques, books, tailoring, food, and wine. He had another side, the reason for his being there: he knew where the floorboards creaked. Few understood Washington's bureaucracy better than Findley. "Never harbor illusions about the State Department, my boy," he liked to insist with a broad smile and arched eyebrows, "It's beyond redemption!" And indeed, a not completely frivolous image that came to mind of the tangled strands of power, status, rivalry, and ambition in our nation's capital was of a bowl of spaghetti depicting an organizational structure covered with *putanesca* sauce connoting blood and carnage.

The State Department divided the world geographically, with each of five regions encompassed by a "geographic bureau" led by an assistant secretary. Washington's dealings with countries south of our border were gathered under the rubric of American Republics Affairs, or ARA as it was called. Findley's responsibility was to take charge of ARA's people, budgets, and embassies; in short, he was ARA's manager. In this capacity he reached across the Atlantic and summoned me back from Berlin to lead the Washington end of our relations with Panama, the Office of Panamanian Affairs. Findley tapped me for

163

this assignment because Charles E. Meyer, formerly an executive of Sears, Roebuck and now President Nixon's assistant secretary for ARA, wanted fresh blood in his bureau and sought to broaden ARA's stalwarts by sending them to other regions. From one divided place to another, I thought—one bisected by a German wall, the other by an American canal.

I knew no one in the ARA bureau except Findley, fresh from London. Initially, peers in the venerable "Latin Club" viewed newcomers like me from other geographic bureaus with suspicion and resentment. Those with depth in the lore of Panama proudly dubbed themselves "Panamaniacs." I would be the leading person in the State Department working full-time on a new Panama.

In dealing with the Panamanian embassy and its ambassador I would, from Washington's perspective, be managing our relations with another government. Most of what I knew about Panama in 1969 I had learned while in the navy fifteen years before, when my ship transited the canal. I understood the importance of the canal as a choke point and was familiar with the movements of ships, their dimensions and characteristics, how the canal worked, and what a two-ocean fleet of interchangeable vessels was about. Fidel Castro remained a troublemaker in the region. In 1968, Panama's quixotic new leader, General Omar Torrijos Herrera, had seized power in a bloodless coup by the National Guard. He was a large and ominous question mark in American minds.

Relations with Panama resembled our ties to no other country in the intensity of domestic concerns, the passions stirred by anything affecting *our* canal. The Office of Panamanian Affairs was not large: eight people including my deputy from the Agency for International Development, his staff, and myself. Crammed with files, this office occupied five small and unappealing rooms on the department's second floor. We sat without glory opposite the Medical Division, where Foreign Service employees and their families were given physical examinations on departing from, or returning to, Washington.

One of our ablest career secretaries, Martha Hayward, with whom I had worked in Berlin, was between assignments and agreed to join me. Together once more through long days, we wrestled with a widely abused "clearance process" requiring others with some degree of interest in a matter to "sign off" on telegrams and memorandums (or decline to without making some changes) before these could be sent to their destinations. Obtaining clearances might take days. True, there were people in other offices and government agencies having legitimate interests, separate responsibilities, and contributions to make to what was going on. The clearance process brought out differences in views and could be creative. It was a way of taking people along in the evolution of policy. Often, however, the number of ego-driven individuals who believed their initials were indispensable to the historical record became ridiculous. Once someone was placed on the list of names and agencies playing the game, it was impossible to get the name removed. The resulting product, diluted by ambiguities and cautions at the lowest common denominator of acceptability, could, if not monitored stubbornly, turn clear thinking into pabulum to be spooned to our embassies in the form of instructions.

I was given two main tasks. The first was to manage, on a day-to-day basis, our efforts to change the treaty relationship with Panama. Earlier negotiations to replace the 1903 treaty had failed. By the time I became involved with Panama in 1969, President Nixon had decided to negotiate new treaties. He recognized the difficulties in continuing indefinitely to play the Yankee role in a dependent Panama while few vestiges of colonialism remained anywhere. Ours was an anachronistic relationship that eroded, rather than supported, our national security interests. Nixon also understood the domestic political hazards of advocating change. Yet the time had come to work out new arrangements that would preserve our needs relating to the canal while granting Panama full independence. This would prove a long and daunting challenge to both nations.

A related responsibility was to understand what General Torrijos was about. He had come to power only months earlier and was an unknown quantity in Washington outside intelligence circles. He was, and remained, an officer in the Panamanian National Guard. Robert M. Sayre, our ambassador to Panama, also had recently arrived at his post. His instructions from Washington were to do his best to get along with General Torrijos and his government. We needed to determine what kind of person Torrijos was, what motivated him, and whether we could have a fruitful relationship with him on the vital issues of treaty negotiations. Our primary goal in Panama was to maintain internal stability to insure the continued smooth operation and security of the canal. Renegotiation was our next objective, but during the Cold War stability was more important.

Negotiating with Panamanians

As national security adviser to Nixon, Henry Kissinger took an interest in negotiations with Panama because he knew Nixon had made up his mind to proceed, but also because he relished the intricacies of any major negotiation. This was one of the rare times when Kissinger delved into Latin American issues. His gaze was on Europe, the Soviet Union, China, and the war in Vietnam. At the core of treaty negotiations were the spellbinding words "in perpetuity," which baldly described the duration of U.S. rights in Panama under the 1903 treaty. With ratification in 1979 of new treaties, "perpetuity" turned out to be seventy-six years.

Led by former treasury secretary Robert B. Anderson, we rekindled our end of the negotiating process through low-key efforts to define the leading issues and priorities and develop a negotiating strategy based on realistic options. By the time I left Panamanian affairs, we knew in broad terms where we were heading. The U.S. bureaucracy had coalesced at this level of consideration, but we were still in the "preliminary and exploratory" stages of our discussions with the Panamanians. Their representatives—lawyers, diplomats, and businessmen—were on familiar ground in the maze of details and technical issues affecting the canal and its surrounding zone. Nationalists all, they articulated Panama's positions forcefully and sometimes hotheadedly but remained careful listeners. I kept in mind that Panamanians considered themselves to be fashioning nothing less than the future of their nation. For them there could be no higher stakes than these. They would become founding fathers as Panama gained full independence for the first time.

For us, the use of a secure canal and its commercial and strategic benefits mattered most. Panama's negotiators understood, but tried to discount, the depth of antinegotiating sentiment in Congress and among the public and the pressures from lobbyists and citizens' groups that hobbled our talks. This was democracy American-style, and they considered such factors to be our problems, not theirs. I had the impression that through lifetimes of association with Americans—the gringos—Panamanians read us well as individuals and negotiators, better than we understood them. Put differently, they felt more attuned to our culture than we did to theirs.

Key issues were not resolved until the end, as both sides sought to maximize their gains. To allow for this approach, the negotiators told each other that nothing was agreed until everything was agreed. What emerged were the treaties of 1977, ratified in 1979, that provided for Panama's phased and full ownership of the canal and the Canal Zone by noon on December 31, 1999, at the dawn of a new century that seemed to Americans reassuringly far off.

General Torrijos

By the time I entered the picture in 1969, some of our U.S. military intelligence people in Panama knew Torrijos well. Shortly before I arrived at the

Office of Panamanian Affairs, he had ousted a newly elected president, the maverick Dr. Arnulfo Arias, for failing to keep preelection promises to the guard and for attempting to exile Torrijos himself by sending him off to San Salvador as military attaché. The State Department decided that someone at the level of a country director (rather than a more senior official) would be appropriate for any ensuing dialogue with Arias, inasmuch as we recognized Torrijos's government. So it was I who met one Sunday with Dr. Arias, at his invitation, over a brunch in Maryland's rolling countryside during which he sought to convince me that the United States should not support Torrijos.

Arias cut a distinguished figure with his white hair, stylish cane, and Panamanian charm. He looked every bit a president. There was widespread distrust of Torrijos in a Washington long accustomed to dealing with a compliant civilian leadership in Panama, members of an oligarchic elite with whom our government felt comfortable. They were a known quantity with an affinity for the United States and a vested interest in stability in a land where the dollar was the official currency. While we did not favor military coups, I explained to Dr. Arias that we would refrain from intervening in Panama's domestic politics. He seemed to have expected otherwise, given the history of our machinations in Central America. Torrijos was firmly ensconced, however, and Nixon intended to keep Panama on an even keel as we sought to renew our talks over the canal.

Torrijos had the reputation of being a leftist and a nationalist with ties to Castro. He was interested in raising Panama's status—its dignity, as he termed it—and rejected the Panama Canal treaty drafts negotiated in 1968. In a Cold War climate, and with the canal at stake, we would be negotiating anew with someone who not only wanted to change the treaty relationship but also could be expected to take hard-line, demagogic positions on the major issues. What sort of man was Omar Torrijos?

Once I had settled in during the summer of 1969, the time to visit Panama had come. Early in December, beginning on a Saturday, I spent a day and a half with Torrijos, accompanied by Bill Pryce of our embassy's political section, a savvy officer fluent in Spanish. We met the general in his hometown of Santiago, where he had grown up as one of eleven children. When he greeted our helicopter at the airport, his first and unexpected question was to ask how old I was. It turned out we were both forty, a fact that seemed to please him. I saw before me a handsome man in a yellow guayabera shirt, tall, crew cut, muscular, with a beer drinker's belly. His face and lips were full, his eyes dark and large and appealing. His father, he told me, remained a disciplinarian to his children at the age of ninety. Torrijos folded us into his schedule, taking Bill and me to the opening of a new school in a village nearby, then to a hospital and a boys' reform school. He said he spent his weekends with the campesinos, leaving him little time to be with his three children. Watching him with crowds of people, I found him neither charismatic nor demagogic. We had lunch in a Santiago restaurant in which hung a portrait of President Kennedy by a local artist, a naïf whose simple style conveyed his grief.

Torrijos asked us to join him for dinner at his former home, now occupied by the province of Chiriquí's National Guard commander, Major Manuel Noriega. We met Torrijos at a local bar to which he had invited us before dinner. With him was his close friend and ally Demetrio "Jimmy" Lakas, a man of Greek origin, the brawny, rough-cut official in charge of Panama's social security program later to be designated president of Panama by Torrijos. As soon as we arrived at the bar, Torrijos ordered a bottle of Johnny Walker Black and challenged me to a game at the pinball machine. I hadn't played pinball since college and never enjoyed it then, but that evening I had a bit of luck. I do not recall anything about Noriega. Being forgettable in the eyes of an unknown U.S. official would have suited the man, in any case.

Torrijos considered himself "an original," he told us. He had tried wearing a tie and smoking a pipe, "but it wasn't me." "I'm not an intellectual," he said, "but a man of horse sense, like a farmer." He characterized his social programs for Panama as a revolution. Since coming to power, he continued, he was trying to eliminate corruption and give people a better life. Every weekend he was said to give away a thousand dollars to random people and causes. "I have to die here," Torrijos told us, "I have no money and no passport"— meaning, I inferred, that his commitment to Panama was total and that, unlike Dr. Arias, whom he had deposed, he would not be leaving Panama to live comfortably elsewhere should his efforts fail.

About our relations Torrijos claimed that "the United States has no better friend than Panama, but you must help us," knowing I had come to take his measure and assess our prospects. This was what one would expect him to say, and he never later turned against us for long, despite some friendly moves toward Castro and Gadhafi in Libya and his support of the Sandinistas in Nicaragua while the dictator Anastasio Somoza García was clinging to power there.

Torrijos invited us to drive with him through the countryside on the following day, our destination being a favorite open-air restaurant. He had a hangover. Jimmy Lakas was at the wheel, Torrijos in the front seat, with Bill and me in back trying to cope with Torrijos's cigar smoke. The general did not have much to say. Lakas carried a weapon, and we had a follow-on Jeep with soldiers from the National Guard. Over a sunny lunch with wine, the conversation became livelier. Torrijos, his eyes beguiling once more, was in fine humor after food and drink served to us by pert and flirtatious women who fussed over him.

Although I found his sincerity when speaking of social development and the common man's plight in Panama convincing, Torrijos showed little understanding of economics or the role of economic forces in Panama. He was mercurial, and I found a capacity for shiftiness as he equivocated on circumstances surrounding the detention of an American citizen, about which I had asked him. Torrijos was not a sophisticated thinker, probably at that point the kind of person most struck by the conversation he last held. All day long Torrijos was inwardly tense. Despite music and dancing at the party in his former home, he never seemed to relax, nor did he appear to enjoy himself. He remained quiet, withdrawn, and moody.

Eventually I came to respect Torrijos as I kept track of him through our embassy's reporting and he grew in self-assurance and popularity. In time, Ambassador Sayre and I concluded that the United States could negotiate with Torrijos over the canal, a view we made known to skeptical ears in Washington. He was not the ideal negotiating partner, but no proud Panamanian would have been. While Torrijos was critical and outspoken about the U.S. role in Panama, which he accurately described as colonialist, he also was capable of listening to what we said. Torrijos was able to hold a rational discussion, a necessary quality in dealing with Bob Sayre, a slight and wiry native of Hillsboro, Oregon, who could be equally hard-nosed, blunt, and persistent in laying out our own positions in fluent Spanish. As we engaged in efforts to change our relationships over the canal, Torrijos immersed himself in the negotiating process. Many decisions would need his approval. Often he stalled and vacillated.

Jimmy Lakas as president remained a figurehead who felt uncomfortable in the public arena. I had an agitated conversation with him in his limousine in Washington, while escorting him from the Panamanian Embassy to the White House for a brief call on President Nixon during a celebration of the twenty-fifth anniversary of the founding of the United Nations. The president of Panama turned to me and asked, "Jesus, Brandon, what the fuck am I going to say to Nixon?" "Just be yourself, Jimmy," I counseled, suggesting a few points for him to raise. "He's a president, and you're a president." Their meeting went well, but then I had helped write Nixon's talking points and found an unexpected opportunity to match them with what Lakas now was primed to discuss.

Our official posture toward Torrijos had changed markedly by the end of my tour in 1971. We had endured serious differences with Panama's astute and tenacious negotiators and other problems in our relations but overcame the hurdle of attributing bad faith and hidden motives to Torrijos as an individual. Bob Sayre and succeeding ambassadors developed effective relations with him. Nixon had a global, strategic foreign policy agenda and never wavered in his decision to proceed with canal negotiations, politically charged at home and in Panama though they were. As with his overture to China, Nixon was not lacking in courage in foreign affairs. In the end, we reached an agreement that was fair and honorable for both sides. In 1981, Torrijos was killed in an unexplained plane crash in Panama during bad weather. "I have to die here," he had told Bill Pryce and me.

Ratification

In 1977 President Carter submitted new canal treaties to the Senate for ratification. They inspired the longest, most emotionally charged, and ugliest debate over foreign policy during the Cold War. For months in advance, Carter worked with true grit to gain support, risking his popularity and prospects for reelection. For him the anachronism of the U.S. role in Panama had become a moral issue. Eventually, thanks to last-minute buttonholing of senators by Majority Leader Howard Baker, Carter prevailed by one vote. When I asked Senator Baker about Torrijos years later, he replied, "You know, I kind of liked the guy," and I understood what he meant.

Thirty years after my brunch with Dr. Arnulfo Arias at a Maryland country inn, Panama held its scheduled elections in May 1999, seven months before the canal would be turned over to the Panamanians. The leading presidential candidates were Martin Torrijos, the thirty-five-year-old son of the late general, and Mireya Moscoso, fifty-two, Arias's widow—she was forty-five years younger than her husband when they married. It was a fair and open contest between moderates in which the canal played no role. In macho Panama, Mireya Moscoso won. Martin Torrijos succeeded her in 2004.

Mark

Our son Mark was born in September 1970, filling our home in Quebec Street with his gentle, cheerful presence. Not much of a scholar until the end, he would complete his studies at Northeastern University's School of Journalism with a full-power surge to magna cum laude. His writing skills turned

out to be strong, and his career interests would lie in communications technology, television, and public affairs. For two years he worked on these matters in Egypt. He would become an indispensable adviser to me, across oceans
if necessary, when my Macintosh acted up irrationally. One learns from one's
children.

13

EAST BERLIN

1974 to 1976

Late on the morning of September 4, 1974, in the seventh-floor Treaty Room of the State Department, the United States formally entered into an agreement establishing relations with the German Democratic Republic. I was there to witness an outcome, with its own logic, of Willy Brandt's concepts of inner-German relations that I had closely followed during my assignment to West Berlin in the mid-1960s.

I stood among dark-suited officials at a small ceremony to watch the assistant secretary of state for European affairs, Arthur Hartman, sign for the United States. We had agreed among ourselves that our side would flash no smiles for the photographers, even during customary handshakes as copies of the agreement were exchanged between signatories. We let the East Germans know that for us this would be a sober, businesslike event taking place without fanfare at a subcabinet level of government. Both German states had become formal members of the United Nations in 1973, further opening the door to international acceptance and normalization of their status. We were recognizing the GDR to remain in step with the Federal Republic of Germany, France, and Great Britain, who had already done so, the three Western Allies having taken their lead from Bonn. We were the 111th nation to acknowledge the diplomatic existence of the German Democratic Republic.

On that day also, the White House announced the appointment of former senator John Sherman Cooper, a liberal internationalist Republican from Kentucky, as the first American ambassador to the GDR. Although Richard Nixon had nominated Cooper, it fell to his successor and Cooper's friend from congressional days, Gerald Ford, to announce the appointment. So solid was Cooper's standing in Washington, despite his opposition to the war in Vietnam, that he was acceptable to Nixon, Ford, and Kissinger. The State Department was looking for someone with experience in Berlin to become the deputy chief of mission, the DCM. I let Hartman know I wanted to be considered for this post.

Senator Cooper and I first met at Henry Kissinger's suggestion during Cooper's call on the secretary of state as ambassador designate. He stopped by my office to chat, knowing I was interested in becoming his deputy. At seventy-three, Cooper was a tall, lean man of noble profile, his features crowned by a full head of wavy white hair, his eyes dimmed and shoulders slightly stooped by age. He looked older than his years and moved with a stiffness suggesting arthritis. I found him a reserved, soft-spoken southern gentleman with the demeanor and formal manners of an earlier time. He knew little about East Germany. At the end of half an hour, he seemed satisfied we could work together.

I was being sent back to Berlin to keep its Four Power status in mind while we took the historic step of opening an American Embassy at the very heart of détente in Europe. Unlike the Russians, we did not feel threatened by a future unified and democratic Germany free of occupation forces: this remained our long-term goal. Improving the inner-German relationship was one of the mainstays of the foreign policies of the Federal Republic, pursued within the framework of its alliance with the West. The establishment of Allied embassies in East Berlin, however, seemed to GDR authorities evidence of a further wearing down of Western resolve, a concession and a milestone toward a permanent division of Hitler's Germany in ways serving their own interests. The Western Allies were aware, and wary, of this view but believed in the soundness of establishing embassies of their own, persuaded that time was on their side. The Allies had no "exit strategy" over nearly half a century because no sustained thought was given to leaving Berlin or withdrawing militarily from Germany, and they had not abandoned the ideal of German unity.

Getting Ready

Launched into my new assignment, I brought myself up to date on German issues and arranged to leave for Berlin in October. Because of school schedules in Washington, Mary and our four children would not be joining me until Christmas. Although I was to become the first American diplomat accredited to the German Democratic Republic, we would not be charting unknown waters. The embassies of Great Britain and France had been functioning fairly well in East Berlin for nearly a year, and their pioneering experiences would help us.

By this time Elwood Williams III, the German expert of my earlier years in Berlin, had retired. I spent many hours at the German desk talking with those in Washington managing our relations with Berlin and both Germanies. Some, like David Anderson, the country director, had been my colleagues in West Berlin. The "Berlin Mafia" was alive and well. I visited specialists on the Soviet Union and NATO in their State Department offices and talked with European experts at the National Security Council. I spent an afternoon at CIA headquarters in Langley, Virginia, conferring with analysts and asking what topics of reporting from the new embassy would be of particular value to them. What were the important gaps in our knowledge and understanding? I read secret biographical profiles of leading figures in the GDR and studied their photographs. We discussed intelligence sharing at the embassy and the responsibilities of a case officer the agency was proposing to assign there, subject to Cooper's approval. Eleanor Dulles gave me her thoughts about Berlin, emphasizing that I should keep in mind how Berliners on both sides of the wall would perceive the establishment of our embassy.

I made a special effort to become acquainted with people on the management staff of the Bureau of European Affairs on whom we would depend for administrative support in Berlin. Setting up a new embassy would occupy much of my time as DCM. I had known and liked the bureau's director, Joan Clark, for many years.

From my desk in Kissinger's Policy Planning Staff, where I was working at the time, I arranged a daylong academic seminar for Ambassador Cooper. It would include some of the leading scholars on Germany as well as Professor Hans Morgenthau, the guru on international relations whose writings I had studied at Princeton. Arthur Hartman gave a luncheon for the group in one of the official dining rooms. What we gained during that day was a fresh perspective, through the eyes of historians, on what the new relationship augured and what they believed we should seek to accomplish.

The Tenor of Relations

The ties to emerge between the United States and the GDR would be qualitatively different from our relations with other communist countries such as Poland and Hungary. We expected those nations eventually to regain their independence and become more or less as we had known them before the war. Agreement on the postwar status of Germany, however, had not been reached among the victors of World War II. The ultimate fate of the GDR remained a conundrum in Central Europe.

We were coming reluctantly to East Berlin, where Moscow was the GDR's patron. In a low-key relationship, we would not deem the GDR a proper partner for handling European issues, nor did we intend to enhance its standing by treating the regime as if it were. We were there to start a conversation. In East Berlin we would not be adding our voice to discussions on relations between the two Germanys, this being the province of the government in Bonn and its representatives in East Berlin, both keeping us well informed. Nor, as we expected, would the GDR's foreign ministry be raising such matters with us.

Constraints like these would condition our behavior in Berlin throughout the relaxation of East-West tensions during détente. Both Germanies were benefiting from détente in the inner-German context and making progress on some of the issues before them. In the evolution of détente we would remain bystanders in East Berlin, detached from the dialogue progressing in Eastern Europe in new if limited ways. Ever correct and courteous, we would deliberately maintain our distance from one of the world's most repressive regimes. Instinctively we would know what seemed appropriate to discuss and what did not. No one needed a checklist.

The United States had few interests that were specific to the GDR. We wanted to understand the GDR in greater depth and would seek meaningful discussions with its officials about conditions within the country. Cooper's main objectives in the new relationship were to establish respect for the United States on the part of the regime and a more favorable image of our country in the eyes of East Germans; to keep the performance of his embassy within the bounds of postwar Allied rights, responsibilities, and practices (a task he left to me); to lay the basis, on the scene, for what we recognized would be a long and arduous process of dealing with restitution claims and other concerns of American Jews; to advance our modest commercial interests in the GDR; and to arrive at a consular convention with its government in order, among other reasons, to protect American citizens within its borders. These were not small matters and would draw upon the traditional diplomatic skills of negotiation and dialogue and a steady, painstaking pursuit of well-defined objectives. When our interests and those of the GDR meshed, we anticipated favorable results quickly.

We would also report to Washington and European posts our firsthand impressions and analysis of the East German scene, work at the heart of a diplomat's calling, turning us into near-journalists. Until our arrival, some of this had been done at a remove by the Eastern Affairs Section of our mission in

West Berlin and by various intelligence entities. Our responsibilities as an embassy would not include reporting on military affairs, although there were more Soviet divisions in the GDR than anywhere else outside Russia: 350,000 soldiers constituting the spear of an invasion force that could assault NATO in Western Europe. Such matters were handled in Four Power channels dating back to the end of World War II.

Within the limits of what could be accomplished in two years, Cooper would address his objectives in a series of first steps, the most important of which was getting our relationship off to a correct start. *Correct* was his favorite word on the subject, reflecting principles, a lawyer's mind, and his view of what should be the style of his embassy's performance. *Correct* meant without prejudice, but not without reserve. Ambassador Cooper never expected to produce warmth or openness in the relationship, even during détente with the Soviet Union. He was realistic in that appraisal.

Establishing the Embassy

As I prepared to depart ahead of Cooper to serve as chargé d'affaires, discussions at the State Department addressed how and where I should first appear in the GDR. One view held that I must be driven through Checkpoint Charlie from West Berlin, thereby emphasizing the city's unchanged occupied status and the existence of Allied as well as Soviet rights there. The other view maintained that, because we now recognized the German Democratic Republic, I should land on its territory after departing by air from a foreign capital as would any other newly arrived diplomat. The East German protocol staff at the foreign ministry would then be able to go through the customary formalities of greeting a new head of mission at the airport.

On the arrival question, Cooper and I argued that, despite the nature of the regime, East German officials should be treated with visible respect, consonant with proper diplomatic behavior on our part. That may seem a small point, but it was not. In diplomacy, communication takes many forms beyond discussion. My itinerary would send a message about our view of the quality of the new relationship in our own eyes and the extent to which we intended to treat the GDR as a normal partner in international affairs. Arthur Hartman, a man of sensitivity on such issues, decided the matter in Cooper's favor. To send a balancing message, I stopped off in Bonn to engage in courtesy calls at the Federal Chancellery, underscoring our support for West Germany's interests in the inner-German relationship. Afterward, I flew to Copenhagen and then on to Berlin.

On landing at Schönefeld Airport in East Germany on that wet late afternoon, I was officially greeted by the foreign ministry's deputy chief of protocol. We exchanged the pleasantries and platitudes appropriate to the occasion, which to me seemed to have more gravitas in German. Also at the airport was Felix Bloch, a Foreign Service officer at our mission in West Berlin (USBER), who escorted me to my temporary quarters at the Hotel Unter den Linden, a seedy place but then the best hotel in East Berlin. Unfortunately, a photographer took pictures while I was registering at the front desk that led to an article in the *New York Times* about the first U.S. diplomat to arrive in East Berlin. This was not what the Coopers or I wanted. German newspapers carried similar stories and photos. David Anderson called from the State Department to tell me to lower my profile because the Coopers were miffed. They were insisting that John Sherman Cooper be known as the American diplomat who opened the U.S. embassy in East Berlin. Not an auspicious beginning, I thought.

In further deference to Cooper's wishes—no one in Washington was willing to challenge him on *this* diplomatic nicety—I was not authorized by the State Department to present my credentials as chargé d'affaires. Thus there would be no officially established American embassy in East Berlin until Cooper himself arrived. That scenario confounded people at the foreign ministry, who could not understand why I hadn't produced Kissinger's letter. I sought to overcome this by telling them it was the American practice (how would they know differently?) to present such letters immediately before an ambassador's arrival. Another awkward matter was Cooper's insistence that the embassy not fly its flag until he had formally presented his credentials, and again I used the same explanation with the East Germans. As a practical matter, however, I was not impeded in my ability to do what needed to be done, even while operating in a diplomatic limbo. It is highly unlikely that a professional Foreign Service officer, about to become an ambassador, would have insisted on similar arrangements. For the politically minded Coopers, however, public recognition at home of their pioneering presence in Berlin was important.

The State Department had sent an advance team to East Berlin months before led by Joan Clark as executive director of Hartman's bureau; she focused on finding and leasing office space and housing, difficult but necessary spadework in preparing for our arrival. Clark's team was supported by the GDR and our mission in West Berlin, with Felix Bloch assisting her efforts in East Berlin and during subsequent transactions with the East Germans. Bloch was to become our economic counselor at the embassy. (Years later, Felix was accused of spying for the Soviet Union during a subsequent assignment as DCM in

Vienna but was not indicted. As his supervisor, I found Felix rather cold and sardonic but skilled in his work.)

By the time I arrived, modest office space had been acquired in a newly constructed building near the Brandenburg Gate, but it was not yet ready to occupy. A house had been found for me on Mayakowskyring, but I could not move in until its rooms were painted and furnished. Anticipating the arrival of my family, I sometimes drove there on a Sunday in winter's cold wet air. From the windows of the empty rooms I examined our future surroundings through a latticework of black and barren branches filtering light from an ashen sky. Our home-to-be was a gloomy villa alongside a park with a stream and ducks, small wooden bridges, and what would be my favorite bench. Its narrow kitchen became more serviceable once we had installed modern equipment from West Berlin. When our books and pictures arrived, along with the few items of furniture with which we traveled, this became more like a home but never a place one would call cozy or welcoming. In springtime, the children played with their American friends from the embassy, throwing balls in our garden with its fruit trees, or bicycling through the villagelike neighborhood of Pankow. They did not form friendships with East Germans their age, as none seemed to be living nearby.

I spent several months at the Hotel Unter den Linden in a cramped and shabbily furnished room with a bed that was too short, trying to stay beneath a satin-covered quilt that slid off and landed on the floor. A wardrobe built of plywood and covered with Formica took the place of a closet. For weeks this room at the end of a hall on the top floor was our embassy. Outside the door there was a chair occupied twenty-four hours a day by uniformed East German policemen for my "protection," although there were few safer places I could be than in East Berlin, even with Yasir Arafat's PLO offices close by. We assumed that what we did was monitored by the East Germans. The hotel served as temporary living quarters for our staff, at its peak numbering twenty-three Americans, including our marine guard detachment. If we wanted to have sensitive conversations, we walked outdoors. One of the most annoying things about the hotel was that every morning, at around five, the coal delivery truck dumped its huge load in the courtyard with a crash that made one think a whole wing had collapsed. I never got used to this. When Mary and our children arrived toward the end of December, we spent a joyless Christmas at the Hotel Unter den Linden, Mary apprehensively contemplating our future in East Germany.

Next to appear after me were James and Aniko Gaal Weiner. Jim, a Foreign Service officer from Swampscott, Massachusetts, was our administrative counselor and an anchor to windward for all of us. His East German counterpart, Herr Manfred Löffler, presided over the Dienstleistungsamt, or Diplomatic Services Agency, on which we depended for housing, office space, and carefully vetted East Germans who would work for us as drivers, household staff, and embassy messengers and receptionists. (They were not vetted all that carefully, as Löffler yanked the ambassador's driver, one Herr Künast, for routinely transporting pornographic material through the wall in the trunk of the Cadillac to resell in sexually inhibited East Berlin.) In keeping with the regime's satisfaction with our presence, Löffler was as responsive as he was able to be, which was not usually very responsive in terms of our needs.

Aniko, thirty-two and new to Foreign Service life, already was a citizen of the world. Hungarian born with Magyar flair and a musical voice, she was tall, auburn haired, and ceaselessly elegant. She volunteered to help people settle in and added color and liveliness to the decor of our office suites at Schadowstrasse 6, which became the chancery. Aniko and our bluff and burly marine gunnery sergeant, through purchases from shops in West Berlin, made a cheerful home of the "Marine House" on Leipzigerstrasse along the Berlin Wall. The embassy's apartments there, much in need of decorating, were part of a vast and aesthetically moribund housing project built of prefabricated concrete panels with a gritty look. Berliners disparaged such buildings, which appeared like dominoes in rows throughout the Soviet Bloc from Warsaw to Havana, as "Russian style." Our perch on Leipzigerstrasse would remain muddy, noisy, and under construction for unpleasant months to come.

We depended on our mission in West Berlin for logistical support and crossed through the wall frequently. As diplomats accredited to the GDR, we were issued red identity booklets and were all but waved through by guards who now saluted us. Our shopping was done in the West, and often we ate lunch there; eventually our children attended an American school there; we went to movie theaters there—these contrasting experiences serving as paroles from the shuttered atmosphere of East Berlin. At the end of a day we returned to East Berlin, and soon this felt like coming home, although from Checkpoint Charlie onward the ride was like driving through a Chicago warehouse district at night. Telly Savalas, star of television's *Kojak* series, visited East Berlin for an afternoon, and Jim Weiner met him at Checkpoint Charlie. Surveying the scene he asked Jim, "You mean you actually *live* here?"

Soon after my arrival we were assigned a communications officer. Until the embassy moved several years later to a permanent chancery with a fully equipped communications center, his responsibility at the end of the day was to take a sealed pouch of telegrams and diplomatic correspondence to West Berlin, along with our personal mail, to be sent onward by USBER's communicators on the Clayallee. In the morning, he would again take an embassy car, drive through a checkpoint at the wall, and pick up messages and mail that had arrived during the night.

One evening early on I had written a telegram ready to be sent from West Berlin, telling our communicator, Bob Walker, I would take it myself because I needed to be there anyway. Bob drove me to USBER, where I dropped off the telegram and had dinner with friends. Afterward I took a West Berlin taxi to Checkpoint Charlie, which was as far as the driver could bring me. By then rain was descending in sheets, and I had neither a hat nor an umbrella. I walked through the checkpoint. My hotel was long blocks away through deserted, dimly lit streets. Cold rainwater ran down the back of my neck and squished in my shoes. Far from feeling downcast, I recognized this drenching trek to be one of the high points of my life as a diplomat. I was born, I felt, to push ahead through a soaking night along the empty streets of East Berlin, and this was worth doing. Like the gutters around me, my spirits overflowed. With no one to watch, I improvised on Gene Kelly just dancin' and singin' in the rain.

Throughout East Berlin spying competed with countermeasures to preserve secrecy. Police booths placed before the homes of American officials were manned around the clock for protection against undefined threats. They were in fact posts from which to observe who came and went and to discourage unauthorized East Germans from approaching.

We asked Herr Löffler to take down a wall in our embassy, not telling him we planned to install a "bubble" in this enlarged space. A bubble was a secure and shielded enclosure the size of a miniature conference room, set two feet above the floor and away from the walls and ceiling that surrounded it. One could speak openly in a bubble. A stream of crates containing the transparent acoustic blocks that would constitute our bubble began arriving from West Berlin. After visiting Seabees assembled it, we met often in this sterile, cramped, and chilly room of poor and noisy ventilation. Each time the hatch door opened, a gasping sound escaped reflecting slight differences in air pressure that could cause giddiness or nausea once inside. Working in this see-through capsule surrounded by insulation and cables on the floor seemed like orbiting in outer space with the State Department as Mission Control. The West Germans and we offered a contemporary and vaguely Scandinavian conference room ambience. Interiors of British and French bubbles brought to mind a gentlemen's club in Leeds that had known cheerier days. None was comfortable. In other settings one pointed to the ceiling if someone verged on discussing things not to be overheard, sign language understood everywhere behind the Iron Curtain to be a warning of hidden microphones.

From the East Germans: Accommodation and Despair

Reflecting on how time flows for Germans is instructive. A German's age tells a lot about the person, and Germans inevitably are aware of their origins in time and where they fit into its passage. They are shaped by their history. Hitler came to power in 1933. The wartime Allies, including forces of the Soviet Union, defeated him in 1945. Terrible as the *Hitlerzeit* was, it endured for twelve years. East Germans and East Berliners afterward lived under Soviet occupation, albeit with a German government imposed on them until 1990, or forty-five years more. So during fifty-seven years the East Germans knew no rulers other than the Nazis, the Russians, or their own GDR leaders subservient to Moscow. Ever fewer could recall what freedom under the Weimar Republic had been like. For the young after the wall came down all of this belonged in history books. They felt themselves disassociated and liberated from such epic events, rooted as they were in a different place in time.

Many generations in the GDR grew up without accurate knowledge of democracies or how they functioned in other parts of the world. They were taught Marxist-Leninist ideology and were made to interpret history and their surroundings within that framework. When the division of Germany ended, a person thirteen years old as Hitler came to power was by then seventy. It was those people, and still others more advanced in years, buffeted by Hitler, the Russians, and their own quisling leaders, who would undergo the greatest shocks and dislocations as Germany was united. Psychologically, their working years behind them and living in retirement and, for many, widowhood, they would become the most disoriented when freedom befell them. I recall television images of young men and women at a breach in the wall exulting in their liberation and of dazed and forlorn older people feeling helpless in such upheaval.

The East Germans considered their system a form of social security, providing housing, education, employment, health care, pensions, and, when that day came, cremation. As inefficient and inadequate as these services were, one could rely on them from cradle to grave. The East German regime did not allow its citizens to feel in charge of themselves, managing their lives to the point of telling workers and their families where to spend summer vacations.

When freedom came with the elimination of the wall, the infrastructure of a communist society collapsed. Citizens of the former GDR were challenged to figure out how to get on with their lives by making choices of their own under radically altered circumstances. Both Germanies were in the throes of coming together, but their institutions could not mesh.

East Germans had developed a sense of identity and at times pride in their citizenship. Pride was evident in sports events, for example when a victory for the GDR's athletes (on steroids or not) was greeted with jubilation. A minority were true believers, Germans who thought in terms of isms, old-time marxists who had helped defeat fascism and unswervingly maintained that communism was more equitable and just than capitalism. For them Berlin would always be the Red City.

True, people living in the GDR watched West German television—the regime was unable to jam those broadcasts. East Germans, again older people especially, were not convinced they wanted to live like their cousins on the other side. They were shocked by crime rates, by violence and nudity on the screen, by materialism in its acquisitive aspects, and by other signs of what they saw as moral decay under capitalism. Yet they could not help but be impressed by the freedoms and opulence of the West: fancy cars to drive anywhere one wanted; ingenious kitchen appliances to chop vegetables and brew coffee; stylish clothes and seemingly endless varieties of food, drink, cosmetics, and cigarettes. They envied their countrymen's freedom to choose among affordable consumer goods of high quality. I came to understand their ambivalence stemming from an ingrained sense of propriety and stoic efforts to make the best, with dignity, of a hard way of life. As they watched Western television, young people found more to wish for and emulate, more to want to take their chances on.

East Germans dreaded the state security police, the Stasi, who managed to keep book on nearly everyone. They hated the wall, what it represented, and what it was doing to them. Years later, as the regime was crumbling, demonstrators in the streets shouted "Mauer weg! Mauer weg!" or "Get rid of the wall!" I found East Germans feeling wronged and humiliated by their regime, sometimes masking their resentment with arrogance, bitterness, or anti-Americanism, but more often keeping silent. An abyss had fallen between them and people enjoying freedom. Our (and Herr Löffler's) few German employees at the embassy occasionally lifted the veil shrouding their emotions. The most I felt I could say was, "Es wirt besser sein," things will get better. As an American diplomat, I was in any case one of the least likely people in whom an East German would confide.

The Soviet sector had changed little since I visited it five years before while stationed in West Berlin. Some renovation and restoration of historic buildings, even of a few prominent churches, were underway by the midseventies. A foreign ministry of surpassing ugliness had replaced the architect Friedrich Schinkel's masterpiece, the Bauakademie. East Berlin's once fashionable stores along Unter den Linden still were largely empty, their windows displaying goods unavailable inside. People on the sidewalks remained withdrawn and reserved, especially toward foreigners from the West. There was little sign of bustling— the quick steps of a vibrant city's men and women with thoughts pressing on their minds and appointments to keep. Lovers flirted as they strolled along Unter den Linden: they were a warming sight and made a few people, including me, smile. The atmosphere of oppression, the absence of gaiety, sparkle, vigor, or spontaneity, remained the same.

During my walks in our neighborhood of Pankow, I might pause to look at a row of apartment buildings blackened with grime and wearing the scars of war. Coming upon these lifeless structures with their windows for the moment blank, I might feel the unease I sensed in Edward Hopper's paintings of abandoned streets and shadowed storefronts. Something was wrong. Much had happened here, but the people of this place were elsewhere. Time appeared to have erased itself, leaving evidence of man's works but not his presence. Intimations of cruelty, drunkenness, and lust—of the loneliness of old people in dark rooms and of suicidal despair—permeated the atmosphere in East Berlin. No writer of English caught the enduring tension between Berlin's decadence and its visceral appeal, the mood of *Cabaret*, better than Christopher Isherwood in his *Berlin Stories* of the 1930s. I felt that appeal and was drawn to it. Hildegard Knef's song "Ich Hab' Noch einen Koffer in Berlin" (I've still got a suitcase in Berlin), popular while we were living there, spoke to such ambivalence and a Berliner's longing for her city. Marlene Dietrich herself, the "Blue Angel" from Schöneberg, died in Paris but was buried, as she wished to be, in Berlin.

Both sides of Berlin, in different ways, had long since recaptured the artistic vitality for which the whole city was renowned in the prewar times of Dietrich, Berthold Brecht, Kurt Weill, Käthe Kollwitz, and George Grosz, among many others. Herbert von Karajan led the Berlin Philharmonic in West Berlin, and Walter Felsenstein staged breathtaking operas in the East. Talented writers, painters, dancers, and actors lived on both sides of the wall, but the lack of artistic freedom in the East was palpable.

By 1974, buildings close to the wall had been razed. A leveled death strip between East and West was widened, fortified by more efficient watchtowers and barriers and patrolled by killer dogs on leash-lines connected to an overhead wire that allowed them to roam the strip freely. At night, blinding lights illuminated this gash through the city. Most prominently in view from the eastern side in the softer glow of West Berlin's lights was the publisher Axel Springer's building near Checkpoint Charlie beaming news headlines into East Berlin. A large, illuminated, starlike logo of Mercedes-Benz, chillingly blue and metallic, rotated slowly on the rooftop of another building close by. These displays were metaphors for life on freedom's gaudier, richer, more vital and vibrant, capitalistic side. East Berliners were poor relations with their noses pressed against the windowpanes of the affluent, outsiders harboring their own thoughts and longings while peering in.

Ambassador Cooper...

At the end of President Eisenhower's first term, John Sherman Cooper was enjoying his year in New Delhi as ambassador to India and Nepal. When Kentucky's democratic senator, Alben Barkley, died shortly before the 1956 elections, political pressures from Eisenhower and Kentucky Republicans obliged him to run for Barkley's seat. Cooper served in the Senate, off and on, from 1956 to 1973, becoming a member of the Foreign Relations Committee, a much-sought-after assignment during the Cold War. The committee's chairman was his friend from Arkansas, J. William Fulbright.

During the 1972 elections, Cooper campaigned for Richard Nixon in his home state. By then he had decided to leave the Senate to practice law in Washington. The election handily won, Nixon told Cooper, according to the senator's personal assistant, Trudie Musson, that he did not want him to leave government service and intended to offer him an appointment of some kind in foreign affairs. For a time it seemed this might be as ambassador to Luxembourg, a delightful post and a quintessential, if largely unchallenging, political plum. The embassy to East Germany was about to be established, however, and Cooper became Nixon's choice for the ambassadorship, in part to provide political cover for his decision to enter into relations with the communist regime that built Berlin's wall. With Cooper's ties to the Senate, smooth confirmation was assured. According to Musson, when Nixon called to congratulate Cooper after Ford's announcement of his appointment, the former president said, rather oddly, "Remember, I thought of it first."

Cooper's wife, Lorraine, began exhorting Secretary Kissinger at Georgetown dinner parties to speed up her husband's departure to a place that seemed to her enveloped in Cold War glamour. Winston Lord, head of the Policy Planning Staff at the State Department, told me Kissinger had asked him to expedite Cooper's departure for East Germany to "get that woman off my back." Senator Theodore F. Stevens of Alaska, according to Musson, asked Kissinger at the end of July 1974 when, exactly, Cooper would be going to East Germany. "Lorraine won't forgive me if it isn't soon," Kissinger replied, and Stevens so informed Cooper. Lorraine, who would have been delighted to know all of this, was thus instrumental in having her husband appointed and dispatched on his mission to Berlin sooner than Kissinger, who wanted to avoid signals to the Russians and East Germans of eagerness on the part of the United States, would have liked.

Cooper's overseas experience, beyond military service in Bavaria at the end of World War II and travel with congressional delegations, was limited to the brief ambassadorial stint in New Delhi. A man originally of modest means, born in 1901, Cooper came from Somerset, in Pulaski County, Kentucky, where he had been a circuit judge. He had political acumen, was neither naive nor easily misled, and knew how to gauge people for their integrity. He saw the whimsy in life and had a strong sentimental streak. A man of emotions, Cooper was treated for depression in the early thirties during years that were hard on him and his family in Kentucky. His strengths derived from his family and his experiences in public life. Cooper was endowed with firmly rooted values, patriotism, optimism, and sound instincts. He liked a good story, off-color or not, and joked and laughed readily. He enjoyed the company of women, whom he charmed and flattered mercilessly. President Johnson had appointed him to the Warren Commission to investigate Kennedy's assassination. Cooper told me he believed its findings to be hurried but accurate.

He was hard of hearing. Like many older men—Averell Harriman, for example—Cooper was reluctant to use his hearing aid, and communicating with him was always difficult. Harriman, I noticed, usually turned off his hearing aid during Secretary Rusk's staff meetings. I soon opened any conversation with Cooper with a short sentence to get his attention and then repeated it, because his first response, invariably, was "WHAT?" Our German hosts learned to adjust to this. The East Germans recognized his depth of character and respected Cooper for his public record, advanced years, and old-world manners. He looked the scripted part: polished black London-made shoes, suits tailored by L. G. Wilkinson in Hanover Square, and a jauntily placed fedora from Lock's.

The Russians bestowed their approval through Piotr Abrasimov, who had been the Soviet Union's ambassador in Berlin for many years. The East Germans and Russians were pleased beyond their expectations not only to have U.S. representation in East Berlin but also to have gained it through a person of Cooper's renown rather than through an obscure career diplomat. Our presence, and the American flag faffling from our fifth-floor office, represented to them the West's completion of a legitimation process—their much-sought *Anerkennung*, or recognition—that had begun on the Allied side when the French and British opened their embassies. The United States, and Cooper specifically, was the prize catch.

Shortly after he arrived, Cooper wrote by hand to Trudie Musson with some fatherly advice for her as she was preparing to leave Washington for Berlin. "It is cold and rainy here," he told her, "so bring a good sweater—perhaps a sleeveless one—which I find useful, your umbrella, and some boots, rubbers, etc. to keep your feet warm." Having had a month or so to size up his embassy, he ended on this reassuring note: "Don't be scared, just come on."

Cooper spoke no more than five words of German, which did not prevent him sometimes from getting along remarkably well with Germans who spoke no English, communicating with them in ways that were mysterious. Not long after the embassy opened, the East Germans appointed a new foreign minister, Oskar Fischer, and Ambassador Cooper was invited to make a get-acquainted call. Cooper and I arranged to meet beforehand in front of the Hotel Unter den Linden, where all of us were living, rather unhappily, at the time. I arrived from the office to find Cooper standing outside in the sunshine, eating a wurst (the German version of a hotdog) and chatting animatedly with the street vendor. I do not know what common language they found. Cooper was nearly finished with his wurst when I suggested we start our walk to the foreign ministry, or we would be late. He folded a flimsy wax paper napkin around the remaining part and stuck it into his overcoat pocket.

When we reached the ministry, we were escorted into the foreign minister's large and oppressively furnished chamber, where an unusual performance ensued. Fischer seated himself close to Cooper on a couch and, leaning forward, stared intently into his face. His behavior was disconcerting to Cooper, and I found myself trying not to laugh. Ours was essentially a courtesy call, with Fischer mouthing platitudes and Cooper defining, once more, the principal objectives of his mission. We finally left this extraordinary scene and strolled back to our hotel, chuckling about the meeting just ended. Cooper imitated the foreign minister by sticking his face close to mine, just as Fischer had done with him. We found the episode incomprehensible.

While Cooper was imitating Fischer, I kept thinking about the wurst in his pocket. I knew that his personal assistant, Trudie Musson, would soon discover this greasy leftover, as she had discovered so many other odd things in her boss's overcoat pockets, which she had learned to check from time to time. Trudie, fully attuned to the Coopers, quickly got the hang of her Foreign Service work and became indispensable. In conducting preventive diplomacy of her own, she provided a bridge between the Coopers and me. Thanks to her tact and foresight, misunderstandings were avoided many times.

Cooper, always a bit careless, forgot things like that leftover wurst rather easily. In his first few weeks at the embassy he received a security violation pink slip each night from the marine guard who inspected our offices after we left. Cooper discarded everything, including classified papers, into his wastebasket. Our marines finally designated the wastebasket as a classified area so that anything in it, no matter how unusual, would go into the burn bag at the end of the day. Cooper was contrite after each violation and apologized to the marines but never changed his habits, although he saved the pink slips in his desk. The marines loved him. Whenever one of them was promoted he assembled all of us in his office, the marines appearing in their dress uniforms. As he slowly read the standard and rather prosaic citation of service to country, his voice began to quaver. By the end we were all fighting back tears. "Don't cry," Lorraine admonished him before these ceremonies.

... And His Wife, Lorraine

Mrs. John Sherman Cooper stemmed from an earlier era in the evolution of American customs and manners. She was the last of a socially oriented and elitist generation whose women participated as hostesses in the diplomatic partnership of an ambassador and his wife, deriving pleasure from bringing people together in their official residences. William Walton, in his book about Washington society in Kennedy's day, *The Evidence of Washington*, likened Lorraine to Mrs. Lightfoot Lee, the heroine of Henry Adams's novel of politics, *Democracy*. "What she wanted," Adams wrote of Mrs. Lee in 1880, "was POWER." An accompanying photograph in Walton's book shows Lorraine on a sofa at her N Street home looking coy in a long white dress and shawl.

Lorraine Cooper had married and divorced rich and prominent men twice before and remained childless. She was a force to be reckoned with on Washington's social scene, where her invitations were prized. She held an annual garden buffet at N Street to which the invitations read, simply, "In Honor of the United States Senate." A large portion of the Senate as well as other luminaries showed up, making this a major event for Washingtonians and the society pages of their newspapers.

Slight and delicate, celebrated for her taste in clothes, Lorraine favored big hats and parasols as protection from the sun. Her name appeared for many years on the "best dressed" lists of fashion writers. A prominent nose dominated her features, but Lorraine, *jolie laide*, knew how to tame a photographer's lens. She was a stickler for proper behavior and could be formal, snobbish, or uppity, as the moment suited her. She was hard on herself as well, criticizing her own actions to people close to her when she felt she had made a misstep. In her self-doubt and vulnerability she could be easily hurt by others.

Lorraine's political instincts were as sharp as her husband's, better honed because she acted on them more calculatingly. Her assessments of others were insightful as she picked through their strengths and weaknesses, no flaws on the surface more galling to her than poor manners or tasteless clothes. Lorraine had a fine sense of what motivated people, and her tongue turned sharp when she was displeased. Her conversations, however, were full of humor about the human condition, sometimes at her own expense. She laughed loudly with others around her in a deep, coarse smoker's voice. She adored good-looking men, sparkled around them, flirted with them in coquettish glances, and made them feel like scintillating lords of the universe. She was the perfect dinner partner, knowing when to "turn the table" by shifting conversation from left to right and back again, course by course.

She could behave outrageously. One afternoon, before smoking bans existed, Lorraine and I were having lunch at Martin's, in Georgetown, when a woman seated nearby politely asked her to put out her cigarette. Lorraine fixed her with a regal look and replied, irrationally, "Why don't you go live in a kibbutz!" Then she continued smoking as the target of this thrust stared at her in open-mouthed disbelief. A native Californian who had not attended college, Lorraine was well read and bright. She was self-created. When Lorraine was young, her mother remarried an Italian prince and moved with Lorraine to Italy. Lorraine spoke good French and Italian and had studied Russian in Washington with the help of her friend Sergei Cheremeteff, my wife's grandfather.

Cooper had character and charm; Lorraine, style and shrewdness. Cooper married her sooner than they had planned so she could accompany him to New Delhi as his desperately needed hostess. They would remain in love. In command of a large, turbaned staff at Roosevelt House, Lorraine was thrilled by a brief exposure to embassy life on a sweeping scale. This was an experience she intended to replicate in Berlin, unrealistic as that ambition was. Always supportive and defensive about John, she spoke lovingly of him even when he was in one of his withdrawn, vodka-flavored moods. About the harsh realities of the East German scene she understood practically nothing.

Lorraine brought to shabby East Berlin cherished memories of the Washington dinner parties she had so often given and attended. For her an invitation to dinner was an invitation to theater. It offered the promise of encounters in nuanced settings as understated as a whiff of perfume from a dress. Her guests, looking elegant, she hoped, were the dramatis personae of these plays, and they had been chosen carefully. How they were seated, who next to whom, and which ones would be accorded places of honor for all to notice inspired a performance to be reviewed and applauded in flowery toasts over dessert and champagne, once someone had ding'd the rim of a glass to create silence.

On arriving in Berlin, Lorraine was sixty-eight and brimming with energy. She made an effort to learn enough German to handle pleasantries and had, far more than her husband, a sense of adventure. Romantically, she fancied the Coopers doing in East Germany what she believed the David Bruces had accomplished in China. They were both pioneering Americans bravely carrying their country's flag into hostile, unexplored territory. Evangeline Bruce was a friend and role model, and an admiring Lorraine reflected her elegance and savoir faire. Intensely patriotic, Lorraine displayed her feelings in unpremeditated ways that made hers an enthusiastic voice for our country. On one occasion in Berlin, however, she also waxed enthusiastic about the GDR during an East German radio interview, demonstrating her lack of knowledge and raising eyebrows among fellow diplomats. Our annoyed country director at the State Department, David Anderson, called me later, asking me to turn down her volume. I said I couldn't and Cooper wouldn't.

My relationship with the Coopers was uneasy in Berlin, although John and I made an effective team and worked well together. We had no differences on substantive matters, whose management he left to me while he remained largely disengaged. However, there were periods of strain stemming from Lorraine's vision of what the American ambassador's residence in East Berlin should become. A competent but harassed and thwarted Jim Weiner thought of her as living almost wholly outside reality. He recalls her saying to me, "Mr. Grove, some people have bad taste, some have no taste, and some have good taste. You have no taste." Joan Clark at the State Department never was able to satisfy Lorraine, try as she might. Soon enough, however, Lorraine was contentedly serving tea and cucumber sandwiches to her newfound friends among the diplomatic wives of marxist East Berlin. Cucumber sandwiches are the Proustian madeleines of diplomacy.

They Settle In

In mid-December 1974, Ambassador and Mrs. Cooper arrived at Schöne-feld Airport in East Berlin. The ambassador made a brief statement before they were whisked to the Hotel Unter den Linden. Long before, Weiner had arranged that two rooms be joined by knocking out a wall so the Coopers would have a little more space in which to move about. With them from N Street came two butlers, Michael Mangan and Thom Hanson; Mrs. Cooper's Salvadoran cook, Delia Alfaro; her personal maid from Guatemala, Carolina Rios; and two decorative black-and-white shih tzu dogs, males forever at it. Gingerly, the Coopers settled into their overheated suite with its collection of East European smells and laughably inadequate wardrobe space for Lorraine's clothes. The early morning crash of coal deliveries would have the same effect on them as me, making them sit bolt upright in their beds.

On their first night, the Coopers chose to have dinner by themselves in a corner of the hotel's dining room. The following morning, Jim Weiner and I took them to the home Joan Clark's advance team had chosen for them. This was the best they could find. It turned out to be a modest Victorian villa sur-rounded on three sides by a cemetery. It had a cramped 1930s kitchen and small rooms, none of which opened onto the other, each accessible only from a confined entrance hall. Delia, Thom, and Michael looked shaken. At first, words failed a stricken Mrs. Cooper; I could only guess at what was running through her mind. Pioneering or not, how could they invite friends in Wash-ington to stay at such a place? A Foreign Service couple would have adjusted, even to the surrounding graveyard. It took only a few minutes, however, be-fore the ambassador asked me, not jokingly, "When's the next plane home?"

Anticipating their reaction, Weiner and I had a fallback plan. I had told Herr Löffler the Coopers would never move into the house at the cemetery and asked him to show Jim and me one of his shoe-box-shaped residences in the notorious diplomatic compound. There were about twenty of these in a kind of Levittown for ambassadors. Surrounded by a high fence, they were conveniently located. Some attempts at landscaping had been made, but over-all it was not a pretty sight. Inside these residences, a central hall with a broad stairway running up the left side divided a symmetrical interior. Empty, they conveyed a feeling of being on a battleship. Yet they had big kitchens, spacious dining rooms, several large bedrooms, good closet spaces, and ample baths. They were well designed for entertaining. The lawn in back could accommo-date many guests. Had we shown one of those houses to the Coopers first, we would have heard the same question from the ambassador about the next plane home. But, after seeing the best traditional prewar housing the East Germans could provide, the shoe box would look better to them, Jim and I reasoned.

The Coopers, still upset by the prospect in the graveyard, asked me to join them for a room-service dinner on their second night. A table was wheeled in, deftly circumnavigating the suitcases and boxes on the floor. I described the shoe box, pro and con, and claimed it had potential. I suggested that Mrs. Cooper could work with the basic structure and transform the interior in ways no other diplomats had dreamed of doing. If they were interested, Jim Weiner would arrange a visit to the diplomatic compound the next day so they could see the challenge and feel the inspiration for themselves. The moment we entered the house, there was a gleam in Lorraine's eyes. She was a talented creator of interiors, and it did not take her long to assess the possibilities. Thom was a decorator as well as a butler, and he too saw what could be done.

Lorraine transformed her shoe box. She hung red damask on the walls, borrowed paintings from the National Gallery of Art in Washington, D.C., with the help of the gallery's director, J. Carter Brown, and strategically positioned the miniature orange trees we had found for her in West Berlin. "It should be like walking into a big red rose," she told Craig Whitney of the *New York Times*, who was writing a piece about her. The Coopers were happy in their new home. I found Lorraine behind the house one day on her knees in jeans under a wide straw hat, digging holes for the plants she had brought over from West Berlin. Aniko later spotted her at the Meissen china display window on Unter den Linden. Lorraine, wearing a chiffon dress and strippy high-heeled shoes, was holding a matching purple parasol over her head. The contrast to East Berlin gray was stunning, Aniko reported.

Weiner had a difficult time with Mrs. Cooper as she probed the outer limits of the U.S. government's procurement policies. Wooden toilet seats made the point. Lorraine had heard her friend Jacqueline Kennedy observe that wooden seats were better in winter because they didn't feel as cold as plastic ones. So she insisted on wooden seats, Berlin turning cold in winter, and her husband added them to a list of items ordered for his residence. I told the ambassador that Washington and we had been as responsive as possible to his many requests. Wooden toilet seats were then more expensive. If we sent a telegram to the State Department with such a request, it would not be long before some mean-spirited person would leak it to the *Washington Post*. I suggested that if wooden toilet seats were needed, they should be bought privately. Lorraine was highly annoyed, Trudie Musson told me later. I never heard about toilet seats again but did notice they had been installed.

I forever walked a thin line in East Berlin. The State Department believed I was too supportive of the Coopers and too willing to be an accomplice in their demands. The Coopers thought I was excessively cautious, too much the rule-book bureaucrat. At the embassy, however, Cooper made it plain to Weiner and me that he wanted to be kept on the narrow path of compliance with the rules in the book. "I never took a bribe," said this former judge and senator with pride.

Poor Jim Weiner. He met his downfall with Mrs. Cooper in the air freshener incident. I do not believe she ever spoke to him afterward. This air freshener was a liquid dispensed with an eyedropper into narrow, grooved rings placed on top of lightbulbs to combat odors such as cigarette smoke. The liquid was agreeably scented and emitted a delicate smoke of its own when subjected to the heat of a bulb. Jim had never come across this before. On the evening in question, an elegant diplomatic reception at the Coopers during which a British-accented Michael formally announced arriving guests at the top of the stairs, "His Excellency the Ambassador of Sweden, Baron Rappe!" Jim spotted a smoking bulb and shouted "FIRE!" Shoving his way past orange trees and through startled guests, he smartly yanked the lamp cord from its socket. When his gaze met Lorraine's as he sought approval for having saved her evening from a blaze, Jim encountered only a withering, icy stare and understood that somehow, and once more, he had failed her.

Working in East Germany

The foreign ministry designated two officials to maintain regular contact with our embassy. One was the gnomelike Dr. Hans-Otto Geyer, who headed the U.S.-Canada-Japan Section, and the other was his immediate superior, Under Secretary Horst Grunert, a man of considerable charm and tact who later became an effective East German ambassador in Washington. I usually met with the former, Cooper with the latter. We were advised to request appointments with other government officials through Dr. Geyer. We were also asked to submit guest lists in advance of our social functions if they were to include East Germans and cite the subjects to be discussed. We complied only to the extent of inviting East German officials through the ministry's protocol office.

At the top of the East Germans' agenda in Washington was their effort to obtain respect for and acceptance of the GDR as a sovereign and independent state. They sought to establish an image of openness and cordiality. Good relations between us, they said, were to be expected. In Washington later on, a newly arrived Ambassador Grunert would fit right in with his bonhomie and good manners, suits with a Western cut, and frequent entertaining. He would profit from our impulse to welcome newcomers indiscriminately. No one would be asking him to submit his guest lists and conversation topics to the State Department for approval, either.

In East Berlin, Geyer and other GDR bureaucrats were correct and courteous and as distant as were we. Periodically, they treated us to pro-forma comments on the wonders of communism, but generally our dealings with East German officials were businesslike. Interested in making political capital out of our new relationship, they sought to accommodate and not offend us. Occasionally, however, Geyer offered some barbed remarks about the failures of capitalism. He was a hard-line, dedicated marxist, stubborn and Prussian, making him a worthy adversary. But he also had a sense of proportion and offered a sly smile in appreciation of our position. We managed to get along satisfactorily with this schoolmasterish personality who, while talking animatedly, sprayed saliva through the spaces between his front teeth.

Dr. Geyer fancied himself a bourbon connoisseur, a crack in marxism we duly widened. At Christmas, we gave liquor or American cigarettes, or both, to East Germans who worked closely with us. Our best bourbon went to Dr. Geyer. No one ever refused gifts. We were careful to make certain we could not be accused of passing bribes, adhering to the pattern of gift giving that had become acceptable in the diplomatic community. Some of our Middle Eastern colleagues, however, engaged in lavish greasing of the skids in the spirit of a Christmas foreign to their beliefs.

On issues of policy and the bilateral relationship, Cooper did not intend to go further in dealing with the East Germans than Washington was willing to accept. But he had differences with the State Department over tactics. Cooper did not appreciate guidance on *how* he should meet his objectives. Like any good ambassador, he believed tactics were his business. The politically prominent and respected Cooper inspired a certain awe in Washington, along with needless concerns that in East Berlin he might stray from the well-trodden paths of Allied practices by taking initiatives of his own and causing trouble. As Cooper's deputy and the ranking Foreign Service officer, I felt David Anderson's breath on my neck more than did anyone else.

The Western Allies, West Germans, and we worked together every day on Berlin and GDR issues. Inevitably, the federal government in Bonn shouldered the greatest burden of dealing with the East German regime. Focused on inner-German relations, Bonn's interests were far more numerous, intense, and immediate than anyone else's. In a rare departure from practice, the federal government sent as its first representative to East Berlin a political appointee, Günter Gaus, who previously had been editor in chief of *Der Spiegel*. As with the selection of Senator Cooper, Gaus was a widely respected public figure. For West Germans and their distant hopes for unification, it was important that their mission in East Berlin not be perceived as a traditional embassy, but rather (as they termed it) as a Permanent Representation. The GDR could not be treated as a foreign country. In his dealings with GDR authorities, Gaus was aggressive, tough, and precise on the issues.

My interlocutor at the West German mission was my opposite number, Hans-Otto Bräutigam, a consummate diplomat who later became Bonn's ambassador to the United Nations and, after unification, minister of justice in the former East German state of Brandenburg. He left his foreign service, he told me, "to work in a direct way on reunification." Had there been separate agendas in Allied relations with the Soviets or East Germans, personal jealousies, lack of competence in Allied embassies, or in the West German mission, we might have faced serious difficulties. To avoid any prospect of this, and in a pattern of Allied and West German collaboration well established in West Berlin, we who were deputies at our missions and Bräutigam met together once a month over lunch to compare notes and coordinate our efforts. We rotated meeting places in West Berlin among ourselves to underscore that we were engaged in teamwork.

Our embassy set about finding and registering American citizens for whom we had consular responsibilities. They were few in number, several of them in the opera company. We urged the GDR to vote with us on certain UN resolutions and other issues in multilateral diplomacy. Our interests converged sometimes, and we strengthened relations by discussing multilateral affairs. We followed negotiation of the Law of the Sea convention with them, on some of whose key issues the GDR, the Soviet Union, and we held similar views. This was a favorite topic of Dr. Geyer's. We also became involved in property restitution questions. Buildings owned by Americans, some of them Jewish, had been seized by Nazis or later confiscated by communists, sometimes both. Such cases were complicated and tended to set precedents. Progress, as we knew, would be slow.

When we raised practical matters about untended Jewish cemeteries in Berlin, a subject of special interest to Jewish organizations in the United States, the East Germans were forthcoming. We had several concerns in this matter: the location of burial records, some of them of Americans; replacement of tombstones that had been removed or vandalized; and fixing responsibility for cemetery maintenance. Leaders of the GDR would not officially declare their people's part in the murder of millions of Jews during the Nazi era and refused to consider financial compensation for Jewish victims. Their focus remained on the communist victims of National Socialism, and they excluded Jews from this picture.

Our small U.S. Information Service sought to explain America and its values, beginning modestly and in a light vein with invitations to a selected audience for a showing of the song-and-dance film *That's Entertainment!* Our venue was the Diplomatic Club, a creation of the foreign ministry rarely used by diplomats. The Coopers presided as hosts at this first large event during their stay, Lorraine dressed for Paris. Spirits soared, and there was much humming of tunes afterward over drinks and a buffet table laden with the finest offerings from the food halls of West Berlin's KaDeWe department store. "Propaganda," apparently to be found even in a song such as "Singin' in the Rain," became the most sensitive area of our activities, one Dr. Geyer found threatening and sought to constrain and subtly disparage. He managed during that festive evening to enjoy our bourbon, nonetheless.

A State Department team of lawyers and consular experts, with myself at its head, and a GDR team led by Dr. Geyer successfully concluded negotiations in Berlin for a consular convention to protect our citizens. In this, the United States was the side seeking such arrangements, having the most to gain from them. Two sticking points concerned notification of arrests and access to prisoners, common issues in dealing with authoritarian regimes. In these first negotiations since relations were established, I found the East Germans formal and proper to a fault, but willing to engage in banter if they thought things were going well. They sought to be as accommodating as possible but dug in their heels on matters of greatest concern to them.

I experienced the benefits, as did Dr. Geyer, of knowing the other side's language and thus being able to use the time taken by an interpreter to think ahead to the next round of tactics and responses once it became my turn to speak again. Body language conveyed reactions we would not have put into words nor wanted in the record. Much of the understanding gained in face-to-face negotiations of any kind results from physical interaction, deliberate or unintended, as each side recognizes facial and body signals of which no traces will remain. Such knowledge is useful feedback.

Earlier I described the isolation we felt while living in West Berlin in the midsixties. The sense of being cut off was even more pronounced in East Berlin ten years later. We could, however, travel outside Berlin into East Germany after obtaining the necessary clearances from the Dienstleistungsamt if we intended to stay overnight. On day trips we could drive wherever we liked, except in areas restricted by the Soviet military. Local Vopos (Volkspolizei) wrote down our license plate numbers at various points along the way.

To visit the countryside was to travel backward in time. I had known Germany nearly forty years earlier. Now, in the midseventies, it appeared that little outside East German towns and villages had changed. Tree-bordered roads were old, narrow, and cambered, with drainage ditches along their sides. Farmhouses had not been painted in a long time. It all recalled a tranquil softness, as in farmland paintings of the nineteenth century in which fields of dark earth were worked by peasant women in head scarves and bulky clothes bending low to reach the soil.

Our embassy participated in the Leipzig Trade Fair in September 1975, the first year after U.S.-GDR relations were established. Erich Honecker, the Socialist Unity Party's chairman and de facto leader of East Germany, accompanied by his camera crew, made a point of visiting our spectacularly modest booth of trade catalogs in order to chat with a pleased Cooper. The embassy's economic officer, Alan Parker, remembers Honecker speaking animatedly about having sat beside President Ford at the conclusion of the Helsinki meeting of the Commission on Security and Cooperation in Europe. He evidently regarded a protocolary seating arrangement as a victory for East German respectability; for him, it had produced a legitimizing photograph.

Erich Honecker was smoother, worldlier, and less doctrinaire than the squeaky-voiced Walter Ulbricht, who preceded him. Khrushchev agreed that Ulbricht could build a wall; Honecker directed its construction. If our relations with East German officials such as Dr. Geyer could be described as two-dimensional—formal, yet not without traces of humanity—our rare encounters with Honecker himself, whom I saw only at official functions, were one-dimensional. Black-rimmed glasses dominated his features, and the wary eyes that looked out from behind them worked themselves on such occasions into feigned affability. Everything about him seemed tensely self-controlled. Cooper, with a southern politician's instinct to reach out to others, found Honecker impervious to his warmth.

Especially irritating to Western diplomats was Honecker's fawning, sycophantic behavior toward Soviet Ambassador Abrasimov on public occasions, particularly his protestations of gratitude for the Russian presence in his country. "An obsequious toady," a British colleague muttered to me. Yet, to give Honecker his due, running a Germany that would be satisfactory to the Russians was a difficult, if not impossible, task. Alan Parker saw Honecker as trying within modest limits to ease the plight of the German population, probably in the face of Soviet indifference or hostility, given the lower standard of living in the Soviet Union. In his private contacts with East Germans, Parker found them unafraid to disparage their own government but deeply fearful of "the Ivans" and unwilling to comment on the Russians.

A Social Life of Sorts

For many diplomats and their wives, unburdened by Allied concerns, the social scene in Soviet-occupied East Berlin added up to little more than ennui. Barred from contacts with ordinary citizens of the land, we Americans were kept busier than we liked (except of course for Lorraine, who could never have too many engagements), compelled through diplomatic custom to attend receptions and national day festivities where we encountered the same faces time and again. The people at these affairs seemed interested primarily in drinks and hors d'oeuvres, hoping there would be enough of the latter to constitute dinner. When a buffet table manifested itself, guests circled the food like pigeons in a park strutting for crumbs, jostling each other and planting themselves in spots providing access and turf rights to some delicate morsel or other. Appraising glances over the rim of a glass at each new face were part of everyone's search for a frisson, a measure of relief from cocktail party persiflage that had a way of repeating itself.

Other diplomats were interested in us, beyond formal pleasantries, as quotable sources of information and dispensers of much sought after invitations to the fabled Cooper residence with its scents and orange trees, the best destination on Berlin's diplomatic merry-go-round. There one found gin martinis chilled to perfection, Kentucky sour mash, and enticing presentations of things to eat. Rarely were unmet East Germans among us; instead we got the usual smiling representatives of the foreign ministry, each of whom bowed to his hosts on arriving and leaving and seemed inordinately thirsty, hungry, and uncommunicative. Junior members of diplomatic staffs, less shackled by the demands of custom and protocol, and with West Berlin to play in, had a lot more fun and gave rise to envious gossip.

Quite a few non-Allied ambassadors stayed closely informed through easier ties to the GDR's *nomenklatura*, viewing their Berlin assignments in strategic terms. Among them were the representatives of Sweden, Pakistan, Egypt, and Portugal. Drawn from the ranks of their countries' top diplomats, as were the West Germans, with the exception of Günter Gaus, they were delightful people, as were their wives, whose talented number included a portrait painter and a poet. They, and Bonn's capable diplomats, became important contacts for us because of our limited access to East Germans of any stripe. We also could not have productive relations with ambassadors from East European countries who, monitored as they were by each other, the Soviets, and their GDR hosts, kept us at a polite distance. When a socially correct opportunity like July Fourth came along, they enjoyed our hamburgers and drinks, and some hinted they wished relations could be more cordial. We managed such contacts carefully with these constraints in mind.

Lorraine, far removed from Washington's more sophisticated swirl, felt confined in the little pond of East Berlin and drew upon her imagination to stay afloat. While Cooper was meeting with President Ford in Warsaw after the Helsinki Conference, Lorraine invited the suave Portuguese ambassador, on whom she had a crush, the dashing Swedish Baron Rappe, on whom she also had a crush, our handsome economic officer, Alan Parker, and me (both of us briefly alone at the time) to attend an opera in West Berlin. Forming a horseshoe in black tie around an exquisitely gowned Lorraine, although this was not a formal evening, her four courtiers sat around their queen in the best box and attracted no small notice, to their delight, as poor relations from the East showing the West a thing or two.

To celebrate the two hundredth birthday of the United States on July 4, 1976, the Coopers gave a garden party unmatched during our stay. American embassies across the globe were encouraged to make this a special occasion, and Lorraine rose to the challenge. Her moment had come. Word reached Jim Weiner and me, through Trudie, that the limits of government procurement regulations were to be stretched taut, and even Cooper stayed out of the way. We began by asking our unenthusiastic embassy in Pakistan to have made for us, and shipped by air, a huge red-white-and-blue *shamiyana* festive tent. Lorraine had Thom drape bands of colored bunting from the rooftop of her shoe-box home, making it look like a Christmas gift in the *Nutcracker Suite*, as seen by the mice. Trudie's grandmother shipped five hams from Kentucky. Small American flags were placed among the flowers on each table inside the tent. We borrowed a U.S. Army band from West Berlin, put the Russian Abrasimovs at the head table, champagned and fed Berlin's diplomats as never before, and danced until midnight. Caught in the mood, Ambassador Abrasimov had leaned toward Lorraine and said, "Let's start the dancing." She looked regal and aglow with pride. Cooper himself cut a debonair figure in his Yale getup of white trousers and blue blazer, with a red rose in his lapel. The only East Germans present were the handful of functionaries designated by the regime to attend. But everyone, including Dr. Geyer, who bowed and sprayed his thanks upon us, took their little flags home. Marx rode a back seat that night.

A Love Story

A slender, dark-haired woman from the West and I, both living in East Berlin, found ourselves in failing marriages. She was thirty-five, and I ten years older. I first met her at a dinner party in diplomatic surroundings, seated beside her according to protocol, and another time at a showing of *Casablanca* in an American's home. Sitting on the floor I looked up at her and caught her eye as tears welled at the movie's ending. We reached across our separateness, looking at one another more closely, each musing about the other afterward. Later on we began to feel we wanted more than brief encounters and while dancing conspired to meet in West Berlin in the parking area of a battered Reichstag. We drove separately through checkpoints at the wall, she arriving first and I parking next to her. Inside her car on a winter's day, holding each other while we kissed, we laughed as the windows steamed up. When I was free to leave my work from time to time, we saw each other in West Berlin. As our love grew stronger, we made plans to meet in London, where, unsure of how to find one another, we decided to look for each other at an appointed hour in the main hall of Victoria Station. Each time we were fated to return to the prison city of East Berlin, where love hid her face. Soon, as in *Casablanca*, we parted.

Relations with the Soviet Embassy during Détente

During the Cold War years of 1969–1979, a decade of détente occurred because it suited the interests of both powers simultaneously. A product of Kissinger's reasoning, détente was put into practice by Brezhnev and Nixon. It provided relief from the ever-present threat of nuclear warfare. This thaw in the Cold War did not diminish underlying antagonisms but permitted a change in the quality of relations on the surface, as well as small steps toward normality. The war of words between the superpowers became less ferocious. Détente allowed the Russians to focus on issues elsewhere, as in China and, to their eventual regret, Afghanistan. In East Germany in 1971, the Soviets replaced Ulbricht, long in the tooth and a hard-liner on inner-German relations, with Erich Honecker as party chairman.

The joint *Apollo-Soyuz* space flight, in which spacecraft launched by the two superpowers docked in outer space, became a symbol of the potential benefits of cooperation between Russia and the United States. Berlin was a barometer in this relationship. The American embassy was established at the midpoint of détente. It came naturally to both sides during that time to reflect a changed atmosphere through their statements and diplomatic postures. In East Berlin we displayed more humanity toward one another, as the real people we were occasionally looked out from behind our official masks.

Members of the East German regime were not international actors in dé-tente but spectators, uneasy about a shift in Cold War politics that warmed relations, at least superficially, between their patron and the United States. During this period Ambassador Abrasimov permitted a few rays of light to fall between himself and Honecker. Abrasimov took to greeting Cooper warmly at receptions, holding up the receiving line in a bit of theater for all to notice. Berlin's diplomats, and even the general public, watched in fascination as a temporary rapprochement between the Cold War superpowers played itself out on the world scene and, more immediately, in the confrontational setting of Berlin itself. Where might this lead?

Piotr Abrasimov by then had served in East Berlin, on and off, for more than ten years. He had recently returned from two years as the Soviet ambas-sador in Paris, a posting neither he nor his unobtrusive wife seemed to have enjoyed. Previously his career had taken him to Pyongyang, North Korea, as number two and to Warsaw as ambassador, posts with heavy responsibilities for a Soviet diplomat. His total service in the GDR would add up to seventeen years, and he was proud of the fact that he spoke no German. As he began a social relationship with us in 1974, we soon perceived that Abrasimov neither respected nor liked Germans, as his asides in conversation made clear. His dis-dain reflected a Soviet attitude that Abrasimov, in the spirit of détente and social conviviality, felt he could express to us, believing that, as allies having fought side by side in defeating the Germans, we would agree. We did not, but didn't say so. Ironically, East Germany during the Cold War became the Soviet Union's most reliable ally. Abrasimov's task was to manage this relationship.

An energetic, gray-haired, and well-rounded man of medium height, Abrasi-mov had a lighthearted side that sometimes appeared forced. He was intelli-gent and quick-witted, artful, assertive, and supremely self-confident. I could not help thinking he must have been difficult to work for. As a member of Brezhnev's inner circle and eventually of the party's Central Committee, Abrasi-mov had political clout of his own that counted in Moscow. In the latter capacity, and prior to his return to Berlin, he had been responsible for senior-level diplomatic appointments. On learning this, I marveled at his fate in returning to the GDR, momentarily overlooking the fact that, for a Russian, Berlin, like Washington and Peking, was a front-line diplomatic assignment. Born in Belorussia, as were Brezhnev and Andrey Gromyko, Abrasimov when we met him was sixty-two, eleven years younger than Cooper.

Abrasimov and Cooper went out of their way to develop cordial ties, which proved easy to do. Cooper was not a naturally effusive person, nor was Abrasimov, but they soon warmed to each other. The Soviet deputy chief of mission, Anatoly Gromyko, son of Russia's foreign minister, had been posted to East Berlin shortly before my arrival and was my counterpart in many discussions. The Gromykos spoke English. The Abrasimovs required interpreters, as of course did we. The Russians provided them.

The Abrasimovs began to invite the Coopers, the Groves, and the Gromykos, Anatoly and Valentina, to their residence for dinner. The Soviet Embassy covered nearly a city block along Unter den Linden near the Brandenburg Gate and served as chancery and residence. Its awe-inspiring exterior proclaimed the authority of a proconsul. Small dinner parties were held in the private quarters upstairs, far more intimate than the formal halls below. Furnishings at the Abrasimovs recalled the opulence of czarist times in a gilded, overstuffed way. Soviet officials in powerful positions adopted this turn-of-the-century style, perhaps in the belief that it would remain forever fashionable; in any case, they had little else from which to choose. Paintings from the school of Social Realism—happy people at work on tractors—hung incongruously on the walls. The Abrasimovs lived comfortably. They had an efficient Russian household staff and all the food and drink from West Berlin they might want. Dishes at these dinners were tasty, as meals came to the table in elaborate courses. Caviar arrived by the kilo, it seemed, which was fine with me.

Evenings with the Russians were at their instigation. Only once did the Coopers lure the Abrasimovs to the home that was like "walking into a big red rose." This was on the occasion of the departure of the British ambassador, the representative of a wartime ally. Trudie Musson, who was present, wrote to her grandmother in Louisville afterward that Lorraine "had coached me that if she saw me once without a smile or a laugh she would poke me in the ribs."

Valya Gromyko was glamorous and blond, lively, westernized. She was Anatoly's second wife and showed an engaging streak of rebelliousness in her little digs, openness, and laughter. She and Mary were the loud ones at the table, but Madame Abrasimov concealed any displeasure this might have caused her. Valya occasionally went to West Berlin with my wife to look at fashions and buy perfume. She was flirtatious and a smooth dancer, as I would discover at our Fourth of July party. I liked her. Our Russian hosts were aware of Mary's background, not least because Moscow's main airport bore the family name, but they never referred to it.

Anatoly was not a person toward whom I could feel close, although he was courteous and sometimes tried, in clumsy ways, to be affable. In conversation he saw himself as a lecturer of rare wisdom. Your function, if you played his game, was to listen: rapt and respectful. I found him vain and pompous, an aggressive marxist conscious of his status as the son of the hard-line foreign minister known to the West from his UN days as "Mister *Nyet.*" Before the war, his father had been posted to Washington with his family as the embassy's political counselor. He then became ambassador during the war years and, in 1946, the Soviet Union's permanent delegate to the United Nations. Anatoly had learned a bit about the United States and other Western countries. Nominally, he was an expert on Africa.

The most festive occasion at the Abrasimovs was a dinner celebrating the *Apollo-Soyuz* docking in space on the day after the event itself in mid-July 1975. For two days U.S. and Soviet astronauts carried out joint experiments while orbiting the earth. This time our economic officer, Alan Parker, and his Swedish-born wife, Inge, were included. We sat down to a colorfully decorated table that might have been prepared for a birthday party, but here the theme was outer space and spacecraft, not an easy one with which to grapple. Anatoly proposed that we sign and exchange the typed menu cards, and we did so. There was a hollow ring at times to the toasts and joviality, because all of us recognized that the fundamental obstacles in U.S.-Soviet relations, among them the Berlin Wall standing only a few hundred yards away, remained unchanged. Nevertheless, the corny decorations and our hosts' pride in them, the elaborate efforts to please American guests, were touching and welcome.

I particularly recall Cooper's explanation to Abrasimov one evening of our impending 1976 elections; the topic arose probably so Gromyko could send a report to the Kremlin on Cooper's views. Cooper sat back after dessert and described our democratic process with homespun eloquence. In his soft voice and candid way, he talked about Somerset, Kentucky, where he was born, his experiences there as a judge, the political life and concerns of near-poor people in Pulaski County. He touched on the key elements of the 1976 elections, the personalities involved, the issues being debated. In wishful thinking he predicted Ford would win over Carter. Abrasimov became absorbed in Cooper's account. He obviously had not before heard a lucid explanation of our political system from someone with a personal understanding of it who had played an important role within it. After a few half-hearted comparisons, Abrasimov gave up trying to praise the Soviet system. It was not that Cooper had made a convert of him; of course he hadn't. Rather, Abrasimov, and even Gromyko, seemed to have gained fresh insight and respect for the United Sates in ways they had not anticipated. Dialogue had occurred in one more area where previously there had been standoff.

We reported to Washington the substance of these social affairs in cables I would write and review with Cooper, but I doubt there is a record of this exchange. None of us foresaw the failure of communism in the late 1980s. We had few expectations of even modest change in that system, although intuitively we knew that some day it must fail. There were always first steps along a new path, however, and the different tenor of our relationships in East Berlin during détente gave us small hope for a better future. Shootings continued at the wall of East Germans trying to escape, with protests routinely lodged with Abrasimov by the Allies in West Berlin. The U.S.-Soviet relationship could not blossom into friendship in occupied Berlin.

A year after both of us had left Berlin, I saw Anatoly again during my visit to Moscow while he was director of the Soviet Africa Institute. Calling on him at his office, I brought a gift of perfume for Valya. He was stiff and formal, and we no longer had the give-and-take we had cultivated as diplomats in Berlin. Ours had been a professional relationship, and he seemed to feel we no longer needed each other. He was right, of course, but I couldn't help regretting that we were unable to use our association to greater benefit, deriving from it a more open and continuing dialogue as responsible people on opposite sides of an epic dispute. The Cold War had sponged us up.

My Surprising Stasi File

When the Berlin Wall collapsed in 1989, the Federal Government in Bonn took possession of the state security records of the GDR and, in time, permitted people who believed they had been targets of surveillance to apply for copies of their files. It seemed that the communist regime had turned half of East Germany against the other half, neighbor secretly reporting on neighbor about ideological conformity and behavior. Some 1.5 million informers had kept a Stasi staff of eighty-five thousand regular employees busy compiling 4 million files on East Germans, 1 million on West Germans, and about two hundred thousand on foreigners, according to the *New York Times*. Stasi head-quarters were in the Normannenstrasse in a large innocuous-looking building that sent chills through anyone who knew what went on inside.

In the course of writing this memoir I applied for my dossier, knowing that security agencies during the Cold War routinely kept track of foreign diplomats, especially those from "hostile powers," the term used by the GDR's intelligence organs to characterize the United States. The East Germans, more-over, enjoyed a reputation for sophisticated counterespionage techniques. A year later, and for a processing fee of about ten dollars, I received in the mail from Berlin more than two hundred pages of photocopied material clamped together at the left-hand margin.

The covering letter provided an explanation of office symbols and described the material. Occasionally a paragraph or sentence was blacked out, presum-ably to protect another person. My file was maintained by Hauptabteilung II/3, the division within the Stasi responsible for guarding against U.S.-directed espionage. What had the Stasi been gathering on me? How successfully had the vaunted East German intelligence apparatus penetrated our embassy? What techniques had they used? Who had helped them? Gingerly, I began to read, and the more I read the more astonished and oddly disappointed I became.

The first 175 pages were summaries of intercepted telephone conversations from my office. Our home phone apparently had not been tapped. I was pleased to see how many people I had arranged to meet for lunch in West Berlin during the course of two years, and how effectively we avoided talking about sensitive matters over the telephone. A second category of material contained summaries of my official conversations at the foreign ministry, and these were recorded with professional competence. There was, for example, a report of a luncheon in the countryside offered by senior foreign ministry officials to the Coopers, the Parkers, and the Groves as a gesture of friendship and the warming of relations. I remembered it as a pleasant and relaxed event at the ministry's rustic guesthouse, with some of my favorite German dishes and wines. This report was based upon tapes, the gracious "Frau K." sitting next to me apparently having been wired for the occasion. Or perhaps the micro-phone was in the floral centerpiece, a hoary practice in the intelligence world.

A third section consisted of photocopies of letters and envelopes received by me through the East German mail arriving at my office. Some, such as invitations, had been sent from embassy to embassy; a few came from abroad. I was touched to reread my father's Christmas letter of 1975 and to see a photo-copy of the check he had sent. There were also a few notations about the movement of my car outside Berlin.

The fourth category was odd, made up largely of photographs of my wife's shopping lists and pages in her address book. Hauptabteilung II/3 was also treated to an otherwise blank page on which someone wanting to restore ink to the dried-out tip of a ballpoint pen seemed to have drawn circles in frustration. Nothing more. All of this was raw, unevaluated data, compiled without comment or analysis, and essentially without value. Intelligence gathering, and particularly analysis, is a labor-intensive process requiring priorities in the use of analysts' time. In vain I searched for an assessment of my intentions or skills as a diplomat, an intimation that I was someone II/3 had better keep an eye on. Quite the opposite: they didn't care *what* I did. Neither Cooper nor I wanted to become sinister figures. We were straightforward representatives of the United States whose agenda was as we portrayed it to the East Germans and whose work was in the open, except for one low-ranking and not particularly competent CIA case officer whose chief targets were communist countries represented in Berlin.

My file led to a few conclusions, nevertheless. It held nothing of a classified nature, suggesting that if the embassy had been penetrated the record was somewhere else. Our regular mail was screened, opened, and copied at a central point, probably in cooperation with our (and Herr Löffler's) East German receptionist at the front desk, whom we all liked. There was no evidence of the existence of listening devices in the embassy or my home. Our East German maid was no Mata Hari and evidently functioned without guidance in photographic endeavors, on a par with her housekeeping skills. I acknowledge the following code-named individuals cited in the covering letter to my file as having been agents working on my case: "Melani," "Christian," "Ritter," "Erich," and "Windmüller." In subsequent correspondence those people were identified to me by their real names, unknown functionaries in a gray world from small towns in East Germany.

Lorraine a Final Time

After my stay in Berlin, the Coopers and I became close friends. I saw Lorraine for the last time in June 1984 at their house on N Street. She was in good spirits, having called me on the spur of the moment to come over for a drink. When she opened the door I noticed her lipstick was askew. In her blue-green library we talked about people from Berlin and our adventures there, Lorraine guffawing in her rasping laugh. She was proud of what she and John had accomplished. She asked, mentioning her name, whether I had had an affair with the woman in the love story. "The way you looked at her?"

she probed with a smile. I said no, and she saw this wasn't true. When I left, Lorraine did not accompany me to her front door, as she always had, but turned away and went alone to the wooden porch overlooking a walled garden below. I watched her for a moment, then let myself out. Hours later she suffered a stroke and remained unconscious. I was not to know until morning that I had poured the last glass of champagne anyone would be able to offer her. Lorraine left with her flags snapping, one of the last embodiments of a determined and mannered breed of Washington women, like Mrs. Lightfoot Lee, whose considerable power resided in the social settings they created for themselves and their men.

Berlin's Wall

The Berlin Wall was an ever-present reality, a physical reminder of the East-West split that assumed an eerie existence of its own in representing to the world the division of Germany and the chasms of the Cold War. One spoke of the wall with casual familiarity, and writers of English soon began to capitalize the W, giving this barrier a form of respectability.

The wall slashed through the middle of a once bustling and thriving city. It ran across land and was extended over water by marker buoys. In a well-publicized incident during May 1975, while Cooper and I were there, a five-year-old girl drowned in the River Spree because East German border guards prevented a West Berlin fire brigade from reaching her. Not only did the wall itself have a terrifying effect, so did the shabby areas surrounding it, the empty lots along Leipzigerstrasse, where anything that might serve as a hiding place had been razed. It was a hideous sight. A wall built by their own leaders without the involvement of Soviet forces locked up the East Germans.

The wall had one particularly sinister aspect: it brainwashed us. We believed the wall would stand for decades more and accepted its presence as an immutable fact. It insinuated itself into our thinking as an enduring symbol of the tyranny of a communist regime over its own people.

On the evening of November 9, 1989, a forty-year-old East German regime peacefully, almost casually, opened its crossing points at the Berlin Wall permitting thousands of astounded East Germans to surge into West Berlin. All other border crossing points between East Germany and the Federal Republic also were opened. This did not happen as originally intended.

The Socialist Unity Party's Central Committee earlier that day decided to change the GDR's travel regulations in a long-considered response to the country's soaring debt, to angry demonstrations for freedom throughout the GDR, and to the economic and political implications of a steady flow of East Germans to Hungary and Czechoslovakia, whence they could continue to the West. The draft text of a new travel measure decreed, "Starting immediately... [a] temporary transition regulation for travel abroad and permanent exits from the GDR are in effect.... Ground for denial will only be applied in particularly exceptional cases." This regulation kept intact requirements for passports and some of the GDR's other customary travel procedures. The process for announcing and implementing the decree then broke down, and thus do affairs of the world unfold.

A hapless official named Günter Schabowski, a party politburo member and spokesman, found himself some three hours after the committee meeting standing before a live and previously scheduled press conference for GDR and international journalists. He was about to take his place in history. He had not attended the Central Committee's deliberations, nor had there been time for him to study the text of the draft regulation scheduled for release on the following morning at the cautious hour of four a.m. And so, according to the transcript, he said in part:

> SCHABOWSKI: ... We have decided today, *um*, to implement a regulation that allows every citizen of the German Democratic Republic, *um*, to, *um*, leave the GDR through any of the border crossings...
>
> QUESTION: When does this come into effect?
>
> SCHABOWSKI: (Looks through his papers...) That comes into effect, according to my information, immediately, without delay (looking through his papers further...)

The Ending

I was in Tunis in November 1989 when the wall opened. In the newspaper delivered to my hotel room with breakfast, banner headlines proclaimed the event. Having lived in both sides of Berlin, I was stunned as I began slowly to comprehend the enormity of the event, its irreversibility. My emotions were of relief rather than a rush to joy, of weariness rather than a sense of triumph; they were those of someone reaching the destination of a long and hazardous journey. With Berlin free and open, the Cold War would be over. Germany would no longer remain divided. The threat of nuclear war between the superpowers was gone. Just as the building of a wall had symbolic meaning, so did its crumbling. I was eighteen as the Cold War began and was now sixty-two.

Yet our government remained silent. An inspiring statement from President

Bush was needed and expected, a coda from the victor paying tribute to sacrifice and validating for the young, especially, the meaning of the Cold War's outcome and what it told about freedom. We led the West in the Cold War but became tongue-tied at its end.

Future historians, and documents on both sides coming to light, will point to opportunities missed or misunderstood. While I doubt a better or more enduring framework than containment could have been devised to avoid nuclear war and achieve the global objectives of the West, there had been little debate on how to end the Cold War. Troubling questions remain: did the Cold War need to last so long and cost so much in life and treasure?

I spoke briefly with former president Gorbachev in April 2001 at a social event in the Library of Congress. Through his interpreter I told him I was a retired American diplomat who wanted to thank him for allowing the Berlin Wall to open peacefully and for what he accomplished in the months that followed. He grinned, patted me on the shoulder, and replied, "A diplomat is never retired." Then he nodded his thanks about Berlin.

Aftermath

In 1990, as director of the Foreign Service Institute, I returned to East Berlin nearly fifteen years after I had left. The wall was open, although it remained standing, and the Cold War was over. Our embassy had arranged a luncheon with several former East German officials. One was a man I had known when he was a young diplomat working for Dr. Geyer. I was amazed to see him again and asked what he and Geyer had thought of the Americans in 1974, when Cooper and I established our embassy. Sounding nostalgic, he said we were always correct (his word) and open and that Cooper was respected and liked. Our "correctness" in relations had been appreciated. He thought life would not go well for East Germans. I sensed he feared that West German arrogance and attitudes of lording it over poor cousins would make themselves felt. Disparities of wealth and spirit would persist. In that he was right. How the world had changed for all Germans.

I would like to walk with the woman in the love story through an open Brandenburg Gate, look around, and take time to reflect and remember. Then, to celebrate the city's freedom, we might cross to the lavishly rebuilt Adlon Hotel for tea and stroll along the now fashionable street where the music of "Singin' in the Rain" came to me one happy, dark, and drenching night a long time ago.

14

JONESTOWN

1978

Seven years after dealing with Panama, I returned to Latin American affairs in a position at the State Department giving me responsibilities for our relations with Mexico, Central America, and the Caribbean. One event in the course of my work was so grotesque and widely known that it dominates my memories of this time. The self-inflicted tragedy at Jonestown was an American Gothic tale without equal.

On the evening of Saturday, November 18, 1978, I was working late in my office at the State Department when John Burke, our ambassador in Georgetown, Guyana, called. He told me shots had been fired at a landing strip near the Jonestown community of Americans living in a "Peoples Temple" close to the Venezuelan border. I had never heard of Jonestown. Burke's preliminary information was that Representative Leo J. Ryan, a California Democrat, had been killed. Burke spoke calmly and precisely. I reviewed the notes I had been making while he talked and told him I would pull together a team in the State Department to deal with this and notify the congressional leadership.

Ryan and members of his party were preparing to board two chartered aircraft at the end of a visit with the Reverend Jim Jones, the temple's founder. Ryan's chief purpose on this trip was to determine whether those living in the commune, most of them African Americans from California, were free to leave if they wanted to. Accompanying Ryan were some fifteen members of the temple who intended to return to the United States, two congressional staffers, nine members of the American media including an NBC camera crew, and a delegation of eighteen "concerned relatives" from California. Also in the group was Richard Dwyer, a Foreign Service officer who was the deputy chief of mission at our embassy in Georgetown, serving as the delegation's escort.

Jones had predicted to his followers, we found out later, that a crisis would one day threaten the community's survival. When that occurred, he said, everyone must be prepared to kill themselves. Mass suicides "for the glory of socialism" were rehearsed in weekly drills called "white night," according to Deborah Layton, an earlier defector. Congressman Ryan's visit, lasting a day and a half, permitted him to ask Jones and others probing questions about the commune. Ryan's presence with an ever curious press group in tow, and the defection of some fifteen of Jones's followers, posed a threat to Jones and in the end triggered him to stage his calamity. By the time Ryan and his party were ready to leave for the airport to return to Georgetown, Jones apparently had become convinced that the temple's isolation had been shattered and that under outside scrutiny it could no longer survive on his terms.

At the sound of gunfire on the grass landing strip while Ryan's group was boarding, the first pilot took off in panic and on reaching Georgetown provided an initial, sketchy account of what had happened. Fanatical followers of the Reverend Jones killed Ryan, three members of the media, and one defector. Others were wounded, including the embassy's Dwyer and a female congressional staffer. Dwyer, shot in the thigh, managed to take charge through the night at a scene where the dead and injured lay unattended. "He was tireless, firm, and brave," wrote Charles A. Krouse, a *Washington Post* foreign corespondent also wounded on the airstrip.

Learning only that a member of Congress had been murdered, I alerted Warren Christopher, then deputy secretary of state. He instructed me to call our embassy and keep the phone line open, making it permanently available to us—a wise procedure in crisis management in the days before the advent of cell phones. The media would pour into Guyana with an overwhelming need for telephones, but the State Department was never without a voice link to its embassy. The department's desk officer for the region, Richard McCoy, knew about Ryan's travel, having briefed the congressman and his staff about Guyana and the Peoples Temple before they left. With Ashley Hewitt, director of Caribbean affairs, and McCoy, I took preliminary steps toward organizing what would become the largest task force operation in the State Department during peaceful conditions. The three of us kept forcing ourselves to think ahead.

McCoy, an energetic young Foreign Service officer of cheerful disposition from Paterson, New Jersey, had recently served in Guyana. While there he had visited Jonestown twice in chartered aircraft to offer the embassy's consular services and have a look around. We learned from him that the Peoples Temple was an isolated community of nearly one thousand American religious cultists presided over by the Reverend Jones, who had brought his followers from San Francisco to this remote place to establish a utopian commune. McCoy had noticed in Georgetown that Jones's declarations of pseudo-marxist religious beliefs were tailored to his audiences, emphasizing either the religious or the socialist aspects of the temple. The government of Guyana, under President Forbes Burnham and his People's National Congress Party, practiced a form of socialism. Burnham approved of Jones and his followers for political and national security reasons: political, because of Jones's purported ideological bent (such views from an American were welcome); and security, because Jones had promised to assist Burnham in developing the northeast territory. The presence of so many Americans would serve as a trip wire against Venezuelan incursions based on that nation's claims to the region.

McCoy well remembered his brief visits to Jonestown. He recalled a vista of about six hundred cleared acres of farmland for growing fruits and vegetables, a piggery and chicken coops, wooden barracks for dormitory living prefabricated by the community's sawmill workers, and generators to provide electricity. There was a doctor and a medical unit. Funding came from followers who turned over their Social Security checks to Jones. They were American citizens minding their own business and not breaking any laws, McCoy felt. When two cultists said they wanted to leave, McCoy took them back with him. In short, the Peoples Temple seemed to McCoy to be functioning as a more or less rationally organized place where tensions, if any, were well concealed from a curious American embassy official.

Jones himself, as McCoy remembered him, was a stocky white man of dark complexion and medium height in his late forties. He habitually wore dark, light-resisting glasses through which he could direct an unwavering, even menacing focus into the eyes of another person, thus adding to his ability to intimidate and manipulate his followers. He professed to be a humble man of faith and socialist ideals and sounded serious-minded, McCoy said. Well connected politically in the United States, Jones had called on Guyanese officials in 1976 to introduce a visiting lieutenant governor of California, Mervyn Dymally. What remained obscured on casual contact were Jones's obsession to control his followers and his cruelty toward them, his paranoia, and his conspiracy theories about the CIA.

Horror Heaped on Horror

Our initial focus at the State Department was on Ryan and his party and what had happened at the airstrip. We had no idea that a mass suicide including murders of children by their parents might have taken place. Hewitt and I telephoned the congressional leadership and the California delegation to brief them and provide phone numbers for them to reach us. Not many hours later, British-trained Guyanese troops arrived at the Jonestown settlement and reports began filtering back through our embassy.

Ambassador Burke told us that Guyanese soldiers at the site were finding many dead, at least three or four hundred. It appeared that nearly all the adults had killed themselves. A few had been shot. I passed this sketchy information to Christopher, awakening him at home and recommending it be released. He agreed. Included in our hastily assembled task force was a woman from the State Department's Bureau of Public Affairs who, through the night, was our liaison to the media. I wrote on a yellow pad that our ambassador in Georgetown had informed the State Department that the government of Guyana had told him there were mass suicides involving many Americans in the Jonestown commune, the number as yet unknown. I read this statement again to myself and have never forgotten the sinking feeling I had as I tore off the page and said to our public affairs person, "Please release this." After I had irretrievably done that, I wondered during a moment of self-doubt whether I had lost my mind or perhaps was dreaming. This would be the State Department's first public alert.

Soon we acquired a better understanding of what had happened. While flying over the site in daylight, Guyanese forces observed what appeared to be clothing on the ground drying in the sun in an enormous, colorful patchwork of different patterns. Those were, in fact, the clothes on the bloating bodies of people who had fallen on top of one another after drinking a brew of Kool-Aid laced with cyanide prepared by Jones and his lieutenants. The deaths were confirmed. At a meeting in my office on Monday, Hewitt reported that the first U.S. military plane was preparing to take off for Jonestown to begin identifying and recovering the bodies of those American citizens. He had asked the military to load five hundred body bags. I grimly told him to make that a thousand, as McCoy suspected there would be around that number at the temple who had committed suicide or, in the case of children and possibly others, had been murdered. As it turned out, 909 Americans died at the insistence of Reverend Jones, who was shot by someone else in the pavilion from which he directed the slaughter through a bullhorn.

Dealing with reporters whose questions were endless, and having few insights to offer, was an overwhelming task for the State Department's press spokespersons. About one hundred reporters, photographers, and television cameramen descended on Georgetown, vying to find rooms in the capital's two European-style hotels. I could feel people's minds straining to come to terms with the enormity of it all. There was no logical explanation, no context within which to make these events intelligible. All of us were searching for facts to hold on to, things known to have occurred. In this need, a stream of gruesome photographs helped.

McCoy's role was indispensable. He kept his emotions in check and bore a great burden day after day as we turned to him for knowledge and understanding. For him the strain erupted only afterward when, for another month, remembering the children he had seen at the temple, he suffered from mental exhaustion and questioned his further commitment to a Foreign Service career. In the end he stayed on, becoming a specialist in consular affairs. All of us involved with Jonestown became emotionally engaged: depressed, angry at Jones and his followers, confused, feeling somehow defiled ourselves, stunned that such a thing could happen, that Americans could behave that way.

Guyanese soldiers found a tape recording of Jones and the hysterical sounds of mass suicides in the pavilion, the reel still clicking on its spool. Asked by my FBI counterpart whether I wanted to hear it, I declined. Why would I want to, and let those sounds haunt my sleep? There was nothing noble, uplifting, or heroic about this occurrence. Jonestown was a human disaster played out in the jungles of Guyana driven by the misplaced faith of American men, women, and even children in a man who was a monster. It bore no consequences for U.S. foreign policy. There was no Cold War dimension. More than anything else, the Jonestown suicides underscored civilization's thin veneer.

Yet the State Department was engaged in many ways, through our embassy's communications with the Guyanese government; State's responsibility to keep Congress informed; its obligation to notify family members of what had happened and to handle telephone calls from an agitated public; the need to develop a media strategy and keep the media as accurately and fully informed as possible; the requirement to coordinate what was being done elsewhere in Washington among other agencies involved; a responsibility, in the early stages of the disaster, to send situation reports to our ambassadors abroad so they could speak informedly; and the challenge of working with the Pentagon to identify and repatriate nearly one thousand human remains.

The House International Relations Committee immediately launched an investigation into "all aspects" of the murders and suicides at Jonestown. I was asked to handle this matter within the State Department and, working with two of our lawyers, compiled several thousand documents—all we had, including my scribbled notes—to be turned over to the committee's staff. They were satisfied and wanted the matter behind them. Hearings were not held. An unavoidable and unresolved issue in Washington for a time was who, within our government, would pay for the use of airplanes, body bags, forensic work, and the like. State and Defense ended up sharing the costs of this senseless tragedy borne, in the end, by the American taxpayer.

15

JERUSALEM

1980 to 1983

"Jerusalem is mournful, and dreary and lifeless. I would not desire to live here." So wrote Mark Twain in 1869 in *The Innocents Abroad.*

My assignment to Jerusalem came unexpectedly. By the winter of 1979 I had finished working in Washington on our Central American and Caribbean ties and expected to become ambassador to Haiti. While preparing for that appointment, I received a call from personnel. Due to the urgency of implementing the Camp David Accords between Egypt and Israel, concluded in September 1978, Secretary of State Cyrus Vance, who normally took no interest in assignments below the ambassadorial level, had decided to select the new consul general in Jerusalem himself. Would I be interested in being considered?

Jerusalem was not an embassy, while Haiti was, but it had many of the attributes of a chief-of-mission posting and would be engrossing work. It was the farthest place from my mind. When I asked the staff at personnel why they had thought of me, the answer was that I had the right credentials: I had no previous association with Jerusalem, and neither the Israelis nor the Palestinians knew of me. Initially, at least, I would not be a problem to either side. That was not wholly reassuring.

Feeling uneasy about heading a post of such complexity in one of the most emotionally charged places on earth, and without the benefit of other assignments in the Middle East, I went to Philip Habib for advice. Phil was under secretary of state for political affairs, traditionally the most senior position for a Foreign Service officer. He knew the region as few did and took an interest in his younger colleagues. I told him Jerusalem intrigued me. Jerusalem, he replied, was "the big time," and I would be foolish to turn down such an

215

opportunity. "You will learn," he assured me. "Look around, pay attention to what people are telling you, and come to your own conclusions." Neither of us suspected that in a matter of months we would be working together closely in that ancient city.

I knew little about Jerusalem and would be obliged to start from scratch. A bright, coolheaded, tough, and exceptionally competent young Foreign Service officer, James "Jock" Covey, working on the Israeli-Arab desk in the State Department, arranged my briefings and shared his insights. I admired his precision and his ability to keep emotions disentangled from analysis. Soon I would defy the system and choose him over more senior candidates to become my deputy.

The Holy City

Jerusalem returns to me through memories of its sunsets and sunrises in uncontaminated air twenty-five hundred feet above the sea: one climbs to reach Jerusalem. Never before had I seen such soft and rosy hues. Yet the place was haunted by its past, the intersection of three monotheistic religions and conflicting ideas about who should control the Holy City. Christ, when he reached the summit of the Mount of Olives, is said to have gazed on Jerusalem and wept. Today, he would perhaps weep again. I will tell about Jerusalem as I found it in my time. I was fifty on arriving.

This was a place of people with head coverings: Israeli men with skullcaps, or *kipahs,* pinned to their hair; Palestinians with kaffiyeh scarves and headbands; Greek Orthodox priests whose hats resembled inverted flowerpots; Armenian priests wearing a triangular black headdress symbolizing Mount Ararat, the traditional landing site of Noah's Ark; Christian nuns in their distinctive garb; and tourists who would wear anything, no matter how ridiculous, to shield themselves from the sun.

Jerusalem was a city of distinct neighborhoods with its core inside the old walls. The Mea Shearim, or "Hundredfold," was home to ultraorthodox Hasidic Jews. There, men in black wore a heavy eighteenth-century Polish garb of fur-trimmed hats and leggings, and women, childbearers and homemakers only, were completely covered except for their hands and faces. The side curls worn by men and boys were said to honor King David, who was believed to have worn them as well. Life's main purpose for men was study and prayer. Secular activities were disdained, and the ultraorthodox could refuse military service. Talmudic study houses in this poor ghettolike enclave, some just ordinary rooms, were filled by bearded men in white shirtsleeves examining sacred texts, phrase by phrase, as they sat rocking and muttering at their desks. A Jewish friend, wearing a light summer dress from Paris exposing her arms, told me she was spat upon by a man in Mea Shearim.

The more-than-century-old American Colony Hotel with its tranquil inner court and muezzin in a mosque nearby, whose call to prayer reminded Muslims of their duty to God, was situated in the Arab quarter of Jerusalem. The Colony was an oasis apart from the traffic noises and smells and shouts coming from the streets outside. Its courtyard, designed around a fountain and lily pond, was one of the celebrated gardens of the Middle East. Courtyard fountains were symbols of wealth in the Muslim world: their cooling jets consumed precious water, and the steady sounds of splashing induced repose. Once a pasha's palace for his harem, the Colony was a refuge in Ottoman style for journalists and others who decided not to stay at the King David Hotel in West Jerusalem, despite its unmatched views of the Old City. This was a place for Westerners and Palestinians to meet with ease as they huddled in conversations over ashtrays and coffee cups. A subtle aura of deal making and trysting floated in the air. An American expatriate, Freddy Weisgal, played jazz on the piano in the red-walled bar for his many friends, including me.

The American Colony was founded at the same time as the Mea Shearim, not far away. The Spafford family of Christians had migrated from Chicago to Jerusalem after the Great Fire of 1871. Soon they and other Americans were training Arab and Jewish mothers in child care, teaching English, and nursing the sick. In my day, Horatio and Val Vester managed the hotel, and we became friends.

At Easter, Father Jerome Murphy-O'Connor, my sons Paul and Mark, a few friends, and I rose in chilly darkness to meet on the Hill of Evil Counsel from which we could look toward Jericho. "Father Jerry," an Irishman who had spent decades in Jerusalem, was a leading archaeologist and writer of guidebooks to the Holy Land, a lean and learned man who lived for his studies yet enjoyed the pleasures of good company, especially young people. As the sun's rim appeared we heard dogs bark and roosters crow, energizing sounds of a new day in the valley. Father Jerry read from the Bible while other groups of worshippers sang hymns. Then we enjoyed an Easter champagne breakfast spread upon the ground. In a different way Ramadan, the monthlong Muslim holiday of fasting from dawn to sunset to make people mindful of the poor, touched us in its nobility and self-denial.

My favorite place in Jerusalem lay hidden in the Arab Quarter. Walking downhill through narrow streets toward the Temple Mount, I could turn into a small and empty square, one side of which was open to an astonishing view.

Below were the red tiled roofs of cramped Arab homes, cats stalking across them. Straight ahead, also below, was the Western Wall with the golden Dome of the Rock above it. Beyond the Old City the spire of a Christian church rose from the Mount of Olives. All of this visible in one frame. I went there because this sight was such a powerful physical representation of the confluence of three ancient faiths in Jerusalem. I could stand in that peaceful square and see evidence in stone of the great crosscurrents that had shaped, with so much bloodshed, the city's course through history. Religion surrounded you in Jerusalem, swirling about you like a whirlpool. There, you could not avoid thinking of gods. Jerusalem was humbling. After a trip abroad I did not feel fully returned until I had walked to the Wall and touched it with my fingers.

Jerusalem was a place of many cycles of religious observances, none more solemn than Yom Kippur. During that time of atonement and soul-searching the city came to a silent standstill. I recall walking with my son Mark down King George V Street, a major thoroughfare now deserted. Eleven-year-old Mark spread himself out in the middle of the street, looked up at the sky, and laughed, celebrating the absence of people and traffic. We turned into Mea Shearim and no longer spoke. Its narrow streets were hot and empty. Only murmurs from synagogues and the buzzing of flies broke the hush. On Yom Kippur a Jerusalem so noisy at other times was filled with the sounds of birds.

Because Jerusalem had no international airport, this city on hilltops was approached from the ground, from either the sea or the desert. In the early 1980s, there was a feeling of having reached a small and quiet place, a sparse and somber enclave where scholarship and gods held sway.

Israel's Settlements

In contrast were the Jewish settlements expanding on Arab land along East Jerusalem's municipal boundaries. They were solid apartment complexes serving also as walls against Palestinians, interrupting the skyline in their newness like discordant notes of music. They offered middle-class Israelis having jobs as far away as Haifa spacious, subsidized housing with tax benefits and spectacular views. Settlements built by Arab labor were crowding a city of open spaces and squeezing it toward its ancient core, changing the way it felt to live in Jerusalem. The Old City was becoming quaint, less a seamless part of Jerusalem as a whole.

Following Israel's victories over its Arab neighbors in the 1967 Six-Day War, Jewish settlements spread across the Israeli-occupied West Bank, Gaza, and the

Golan Heights in Syria, appearing on hilltops and at other strategic sites. The Fourth Geneva Convention, to which Israel was a signatory, stated that "the occupying power shall not deport or transfer parts of its own civilian population into the territory it occupies." Yet Likud and Labor governments alike built settlements. They were "facts on the ground," in their patron Ariel Sharon's phrase. Over the years the U.S. government followed the growth of settlements on occupied lands with concern but did little about these metastasizing obstacles to peace other than issuing the rare protest noting their expansion.

Settlements could serve as remote strategic outposts for ideologically driven Jews eager to push Palestinians off land on which they had lived for centuries in order to claim a biblical Judea and Samaria for themselves. Settlements outside the cities usually began with mobile homes on hilltops quickly to be converted by the Israeli government into self-sufficient enclaves with connecting roads, diverted water, electricity, and lavishly irrigated farmlands. "The settlements are Israel's answer against the establishment of a Palestinian state," Defense Minister Sharon stated in 1982 while I was in Jerusalem, as reported by Ari Shavit, an Israeli journalist for *Haaretz*. Sharon made this pronouncement at an official ceremony transferring an army outpost to civilians building a new settlement. Soon their bulldozers would uproot old olive trees and destroy the vineyards and livelihoods of Palestinian families living nearby.

Some perspective will help. In 1982 during my stay there were about one hundred Jewish settlements on the West Bank and in Gaza with a combined population of more than twenty thousand Jews. By 2004 there were approximately two hundred thirty-five thousand settlers in these areas living in a great many new settlements, with an additional one hundred eighty thousand Israelis living on former Arab lands around East Jerusalem—roughly a twentyfold increase in settlers inhabiting occupied territory.

The ancient city of Hebron on the West Bank disturbed me viscerally. I found something crushing and evil about the place, a moral blindness on the part of Jewish settlers. I never walked its streets, nor did I choose to eat there. I made it a point, however, to drive past a settlement established by religious zealots, some from Brooklyn, in the very heart of Hebron. Hadassah House in the former Jewish quarter, its ownership disputed, was established in an old Arab building of stone three stories high near the central square and mosque. On its rooftop were searchlights trained downward, sandbags, and a guard shack manned by settlers brandishing Uzis. A large blue-and-white Israeli flag bestowed the look of a military outpost with a message of contempt for Arabs. Outside were strung coils of barbed wire. Female settlers in their shorts and

T-shirts hung out the wash. To me, understanding the capacity for hatred on both sides, that settlement was an unnerving sight. In 1994, an Israeli from a large settlement nearby massacred at least twenty-nine Muslim worshippers at the Mosque of al-Haram al-Ebrahimi, believed to have been built above a cave holding the tombs of Abraham and his family. Some settlers at nearby Kiryat Arba venerate the assassin's memory.

On my visit to Washington in February 1983, I was summoned to the situation room of the White House to brief President Reagan on settlement activities. Vice President Bush, Secretaries of State and Defense George Shultz and Caspar Weinberger, Reagan's senior staff, and several other members of his cabinet would attend. During an eerily white night before my presentation, the heaviest snowfall in many years descended on Washington. Rising early, and in boots borrowed from the friends with whom I was staying in the suburbs, I trudged along roads barely plowed to reach the Executive Mansion.

The purpose, I was told beforehand by an NSC staff member, Geoffrey Kemp, was not to open the issue for debate but to sensitize the president to the political minefield settlements represented at election time. I was to convey the thought, delicately, that anything unscripted he might say on the subject would have repercussions in the Middle East. The problem of settlements was not new to this group, but the rate of their expansion was. My maps and blown-up photographs of what they looked like, available at the NSC, held everyone's attention. I sensed concern in the room. Only when I touched upon water issues on the West Bank, however, did the president perk up. Owner of a ranch in California, Reagan recounted in lively ways stories of his times on horseback in search of watering places.

Was it already too late for our leaders, as true friends would do, to talk privately with successor Israeli governments and warn them against their self-destructive miscalculations in annexing the occupied territories through settlements? Israel's need for security was beyond question. Bipartisan support for this principle was a basic tenet of U.S. policy in the region. But our failures to be candid and firm with the Israelis about settlements, to the extent anyone considered such initiatives, were based not on foreign policy concerns but on domestic politics—perceptions of a "Jewish vote" and the influence of lobbyists supporting Israel. There was in fact a diversity of opinion among American Jews about the settlements. Long before I arrived, the United States and Israel had not been acting in our mutual interests. In Congress and the White House political will for urging change in Israel's settlement activities, especially during election seasons, was entirely lacking. But no, it was not too late.

Medieval Practices, Modern Politics

King Louis XIII of France in 1621 appointed the first resident foreign consul to Jerusalem, "for the glory of God and the comfort of pious persons who
go devoutly to visit the holy places." He meant French pious persons. An
American consul appeared in Jerusalem in 1844. The various diplomatic rep-
resentations there during the 1980s dated back to the Ottoman Empire and
were at the elevated status of consulates general. They were neither embassies
nor traditionally subordinate consular posts as, for example, Milan was to
Rome. They functioned independently of embassy supervision and reported
directly to their capitals.

The U.S. view of Jerusalem was (and is) that its ultimate status would be
determined when the parties involved reached a mutually satisfactory agreement.
Following the 1967 war, Israel annexed the eastern, largely Palestinian, part of
the city. All other governments and we maintained that the city's status needed
to be resolved through negotiation. Only Costa Rica and Guatemala eventually situated their embassies in West Jerusalem. Along with other nations having embassies in Israel, the United States did not move its mission from Tel
Aviv to Jerusalem, in recognition of broader legitimate interests, among them
those of Christians, in the city's ultimate status, and to encourage peaceful
agreement between Israelis and Arabs. Settling the fate of Jerusalem will likely
be the last hurdle in achieving a comprehensive peace in the region.

Arriving at Lod Airport in Tel Aviv in the winter of 1980, I was met by two
members of the consulate's staff, in whose company I rode for the first time
up the hills to Jerusalem. When we reached my future home and the high iron
gates swung open to old trees and an oval lawn bordered by rosebushes and
shrubs, I saw why this Ottoman residence was one of the most striking prop-
erties owned by our government abroad. Stately yet welcoming, its rough stone
face covered with vines climbing beyond tall windows, it conjured up visions
of the history that enfolded it. As in a medieval castle, the walls were three
feet thick, cooling in summer and warming in winter.

I opened the front door and, like Alice going through her looking glass,
drew a deep breath and stepped across the threshold into a new life. Once my
suitcases had been carried upstairs to a large bedroom with a vaulted ceiling
and an overhead fan, I climbed the separate steps to my office on the third floor
and signed a telegram to the State Department reporting that I had arrived
and taken charge. Looking around at the worn furnishings I sensed an old-
fashionedness, a lingering whiff of British Mandate times. I had feelings of

possession and intrusion, an instinctive respect for events that had taken place and for the people involved in them who had lived here.

The residence was permeated by echoes of its past. They made pleasant sounds, and I thought myself the custodian of this old house and the definer, for a while, of its future. The long, arched living room with a marble fireplace and three oriental rugs set end to end contained the tables, sofas, and armchairs from which Philip Habib and his team would plan Arafat's expulsion from Lebanon. A large octagonal mirror in an elaborately gilded frame hung above the fireplace. I gazed into it as I did into any aging mirror, searching for the faces of those who had looked into it before and registering my own as among them now. We, and all else the mirror saw, were enshrined in its opacity: visits of the famous, Arabs in their anger, lovers on a Persian rug.

This was the extent of my official installation. I was not accredited to the government of Israel and therefore did not have an *exequatur*, a formal document normally issued to a consular officer by the host government acknowledging the right of that officer to discharge consular responsibilities. I was able, as my predecessors had been, to visit the foreign ministry in Jerusalem, where I was accepted as an American official exercising consular functions in the city. My calls were on the chief of protocol and the head of the consular division. Both were seasoned Israeli diplomats who received me cordially. We had the normal consular workload: Americans getting arrested, being born, dying, running out of money, losing their passports. Religious extremists and disturbed people fancying themselves personages out of the Bible visited us as well. Ours was the largest official foreign presence in Jerusalem, as it was nearly everywhere else in the world.

France, Belgium, Spain, Sweden, Great Britain, Italy, Greece, and Turkey also had their consulates general in the city. Nearly all were one- or two-person posts. By custom the Vatican's representative was first among equals with us. We formed a small and closely knit consular corps, all of whose members bore responsibilities basically similar to mine. Existing by our wits like medieval envoys, we were a band of diplomats denied normal contacts with a host government.

The consuls had different degrees of access to Palestinians based upon traditional ties and the politics of the moment. After the Camp David Accords, the United States was perceived as the instigator of Egypt's defection from Arab ranks, a strategic change that neutralized the most powerful Arab military force in the region aligned against Israel. The more radicalized Palestinians refused to meet with American officials. Informal monthly luncheons of the consular corps, held on a rotational basis, amounted to discussions of how each of us viewed the situation on the West Bank and in Gaza, and more broadly the Israeli-Palestinian relationship. They provided opportunities for me to brief my colleagues on the lack of progress in the peace process envisioned in the Camp David Accords and, later, on U.S. involvement in Lebanon through Philip Habib's negotiations.

As a consular corps we maintained formal and traditional ties to the Greek, Armenian, and Russian Orthodox patriarchs and to the representative of the Holy See. For the United States these were matters of observing custom and showing goodwill; our government usually separated church from state in its dealings, although we were officially represented at the Vatican. For the Greek consul, in particular, religious ties were his most important responsibility. The Frenchman remained vigilant to the comfort of pious persons as Louis XIII had commanded. Elaborate banquets in our honor offered by the patriarchs took place in a medieval courtlike atmosphere. We were thumped into a patriarch's presence by his *kawass* wearing baggy pants and a tarbouche on his head. This Arab attendant in Turkish garb carried a long and heavy metal-tipped staff he banged on stone floors to announce our coming and to clear an imaginary path through nonexistent throngs. The American consul at one time had his own *kawass*, as I knew from his staff encased in a slender glass box on a wall in my office.

Living and Working at the American Consulate General

Before leaving Washington, I was briefed on the ties between our embassy in Tel Aviv and the consulate general in Jerusalem. Harold Saunders, then assistant secretary of state for Near Eastern affairs, a wise and gentle man, reviewed that relationship with care because historically it had been troubled. Maintaining the independence of Jerusalem as a Foreign Service post was important, he said, and just as important was that I be perceived as maintaining it. There had been periods during which ambassadors and consuls general taking sides in Arab-Israeli disputes were not speaking to each other. Hal pointed out that Sam Lewis, now the ambassador to Israel, had a strong personality; he hoped I would resist any efforts by the embassy to encroach on Jerusalem's responsibilities. I replied that I had known Sam for a long time and had no reason to expect difficulties. As it turned out, Sam and I did not argue about our respective roles or "turf." Friction between our staffs was minimal, because Sam and his deputy, Bill Brown, and Jock Covey and I monitored the relationship carefully. Sam once asked whether he could use my residence for a social occasion at which he would be the host. I replied that in other people's eyes this might cloud our position on Jerusalem's unresolved status. He thought for a moment and agreed.

I attended weekly Country Team meetings at our embassy in Tel Aviv. Reporting on West Bank developments and participating in discussions of U.S.-Israeli relations, I provided a Jerusalem perspective. Lacking channels of my own, I occasionally urged the embassy to take initiatives with the Israeli government concerning the Palestinians. U.S. military attachés in Tel Aviv reported on the West Bank and its occupation authorities. One day on the road to Tel Aviv shortly before Israel's incursion into Lebanon, my driver began overtaking a long column of flatbed trucks carrying tanks northward. I counted the tanks and provided their number to our embassy's military attaché as a further indication that Israel was preparing to invade Lebanon.

The commute to Tel Aviv was rich in human interest for someone like me who enjoyed the passing scene. Observing traffic was like watching film set on fast-forward to the sounds of horns blowing. In Tel Aviv I noticed a taxicab waiting by itself at a red light. Seconds after the light turned green, with no one ahead of him and therefore without provocation, the driver leaned on his horn in a Pavlovian reflex. His action reminded me of an Israeli's zest for living and of my favorite toast, *L'Chaim*, which in Hebrew means "to life."

Social occasions at Sam's residence above the sea on the outskirts of Tel Aviv provided opportunities to share my thoughts with a broad range of Israelis. They were interested in hearing the observations of someone in daily contact with Palestinians, and they were curious about Washington's man in Jerusalem. Sam and I stressed that the United States had only one set of policies for Jerusalem, Gaza, and the West Bank. Visiting officials and journalists gained the same perspectives from me as they did from Sam. In this I differed from other consular colleagues, some of whom would have considered trafficking with their embassies in Tel Aviv an abandonment of virtue.

Sam introduced me to Defense Minister Ariel Sharon at a social function honoring an American artist. He hoped that, by meeting me, Sharon might become less suspicious of the consulate. Instead, Sharon said gruffly that he knew who I was and what I was doing. He was scathingly critical of me and of my staff, whom he accused of coddling the PLO. I replied that because Minister Sharon was well informed, he would know that no one at the consulate had any contact with the PLO. He turned his ample back to me, and we left it at that. As I took his measure in the early eighties, it appeared to me that Sharon considered every Palestinian an enemy and less than fully human. Once you start seeing people that way you're in trouble, I thought to myself.

Our consulate general in Jerusalem was the only Foreign Service post where

Israelis and Arabs worked side by side. When there were disputes, they had to do with circumstances at the office and were not politically motivated. I was struck by how disposed both sides were to working together and how well they succeeded in doing so. When a Palestinian employee had her baby, Israeli staff members might go to the hospital to visit the mother and child. The reverse was true. We were a diverse family at the consulate general, but an extended family nonetheless. Nearly all of our local employees had been working there for a long time. The residence staff, especially the head gardener, Sayed, had been with the consulate for decades; most were Jordanians living on the West Bank who had stayed in their villages after the Six-Day War.

When Jerusalem ceased to be a divided city in 1967, we kept our Ottoman-style building in East Jerusalem, near the American Colony Hotel, and carried out consular, informational, and cultural activities there. We never afterward were able to put to rest a canard that we maintained two consulates in a united Jerusalem: one for Arabs in the east, and another for Jews in the west. All consular work was performed in East Jerusalem, and Israelis seeking visas went there. The consul general and the political, economic, and administrative staffs occupied the compound on Agron Road, in West Jerusalem. Its top floor housed our communications equipment, and the load eventually became a structural problem. Turks had not built this home for a pasha with electronic communications in mind.

If I speak in the first-person singular about my new home and living there with only my children, it is because Mary and I had separated before I set out for Jerusalem. Separation and divorce were as common in the Foreign Service as elsewhere in American life, but a nomadic existence in stressful places added its own irritants. From the outset of my career the work I did was demanding and time-consuming, always something new for me away from a home with small children. Mary did not enjoy the social obligations of a diplomatic life. Earlier than either of us realized, we had become distant people with different goals and interests. In East Berlin we recognized that a tragedy had occurred. Divorce, even when the best outcome in a failed marriage, is a heartbreaking decay of love and trust, a confession of failure by two people once pledged to each other and full of hope for their days together.

In the most painful moments of my life, I told our children in the parking lot of Annunciation School in Washington that their mother and I soon would be living apart. Having heard quarrels enough, they were not completely surprised. A divorce would follow, I said, and I would be leaving for Jerusalem by myself. Months later our younger sons, Mark and Paul, joined me there and attended the Anglican School. Jack and Cathy, already in Washington's secondary schools, visited during summers while the two boys returned to their mother in Washington. This was hard for our children, who were shocked and hurt and bore scars that remained with them. But we managed in the end. Looking back on difficult years, I admire all the more the maturity, dignity, and inner strength of each of them in coping with family misfortune.

In the early 1980s, one's personal safety in Jerusalem was not the problem it later became. Our consulate had not yet been transformed into a fortress. I walked freely without a bodyguard, although I avoided crowds and told my children to do the same. Our stay ended before the intifada, or shaking off, began, before warfare broke out on the West Bank, and before Palestinians armed themselves with more than rocks and Molotov cocktails or became suicide bombers. There was a calm of sorts following the 1967 war and a grudging coexistence between Jews and Arabs, whose economies required each other, that made it at least conceivable to think of measures of reconciliation such as autonomy for the Palestinians. A lasting peace seemed tantalizingly possible.

Jock Covey and I began a typical day with an informal staff meeting in my office after reading the overnight cables from Washington and from other posts in the region. I might next meet with Palestinians and then have lunch with a visiting American, a journalist, or Sam Lewis if he was in town. There were daily phone calls to our embassy in Tel Aviv, sometimes attempted on a secure phone that rarely functioned properly in its soundproof booth. Afternoons might be devoted to visiting mayors and other prominent figures on the West Bank and observing settlements to report on new activities. At the end of the day I dictated the cables from me that needed to go out and mused about things in general with Jock. Throughout I was assisted very skillfully by Martha Hayward, who had served with me in West Berlin and while I was country director for Panama.

Dinner followed with my sons or Israeli friends, or perhaps with a jolly and rotund Father Godfrey Kloetzli, of Terra Sancta College. Father Godfrey was an honorary member of the consular family who was an archaeologist and a popular tour guide to the holy places of three religions. A bon vivant in a brown Franciscan habit with a rope tied round his waist, with his remaining hair forming a wreath above his ears, he reminded us of a latter-day Friar Tuck. The consulate's staff became his personal flock, year after year, no matter what anyone's religious beliefs might be. He was someone gentle with whom all of us could share our troubles.

Many enjoyable hours were spent in my office, or over a meal, conversing off the record with American and foreign journalists. We socialized with locally based reporters and stringers for newspapers and networks, whose families and ours became friends. I briefed columnists, commentators, and television anchors traveling through the region.

Diplomats and reporters lead similar lives. For the diplomats, journalists are sources of gossip and funny stories, astute thumbnail sketches of people, unique points of view, tea-leaf readings, and pragmatic assessments. Their conversation is unadorned. They are on the alert for the next story, what it portends and its underlying meaning.

The good ones live in the glare of realpolitik and are not easily taken in. Each side gives as much as it can and usually receives the same in return, with both sides being the wiser for it. The diplomat learns from the journalists' questions what they believe are the elements of a situation, and this may provide ideas for the diplomat's own reporting. Each has insights and information the other wants; both light the darkness. They are competitors, and the diplomat is an actor on the scene. By deciding what to report, and through their commentaries under bylines, journalists may also become participants in what is going on. But for the journalist, no matter how close the friendship, the story comes first.

Hal Saunders at his State Department desk in the Near East bureau might on a given morning have read in the *New York Times* an article by David K. Shipler about the West Bank. His inbox would yield my own classified telegram on the same topic, the subject matter of which David and I, coming from different angles, might have been chewing over on the previous day. David and I both intended to inform the reader, but my perspective would also address policy implications and recommendations for action.

The Israeli press and radio criticized our consulate whenever they could. Israel's free press was lively and occasionally vicious, and few escaped its barbs. There was no full-blown reporting on the consulate, but we got the occasional dig about visits to Palestinians, Israeli hard-liners in the media denigrating us as "Arabists" or PLO sympathizers. Ordinary Israelis and Arabs who watched the news and read their papers accepted our presence and what we were doing as a matter of course. The consulate had even fewer contacts with the Arabic media. Arab journalists tended to be leftist, shrill, and vehemently opposed to U.S. policies, especially to the Camp David Accords.

The way in which some Israelis and Americans applied the term *Arabist* could be misleading. An Arabist was someone who had learned Arabic and perhaps Hebrew, studied the cultures, lived in the region, and made the Middle

East an area of professional specialization. Would anyone today doubt that knowledge of Iraq and Iraqis is a vital requirement of our diplomatic skills? Until the 1980s, few Arabists, no matter how interested they may have been in serving in Israel, jeopardized their State Department careers by learning Hebrew and then working in Tel Aviv, since the likely consequence was that they would not thereafter be welcomed in Arab states.

In 1983, my prospective appointment by President Reagan as ambassador to Kuwait foundered when the Kuwaitis publicly turned me down as sympathetic to Israel—and therefore unacceptable—on the basis of my service in Jerusalem. The city's commiserating mayor, Theodor Kollek, wrote to me in Washington: "Brandon, sorry for all the trouble you had because of your Jerusalem assignment. Yours, Teddy." Nonetheless, in more recent decades, there has been a growing cadre of Arab-Israeli experts in the Foreign Service exemplified by Edward "Ned" Walker, who served as ambassador to the United Arab Emirates, Israel, and Egypt, following which he became assistant secretary of state for the entire region.

The Camp David Accords: The View from Jerusalem

I arrived in Jerusalem sixteen months after the Camp David Accords brought mutual recognition and peace to Egypt and Israel. During nearly two weeks of summit diplomacy pounded into shape by President Carter at his retreat in the Catoctin Mountains, these accords were marked at critical points during their negotiation by threats from both sides to leave. Suitcases were packed and unpacked. In the end, the accords also produced a loose framework for settling the future of the West Bank and Gaza. During a first stage, the occupied territories were to achieve "full autonomy" under an elected self-governing Palestinian authority to serve during a five-year transition period. In a second stage, to begin no later than three years after the self-governing authority was established, agreement on the "final status" of the region was to be reached. At best the clock would tick slowly. The concept was intentionally vague, neither Israel, Egypt, nor the United States wanting to be locked into specifics.

A summit meeting in diplomacy is the biggest gamble of all if the outcome has not been precooked at lower levels to within minutes of serving time. Public expectations become unrealistically high. The media tend to focus on personalities rather than issues. There is no more valuable investment of a nation's prestige and authority, no further court of appeals in the event of a breakdown. When summit diplomacy collapses, violence can ensue. Yet, sometimes summitry does work in free form. Photographs of handshakes between Anwar

Sadat of Egypt and Menachem Begin of Israel, with Jimmy Carter in the middle, all three looking a bit astonished at what they had accomplished, raised long-dormant hopes for a resolution of the Israeli/Palestinian stalemate. Peace between Egypt and Israel would endure, but the awkward formula for autonomy, bearing President Carter's signature as well, was destined to become a footnote to history.

My main task in Jerusalem, nevertheless, was to elicit support from Palestinians for the Tinker Toy autonomy process offered in the Camp David Accords. To borrow from Ecclesiastes, this was a striving after wind. Moderate Palestinians mistakenly saw no role for themselves in finding better ways to resolve their problems, nor were they willing to articulate more than their complaints, although Palestinian elites had a sophisticated understanding of democracy and basic human rights gained in part from Israel's example. Ours was not a dialogue of competing ideas on which one could build. In their disorganization and apathy, their sense of victimhood, Palestinians did not produce initiatives or counterproposals of their own. All was left to a corrupt Arafat living abroad and bent on terror, who kept a tight grip on the Palestinians and made his authority felt in Amman, Riyadh, and elsewhere in the Muslim world. In frustration I sent back cables to Washington with such headings as "Palestinians at a Crossroads" and "The West Bank: Peace Has Become a Necessity," using the one diplomatic avenue open to me, an ability to inform my government of what we in Jerusalem observed and analyzed.

My colleagues at the other consulates viewed the accords as stillborn and told me so from the outset. Their capitals did not support the U.S.-sponsored autonomy process, and the consuls did not promote it among Palestinians. In fact, they joined the critics. Begin's government was not putting its shoulder to the wheel. As instructed, I was determined to soldier on as long as possible in a hopeless cause, bracing myself for unhappy reactions from Washington to my candidly discouraging reports—the proverbial messenger waiting to be shot. There was nothing positive to say. While I had general guidance from Washington on promoting the accords, it was up to the consulate to be the advocate, devising strategies to meet our aims with Palestinians while keeping Washington informed of prospects. In principle this was a desirable situation for any diplomat: the fewer instructions, the greater the latitude in strategy and tactics. But when the objective of obtaining Palestinian support was unattainable and experts in our government knew this, the consulate's efforts turned into a charade, and American credibility in the region suffered.

The consulate's chief value lay in its continuing presence in Jerusalem as a symbol of the unresolved status of the city. During three years I was instructed only once to go to the foreign ministry, and predictably this concerned a consular matter. We contributed to Washington's understanding of the region through a steady flow of analysis about Palestinian attitudes and behavior, along with reports of Israel's settlements and occupation practices. We told Palestinians the U.S. government had no sympathy for Israel's violations of human rights such as illegal land seizures, dynamiting of homes, collective punishment of Palestinian families, arbitrary arrests and detentions, or the acts of brutality by soldiers and militant settlers occurring with increasing frequency. We deplored with equal fervor ambitions of the Arabs to annihilate Israel, assassinations of Israelis, usually in Europe, and Arafat's central role in all of this.

In April 1981, during Secretary of State Alexander Haig's first visit to the Middle East, I briefed him over breakfast on his balcony at the King David Hotel, the golden walls of the Old City aglow before us. I told him it was common knowledge among my Israeli friends that Sharon was seeking any excuse to invade Lebanon. Arafat and his PLO had their headquarters in Beirut, and Sharon would be tempted to settle the Palestinian issue in Beirut itself, once and for all, by force.

Notables and Mayors

The Palestinians I came to know were for the most part "notables" and mayors, professors at Birzeit University, businessmen, lawyers, doctors, and their wives. Few were professional women. Heading the category of notables was Anwar Nuseibeh, an elderly, aristocratic-looking man who ran the electricity company in East Jerusalem. Descended from one of the most prominent Palestinian families, he enjoyed prestige in the Arab world. He was a proud man, stern but wise, with a limp from a war, who made the Palestinians' case with bitterness politely expressed. He deplored the Camp David Accords as a sellout by all parties of Palestinian aspirations and needs. America's failure to act justly, as he perceived it, was agonizing to him. I felt he had surrendered hope and recognized I would be unable to change his thinking. But I liked and respected him and kept seeing him, believing that talking mattered and wanting him to know that I remained a friend.

Nearly all of the Palestinians with whom I met on the West Bank spoke English and had family or personal connections to Jordan, where Amman was the source for financial support and banking, advanced health care, passports, international transportation, and other amenities for Palestinians. Many had relatives living in the United States or studying there. Beyond criticisms of

Camp David, they generally admired our country and liked Americans. A tedious part of my duties was to sit through the litany of complaints from Palestinians about U.S. policies. Only a few were seriously interested in hearing my views, and time and again I was subjected to set speeches pinning responsibility for the West Bank's miseries on Washington and its dollars flowing into Israel. At the end of such days I felt drained. I might return to Jerusalem hoping to find a cheerful Father Godfrey available for drinks and a family dinner.

Bethlehem was not the imagined little town of Christmas carols but a sprawling, ugly city where hawkers pushed religious souvenirs on visitors from the earth's four corners. "This wood is from the same olive trees as in the time of Jesus Christ!" Few places stirred me less for their strains on credulity than the Church of the Nativity. "If this isn't the birth cave, it's one of the other caves very nearby," I heard a tour guide assure his flock as some were kissing the stones.

I profited from visiting Bethlehem's mayor, Elias Freij, in his roomy office overlooking Manger Square or for dinner at his home. He was a short, stout man with a square mustache and a fatalist's sense of humor about life. Freij was an Orthodox Christian, a moderate, even-tempered, and moral man, someone who did not whine and understood the Palestinian predicament in its international context. He opposed the Camp David Accords and condemned Arafat for his support of terrorism without disavowing him as the legitimate, if miscast, leader of all Palestinians. Who else was there? No other mayor with whom I spoke dared fault Arafat.

I found in Freij the Palestinian I was looking for: open to other views, fair-minded, searching for ways to reduce suffering under Israel's occupation, prepared to speak up as a moderate. He accepted Israel and its need for security. We reinforced each other without any practical effect. As a Christian, Freij had little influence over the Muslim majority of Palestinians. He paid for his courage by becoming something of a pariah on the Jordanian political scene. On one occasion he suffered the added indignity of having the entrance to his home guarded by Israeli soldiers for several days. "For your protection," they told him. That was an offense I brought to Sam Lewis in Tel Aviv with good results.

For a different and more broadly based Palestinian perspective I might call on Karim Khalaf, the former mayor of Ramallah, who was one of two mayors to lose his legs in car bombing attacks perpetrated by the right-wing Jewish group TNT, or Terror Against Terror. Khalaf lived in Jericho thereafter, but I had known him in Ramallah too. He was a flamboyant radical, one of the most outspoken mayors on the West Bank, and dismissive of Camp David. Even after the amputations, Khalaf never lost his fire. When I talked with him in the shade of his orange trees in the valley of Jericho, he was full of sparks and anger toward the Israelis and the Americans, a fount of Palestinian hard-line rhetoric. He, too, was not interested in hearing my views. But he was always, in the Arab way, a warm and welcoming host, unhappy if I did not share coffee and food and take some of his oranges home to Jerusalem.

Israeli occupation authorities deported to Jordan two West Bank mayors accused of being PLO supporters. They were respected leaders among the Palestinians of Hebron and Halhoul, thoughtful men who were not radicals or demagogues. Deportation left their families, who chose to stay on their land, in dire straits. Western governments, including our own, protested Israel's internationally publicized actions. To implement the Camp David Accords, the United States and Israel needed the support of the West Bank's mayors, particularly those of moderation and stature. We required the Israelis' cooperation, urging that they avoid repressive measures on the West Bank and in Gaza.

I decided to visit the wives and children of the two deported mayors in their difficult circumstances to ask how they were faring. In Jerusalem, I was pleased when these women stopped by my office. I recognize now that this gesture on my part, which became widely known among Palestinians and doubtless to Minister Sharon, may have been the most effective step I was able to take in three years to reach out to Palestinians as a credible and humane American official. One of the deported mayors, on a visit to the United States fifteen years later, telephoned me for the first time to express his gratitude.

Arafat and Monica Lewinsky

During my service in Jerusalem and for a decade afterward, American officials were prohibited from contact with Arafat or any member of the PLO. But that would change after the Oslo Accords of 1993, which provided for the reciprocal recognition of Israel and the PLO. I had the unexpected experience five years later, on January 23, 1998, of sitting down to a conversation with Yasir Arafat in his Washington hotel suite. I was among a small group of Middle East experts from the Council on Foreign Relations. Arafat had just returned from a meeting with President Clinton in the Oval Office. It happened to take place during a low point in the Monica Lewinsky scandal. Members of the media, allowed to pour like floodwaters into the president's office at the beginning of meetings with foreign visitors, had little to ask about the Middle East on that day, Arafat's presence notwithstanding, but a great deal on their minds about the president and Ms. Lewinsky.

How many times on the evening news have we watched foreign callers at the White House stare blankly for minutes on end as questions are hurled at our presidents, often uncomfortable ones, having nothing to do with their visits? Inevitably, such guests feel slighted, if not insulted. On the evening news that night, Arafat's discomfort as he sat in the Oval Office in an arm-chair beside Clinton, not knowing which way or even *how* to look, reflected his bafflement over the attention accorded the president and the intern.

I admit to having savored the prospect of an encounter with Arafat, who loomed large yet tantalizingly inaccessible during my years in Jerusalem. Riding up in the hotel's elevator, I wondered what it would be like to shake his hand and, in a few moments, address him as "Mr. Chairman." Arafat was cordial enough in his greetings, looking everyone in the eye and smiling, but soon became taciturn as he expressed disappointment at what he felt was a flagging U.S. role in the struggle to define a Palestinian state. He appeared distracted and had nothing positive to say. I noticed the trembling of his lower lip and of his small, almost feminine hands and became annoyed by his habit, as he spoke, of adjusting his kaffiyeh headdress. Arafat's answers to our questions were perfunctory and querulous, delivered in Arabic, although his English was adequate. He seemed to me smaller than life, less forceful or compelling in voice and presence than his public persona or propaganda suggested. His stubble of a beard gave him a slovenly look. I searched for signs of warmth or compassion beyond the carping in what he said but found nothing that morning. More disappointing was Arafat's avoidance of a larger vision in talking with a group receptive to such perspectives.

Walking home afterward, I recalled Karim Khalaf and other radical Palestinians I had known on the West Bank. Unlike Arafat, they were living day after day under the pressures and injustices of Israeli military occupation, Khalaf having lost his legs to Jewish terrorists. I did not remember Karim as bitter or petulant. He had a kind of exuberance about being Palestinian, an openness in his anger that made him easier to read, more consistent, and seemingly less duplicitous. His protestations finished, he became cordial and relaxed. Disagreeing with Karim, I understood him as a person.

An Evening in Batir

It seems incongruous as I write in a time of mass slaughter among Palestinians and Israelis to recall a solitary death in the early 1980s. Simply, this is about the shooting of an adolescent girl and its impact on me as I learned from her parents what had happened. The snuffing out of her life remains a metaphor in my thoughts for the larger conflict itself.

Mohammed Latif, our majordomo at the residence, lived in the village of Batir near Jerusalem. One day he invited my sons and me to his home for dinner. We stopped to visit a friend of his nearby whose teenage daughter had been killed while walking home from school a few days before by a stray bullet fired by an Israeli soldier. Such incidents prior to the intifada were rare. Mohammed wanted us to meet her family. The girl's parents did not lash out at me; they spoke of their grief quietly and with somber dignity. They told me they were unable to understand why the United States did nothing as violence increased on the West Bank and innocent people like their daughter were killed. They could not accept—few Palestinians could—that we did not have the power to curb the Israeli government if we chose.

Sitting with them at dusk on their stone terrace in Batir, looking over the vineyards in the valley below and hearing the father speak of this tragedy, I found my thoughts and feelings providing a deeper understanding. The mother showed me a photograph of her daughter, a smiling girl in her teens with dark braided hair like that of my daughter Cathy. The immediacy of their loss was poignant, as were the composure and resignation with which it was accepted and conveyed to me. No angry mob could have had anything like this effect on my understanding of the human toll of occupation. There was also, I realized, a price paid by the occupiers, young soldiers many of whom found the brutal aspects of their duties repugnant.

In Jerusalem later that night I worked on a cable, "The Dark Side of Israeli Occupation," drawing on the evening's conversation and its mood, trying to make a real person of this innocent victim of the Arab-Israeli conflict whose name I did not know. One girl dead. Words flowed through my fingers into the typewriter as I sat alone for a long time in the quiet of my office, determined to avoid hyperbole in conveying the essence of that event. Rarely did our reporting arouse so much comment. My words struck a chord of understanding among colleagues in the Middle East, including Tel Aviv, but especially in Washington, where I was told Secretary Shultz read what I had written. In a short time my cable would be forgotten, but I did not want the girl to be forgotten. The conflict would continue, and our government would not change its stance toward Israel.

I wrote about that girl and recall her now, because death is bestowed singly on each of us and has meaning. After all the negotiations, signings of accords, photo opportunities, cheering, and peace prizes, the accomplishments of states-men seep into the lives of remote and ordinary people and carry consequences for everyone. I asked myself, after dutiful years in Jerusalem peddling accords that couldn't work and reporting on settlements that wouldn't stop, what remained of personal, if painful, satisfaction from my efforts. In a way mean-ingful to me, this lay in writing about a girl who had needlessly been killed and in visiting the wives of two mayors who had wrongfully been expelled.

A Peacemaker Views His Peacemaking

In March 1983, former president Carter and his wife, Rosalynn, visited Jeru-salem and spent part of a day traveling with me on the West Bank. In retire-ment, Carter seemed more relaxed and at peace with himself. The three of us sat in the back of an armored limousine, provided by the Israeli government, in which Carter and his wife held hands and she kicked off her shoes. An Israeli security officer speaking fluent English rode in front, and security vans preceded and followed us. Carter, a cosigner of the Camp David Accords, already moribund as they applied to autonomy, wanted to meet Palestinians and hear their views. As I had determined beforehand, most of my contacts would be willing to see him only in my home. Carter visited Ramallah, where Arab youths threw stones at vehicles following his motorcade. We drove to the huge settlement of Ma'aleh Adumim, a sight that shocked the Carters.

Jimmy Carter's interest in the Palestinian-Israeli relationship was deep, and he felt sympathy for Palestinians. His lined face, with its muscles often tense, told much about his ability to concentrate. His questions and how he followed up on them reflected the pragmatic, fact-gathering, and analytical bent of the naval engineer he once had been. Small talk did not interest him, and his eyes stayed cold. But he seemed to me, as he sorted data into categories of right and wrong, a man of exceptional religious and moral roots. The Carters pro-foundly enjoyed their visits to religious sites under the tutelage of Father Godfrey. By the end of his stay in Jerusalem, Carter recognized that the benefits of the Camp David Accords were limited to the rapprochement be-tween Israel and Egypt he had brought about. He had seen for himself that the Camp David formulas for autonomy, rejected outright by the Arab states and tacitly by Israel, were unacceptable to the Palestinians and had become ir-relevant.

During a press conference at the King David Hotel on the last day of his visit, Carter did not equivocate. Asked by David Shipler of the *New York Times*

about the failure of the Camp David process, Carter replied that one reason was "the sharp disparity between the concept of full autonomy as offered by Prime Minister Begin and his government on the one hand, as contrasted with the concept that both President Sadat and I had at the conclusion of Camp David. . . . I never considered that the definition of autonomy would be so narrow as has been preferred by the Israeli Government." In key areas, such as water and land, "the offer of autonomy did not remain." Seeing Jewish settlements on the West Bank, he said, had been discouraging.

For me, in a different vein, a memorable experience during the Carter visit occurred one evening of his stay during an elevator ride at the King David Hotel on the way down from Carter's suite to the lobby. Mrs. Carter had felt slightly ill during the day with symptoms of flu, and a doctor had been sent for. She was able to go out, however, and the Carters, the doctor, a security agent, and I filled the elevator as we started off. Carter asked the doctor what was troubling his wife. "Mrs. Carter," came the answer, "has herpes." The silence was awkward as we reflected on this, eyes respectfully lowered. I wished I were at the Dead Sea rather than a few inches from President Carter as he received such unsettling news. Herpes, the doctor explained, takes many forms, including Mrs. Carter's aggravation in her mouth, and with medication all would be well in a day or two. *Whew!* Ground Floor. Everybody out to face the tourists and cameras!

On the evening before their departure, I invited the Carters and our by then exhausted staff to dinner at the Philadelphia Restaurant, our favorite place for Arab food in the heart of East Jerusalem, near the American Colony Hotel. Carter's security people, mainly Israelis, seemed not unduly concerned about his safety. My sons Paul and Mark were included. In that noisy and informal ambience, we were served a banquet at which plates of cold dishes covered the table before the arrival of rice and lamb. Arak was followed by beer. Walid, the young and gregarious owner, buried any resentment about Camp David he may have harbored. We had a lively, almost boisterous time.

Citizens and Cabinet Members Come Calling

I briefed the leaders of Jewish organizations when they came to Jerusalem and developed good relations with them. Sam Lewis had urged me before I left Washington to call on those whose headquarters were in New York. They should have an opportunity to meet me as I prepared to leave, Sam wisely recommended, and to express their views before I took up my duties. From his embassy in Tel Aviv he helped arrange appointments. I saw five or six heads of various Jewish groups, asking their advice and inviting them to visit the consulate. Most took me up on my invitation, which helped build rewarding connections. When they visited they listened to our briefings with concern, and many traveled on the West Bank. I invited Palestinians to join us at the residence, if our visitors wished me to, and most did. I had no difficulties getting Palestinians to come to these functions. They were more tolerant of Jewish leaders than of U.S. government officials. Their hostility was directed against our policies, not against Americans or Jews as such.

Official visitors arrived frequently. Cabinet-level Americans stayed at the King David Hotel near the consulate. They arrived at Lod Airport in Tel Aviv and then headed to Jerusalem in roaring motorcades. If the visitor was Secretary Shultz, I would meet him and his entourage, including Sam Lewis, at the hotel's entrance, along with the manager and additional Israeli security guards. We would then make our way through the crowded lobby toward two small elevators. The question of who would ride with the secretary in such intimacy was the nub of the matter. Sam and I had worked this over before Shultz's first visit, and Sam said: Jerusalem being Jerusalem, why don't you do the honors? The secretary, one security guard, and I got into one of the cramped elevators and rode to the appropriate floor, mostly in silence, especially with Shultz. Photographers snapped pictures of us entering and exiting this narrow conveyance, and that was the point. I tried to look as if I had just learned something important. We called this ritual "elevator diplomacy," and if those vertical boxes could talk, what tales, not just of furtive kisses, would they tell! Before my time, Secretary Kissinger and his little group had once spent forty minutes in each other's company when the elevator got stuck on their descent to dinner. That is an experience I am happy to have missed.

Teddy Kollek: Mayor of a "Unified Jerusalem"

Jerusalem's renowned mayor, Teddy Kollek, was in office during my time, as he had been for many years before and was to be long afterward. When I arrived, I called on him. Ours was a cordial but tough meeting. Kollek told me he was trying to unify Jerusalem in reality as well as in name, and the American Consulate was trying to divide it. He deplored the fact that we held two Fourth of July receptions: one in West Jerusalem and the other in East Jerusalem for Palestinians. When June came around, however, I sent out invitations to two July Fourth events, as was the custom. Teddy Kollek went through the ceiling and wrote an unkind letter to Sam Lewis that Sam forwarded to me for a reply. Diplomatic disputes also concern appearances.

We did not want to hold two July Fourth receptions and were not interested in exacerbating Israeli-Palestinian divisions. I believed, however, there was no other reasonable choice and that the problem had not been created by the United States. If we had attempted to hold just one event, no Palestinians, in those days of resentment over the Camp David Accords and worsening West Bank repression, would have come, thereby creating a breach in our relations difficult to repair. The other consuls all felt obliged to offer separate receptions on their national days, something that troubled Kollek less. I saw no way to satisfy the mayor and at the same time continue an open, if not particularly fruitful, dialogue with Palestinians. I had been able to bring Israelis and some Palestinians together socially at my home, but during 1980–1983 that would not have worked at a public function. A change in U.S. behavior in a matter such as this would have sent confusing signals as to our motives and timing.

So we entertained Israelis in the shaded summer garden of the residence, along with prominent Americans in the Jerusalem community, journalists, a protocol person from Kollek's office (the mayor himself, of course, did not come), and friends of mine such as former supreme court president Yoel Sussmann; Chancellor Avraham Harman of Hebrew University; Walter Eytan, founder of Israel's foreign service; the writer Amos Elon; their wives; and a variety of religious leaders in their robes and headdresses. Our consular colleagues attended this pleasant, elegant garden party that managed to have a softly filtered 1920s look, with women in light summer dresses and broad-brimmed hats and some of the men in blue blazers.

The second celebration was held the following evening in East Jerusalem on the roof terrace of the American Colony Hotel. This was a smoky feast of grilled meats and Arab dishes, lit by strings of colored lights and animated by the thumps, tambourines, and seductive songs of Arab music. Palestinians attended this affair in great numbers, bringing their families and uninvited friends. Camp David was put aside. Journalists, religious leaders, and some Israelis came to both events, including Israeli reporters and columnists who enjoyed friendships with Palestinians. Our consular colleagues arrived once more as we celebrated late into the night with the Vester family, who for so long had been associated with the American Colony.

Those July Fourth parties bedeviled us during the time I was in Jerusalem. I gritted my teeth and held them anyway and finally was able to pacify Kollek in the matter as he watched and deplored the deterioration of conditions for Palestinians on the West Bank. At stake, I reminded him, were our contacts with even moderate Palestinians. Kollek often came to the residence, where his preference was to sit on the floor with his legs crossed like a Buddha, while our guests talked with him about Jerusalem and his plans for its future. I took congressional delegations to see him or, if their stay was short, gave a reception and invited Teddy. One hostile congressman, on returning to Washington, told a columnist that the consulate staff and I "favored the Arab side." When Teddy read this he called the congressman and rebuked him.

I also spent time with Teddy planning the visits of American officials. During my stay, when cabinet-level Americans toured the sights in predominantly Arab East Jerusalem, I, but not Kollek, would escort them, although Teddy rightly considered himself mayor of the whole city. In 1983, when Caspar Weinberger was scheduled to visit Jerusalem, I cabled the State Department arguing that the practice of having the consul general escort an American official within East Jerusalem, while Kollek acted as host in West Jerusalem, was an anachronism. Kollek justifiably resented this distinction, and Palestinians didn't care. Splitting the city this way was unseemly and ran counter to our interests. We maintained that Jerusalem was one city and yet, when it came to specifics, we sometimes needlessly treated it as two.

I informed the State Department that, unless instructed otherwise, I would ask Mayor Kollek to escort Weinberger through West *and* East Jerusalem. I phoned our desk officer in Washington, after having discussed my proposal with Sam Lewis, to alert the department to this message. Go ahead, he said, and see what happens. I called on Teddy to share the news. Before I could begin, he said to me in his gravelly voice that he knew why I was there and was sick and tired of the usual pitch about visitors. I told him to calm down and listen. I was there to discuss the Weinberger visit. He said he didn't want to hear about it. I then told him we were proposing that he escort the secretary of defense through West and East Jerusalem. Teddy looked at me, stunned. He finally growled: "God bless you!" Weinberger, Kollek, and I traveled around all of Jerusalem in a minivan. When we alighted inside the old walls, Teddy turned to Weinberger and said: "You know, you're making history!" I had briefed Weinberger, and he understood the reference. This is what passes for progress in the Middle East.

Teddy took pride in the acres of flowers he had ordered planted in Jerusalem. There were small parks, and flower beds divided the boulevards. Driving around the city in his battered Volkswagen Beetle, Teddy occasionally spied someone picking a flower. He would slam on the brakes and pounce on the unlucky person. "What would happen to this city if *everybody* picked its flowers?" he bellowed. The target of this outburst from the mayor would be mortified, but what can you do with a flower once you've picked it?

Writ of *Ne Exiat*

One of my purposes in returning to Washington during the spring of 1983 was to be present in court for final divorce proceedings. My marriage no longer held together, even at its edges. Mary, living in Washington, had changed lawyers and thus had someone new working with her. One afternoon as I was briefing members of the State Department's Policy Planning Staff on Palestinian attitudes, two federal marshals appeared in the outer office with a warrant for my arrest on a writ of *ne exiat*, an order issued by a judge when someone is believed to be intending to flee a country to escape the law. A secretary came into the conference room where I was speaking, interrupting me with a note saying I had visitors outside who told her they could not wait. The most surreal experience of my life was about to unfold.

Thoroughly confused, I left the briefing to confront the marshals. They walked me down a corridor and frisked me in a men's room fortunately free of colleagues relieving themselves. After assuring my captors I wasn't going to bolt and did not require handcuffs, I was escorted from the building through its front entrance into an automobile across the street. The marshals drove me to the District of Columbia Jail, where I was allowed to make one phone call. After I talked with my lawyer, Peter Sherman, I was taken to a large area with holding cells filled by the newly apprehended. My arrival was jeered by fellow inmates, a suit and tie setting me apart in a sea of T-shirts and jeans. On instructions from a policeman seated at a table I began emptying my pockets for an inventory of everything I possessed; my calling cards were duly counted. The next two hours were spent in a private cell reserved, I thought with what humor I could muster, for errant diplomats. With time to pace and think once my shock was overcome, I recognized that this shabby ploy intended to embarrass me and hurt my reputation, which it briefly did, was so witless it would probably help me in divorce proceedings, which it also did.

Receiving word that bail was on its way, the head jailer unlocked my cell and escorted me to his office to wait in improved surroundings. There I sat facing rows of nude playgirls taped to a wall: proud breasts, spread knees, nothing left to the imagination. Peter Sherman provided the stipulated $1,000 in cash, and again I breathed free air. The following morning an irritated judge vacated his own order and rebuked Mary's lawyer for her tactics. In its Washington features column a few days later the *New York Times* alluded to this incident without mentioning my name, lightheartedly depicting me as a Foreign Service officer involved in divorce proceedings trying to elude federal marshals in a merry chase through the halls of the State Department.

Gaza: The Strip on the Other Side of Israel

The Gaza strip is a largely sandy, narrow rectangle of land extending twenty-three miles along the Mediterranean shore. Surrendered by Egypt during the 1967 war, it abuts the Egyptian coast. In area Gaza is roughly twice the size of Washington, D.C., but its population density is one of the highest anywhere.

More than one-half of its inhabitants live in refugee camps dating back to the establishment of Israel in 1948. Arab states refused to grant Palestinian refugees citizenship, and Israel did not permit their repatriation. The United Nations under its Relief and Works Agency has ever since administered these camps. While spending the summer of 1951 in Cairo with my parents, I visited one of them and found living conditions predictably appalling. Gaza remains in stark contrast to the West Bank in the ways its people and buildings are jammed together and in the economic and social consequences of refugee camps overwhelming local life. Gaza is a place where people's fortunes decline.

With resentment flowing through their veins, generation upon generation of pent-up, unemployed men and women have been raised in such camps. In my time Gaza's problems existed on a smaller scale, and there was a semblance of order in the employment of men as fishermen and day laborers on the Israeli side. Gaza was not yet the powder keg it would become.

I usually asked my Palestinian driver, Ibrahim, to return me to Jerusalem by starting off on dirt roads coursing through a refugee camp along the shore where I could see the squalor for myself. The lessons Palestinian youths were being taught by their elders were troubling. They were learning to hate Israelis, to taunt their forces, and to see an Israel backed by the United States as the cause of their suffering. Under Arafat and the militant Islamic Hamas movement they would become radicalized, armed, and suicidal terrorists who would enter Israel to create mayhem and threaten its security. Years later I watched newscasts of these youngsters, now men, leading tumultuous funeral processions of comrades they called martyrs. The next generation of boys running alongside were, in their turn, becoming indoctrinated by hate-filled role models. In scenes on television depicting riots, one does well to look at youths in the mob and at what is being graved in their minds to be remembered and passed along through time.

I also went to Gaza for a change of scene and pace, a haven from Jerusalem, a place where I could wear shorts, sandals, and a straw hat. The United Nations maintained a recreational compound there for its own people but available as well to the consuls of Jerusalem. This amounted to a handful of rude, un-air-conditioned cabins by a primitive clubhouse built on a rise above the Mediterranean dunes. A greasy Arab kitchen, buzzing with flies, offered succulent prawns from the day's catch served on a porch of wooden planks shaded by a tattered awning, a porch overlooking an empty sea. With boiled prawns came wedges of lemon, deep-fried potato slices with sea salt, a spicy mayonnaise, and a cold Heineken or two. As surf pounded the deserted beach, water raced up sandy inclines until it had spent itself in green and foamy pools, only to be sucked back and cast up once more in the next thunderous onslaught. So it had been for millennia along Gaza's shore, where powerful rhythms of ebb and flow freed me from stress and time.

On my final visit to the UN club in Gaza, I idly watched from its porch a small fishing boat not far out on a shipless sea rising and disappearing in silky swells. Two Arab fishermen stood working their nets. The boat sank from view into a trough once more and rose, capsized, on the next wave. There was no sign of the men. Nothing. The completeness and finality of their disappearance below that shimmering surface, without sound or apparent struggle, was as if someone had painted them out. Helpless to do anything to save them, I took this tranquil seascape as an omen that the time had come for me to leave Jerusalem and what is called the Holy Land.

My years in Jerusalem were intellectually thrilling, professionally disappointing, and emotionally battering. Never had I lived amid passions like these. I learned how difficult it was for a diplomat there to hold the middle ground and stay sane. I felt trapped in linear history, beginning who knows when, living with ghosts of ancient prophets whose teachings led to good but also to zealotry, slaughter, and misery. Now Palestinians and Jews were opposing each other in an uneven struggle that begged for justice and compromise and, on some far-off day, forgiveness by both sides. I saw psychological barriers to peace building everywhere and wondered how they could be overcome any time soon. Were they destined never to disappear, as some would argue?

The end of my marriage and its harm to my children weighed on me. Alone and depressed on many an evening, wearing the private face behind my public face, I turned to alcohol for solace it did not provide for long. At such times I felt confined within my walled Turkish mansion as the only adult living there. After years of being wed, I hardly knew how to ask another woman out. The first time I barely uttered the words, and to me they had the solemnity of a marriage proposal. At different periods in Jerusalem, I entered the lives of two women, one a Jewish Parisienne drawn to Jerusalem by her friends and faith, and the other an American writer from Michigan. They were sophisticated, warm, and attractive people with good careers of their own, and we became passionate and happy for a while. But these relationships were not destined to last, and their inevitable endings added to my pain. I had no coherent picture of what the future might hold for me professionally or personally. Never had I felt, all at once, more isolated, useless, or exasperated—with Palestinians, Israelis, and my own government, evenhandedly. Locked up in Jerusalem like an insect fossilized in amber, I could do little about my predicament.

Val Vester, still at the American Colony Hotel where Freddy Weisgal had played the piano in the red-walled bar, wrote to me fifteen years afterward. "I think you would hate Jerusalem if you saw how it is now, so built up and surrounded by high rise fortresses. . . . I look back on the period that you were here as a very happy one." I remembered how sad and frustrating my time there had been. Was she, in a Jerusalem now far from small, nevertheless agreeing with Mark Twain more than one hundred years later that the city in a different way was turning "mournful, and dreary?"

Middle East Peace?

As I packed up during my last days in Jerusalem in 1983, I felt profoundly discouraged about the future of the West Bank and Gaza. Carter's autonomy process had quickly run its course. Sharon's settlements were corroding the landscape and the soul of Israel itself. Our map showing their locations in red resembled the skin of a child with a severe case of measles. I saw no prospect for the creation of a respectable entity Palestinians could call their own. Struggles between Palestinians and Israelis were about security and nonbelligerency; land, water, and borders; holy places; the future of refugees and the right of return; the final status of Jerusalem; dignity and freedom in its many forms. Whose land was the West Bank and Gaza, and whose city was Jerusalem? By what rights—lore, history, conquest, deed, use, or occupation—did these lands belong to Arabs or Jews or both?

In the years following my time in Jerusalem there were events of greater promise. I was present when the 1993 Oslo Declaration of Principles was signed on the White House lawn one hot September morning and watched as

Israel's prime minister, Yitzhak Rabin, and Yasir Arafat—Rabin hesitating for a tantalizing moment—shook hands. Their clasp was electrifying, and I joined in a long, emotional ovation that brought tears to war-weary eyes. With Clinton in the middle, as Carter had stood between Begin and Sadat, the scene rekindled a flicker of hope. "Enough of bloodshed is enough!" Rabin proclaimed, but it was not. Soon afterward a countryman assassinated him, as Sadat had been murdered before him, and the flicker blew out.

Regarding Jerusalem itself, the heart of the matter, I suspect a generous formula for municipal boundaries and governance, security for Israel, some form of religious authority over the holy places, and international enforcement backed by the United States will one day prove acceptable to both sides. The status of Jerusalem cannot be resolved in isolation from other issues. Like a wedge-shaped keystone in the curve of a Jerusalem arch, the city is the stabilizing block for a comprehensive agreement. When Arabs and Jews reconcile, Washington will move its embassy from Tel Aviv to Jerusalem. So will other capitals of the world. For us to do so sooner, or unilaterally, would end the credibility of the United States as the reliable, indispensable broker in this conflict by placing us squarely, once and for all, in Israel's camp. The issue of relocating the embassy is weightier than political pandering during our biennial elections or gamesmanship in threatening Palestinian peace negotiators.

Ours will be a busy embassy having to cope with the afterpeace: reconstituted relationships that assume problematic lives of their own once agreements have been signed and are being implemented. This will not be the end for diplomacy. No solution for Jerusalem will be easy to carry out. The role of the United States as peace broker and promoter of democracy in the Middle East will remain central to supporting agreements reached by Israel and Palestine.

And Jerusalem the Holy City? With many new embassies and their staffs, probably two sets of them, demands will arise for land, electricity, and water; more gasoline stations and wider roads to accommodate more vehicles; an international airport; more hotels, apartment buildings, parking spaces, supermarkets, shopping malls, streetlights, nightclubs, theaters, schools, hospitals, and fast food outlets. These needs and accomplishments will be hailed as signs of progress, but I do not plan to inspect that scene for myself.

16

PHILIP HABIB

1982

Israel's invasion of Lebanon under the ill-chosen rubric *Operation Peace for Galilee* began early in the summer of 1982 and became the defining event of my stay in Jerusalem. The world was led to believe that Israeli forces would stop twenty-five miles north of the border as announced by Defense Minister Ariel Sharon, thereby providing Israel a justifiable buffer zone against artillery shells from southern Lebanon.

But the tanks kept moving, and soon it became evident that Sharon intended to go all the way to Beirut to destroy Arafat and his PLO and conclude a peace treaty with Lebanon. Foreign Minister Yitzhak Shamir and Sharon seemed to know more than Prime Minister Begin about plans for an Israeli push to Beirut. Mr. Begin in any case did not intend the Camp David autonomy process for Palestinians to succeed. How could it have in those circumstances?

As coffins of Israeli soldiers returned in a steady file and the further purposes of the invasion unfolded, the mood in Jerusalem darkened. Begin's subsequent depression, his withdrawal and isolation, must also have reflected a growing understanding of Israel's self-inflicted wounds in Lebanon. Among them were the massacres at the Palestinian refugee camps of Sabra and Shatila, outside Beirut, carried out by Lebanese Christian militia forces controlled by Israel. For these massacres Israel's Kahana investigating commission later held Sharon indirectly culpable, prompting his resignation as defense minister. A year afterward Begin himself would resign. His wife, Aliza, to whom he was devoted, was in declining health and died without him at her side while he was on a trip to California.

The invasion of Lebanon polarized Israeli society. Jerusalem's scholars and religious leaders gave the city moral authority and made it the repository of national values. Friends like the writer Amos Elon and his wife, Beth, were asking me rhetorically: What have we come to? Look at the West Bank! What is this country about to do in Lebanon? Supporters of Peace Now were the most vocal protestors. Demonstrations and all-night candlelit vigils were held in front of the prime minister's residence a few blocks from the Consulate. Moderate Israelis and Palestinians alike came to feel helpless against the tide of events. A nation accustomed to attacks from outside its borders was experiencing an identity crisis within. Schizophrenia took hold.

Our Man on Stage

Into this situation strode Philip Charles Habib as leader of a small U.S. negotiating team seeking to dislodge Arafat and his PLO fighters from Lebanon and end conflict in the region. Phil's instructions were no more detailed than that; from the outset, he and his group improvised as they went along. His deputy, quickly to become indispensable, was a Foreign Service officer named Morris Draper. Morris was a large and imposing man with a head of wavy white hair and an inexhaustible capacity for work. He coolly suffered Phil's outbursts, often directed at him, except when he shouted back. I had no idea, nor had Phil, of what was in store for us. What follows is my account of how Philip Habib accomplished a near miracle.

I met Phil while I was serving at my first post, Abidjan, in 1960. He was then a forty-year-old Foreign Service officer. From Brooklyn's ethnic mix of Jewish and Lebanese families (his was Syrian-Lebanese), he grew up with playmates who were nearly all Jewish. With a Ph.D. in forestry, Phil was already recognized at the State Department for his outspokenness and his ability to get to the heart of a matter. He had come to the Ivory Coast gathering material for his National War College essay on West Africa. Ever buoyant, Phil and the consulate's American secretary, Marion Markle, set off in her Volkswagen Beetle for a picnic in the rain forest. In towns along the road, Phil sought out Lebanese shopkeepers to practice his Arabic. Marion reported that he received a hero's welcome. He would later become ambassador to Korea, a participant in the Vietnam peace talks in Paris, assistant secretary of state for East Asia and the Pacific, and finally under secretary for political affairs.

While trying to rekindle negotiations between Jordan and Israel on water issues involving the Jordan and Yarmuk Rivers, Phil and Morris stayed with me in Jerusalem. Phil had barely begun that work when President Reagan named him his personal representative to the Middle East for the larger issues of Israel, Syria, and Lebanon. By that time Phil had retired from the Foreign Service, having suffered two heart attacks stemming from hard-driving work habits, temperamental outbursts, and the consumption of food high in cholesterol. His work on the rivers had been a low-key but important assignment of the kind offered to skilled diplomats after they retire.

Phil's hairline had receded beyond the middle of his head, his darting eyes framed by the black circles of horn-rim glasses resting on a majestic nose. A man of medium height, he was chronically overweight and bore a paunch he patted with evident satisfaction. As under secretary he had regularly pronounced that Foreign Service officers should not take vacations and believed in what he said—this tough guy and loudmouth from Brooklyn. He concealed his tender side. When he expressed kindness to people or thanked them warmly, Phil seemed embarrassed, a caring man shyly reluctant to let this quality show through.

His face expressed the gamut of emotions. My least favorite was a steady, critical glare into the eyes of another (mine, say), chin lowered, eyebrows arched upward, and *not a word said.* He would hold that pose for five seconds and then turn to whatever else was at hand. Phil was renowned for sarcasm, a short fuse to his temper, and ingrained stubbornness. He liked to stride around the room like an actor on a stage, arms waving in the air, delivering his opinions in a monologue without volume control. But he felt deeply about issues in a principled way, and his political instincts and intelligence were of the highest order. He was reachable. Bluster and cursing, mainly for show, were part of his style. Phil took risks with the courage of a bullfighter turning his back on a bull. No one's stereotype of a diplomat, he was among the best.

During his negotiations Phil stayed with me when he was in Jerusalem. He could hold meetings at the residence at any time under secure conditions, and our offices and communications facilities above the living quarters provided immediate support. Phil enjoyed the residence for its spacious and cool comfort and the quality of the household staff, particularly the talents of the butler, Mohammed, and our Arab cook, Ata. In typical fashion, however, he complained that his shirts were ironed better at the ambassador's residence in Beirut. He gorged on the Lebanese pistachios before him. "The best ones come from Lebanon." He loved the rose garden. A plaque has been placed there honoring Phil and his devotion to roses. He viewed the residence as a calming shelter from the world beyond its walls. In his early sixties and with a history of heart problems, Phil found the negotiating process over Arafat and Lebanon grueling. From time to time, I arranged for an Israeli cardiologist to appear at the residence unannounced. Phil grumbled but was pleased to have a checkup. He was concerned that these visits would leak to the press, but they never did.

When his motorcade arrived, I greeted Phil at the front door and took him up our stone steps to a large guest room, where he unpacked and hung up suits in their plastic dry cleaning bags. "A good way to keep the wrinkles out," he instructed me. He stripped to white boxer shorts, T-shirt, and long black socks on thin legs, stretched out on the bed, and started talking. Phil invariably asked about my children and how the members of our household staff were faring. We discussed the garden and its roses and agreed it needed his attention, an issue of priority on his personal agenda. Phil shared with me his concerns about the work at hand. Then he dozed off to loud snores. Soon he would be exchanging views in Arabic with Sayed, our aging head gardener, who wore an Arab skullcap and severely admonished my son Mark when he stepped on the flower beds.

Negotiating from Scratch

The PLO and Israel had been at war since the founding of the PLO, in the 1960s, as a Palestinian terrorist organization dedicated to the destruction of Israel. In 1970 Arafat established his headquarters in Lebanon. Sharon's invasion began on June 6, 1982. Within days, Beirut was under siege by Israeli forces, and it would remain so through August.

During that long summer when Phil's shuttle diplomacy brought him to Jerusalem from Beirut, he was returning each time from the trenches of Lebanon. Bombing and shelling by Sharon's forces, some of the shrapnel hitting the American ambassador's residence where Phil stayed; deception on the part of all parties to his negotiations; the helicopter rides he dreaded; the shouting matches over secure satellite telephones in his efforts to keep Washington by his side—all of these pressures were wringing him dry.

Reagan had given Habib carte blanche to resolve issues in the PLO's departure from Beirut, the Syrians' as well, and the larger effort to achieve peace between Israel and Lebanon. On the secure phone, Phil and Draper worked with Near East Assistant Secretary of State Nicholas Veliotes on day-to-day matters. Despite his bursts of temper, Phil found Washington's bureaucracy supportive, which usually happens when negotiators have access to the top levels of command and nobody at home knows what to do next. When his friend George Shultz became secretary of state and strongly supported him, Phil's efforts gained momentum. Ambassador Lewis, shuttling between Tel Aviv and Jerusalem, shared in these matters as he worked the Israeli side. U.S. Marine

Colonel James T. Sehulster was Phil's senior military adviser, providing expertise and an ability to talk with Israeli and other officers as comrades in arms.
Beyond Phil, only Morris Draper carried the whole story in his head. Phil's
amanuensis, Morris participated in all of the talks in Beirut, Jerusalem, and
Damascus and usually accompanied Phil on his trips back to Washington.

Sam's embassy staff exhausted themselves composing reporting cables. The
writing of telegrams became the principal means for decision making. Someone would produce an initial draft describing what had occurred at a meeting
earlier in the day, what Phil had said to an Israeli official for example, and how
that official had responded. Accounts of meetings tended to be detailed and
constituted a continuing record of events and Phil's reactions to them. They
were the means by which Phil carried his various readerships along, especially
in Washington. Then a two-part process began.

The first step was to decide, on the basis of a draft telegram, what actually
had occurred, especially what Phil had said. This was like watching the Japanese film *Rashomon*. Perceptions of objective reality were not agreed upon easily and could provoke heated discussion, particularly if Phil believed his note
taker had not been accurate in what was attributed to him. We tend to believe
we are more persuasive, more closely on message, than we really are. Dean
Acheson once said he had never read a memorandum of conversation between
two people in which the writer came off second best.

Once this first stage of the drafting was resolved by Phil, a second step was
to assess what the encounter signified and had accomplished, or not accomplished, and to outline the next moves. During this part of the drafting process
policy was set, and discussions with Phil became animated and prolonged. At
their end, Phil usually laid out what he planned to do next, but he did not
seek approval from Washington unless something major was afoot. The record
of Phil's actions that day, and the directions in which he wanted to proceed,
constituted the basis for his future moves. If he had decided to shuttle to Beirut
on the following morning, his reporting telegram would cite the points he
intended to make there. Back in Jerusalem that evening, Phil would repeat the
reporting process into the night. Because the hard-pressed drafters of those
telegrams required time to get them right, the clock's hands were often into
the morning hours before Phil, stretched out on one of the long sofas in my
living room, put his initials on a telegram after a final review, sending it off.
Phil rarely wrote himself. When he did, it was likely to be a short, first-person
telegram to an ambassador in the Middle East or to the secretary of state. He
knew when and how to play his cards at each table and how to put the most
important things in his own recognizable words.

The Israeli government troubled and disappointed Phil. He had direct access to Begin and admired him in some respects but found him frustratingly lawyerlike and sometimes curiously uninformed about what was going on. At Phil's request I occasionally listened in on their phone calls to make notes and sensed warmth and respect in their relations.

While Phil found support in some Israeli quarters, particularly at the foreign ministry, he received no encouragement from Sharon, in whom he lacked confidence. Phil ultimately was able to overcome this problem by appealing directly to Begin. Colonel Sehulster has shared with me his recollections of those times. "Habib's dealings with Sharon were from a position of total distrust. I can recall Habib being furious at something Sharon had told him would or would not occur only to have the opposite happen. He was acutely aware that Sharon was orchestrating everything that happened in Lebanon, and Sharon's arrogance truly frustrated him. This made his trips to Israel even more important, since he, I believe, saw that the only way to control what was happening in Lebanon was to get Sharon's seniors to understand what had to be done and that they so direct Sharon."

Phil felt stymied by infighting in Lebanon among the various factions. His Lebanese origins seemed not to influence his views or emotions. Rather, they helped him understand the courtesies and humor, mind-sets and negotiating styles, of his counterparts in Beirut, as his childhood in a mixed neighborhood of Brooklyn also helped him understand those of the Israelis. During each visit Phil asked me to brief him about the situation on the West Bank, which was relentlessly grim. He was careful to keep such matters separate from the concerns of his negotiations but on a couple of occasions agreed to pass along comments and advice about the occupied territories where they were likely to be heeded in Begin's government.

My functions beyond innkeeper and general manager were limited to providing a Palestinian dimension to our concerns about Arafat and his PLO. There could be no formal role in these negotiations for a consul general working in the diplomatic limbo of Jerusalem. I recognized this and missed sharing in the action, deciding instead to do everything I could to make life easier and more pleasant for those who did.

Offstage

One Sunday afternoon Phil was in a happy mood and looking for something to do. I suggested we visit the gallery of Roman glass at the Israel Museum, one of the best collections, if not the foremost, in the world. When we entered the rooms where Roman glass was on display, Phil became engrossed in delicate shapes and colors and for a long time walked from one beautifully lit showcase to another, totally absorbed in an ancient world, new glass containing old. This was one of the few occasions on which I was able to lure him out of the residence. Arab feasts at Walid's Philadelphia Restaurant with some of the consulate's staff and my children provided others. Phil cherished the quiet solitude of the residence and its rose garden and old trees. He was fond of my children. He greeted my youngest son, Mark, at the breakfast table with a hearty, "Good morning, smartass!" Phil inscribed a photograph of himself to all of us "with appreciation for their support, hospitality and friend-ship—without which it would not have been possible for me to survive."

Occasionally I gave small dinners for Phil and Morris to which I invited officers from the United Nations Forces in Lebanon and interesting people in Jerusalem. Phil was a lively, noisy dinner companion and raconteur. Whenever Phil's friend Brian Urquhart of the United Nations was in Jerusalem, I asked him to dinner with Phil in our dining room with the Ottoman arches. Brian had an informed, intuitive understanding of Lebanon and the Middle East and a profound appreciation of the capabilities and limitations of the United Nations' peacekeeping activities, on which he had worked for many years. I enjoyed taking part in their assessments and reminiscences and seeing Phil relaxed and engaged with a diplomat of similar caliber.

There is particular warmth in the camaraderie and understanding of seasoned diplomats who find themselves on the same wavelength, sometimes within moments after becoming acquainted. Decades of working on world affairs from different vantage points, sizing people up and weighing the meaning of events, create common ground. Eager for insights, gossip, and validation of their views, diplomats take an old-shoe comfort in their ancient and venerable guildship, discovering friends in common or finding they have served, at different times, in the same places. Especially among former opponents, as with Russians in our case, such encounters can be pleasurable. They present opportunities to understand the other side better, to compare each other's perceptions of recent history and reality. It is not that diplomats speak their own language. They don't beyond a few terms of art. As products of uprooted lives, however, and disciplined by careers devoted to interpreting their surroundings to others, they tend to think alike.

Habib's temper tantrums were memorable but brief. Nick Veliotes recalls one of Phil's quick visits to Washington. Phil had asked Nick to draft a telegram on some complicated matter, which Veliotes and his staff promptly did. The draft was handed to Phil, who retreated into Nick's office and closed the door, while the others waited outside in trepidation. Soon enough the outburst came: "GOD DAMN IT!" Phil yelled to their dismay. "Why can't the REST of the State Department do work like this!" It was Phil's way of being complimentary.

One of our junior officers, Carol Thompson, often served as Phil's staff assistant in Jerusalem. He seemed perplexed, at first, to be dealing with a female aide and, unable to help himself, greeted Carol in the morning with a cheery, "Good morning, little lady!" At first she was disconcerted at being summoned to his bedroom to take notes while he sat at a desk in his underwear, but she said that after a while it felt normal—she had, in effect, become "one of the guys." Carol was with Phil one day while he was talking on the phone with Reagan, saying to him: "God damn it, Mr. President, *this won't work! I'm telling you! You can fire me if you want, but this is the truth!*" Like the rest of us she was learning from Phil.

Habib had an ingenious press policy. When he went to the Israeli foreign ministry at the outset of his negotiations, he was confronted after his initial discussions by a jumble of television cameras and journalists. Phil walked to the microphones, looked straight into the cameras, and said: "Ladies and gentlemen, this is going to be a silent movie." He surveyed the startled faces for a few seconds, turned, and left. He would not speak to the press during his negotiations, except for a rare formal statement. He believed one couldn't negotiate in public. The Israeli press, moreover, was notorious for its flights of fancy and tenacity.

During one of his visits to Jerusalem, Phil was unhappy about the support for his negotiations provided by our embassy in Beirut. He was about to return to Washington for a meeting with the president and told me he intended to ask Reagan to appoint me ambassador to Lebanon forthwith. I thanked him for his confidence and said I needed to sleep on it, although I knew what my answer must be. Family members were not permitted to live in Beirut, proba-bly our most dangerous post. The judge in my divorce had entrusted our mi-nor children into my custody, although she knew we would be living in Jeru-salem. At breakfast the next morning, I told Phil it would not be possible for me to go. I had commitments to my sons Mark and Paul from which I could not walk away, especially when they were at ages in which a father's guidance was badly needed. Phil gave me a severe version of the five-second look and made his disappointment clear. He believed in "the Foreign Service first" but accepted my decision, scowling at me from time to time later on and muttering that I should have gone to Beirut. Had I done as he wished, I might have been in our embassy when a terrorist bombing destroyed it. Phil and Morris

Draper were in Beirut then, but not in the building because they were meeting with Lebanese President Amin Gemayel. Sixty-three people were killed on that day.

Final Act

In the end, Phil accomplished the feat of getting Arafat and nine thousand of his PLO fighters to leave Beirut on ships bound for destinations including Yemen, Libya, and Tunisia. Some four thousand Syrian troops returned overland to Syria. The delicacy of putting an American official in touch with Arafat, disputes among contending Lebanese factions, and the tangle of logistical planning for the expulsion itself were daily headaches. Last-minute questions in dislodging Arafat—what weapons could the PLO take with them, who would be responsible at the checkpoints and at the scene of embarkation, how would anyone know whether all of the PLO had left—became matters of immediacy for Phil to resolve. Nothing like this had been done before. Habib, with a weak heart, pushed himself until the curtain came down on Arafat as in a play in which the protagonist of many moods and stratagems takes his audience through a solo performance to the triumphant closing scene.

After Arafat's exodus from Beirut, Habib increasingly was mentioned as a candidate for the Nobel Peace Prize and appeared on the covers of *Newsweek* and *Time*. Phil, diplomat extraordinaire, was the hero of American foreign policy. But such adulation ended in October 1983 when a suicide truck-bombing of barracks in Beirut killed 278 U.S. Marines, in the worst of times for people committed to peace in the Middle East by their presence, actions, and cautious hopes. A Muslim fundamentalist organization calling itself the Islamic Revolutionary Movement claimed credit. "Stay away from this problem," Phil advised me in Washington, in case I should be asked to get back into it.

Not until May 2000, eighteen years after the invasion began, would a frustrated Israeli government under its most decorated general, Ehud Barak, withdraw all of its forces unilaterally from Lebanon without having brought peace to Galilee. More than nine hundred Israeli soldiers, men and women, lost their lives in Lebanon fighting in what turned out to be a futile cause.

Phil died in the countryside of France in May 1992, a decade after the PLO left Lebanon. He had attended a Bilderberg foreign policy gathering and then departed on a tour of Burgundy's vineyards with a French friend of long standing. In his room after breakfast he was felled by an attack of cardiac arrhythmia. At a memorial service in Washington's National Cathedral that his family had asked me to arrange, several hundred of Phil's friends and colleagues, including three former secretaries of state who eulogized him, gathered to salute an American diplomat who was a prince of a man. His daughter Phyllis told me she wanted the music to be happy.

I learned from Phil's biographer, John Boykin, that Phil's father was named Iskander Habib Jamous and that the family name of Jamous somehow got dropped during the immigration process. Had it not, Phil might have been called Habib Jamous, or "Beloved Buffalo." How right that would have seemed, if not in his eyes.

17

AMBASSADORS

Being an ambassador is different from anything done before, whether one has been a career diplomat, a college president, or the CEO of a corporation. An ambassador posted abroad is the president's personal representative, his government's highest-level emissary in residence, its chief actor and observer on a foreign scene. His or her voice is heard in the most senior councils of Washington. Before recounting how I became an ambassador, I offer a few thoughts about this function under our system of government.

An American ambassador's responsibilities are better defined in the president's letter of instructions to each chief of mission than are those of anyone else in foreign affairs appointed by the president and confirmed by the Senate. They are more explicitly set forth than the duties of the secretary of state. They establish an ambassador's authority over the activities of all U.S. government employees in the country of assignment, except for those serving under separate military commands. Our ambassadors are provided official residences in which to live that are intended to represent our people and values and also, in a capital such as Paris where the residence is more like a palace, America's prestige and standing in the world.

As they advocate U.S. policies and engage in public diplomacy, the best of our ambassadors do not keep themselves at the end of a tether from Washington or fall under the spell of a foreign capital. Instead, they perch on an imaginary rock somewhere in between. With both places in sight, and seeking to understand the needs and natures of both, they assess how, in light of mutual objectives and events of the time, each should be guided. In foreign capitals they instinctively seek good relations, even if opportunities for influence and cooperation are slim, as they were in many places during the Cold War, in my case with President Mobutu of Zaire.

Many years ago Ambassador Livingston T. Merchant noted, "The priceless asset of the diplomat is that he is *there*. He is *in* the foreign country, on the spot." Ambassadors are the most senior officials anywhere in government who deal with the totality of our relations with another country. They are responsible for providing strategic, and not just tactical, insight. Our political leaders at home are challenged to piece together, with as much vision, coherence, and popular support as they can muster, the large and shifting floes of foreign policy. To meet this obligation, the counsel of informed ambassadors able to think in broad terms is indispensable.

As John Kenneth Galbraith observed of his days in India, "The job of an ambassador is much like that of an airline pilot—there are hours of boredom and minutes of panic." Yet the ambassador should be the one most able to lucidly define the elements of relations; to understand concerns both locally and in Washington most thoroughly, while appreciating the slow shifts of power in both places; to deal with crises most confidently; to assess the future most astutely; and to anticipate opportunities and difficulties most wisely. This defines the ideal ambassador. Real people, even Galbraith, tend to be flawed: bored, sometimes lazy, and occasionally dead wrong.

Ambassadors represent only their own governments. While secretary of state, George Shultz sprang a little trap on ambassadors making their farewell calls on him before setting off, a trap into which I fell. He had a large globe in his office beside which he liked to pose with a new chief of mission for the customary photo session producing a picture eventually to be displayed on the grand piano of the residence in its silver frame. In what seemed an effort at making conversation, he said, a bit insultingly, "Show me that you can identify your country." I pointed to a large green blob at the heart of Africa. "WRONG!" he deadpanned, "Your country is HERE!" pointing to a large blue blob that was the United States. A worthwhile point to make.

Why Zaire?

As I neared the end of my work in the State Department on Central America and the Caribbean, I never regretted having passed up my first chance to become an ambassador, to Haiti. Jerusalem in my eyes rivaled many an embassy. After three years during which my reporting was closely followed in Washington, I recognized that my turn was coming around once more, perhaps for the last time. I was asked to go to Kuwait, which would keep me in the Middle East.

There is a formal, usually routine procedure in diplomacy called *agrément*, through which one government considers whether to accept an ambassador proposed by another. The Kuwaitis promptly and publicly turned me down at the highest level. I would be coming from Jerusalem, they said, and therefore was biased toward Israel. It was all but unheard of for any diplomat to be refused by another government in a statement to the press made without prior consultation with the sending government, and for a motive as fatuous as this. The State Department waited many months before proposing another new ambassador to Kuwait and received Kuwaiti officials in Washington at midlevels of the bureaucracy during this period.

Unexpectedly I found myself in Washington for nearly a year until another post for which I would be qualified opened up. Without savings in the bank, I eventually succeeded in finding a school for my twelve-year-old son and a place for us to live. Mark was happy at Holy Trinity School and did well there. My son Paul took a year off from schooling to work on a construction project and then as a cook in a Washington café. The State Department, in turn, put me to work on management projects, asking me to improve the handling of its dispersed international communication and information responsibilities, an unexplored field for me but one of importance. The solution I recommended gathered these responsibilities under a new and strongly led bureau.

The State Department's executive secretary, Paul "Jerry" Bremer, proposed that I look at his Operations Center, which was characterized by uneven performance and low morale among senior watch standers. I urged Jerry to step back and see himself as part of the problem. He worked effectively for the secretary of state; there was no doubt about that. He drove himself hard. But while looking upward, as he was obliged to do, he needed also to lead and inspire his own troops, make them feel he had confidence in them, and micromanage them less. In a hectic environment his demands could seem bossy—curt, arbitrary, and short-fused—with rarely a word of praise or thanks. A little more listening and explaining and the occasional human touch would help, I suggested.

Soon the director general of the Foreign Service asked whether I would accept a three-year posting to Zaire, a French-speaking country in the heart of Africa, the former Belgian Congo. I would be returning to that continent a quarter of a century after launching my career in the coastal capital of Abidjan. In the meantime I had not followed African affairs closely, believing my future to lie in the Middle East, Latin America, or Europe. The State Department by then had developed a cadre of people with depth in Africa, specialists groomed to become ambassadors. Zaire was a complicated place, our embassy was large, and the American school was good. I recalled, too, that a tyrannical Mobutu Sese Seko had become the bane of American ambassadors working in Kinshasa, Zaire's capital.

When I agreed to go, cheerfully to be honest about it, the nine-month vetting process of financial, medical, and security clearances began. As confirmation by the Senate drew near, I attended the Foreign Service Institute's two-week Ambassadorial Seminar, during which prospective ambassadors and their spouses, increasingly male, were guided in the ways of the State Department. We were given information and advice on how to run our posts, especially as to where the administrative pitfalls would lie, and there were many. In 1984, Shirley Temple Black, a former chief of protocol and a successful ambassador to Ghana, was the course chair. She was the first person to call me "Ambassador Grove." It occurred to me on the opening morning of the seminar that here I was, about to become ambassador to Zaire because the Hollywood actor Ronald Reagan, president of the United States, had nominated me. Ambassador Shirley Temple, the tap-dancing girl of the *Good Ship Lollipop* and my childhood dreams, was about to tell me how to succeed.

Reagan followed a practice of telephoning his prospective ambassadors, once the White House had forwarded their nominations to the Senate. His ostensible purpose was the formal one of asking whether they would accept their postings, no surprise to them as they had already spent months crawling through the bureaucracy to reach this point. Reagan did this because he enjoyed personal contact and dispensing good news, as well as exercising an agreeable side of presidential power. He was making the important point that ambassadors were his personal representatives abroad, deriving their authority from him. This was particularly necessary for Foreign Service appointees, accustomed to layers of bureaucracy, to understand. Now they would need to lead, not follow.

A White House operator reached me at home a day in advance, giving me a window of time during which I could expect a call from the president. I got myself ready at the appointed hour and asked my son Mark to pick up the telephone extension when the call came through in order to hear the president. This was dad's big moment. After several false rings from unwelcome callers tying up the line, the White House operator finally was on. "The president is calling," she said. Mark scrambled into place, his hand cupped over the speaking end of the extension phone. What a special time in a Foreign Service career and family life! A pause, and then the familiar, husky, friendly voice was on the line. "Mr. Grover?" the president asked, adding an "r" to my name. I glanced at an astonished Mark with an expression that said if you laugh I'll throttle you. To his credit, Mark kept his hand over the phone, although he was starting to tremble. In the brief exchange that followed, I told the president that in Zaire I would do my best for him and our country. "I know you will," was his gracious reply.

18

ZAIRE

★ ★ ★ ★

1984 to 1987

In 1984, as I picked up the reins of our relations, Zaire was a stable and important Cold War ally in Africa. By 1997, the year of President Mobutu Sese Seko's flight into exile and with the Cold War over, Zaire concerned us far less.

The Belgian Congo gained its independence in 1960 along with other colonies of sub-Saharan Africa, including the Ivory Coast, where I was stationed at the time. Five chaotic years ensued. The events in the Congo became one of the biggest news stories of the time. The country subsisted under wobbly leadership veering from the marxist-leaning firebrand Patrice Lumumba, until his murder in 1961, to the Belgian-influenced Moise Tshombe, with others in between. The United Nations intervened in an early peacemaking operation. Its secretary general, Dag Hammarskjöld, was killed in a plane crash on the Angolan border while acting as a mediator. Khrushchev at the United Nations memorably pounded his shoe on his desk during a debate about the Congo. Mobutu would come to power through the cumulative failures of Patrice Lumumba and his successors, whose weak performances unnerved Western leaders. The U.S.-Soviet relationship was stretched taut. In the global politics of the Cold War, the Congo disintegrated as the East German regime built its wall through Berlin.

At Lumumba's behest following independence, the Soviet Union provided modest military assistance to put down secessionists, along with nearly one thousand technical advisors for newly formed ministries, managing for the first time to establish a presence in Central Africa. The Belgian government had ineptly transferred power, and Belgian citizens who stayed behind were subjected to gross mistreatment. After five years of waiting and watching, the Congolese army's chief of staff, Colonel Joseph Désiré Mobutu, took control by staging a coup in September 1965. Soon he would dub himself "The Leopard" and create an order of knighthood around his fantasy. Mobutu acted on a nod conveyed to him five years earlier by the U.S. government, which launched him on his course and brought him token support along the way. Soviet influence ended with Mobutu's accession to the presidency. The Congo's future under his rule was sealed. In Western capitals a sigh of relief could be heard.

A Nod That Changed the Congo

The American nod to Mobutu in 1960 came from the urbane, worldly-wise, and intrepid CIA station chief in Léopoldville (now Kinshasa), Larry Devlin. No American has known the Congo as well as the legendary Devlin. We became friends in Kinshasa, where Larry, no longer with the CIA, represented a diamond firm and the business interests there of Maurice Templesman. The son of a West Pointer, Larry was reared under the banner of duty, honor, country. Due to weak eyesight, he never made it to the military academy himself. He was a tall and strong man, husky-voiced, with a cigarette between his fingers. Impeccably dressed, the tips of a handkerchief poised above his jacket pocket, Larry was a person of charm and continental manners with an Irish twinkle, for women especially, behind his horn-rim glasses. Tough and pragmatic, Devlin was the epitome of the American Cold War intelligence operative. In the fall of 2000, I spent a weekend with him at his lakeside home in Virginia. Our reminiscences would lead me to ask Larry about the circumstances, forty years before, when Mobutu was assured of U.S. support. What had occurred?

But first I wanted to learn more about one of the strangest stories among the wild tales of the Congo. Is it true, I asked Larry over a glass of wine before dinner, that early on the CIA had sent him a tube of poisoned toothpaste with instructions to get it to Lumumba? "It is," he replied. "I was told the instructions came from Eisenhower, but I didn't carry out the order. I was totally taken aback. I knew that refusal would result in my recall, so I stalled by asking questions. I did not believe the action was necessary. Lumumba was not a Hitler; he was not about to start World War III. I knew it was wrong, and it would have involved great danger for all Americans in the Congo, and perhaps for many others. How in the world would I get toothpaste to Lumumba, anyway?" Devlin's delaying tactics worked, even as he dealt with an agency

scientist, marvelously identified beforehand as "Joe from Paris," sent from headquarters to prod him along.

On the following morning, during a walk through wooded countryside, I
posed the larger question to Larry about his fateful encounter with Mobutu
early in 1960. Devlin, working in the CIA station at the American Embassy in
Brussels, first spotted Mobutu that year at a round-table conference between
Belgians and Congolese convened in the Belgian capital to negotiate terms of
independence. Larry found Mobutu, at thirty, highly intelligent, focused, and
idealistic about the Congo's future without Lumumba's baggage of flamboy-
ance and marxist rhetoric. Mobutu had potential, and his youth suggested mal-
leability; his views and actions might still be shaped. Before then he had been
an army sergeant and journalist. Larry concluded that Mobutu, Lumumba's
secretary at the conference, was the most impressive African in the delegation, and he began to steer Washington toward viewing him as the best alternative to Lumumba. While the U.S. government had no specific preferences
regarding a successor to Lumumba, "there was vague agreement that it would
be better if there were someone else," Larry said.

The moment enabling Mobutu to take his first step on the long road toward
seizing power in 1965 came abruptly, Larry continued. On September 9, 1960,
while serving as the Congolese army's chief of staff, Mobutu was holding an
emergency meeting in Léopoldville with other colonels from the regions. No
one was any longer in charge in the Congo. Late that night Devlin made his
way to the palace through UN lines to talk with Lumumba and his foreign
minister. In the waiting room was Mobutu. He wanted the army to take over
"temporarily," Mobutu told Devlin, and sought a guarantee that the United
States would not oppose him. Devlin hedged, but Mobutu pressed, telling
him the colonels would be returning to their regions the following morning.
"The decision must be made tonight," Mobutu asserted.

"I did my best to avoid responding to Mobutu's insistence that I give him a
yes-or-no answer," Devlin recalled. "I realized full well that I did not have the
right to make such a decision. I did, however, know that the U.S. government
wanted Lumumba to be removed from office. I finally gave Mobutu an affirma-
tive reply, knowing that if things went wrong I would almost certainly join the
ranks of the unemployed." Larry woke up the American ambassador, Clare
Timberlake, told him what had happened, and said he could still stop it.
"Timberlake did not hang me out to dry," Larry said. "He, too, was prepared
to face the music if we failed." Mobutu did, in fact, quickly hand power back
to a group of commissioners, who were followed by a succession of inept political leaders until he staged his coup five years later.

When we reached his front steps at the end of our walk Larry paused, lost in thought, a man sorting through an amazing past. Then he said to me, "You and I both know how dicey our work can get!" He grinned and his eyes lit up. We went inside.

A New Ambassador's Objectives

By 1984, when I arrived on the scene, Zaire had long since been brought to ruin by Mobutu. Seventy-seven times the size of Belgium, Zaire was as large as the United States east of the Mississippi River. It had strategically important natural resources, among them copper, cobalt, uranium, diamonds, gold, oil, timber, and coltan, a mineral now used in cell phones. When world commodity prices and especially copper prices plunged in 1973, Zaire suffered a major decline from which, as a consequence of Mobutu's rapacious mismanagement of the economy, it never recovered.

The United States continued to be interested for strategic reasons in a dependable Zaire. Mobutu steadfastly supported us during the Cold War. He sided with us in the United Nations on important issues and twice sent his troops to help defend Chad against Libya. We viewed him as the powerful and enduring leader of a large country surrounded by nine smaller ones he helped keep in the Western orbit. Mobutu was a supportive partner in the Angolan struggle, in which Cuban forces were engaged, and in U.S.-sponsored Southern Africa negotiations. Cold War imperatives, as we saw them, defined our ties. In a domino theory about Central Africa, Zaire was the key piece. We became convinced we could count on Mobutu to provide the staying power we sought, and for many years we were right.

I left Washington in 1984 with three goals in mind. First, the United States was committed to prodding Zaire along a tortuous path toward economic reform. At the time, there were small measures of compliance by Mobutu with World Bank and IMF-mandated economic restructuring, including meeting scheduled debt repayments in the Paris Club, an oddly named organization regulating government-to-government debt. Under duress he sold one of his jets. There was also, through Mobutu's appointment of a few capable people to key positions, barely visible improvement in the economy, giving slender hope that the downward spiral might at least be slowed. I would arrive at the opening, just a crack, of this window on progress, which would be slammed shut before I had gone. Mobutu and his cronies had been plundering the country for two decades and found it hard to stop. To keep Zaire inching toward reform, the United States worked in tandem with Belgium and France, urging the same measures on Mobutu and his ministers to underscore our common views.

The second U.S. objective was to keep the strategic dialogue with Mobutu on world affairs going in our direction. To succeed with Mobutu, I needed to understand his personality and foibles and to develop approaches of my own, fostering as cooperative a relationship as possible. Whatever diplomatic skills I possessed would become engaged. Despite the U.S. government's tolerance of his despotic ways and its support through other means, Mobutu was renowned for grinding up American ambassadors. He had curtailed the stays of three of my nine predecessors since independence.

Our third objective was even more elusive. We sought real progress, in specific ways and cases, in curbing widespread and well-documented human rights abuses. At the same time, we intended to nudge Mobutu toward democratic practices, especially in tolerating opposition leaders and their parties in exile and acknowledging a role for them in the political and electoral processes of Zaire. Mobutu was feared, as was his army, by people in villages who suffered constantly from pillaging, brutality, and rape by underpaid or unpaid soldiers exacting their "pay" from the villagers by stealing food and having their way.

No one in Zaire was able to challenge Mobutu directly, either politically or by force. Opposition leaders like Etienne Tshisekedi and members of his UDPS Party, well-to-do moderates, lived for their safety in Belgium. Our embassy in Brussels maintained low-level contacts with these figures, arousing Mobutu's suspicion and anger. He carried on a relationship with us over the years properly described as love/hate on his part. Ever with us, Mobutu nevertheless remained manipulative, someone who knew his throne was safe but chose not to recall how he came to sit upon it.

As with any dictator, to make U.S. influence felt I would be dealing less with anemic ministries of government than with the autocrat himself. For a while the tenor of relations would depend on the interaction of two individuals, Mobutu and me. Before departing for Kinshasa, I talked with my predecessors. "How did you handle Mobutu?" I asked them. "What should I expect?" Their replies gave me, from different angles, a picture of Mobutu that was all too accurate. Little that he did during my tenure came as a surprise. Not by chance, my predecessors were Foreign Service officers rather than political appointees, each with his own style and ways of approaching Mobutu. In the course of time I developed mine. I recognized that conditions in Zaire—destitution, absence of human rights, disintegrating infrastructure, one-man rule—

were not likely to change much during my tenure, short of the unexpected. The demise of Mobutu was not predicted. Little glamour attached itself to this ambassadorship.

While still in Washington, I decided to call on the Israeli ambassador to tell him of my intention to work closely with his counterpart in Kinshasa. Israel had for many years, and with our support, made serious efforts to win friends and influence governments in African countries. Moshe Arens was away, but his deputy, Binyamin Netanyahu, received me early one evening for forty-five minutes of probing conversation. I felt myself in the presence of a highly intelligent, smooth yet intense, politically attuned, and forceful man who had done his homework on Zaire. I could not miss a steely and domineering quality in his personality.

Accrediting an Ambassador

Ambassadors newly arrived at their posts follow similar procedures leading to accreditation to a head of government or a chief of state. Copies of letters of credence and recall of the previous ambassador, signed by the president of the United States, are delivered to the foreign ministry by the succeeding ambassador. The ministry's chief of protocol explains local diplomatic practices to the ambassador-in-waiting, such as when to fly flags on one's official car, and briefs him or her about the accreditation ceremony. The new ambassador, meanwhile, has time to take charge of the embassy and settle into the residence. Often this home-to-be is in need of painting and repair, sparsely and randomly furnished with basic items but lacking the personal touches of books, pictures, rugs, a favorite reading chair, and other things people routinely take along to make the place a home. It is important for peace of mind to bring personal chinaware with a cheerful pattern, so the eagle on the State Department's gold-rimmed plates isn't staring you in the face over breakfast. Any residence is likely to be dispiriting at first sight.

My formal courtesy call at the foreign ministry in Zaire began pleasantly enough. The chief of protocol had arranged to brief my deputy and me on the evening before I was to present my credentials to President Mobutu. During our conversation, Kinshasa experienced a power failure signaled by one of the loudest thunderclaps I had ever heard. We were the only people remaining in the totally dark building. No candles or flashlights were at hand. The briefing, however, continued. At the end, moving in single file, we slid our fingers along the walls of pitch-black corridors, calling to each other to stay in touch, and made our way cautiously down several flights of stairs to my car outside. Construction work in front of the building had created muddy ruts and puddles that prevented my driver from reaching the ministry's entrance. Despite high leaps toward him, briefcase in hand, I became soaking wet in the evening's final flourish. An apt briefing in the heart of darkness, I suddenly realized.

On the following bright day, three other newly arrived ambassadors and I were scheduled for individual appearances before Mobutu. Diplomats in Zaire were accredited in clusters. We were to be ready at our residences at nine o'clock but did not know in what sequence our motorcycle escorts would whisk us away to the ceremonies. The heavy rains of the previous night had caused a major leak through the ceiling in my son Mark's room, adding urgency to the list of repairs on the second floor of our new home.

Senior members of the embassy's country team were invited to join me at the ceremony. We spent three hours on my warm terrace becoming better acquainted, drinking coffee while work crews attended to the flooding and the roof. Motorcycle escorts for newly appointed ambassadors living nearby wailed and roared as they sped their charges to Mobutu, sounds disappointingly fading away as, once again, they passed us by. Finally the churning reached our gates, which had long stood open, and eight policemen vroomed into the circular drive at breakneck speed, flinging up dust and gravel to the horror of Mark's bulldog, Johnny. At last, I was on my way.

Mobutu Sese Seko

The ceremony to present credentials took place at Camp Tshatshi on the outskirts of Kinshasa. This spectacular setting was not the sort of formal grand chamber used by most governments on such occasions. I saw President Mobutu for the first time at an event staged on a plateau overlooking the Zaire River at Stanley Pool, where measureless tons of water roiling and pounding on rock made drumbeats of their own. A newly arrived ambassador faced this rushing, foaming river while national anthems were played, and it was quite a thrill. Mobutu was making a statement about power: that of nature, that of Africa untamed, and not least his own.

The Polish-born writer Joseph Conrad, I remembered, had stood here nearly a century earlier, before beginning the voyage up the Congo River that so affected him he wrote *Heart of Darkness*. Drawing on figures from the time, Conrad gave us the terrifying Mr. Kurtz, who displayed on fence posts of his garden, as lessons to others, the severed heads of Africans he had disciplined.

Kurtz was a Belgian colonizer who lived upcountry on the river's shore, extracting ivory, rubber, and more from the Congo for a corrupt and mindlessly greedy King Leopold II, who owned what became Zaire, giving nothing back to those whom he tyrannized and pillaged. When the atrocities occurring in the Belgian Congo became more widely known in the 1890s, Joseph Conrad and Mark Twain took part in the first major human rights movement to join forces on both sides of the Atlantic.

I glanced to my right where Mobutu was waiting in the entrance to a large *paillotte,* or thatched hut. I perceived in this glimpse a tall, heavyset figure standing against the dark background of the interior. My first impression was of the gleaming whites of his eyes bordered by black and severe horn-rim glasses. Mobutu was wearing the obligatory *abacost,* whose name was a contraction of a French phrase meaning "down with suits!" These were black, gray, and sometimes brown Mao-like jackets open at the throat and worn with cravats fastened behind the neck with Velcro. The effect was somber, but even here, as with any uniform, the fabric's quality and cut said something about its wearer. Mobutu's head was large and round, with his tightly curled hair covered by a trademark leopard-skin cap made for him by a shop in Paris. He had with him the carved wooden staff of a chieftain, upon which his hands rested in front of him while he stood ramrod straight. It was disconcerting to feel him standing there, watching the new American ambassador intently from the interior darkness of the *paillotte* as the band played and I stood at attention. "Well," he must have been thinking, "here comes another one."

I walked toward him trailed by members of my staff, whom I formally introduced. One of Mobutu's affectations was to insist on being addressed as "Citizen President." I had with me a letter from President Reagan that I had helped to write, and managed to get signed, before my departure from Washington. It described our objectives in the relationship and said some pleasant things about me. I presented the letter to Mobutu, who was pleased. He knew, as did I, that his ties to the U.S. government were not limited to what would flow between us.

Mobutu, I had been warned, tested American ambassadors as soon as he could, and he lost no time with me. "Mr. Ambassador," he said in French, "I want to offer you a traditional Zairian drink—coconut milk. I hope this does not violate your human rights." A clumsy dig, at best. Mobutu was sensitive to our human rights policies and pressures, and I was pleased they were having this effect. I'm not fond of coconut milk even with rum, but assuring Mobutu my human rights were unoffended I did my duty for my country. A former army colonel, placed in power by Americans, Mobutu constantly felt the weight of our influence and his dependence on our support. His pride by now resented this. Toying with an American ambassador must have seemed to him a cost-free form of gratification. So began our dialogue over the next three years.

I would meet with Mobutu many times, often alone or with one or two other Zairians over breakfast or lunch. By the mideighties and after twenty years in power, he was moody, frequently depressed, and increasingly bored with his life. The word *bored* is right. I sensed inner frustrations and a lack of personal fulfillment that did not stem from a greedy appetite at this point but came from an empty place inside. Mobutu had everything money could buy: his beloved yacht *Kamaniola*; residences in Zaire, Switzerland, France, Spain, and elsewhere; women; and jet planes. Yet I thought he was finding these distractions dull and wanting, and, as it turned out, he was ignoring his health. He wielded the absolute power of a despot and had perfected his skills at intimidation. In a deep and rasping voice that reminded me of Henry Kissinger's, he lashed out at underlings from the prime minister to a flustered server at his table. I sometimes felt I was attending an Elizabethan drama.

Mobutu's customary facial expression of irascibility gave him away, bloated lips surrounding a turned-down mouth, a scowl above. He was stiff, peevish, and short-tempered much of the time, someone irritated by nearly everyone around him and in a deeply human way uncomfortable in his chosen role. A lack of self-confidence fed his paranoia. The hoary ghosts of the Congo possessed Mobutu. He liked to go fishing alone in a cowboy hat.

True, in intimate settings Mobutu's tensions eased a bit. He participated, during brief periods that seemed like lapses, in banter and small talk, subtly making it clear, however, that his was the presiding personality and *he* was at center stage. Abandoning his *abacost* he wore aloha shirts, often in wild, rebellious patterns. On such occasions he addressed me with the familiar *tu* and joshed without regard to our roles, although I never relaxed. He liked to tease and denigrate his target of the moment; his humor usually was at someone else's expense, never self-depreciating. His laughter was brief and loud, while his eyes stayed strained and cold. I was the butt occasionally and never found myself on his wavelength at such times. More than once Mobutu played me off against his wife and her identical, equally plump, twin sister. One of them would enter some grand room where we were talking, and Mobutu would ask, "Have you met my wife?" As I rose and answered that I had, he would announce with childish delight, "Well, that's *not* my wife!" He was believed to bed them both.

Mobutu was a generous and caring host. If you were his guest at a small and purely social meal, he insisted on serving you himself from a buffet of mysterious and similar-looking Zairian dishes. These included chunks of meat suffused in a dark brown sauce, Mobutu telling each guest what was about to land on his plate, not helping himself until everyone was served. Some of this food I disguised with *pili-pili*, a weepingly hot homemade red pepper relish. I lived in dread of encountering monkey meat, a special treat in which the hands were prized. Although I had sampled exotic animals, reptiles, and insects in my diplomatic work, I drew the line when it came to monkey. This was too close to home. Pink champagne was Mobutu's drink of choice. Pink champagne and monkey palms on a day to celebrate.

He was building for himself a marble palace at Gbadolite in the northwest corner of Zaire. My diplomatic colleagues and I, who were summoned there from time to time, observed the palace's construction, and that of a fancy airport and Potemkin village nearby, with awe and dismay. Everything seemed made of green malachite or Italian marble. We were appalled to witness such vainglorious and senseless extravagance. Mobutu began spending more and more time in the Oz world of Gbadolite, far from the overwhelming realities of Kinshasa. While he thus indulged himself, the rest of Zaire—all of it—rotted.

Mobutu felt a profound attachment to his country and its soil, the way a Russian feels about Mother Russia. I thought at the time that the worst punishment for him would be a life in exile, despairing in the knowledge that he would never again see his homeland. Its loamy earth, trees, crops, and generous rain, the narrow footpaths on forest soil, the awesome game preserve at Virunga, the muddy, bending river with its mists, the sounds and smells of Africa—all held a tight grip on him. He pined for Zaire each time he left, even while indulging in the luxuries of Europe, and could hardly wait to get home again. When I met with him at his very Swiss-looking estate near Lausanne, he seemed out of place and diminished in a European setting, as if he needed all that marble and wasted space surrounding him in Zaire to define and present himself.

Dealing with the Man

Mobutu was a discerning student of world politics. After nearly two decades in power he was well informed about other African nations and their leaders, among whom he favored Houphouët-Boigny of the Ivory Coast, Omar Bongo of Gabon, and his old ally King Hassan II of Morocco, who would later provide him refuge when he was overthrown. Beyond Africa, Mobutu arrived at so-phisticated assessments of the Soviets, the Chinese, and the United States, asking me pointed and well-informed questions. He respected the Chinese for their organizational abilities and discipline and had no use for Russians. He understood competing aims in the Cold War as they played themselves out in Africa. For him such insight was vital. After all, that was how and why he came to power.

He managed his relations with the United States, Belgium, and France through cunning means aligning him with the West. This suited his three partners, who knew in the diplomacy of realpolitik what each wanted from the other and how to look the other way. I never met anyone who liked Mobutu. Carrying out policies of the West toward Zaire, with their underly-ing elements of cynicism and hypocrisy, was not for the fainthearted, some-thing ambassadors on the scene appreciated better than anyone else. For Mobutu's support, regionally and in forums like the United Nations, and for holding Zaire together under the threat of international communism, we con-tinued to back and reward him no matter what he did.

Mobutu characteristically viewed politics in terms of leaders, weighing their strengths, vulnerabilities, ambitions, appeal, and the price of their loyalties. "That fellow!" he would exclaim when I asked about another African, follow-ing his rejoinder with a clever and usually unflattering thumbnail sketch. Until his last few years in power, Mobutu met with other leaders on a regular basis to keep his knowledge and influence current. He nourished his African con-nections in ways at which one can only guess.

He admired Ronald Reagan. When the president won his second term in 1984, Mobutu called me at home and summoned me to breakfast. He wanted to discuss the elections. Reagan and George Bush had trounced Walter Mon-dale and Geraldine Ferraro, those two opponents of despots and advocates of human rights. I armed myself with statistics from the wire services and brought along a map of the United States. The greeting I received was warm. Sitting beside an enthralled Mobutu, I explained what the results signified domesti-cally and what they portended in our foreign relations. I got in a word or two about what he could accomplish in Zaire to please the new administration, to no avail.

While accurately reading the political profiles of American presidents from Kennedy onward, Mobutu chose not to understand our system of government, preferring to believe a president needed only to instruct Congress on the lev-els of economic and military aid he wanted. This misperception, real or feigned, led him to periods of anxiety in assessing our intentions. When Mobutu felt he wasn't getting his due, he blamed the American ambassador in Kinshasa. Quick to take offense, he was obsessively concerned about imagined slights to his presidency, a mark of his lack of self-assurance. If you understood this sensitivity and subtly made clear that you were talking about valid issues and not demeaning the dignity of his office, Mobutu would at first listen carefully: he needed to assess how threatening the conversation had become. Our dialogue might then deal with some of the contentious aspects of U.S.-Zairian relations. We would for example be able to discuss, albeit briefly, such topics as openness in his government's financial transactions, human rights, and the need for political reforms, all measures he professed to favor but did little to support. No economist, Mobutu was chiefly interested in how to mine the economy to serve his ends and preserve his power. And he certainly knew how to count.

By this time I had developed my own style in approaching Mobutu: comme il faut and clear in message. My tack was to seek progress on issues of political and economic reform by appealing to his vanity and sense of history. I asked him how he thought history would judge him if he failed to take steps toward reform, telling him such measures, were he to apply them, would be applauded. "Think of your place in history!" I encouraged him, with little expectation of persuading him to act in his own best interests. The old black goat of corruption, in this Chinese image, continued to stuff itself on Mobutu's Zaire.

Mobutu had scant concern for the welfare of the people for whom he fashioned a nation of sorts from the wreckage of the Belgian Congo. He was uninterested in discussing economic aid or Peace Corps programs with me, but military assistance was a subject animatedly pursued. He did next to nothing to provide schools and respectable hospitals, roads, water, sanitation, electricity, work, or housing for ordinary Zairians. They, instead, created a submerged extended-family economy of pure genius, understood by no one, that seemed to begin each day with small children collecting plastic bottles from heaps of litter. "The Leopard" took pleasure in exercising power over his people and in basking like a champion at huge, staged rallies. He felt himself accountable to no one, a Daumier figure of satiety and arrogance.

During my stay Mobutu created a small government office for human rights, making quite a point of it with me when it opened without fanfare. Occasionally I would call on the head of this office, Citizen Nimy Mayilika, one of Mobutu's henchmen. I did not get the impression that this citizen felt passionately about the rights of his fellow citizens. For the inhabitants of this great yet cursed land there had been an uninterrupted history of foreign tyranny and indigenous repression since the Portuguese showed up in the fifteenth century.

Jonas Savimbi's War

Our dialogue with Mobutu on strategic matters in Africa, and the rewards he expected from cooperating with us, strongly influenced him. He was delighted by a "black" clandestine visit from CIA director William Casey, who arrived in his windowless C-130 to discuss the civil war in neighboring Angola. Casey was there to tell Mobutu how he might once again help the guerrilla leader "Dr." Jonas Savimbi, whose UNITA movement was fighting the MPLA regime of President José Eduardo dos Santos, backed by Cuban forces and the Soviet Union. Through Mobutu, and along with apartheid South Africa, we were supporting Savimbi. Through Castro and some twenty thousand Cuban troops in Angola, the Soviet Union stood behind dos Santos in another Cold War proxy conflict. When speaking with Casey, Mobutu assumed his most statesmanlike demeanor: a sanctimonious actor on the world's stage pontificating about the region in ways intended to impress (unsuccessfully) his guest.

The Cold War favor Casey asked of Mobutu this time, which Mobutu promptly granted, turned out to be covert U.S. access to Kamina airfield, near the Angolan border but in deplorable condition, to supply Savimbi's forces with sophisticated antiaircraft and antitank weapons. We would restore the airport and its control tower and repair a gaping crater on the runway, leaving vehicles, equipment, and so forth behind. During the return leg of a visit to Lubumbashi in the embassy's plane soon afterward, a few of our military attaché staff and I landed at Kamina—after cautiously finding the crater—to inspect and photograph this hole. The place was eerie. An African caretaker appeared, startled to have found an intruder from the skies with THE UNITED STATES OF AMERICA emblazoned on its fuselage circling and then landing on his runway.

I met with Savimbi several times in Kinshasa while accompanying visitors from Washington engaged in discussions over Namibia and Angola. A guest cottage at Mobutu's Camp Tshatshi, at which we would arrive after nightfall in nondescript vehicles with Zairian license plates, was the venue for these secret talks. Once a self-proclaimed Maoist, Savimbi, now designated by us as a freedom fighter, received an invitation from Reagan to visit his White House while I was in Zaire. He was an elemental man of physical force and energy, charismatic and overbearing in personality, with a solid reputation for brutality and deceit. Savimbi's mustache joined his goatee, forming a thick black oval of hair around his mouth that gave him a threatening, catlike aspect. The questionable title of *Doctor* that he relished stemmed from time apparently spent studying political science at the University of Lausanne, in Switzerland.

From his start with Larry Devlin, Mobutu had become adept at pitting the State Department against the CIA, succeeding in establishing separate relationships within our embassy and thereby maintaining a private channel to Casey at the agency headquarters in Langley. This proved a headache for every American ambassador, vigilant but expecting to be outfoxed by both sides more than once. I know. I was.

Reagan's Special Envoy

Retired U.S. Army General Vernon "Dick" Walters twice visited Kinshasa as a presidential emissary while I was there. He had not yet been appointed U.S. representative to the United Nations, much less ambassador to Bonn. He arrived to underscore U.S. views on the urgency of Paris Club debt repayments and economic reforms in Zaire. In the usual mix we fed Mobutu, however, Walters also stressed the need to continue supporting the rebel leader Savimbi and his UNITA movement in Angola. Mobutu was flattered by these unpublicized visits, which was the whole idea.

Special envoys can help an ambassador by demonstrating through their presence Washington's attention to the relationship. They are heard with care. Such messengers bring an aroma of Washington with them and can deliver unwelcome news in starker terms than can someone obliged to rise the next morning and face another day on the job. They carry with them a message from the president. They can be sent to jolly up a relationship, if that is what is needed, or to talk tough. It is essential, however, that they not meet alone with heads of government or other officials on matters between the two countries and thereby undercut an ambassador's influence. The ambassador needs to note the words of a message as delivered by the envoy, to observe carefully the reactions it elicits, and to be able to participate with firsthand knowledge of the exchange in follow-up conversations that may be required once the envoy has left. An ambassador's position becomes untenable if the host government knows more about his country's diplomacy than he or she does. That would be a valid cause for threatening to resign and if necessary doing so.

Reagan tapped Walters to make these overtures because Walters had an extraordinary influence over Mobutu, and Walters had the legendary status of a special—even mysterious—envoy. His army career had propelled him to the rank of a three-star general. He had served Nixon as deputy director of the CIA and had been associated, initially as a foreign language interpreter, with every president since Franklin Roosevelt, no doubt for his intelligence and personal appeal as well as for his linguistic skills. Walters stayed with us at the residence, where this uproarious raconteur, a fleshy and imposing man of the world, was a prized guest not least in my children's eyes. No one enjoyed travel and adventure more than Walters, a boy at heart. He kept meticulous count of the countries he had visited, and by the time I met him few were left uninspected.

The first time Walters and I went to see Mobutu he was on board his presidential yacht *Kamaniola,* on which we landed in a Zairian-piloted helicopter while the yacht was underway, to Walters's evident discomfort. "Look, it's *moving!*" Throughout the conversation, Walters flattered Mobutu in ways so exaggerated I feared they would cause me problems later on. Nobody could be that gullible, I reasoned. On our way back in the car, I commented to Dick that he might have overdone it. Walters looked at me disparagingly and said: "Anyone who thinks flattery doesn't work has never had any." How right he was. He had read Mobutu correctly on the day he met him years before.

Dick, ever the linguist, was one of few Americans I knew who could accurately recite Mobutu's full name: Mobutu Sese Seko Kuku Ngbendu Wa Za Banga. Roughly translated from the Ngbandi language, it meant, in the polite version, "All-conquering warrior who goes from conquest to conquest." More pungently, what it said was: "The cock who jumps on any hen that moves." Little moved in Zaire that was not pleasing or profitable to its president.

Walters told me over lunch years later that on a trip to Morocco he had visited Mobutu's grave in the Catholic cemetery of Rabat. When I asked him why, Dick replied, "Because in his way he had been kind to me and helped my career."

Mobutu with Reagan

Mobutu made one of his periodic visits to Washington in 1986, and, as ambassadors do on such occasions, I accompanied him on his calls, having arrived several days before to help set them up. During the course of his stay, I flew in an Air Zaire jet with Mobutu and his entourage for a daylong sojourn in New York, where we were to have lunch with a group of businesspeople at Dick Walters's UN apartment at the Waldorf-Astoria. On the return leg I found myself sitting across the aisle and slightly behind Madame Mobutu. I looked up from my book when she summoned an aide, who brought her a small footlocker she asked him to open. Stacked side by side, in a scene from a Mafia gangster film, were rows of U.S. currency bound together with paper bands across the middle. I couldn't read the denominations, but a safe guess is they were $100 bills. And this was *after* her shopping spree on Fifth Avenue.

As the highlight of his visit, Mobutu joined President Reagan at the White House for a "working lunch." This was preceded by a pleasant meeting in the Oval Office during which a few points of substance were addressed by the president and reinforced by George Shultz and others in the room, Reagan glancing often, and without enthusiasm, at the briefing cards in his lap. Our thrust, as usual, was to encourage Mobutu to adhere to IMF and World Bank reforms as necessary steps to get Zaire's economy on a sounder footing. No thought had been given to proceeding more firmly with Mobutu on the need for drastic, positive, long-term political and economic measures in Zaire, an approach out of character for Reagan and considered unnecessary by his advisers. It surely would have made Mobutu seethe, and what effect could it have had? We were in no mood to threaten the man. "Why rock the boat?" the argument in inner councils would have been.

Instead, everyone adjourned to a small luncheon in the Roosevelt Room. Here, a relaxed American president abandoned all thought of serious conversation. He began telling jokes, many of which had communist dolts or the Soviet system as their target. These were dutifully translated into French by one of the State Department's star interpreters (those unsung heroes!), Alec Toumayan. Jokes do not fare well in translation, and these were no exceptions. Mobutu became increasingly baffled. The Americans clucked loyally, although it was clear that for White House figures like Jim Baker and other regulars at the table it wasn't close to the first time they had heard these stories. Mobutu tried to discuss Angola and the broken-down Benguela Railway. Finally, he gave in and told a rather long story himself, in French. It fell flat, although everyone tried his best. In the State Department later on, I asked Alec whether Reagan always told so many jokes. "No," Alec replied wearily, "sometimes he tells more."

Reagan struck me as shrewd and opinionated, incurious, locked in on a few large objectives that were important to him, and impatient with details. But he also was immensely friendly on the surface and brimming with good humor, no pretentious airs about him. During a briefing for him on Zaire he looked around the Oval Office for anyone who had not yet spoken, then asked with a smile whether that person wanted to comment. From his conversation I sensed that a world of horses at the mountaintop ranch in California filled his head. One felt that for him the more onerous duties of the presidency were unwelcome distractions from this private realm, noblesse oblige accepted with a small sigh of resignation. But then all I ever brought to my brief encounters with President Reagan were the miseries of Palestinians and Mobutu Sese Seko. I liked and respected Reagan despite his flaws and superficialities and felt warmed and cheered by his presence. Somehow he was emblematic of our sunny and hopeful side—an American homegrown in the native soil of our heartland.

A footnote to Mobutu's visit before it began lay in the difficulties I encountered from Kinshasa in arranging his call on the president, a matter normally taken for granted during a "working visit" by Mobutu, such was the nature of our Cold War ties. This time, however, we could not get him on the schedule. From the exchange of telegrams with Washington it was clear there was every intention of scheduling a meeting, but somehow a date and time could not be set. I used back channels to colleagues in the State Department, at the CIA, and at the National Security Council to determine what the problem was and finally received an authoritative answer that the holdup was in the president's office itself. Mobutu could reschedule his visit, I said, if the time proved inconvenient. It would be a strong public signal of a change in the quality of relations were he to visit Washington and not see Reagan. "Understood," my interlocutors replied, "but it's a special circumstance and even the White House chief of staff can't do anything about it." I suspected a problem with the president's health. Only later was I told that the hitch involved Joan Quigley, the astrologer consulted by Mrs. Reagan. Mobutu also had his shamans: he might have understood. In the end, he got his meeting with the president and the media attention he craved.

Down by the River

Zaire was exciting to my children, who had not previously seen Africa. The ambassador's residence, neither grand nor particularly large, was a welcoming and airy white building with red tiles on its slanting roofs. The Stars and Stripes flew from a flagpole on the front lawn. A fountain splashed in the oval garden at the entrance, surrounded by the largest and most beautiful poinsettia shrubs we had seen. There were, in fact, seven distinct gardens meticulously tended among the trees and rocks and lawns within the fenced-off compound. I opened the swimming pool and tennis court to others at the embassy and to Peace Corps volunteers passing through.

An ample L-shaped living room and a well-proportioned dining room made entertaining easy. Comfortable family quarters with ceiling fans and guest rooms were on the second floor. The house had central air-conditioning. Windows rising to the ceilings admitted sunlight and varying hues of green from the shrubs and trees around us. Before leaving Washington, I had selected from the State Department's "Art in Embassies" collection housed in its basement a half dozen large paintings by contemporary American artists whose abstract works in reds, yellows, and blues fit easily into African surroundings. Forceful lines and irregular shapes emulated what we found outside in nature's patterns. Our African guests admired them, while more than a few Americans politely refrained from commenting. My successor's tastes were different, I am told, and that was as it should be.

A wide terrace under a striped awning overlooked the back garden and the river, which was broad at this point. Installed on the terrace for many years was Jocko, the parrot, who cried out "Bonjour, monsieur l'ambassadeur!" from his cage and soon took to summoning Johnny, our bulldog, who dutifully waddled up to see what was wanted. I never cottoned to Jocko.

During the day, the great river flowed past only yards away with green patches of water hyacinth as big as city blocks on its surface. We knew when there had been heavy rains upstream because the river moved in swifter currents and turned brown with churned-up mud. At night, the far-off lights of Brazzaville blinked across it. We had not lived by a river—so much moving water—nor understood, before, its domineering presence and force. Each morning and when we reached home in time for sundown breezes, we were drawn to it. We had our breakfasts and lunches under the awning and watched the river, as one does a quivering fire, with fascination. And like a fire in the hearth, its silent waters soothed yet menaced. *I do not know much about gods; but I think that the river is a strong brown god,* T. S. Eliot wrote about an American river wending through summer-green banks.

For three years Mark, living with me, attended TASOK, the large American School of Kinshasa. During one of his holidays we went to the enormous Virunga Game Park on the equator, where, because there was no commercial tourism, we stayed in Mobutu's camp of round white cement cottages built earlier by the Belgians. Food in an unadorned lodge for a handful of Americans—fresh game and fish—was excellent, and so were the wines from France. In our Land Rover we came within a few feet of lions as they ate their kill and vomited hide and other indigestible parts, or simply slept, sometimes as a pair. I watched one male roll over so he could look into the face of his mate alongside. Late at night, bulky young hippos from a muddy stream prowled through our camp making a great deal of noise on lumbering moonlit walks.

At Virunga we saw how animals in the wild lived together in nature's great

domain and under her laws—from insect to elephant, fish to bird. Living life
at its essence, they foraged for themselves and their young, found water, and
yielded to the mysterious instinct to mate. They fought and fed off each other
in an exquisite scrambling of needs and impulses no municipal zoo with its
segregated cages, snake halls, aviaries, aquariums, and drawers full of dead
butterflies could replicate.

We visited pygmies in the Ituri forest, short and nearly naked people, most
no taller than four feet, living in primitive ways. Some carried bows and arrows
and, having made crowns for themselves of twigs and green leaves, danced in
circles, chanting as they shuffled in small steps to the music of rudimentary
strings and drums. Afterward, one of the men wearing only a loose loincloth
asked me in pantomime for cigarettes.

Jack, Cathy, and Paul came from their colleges for the summers. My children were intrigued by African life and culture and admired the Africans
they came to know in open, easy ways. Jack worked in the embassy's general
services section, honing his skills as a carpenter and enjoying the swimming
pool. Paul persuaded our bighearted defense attaché, Colonel Paul Wenzel, to
arrange for him to join the French-sponsored paratrooper training program
for Zairian soldiers. He made three perfect jumps as I watched him on three
harrowing days and won his parachute wings. I later informed a perplexed
Mobutu about my son's accomplishment. Cathy filled in for our community
liaison officer while the latter was on leave and led her own embassy trip to
Virunga. She stood beside me in the greeting line at our large July Fourth
reception in the garden of the residence, wearing a white suit with blue trim
and a big white hat, a very stylish twenty-two-year-old, I thought, and in every
way a gracious representative of our country.

National-day receptions such as our Fourth of July party provided diplomats welcome opportunities for casual encounters. Rather than requesting an
appointment to call on someone in a government ministry, or on another
ambassador, one contrived to come across these same people at receptions
where everyone milled around. The conversation appeared accidental and had
the force of directness inspired by a brief opportunity. You were simply there,
face-to-face with a person to whom you intended to convey a point or ask
a question that might be inappropriate in a less spontaneous, more formal
approach. Others in the room were doing their own diplomatic dances as people turned to different groups, shook new hands, air-kissed scented cheeks,
and faded in and out of conversations. Agendas got advanced in this way, sometimes on instructions from capitals to find the right setting for a well-placed
word or two with a telegram to be sent back on the outcome.

The rites of national days, although useful in this context, were biased against having a good time. Money was not lavished, except by the French, on the food passed around, and it usually was difficult to find something to drink. In Kinshasa, having briefly worked the grand hall of the Intercontinental Hotel where most of these affairs were held, and having been noticed because of my height to be in attendance, I disappeared by means of an escape route through the pantry. Knowing waiters with smiles held the doors open for me. In moments I would reach my driver, M'buaki, and the Cadillac with its little flags: business, if any, transacted; messages, if any, received.

The American Embassy

Located near the ramshackle port in an old building that had a colonial atmosphere to it—especially when the heavens opened up and the power failed—the U.S. Embassy in Kinshasa was then our second largest in Africa, after that in Cairo. On my arrival, I met the staff by walking through various offices in several locations. The head of security had me try on a bulletproof vest I never saw again. I began settling in. As M'buaki drove me to the embassy each day, we passed through a refuse-strewn square. I knew where to look on the corner of one of its dilapidated buildings to spot a barely legible blue-and-white sign proclaiming this square the former Place Léopold, after the Belgian king. In a country with few visible remnants of its past, this simple sign was an inglorious reminder of what once had been.

The deputy chief of mission during most of my stay was Daniel Simpson, who had earlier in his Foreign Service career been consul general in Lubumbashi. Feisty and compact, from Bellaire, Ohio, Dan collected tapes of Zairian music and became an authority on singers, rhythms, and bands. He was a respected expert on the African continent, a first-rate manager, a courageous diplomat, and a valued adviser, a deputy with a fine pen who would say to me about my wilder notions, "Boss, why don't you sleep on it?" or "Let me try my hand at writing this." (Dan would much later succeed me in Kinshasa and tough-mindedly preside over U.S. interests during the rebel invasion of Zaire from the east and the overthrow by the brigand Laurent Kabila of a terminally ill Mobutu.)

Two days after Dan appeared in Kinshasa, I invited him to lunch at my home to have a heart-to-heart talk about how we would work together as a team, a discussion of moment between any chief of mission and a new deputy. "Mr. Ambassador . . ." Dan said on arriving. "Dan, please call me Brandon." "Thank you, sir. Brandon, as you know Chet Crocker [assistant secretary of state for

African affairs] is due in this afternoon. Mobutu's office just called to say Mobutu won't meet with him. Mobutu wanted you to know that Reagan doesn't meet with *any* Zairian officials in Washington, not even with the Zairian ambassador. So Mobutu won't see Crocker." Crocker's seasoned reaction: "That's fine with me." During the months that followed, Dan and I never returned to our heart-to-heart talk, so busy were we pushing wheelbarrows over ruts that nothing sensible would have been left to say.

The embassy's political officers found Zaire's governing process a bewildering merry-go-round. People would be in power as cabinet officers, generals, governors, bank officials, or advisers to the president and twelve months later find themselves out of favor, ousted, even jailed, to be replaced by others who had been thrown out earlier. This process would be repeated, with former outs becoming new ins. Changes were made according to Mobutu's whims and were intended to prevent ministers and regional figures from creating their own platforms of power and revenue. They also served as reminders of who was in charge and able to spread the wealth around.

The exception to this merry-go-round was a small coterie of trusted personal advisers, one or two of whom, I suspected, managed the president's finances and knew the account numbers in Swiss and other banks. Mobutu's team by and large was a kakistocracy, from a Greek word meaning government of a state by its worst citizens; the problem was an old one. Mobutu was a hands-on president at every political turn, and a paid network of spies kept him informed. His power stemmed from control of the military, the media, and the fruits of Zaire's economy. He held a governing philosophy of divide and rule, with payoffs to all and sundry. He micromanaged the issues that mattered most to him. He created for the masses a personal, divine myth about himself in which he, too, began to believe. Through three decades this combination worked for him.

Mobutu was paranoid about the American embassy, which he viewed separately from the U.S. government when it suited him, suspecting us of plotting against him. He believed members of our political and public affairs sections were reaching out to opposition figures at a time when there was no political opposition in Zaire worthy of the name. He was wildly suspicious of the Peace Corps. Toward the end of my stay he impulsively expelled nearly all volunteers for stirring up dissent in the countryside, an absurd allegation. One young man in Bukavu was reported to have made disparaging remarks about Mobutu over beers in a bar, which said something about his information network. Summoned to his presence, I offered an obvious explanation of this trivial incident that fell on deaf ears. Mobutu became furious, shouting at me. I made an effort to keep my replies level, to the point, and unrelenting as I felt myself drifting toward being declared persona non grata, with only a short time to pack my bags and leave the country. Not an altogether bad prospect.

In the light of another day Mobutu decided, instead, that members of the American embassy were to be treated coldly. For months I found myself dealing only with the capable prime minister, a Polish African named Kengo Wa Dondo, which was acceptable to me because I had no formal matters needing Mobutu's personal attention. Chiefs of mission rarely bothered to see the foreign minister of the moment. Now I myself was in for a ride on Mobutu's merry-go-round, a fate that more frequently befell my Belgian colleague. I used the well-oiled liaison relationship between my station chief, Charles Redick, and his opposite number in the netherworld, Honoré N'Gbanda, principal adviser to Mobutu on the most sophisticated of matters, to make sure *le Guide*, as Mobutu liked to be called, understood U.S. annoyance at his performance. Our July Fourth party on the lawn that year was attended by only a handful of middle-ranking officials. I became one of few ambassadors from anywhere to leave Zaire without having the saucer-sized Order of the Leopard bestowed upon him by Mobutu, which was fine with me.

There was little I could say to Washington about Zaire or Mobutu Sese Seko that it did not already know. Policy makers in a Cold War setting were uninterested in altering the status quo through fresh initiatives. My advocacy of reform in conversations with Zairian officials at different levels provided me a bit of personal satisfaction and for a while seemed to have some small effect. Improving human rights practices was always near the top of the American agenda, no matter how frustrating this effort became. Diplomacy on the ground could sometimes be little more than barely keeping things going as we wanted them to. You worked steadily with what there was to work with, until the moment for change arrived, and then you seized it.

It is fair to ask: did the United States, Belgium, and France do more harm than good in the ways they dealt with Mobutu? From the standpoint of their own interests during the Cold War, which were a mix of strategic, economic, historical, and Francophonic, they did themselves little harm because they achieved their purposes in the relationship with scant effort and at low cost, as in the symbolism of Reagan's jovial luncheon for Mobutu. The hue and cry about the sort of leader we were backing was politically manageable in capitals. That we would act as we did in the world of the time was largely accepted.

Harm was done to the long-suffering Zairian, who might have benefited from serious and sustained pressures on Mobutu, coordinated among the three governments and with broader international support, to enact radical reforms. These governments were in no frame of mind, however, to consider pushing a boulder up Mobutu's mountain, knowing his capacity for obstinacy, deception, and delay. At heart he was beyond persuasion. Would it have been realistic, in any case, for us to engage more deeply in the management of Zaire's economy when carefully monitored reform efforts of the World Bank and the International Monetary Fund, over many years and on the ground, were nowhere near succeeding? Would Congress have approved the necessary resources? Did Americans even care about a smoldering crisis in a place called Zaire that did not affect them and was left largely unaddressed by the U.S. media? As for the opposition figures living comfortably in Brussels, they said the right things in general, but most were men of narrow interests in search of power and attuned to its benefits.

Communist Diplomats in Africa in the Mideighties

Among the most active aid donors in Zaire was the People's Republic of China. We discussed development assistance with the Chinese from time to time and noticed that outside the capital they chose sound projects and made them succeed. Chinese technicians in the countryside lived together in cramped, hot quarters and socialized only with each other. Outreach on their part to the local population, except to provide technical training, did not occur. There was noticeable coolness between the Chinese and the Soviets in Zaire in the mideighties, particularly in an environment in which Mobutu favored the former and shunned the latter.

Our embassy's relationships with the Chinese in Kinshasa were cordial. Not much had changed since I observed communist diplomats together in Conakry, Guinea, more than twenty years before. The shift was in relations between the Chinese and ourselves. Their ambassador lived along the river, and we visited each other from time to time. I liked him and thought it worthwhile to explain what the United States was doing in Zaire. He reciprocated. The Chinese had built for Mobutu an enormous People's Palace in Kinshasa, where he was able to hold lavish and wasteful social affairs on a grand scale. Several times at embassy dinner parties, I found myself seated next to the Chinese ambassador's vivacious wife, who spoke neither French, German, nor English. We discovered through a process of elimination that she knew a little Spanish, as did I. We spent our evenings together exploring wide-ranging topics in broken Spanish, our hands filling in the words we did not know. She once told me animatedly that a nine-foot boa had slithered into the garden and swallowed her cat.

The Cold War dragged on. By a quirk of fate, the Cuban ambassador in Kinshasa, a squat and gloomy man built like a wrestler, was immediately behind me in protocol ranking, and we found ourselves waiting in receiving lines together and seated side by side at official dinners. This was a man who knew how to down a meal. In a pleasant way I mined for information about Angola but did not get any.

I rarely saw the Soviet ambassador, who spoke good English and once came to my home for lunch with several other ambassadors. Mobutu barely tolerated the Soviet embassy; his fear of a resurgence of Russian influence in Zaire was genuine. This Soviet ambassador was visibly unhappy with his assignment. He drank too much and became known for a loose tongue and disparaging remarks about Africans. He apparently took a liking to me, however. I did not object to becoming better acquainted, curious to learn more about what my Soviet counterpart was thinking.

Early one evening, he telephoned my office to ask whether he could see me. I invited him to the residence for a drink. There we were, the two of us, drinking vodka tonics while his driver waited outside. My Soviet colleague did not seem to have an agenda. I listened carefully for the message I was certain he had come to deliver. None came through, although he talked for quite a while in a rambling way. I had finished reading a book by Arkady Shevchenko, the ranking Soviet diplomat at the United Nations who had defected, and it was in my study upstairs. I asked the ambassador, in a moment of mischief, whether he would be interested in reading it. He said, oh yes. I began to wonder whether he was leading up to a request for asylum and mentally reviewed what I would do in accordance with well-established procedures worldwide. After another drink, my visitor left with the book, and without my being able to determine why he had come. Afterward I could only guess that some combination of loneliness, despair, alcoholism, or curiosity about Americans drove him to take such a risky step as seeing me alone. If he had harbored thoughts of changing sides, he never signaled them.

I did not give this episode further thought at the time, beyond reporting it in an intelligence channel. Several months later, however, after the Soviet ambassador had left Kinshasa, I read an arresting item in one of our periodic worldwide intelligence summaries. It cited a Soviet foreign ministry report about one of its ambassadors in an unnamed African country who had become friendly with his American counterpart and accepted from him a book by the defector Shevchenko. The report condemned loose and unprofessional behavior. The American ambassador was treacherous. Soviet diplomats everywhere must keep their guard up. I found it amusing and quite a little sad, too. I suspected his driver, probably a KGB operative, had turned him in and assumed my unfortunate Russian colleague was punished for that strange and pointless evening in my living room.

Anatoly Dobrynin, the Soviet Union's ambassador to Washington during much of the Cold War, made a telling comment about African relations in his memoir, *In Confidence*. "In retrospect," he wrote, "I cannot help being surprised at the amount of energy and effort spent almost entirely in vain by Moscow and Washington on these so-called African Affairs. Twenty years later no one (except historians) could as much as remember them." This was a Soviet confession of how little they were able to understand or accomplish there.

Years after the Cold War, I became friendly with a former Soviet diplomat, Alexander Yereskovsky, who had been Ambassador Dobrynin's adviser in Washington on arms control. Highly regarded by American colleagues, he was someone who had a long history of negotiating with U.S. counterparts on such issues. Ever interested in diplomats, I asked him to describe his view of diplomacy. "A diplomat must be a creative negotiator," he began. And, with a smile: "He works eight-hour days—from 8:00 a.m. to 8:00 p.m.—and then from 8:00 p.m. until after midnight. He needs good health, strong nerves, and patience. In Washington's climate conditions are harsh. During the sixties, you know, our embassy had no money to put air-conditioners in the homes of our staff. I believe in the power of negotiations, and that diplomacy should have more answers than yes or no. A modified treaty is better than no treaty. While one of the major tasks of a diplomat is to defend his country's position to his counterparts, that defense isn't made in a vacuum. It is equally important to understand the other capital and to convey the truth back to Moscow. Telling the truth takes courage and can have penalties. 'Shoot the messenger,' as you say." That all sounded familiar.

Mariana

During President Mobutu's visit to Washington in December 1986 I met my future wife, Mariana Moran Fleming, one of the few good things for which I credit the man. I had been a single parent with custody of my younger children, Paul and Mark, since Mary and I separated in 1980 and subsequently divorced. Mark lived with me from my assignment to Jerusalem onward. Cathy and Jack, completing their high school studies in Washington at Georgetown

Visitation and at Maret, spent summers with me, while Mark and Paul visited their mother.

I managed the residences and frequent official entertaining in Jerusalem and Kinshasa, planning guest lists, menus, flowers, and seating arrangements, accepting the life of a diplomat without a spouse. Far from my thoughts toward the end of a grinding, weeklong visit to Washington with Mobutu was the prospect of meeting someone as compatible, interested in the world, elegant, and happy to dance as Mariana.

One cold December evening, out of a sense of duty alone, I accompanied Mobutu from the Willard Hotel where we were staying to the Georgetown home of his friends Harry and Norma Smith. Standing by the stair railing was Mariana, marooned in a sea of Zairian men in their black *abacosts* and cravats fastened by Velcro. She lived across the street and had been invited by a scheming Norma to meet the unattached American ambassador to Zaire. It was at first sight the beginning of love. The next evening we had dinner by the fire at La Chaumière, an intimate, rustic Georgetown restaurant.

Born of a Panamanian mother, Cecilia, in the Alfaro family, and James Moran, her American father of Irish descent, Mariana graduated from Smith College after majoring in art history and Spanish. She had been a founding partner in a Washington antiques business specializing in seventeenth- and eighteenth-century English furniture that thrived during the free-spending eighties and then closed its doors when the economy sagged. Mariana later became a Washington real estate agent for a large firm. She was getting a divorce. Her daughter, Michele Parsons, was beginning a successful career in New York's fashion industry and becoming an inveterate New Yorker.

After we spent time together during my subsequent trips to Washington, I invited Mariana to visit me in Africa. One day over lunch before returning to Kinshasa, I offered her malaria suppressant pills to take in advance of her travel, which she accepted, something I took as a good sign. Mariana arrived in Zaire in time for the June festivities of Fish Day, and I began to show her Kinshasa and its surroundings with a sense of pride in my work I had not felt before. We flew in a helicopter over the cataracts at Livingstone Falls, dipping so low into this churning cauldron that the windows through which we looked caught the spray. On the way back, we landed for the fun of it on a clearing atop a high and steep hill miles from anywhere, wondering whether we were the first human beings to set foot there—and perhaps we were.

In the dusk of Virunga Game Park, on a rise overlooking a seemingly limitless, wild, and primordial plain with no trace of civilization, and believed to be a site of the origins of man and woman, I asked Mariana to marry me. Two armed and bewildered Zairian guards watched us from a distance. In December 1988 we were wed in our apartment in Washington with my son Mark as the eloquent best man. A journey involving many years of living alone ended in happiness I did not expect to find.

Fish Day

Fish Day was an annual festival held in Kinkole, a tiny fishing village near Kinshasa. It provided Mobutu a relished opportunity to make his State of Zaire address before an enormous crowd and hundreds of drummers and dancers dressed in brilliant colors.

Mobutu employed the catching and marketing of fish as metaphors for life in Zaire and dwelt on the symbolism of the great river as provider and life force. His speech, entirely in Lingala, lasted more than two hours, while some sixty ambassadors and their wives sat under the sun in a variety of head coverings. The Japanese ambassador knotted his handkerchief at its four corners. My German colleague sported a Disney cap with a Donald Duck logo. Ambassadors who had been to Kinkole before brought books to read. People slept. Not a single diplomat, including other Africans, understood Lingala. Mariana squirmed under her large straw hat. I retreated into a semistupor under mine.

At the end of this Fish Day ordeal the chief of protocol announced on the public address system that a luncheon would be offered to the diplomatic corps. We were advised where to gather and in a wilted thirsty state reclaimed the air-conditioned comfort of black automobiles and proceeded to our common destination in a diplomatic disgorgement from Kinkole. On disembarking in the countryside at an empty hall with limited plumbing, the men gallantly repairing outside, we were in due course told by an overwrought protocol official that our meal would be provided at a different place. We all climbed back into our cars parked in disarray on a narrow road, each with its proud little flag. After our drivers painstakingly formed a file again, M'buaki distinguishing himself at the wheel, we proceeded through billowing dust to the new location several miles away.

Soon, when we had arrived at N'sele, Mobutu's grand Chinese-style pavilion outside Kinshasa where fountains gushed, we were relieved to behold a splendid lunch set under a large white tent. It included French wines and melting cheeses along with a barbecue of local fish and meats from Belgium grilled by a chef from Buenos Aires. Before an artificial waterfall, voluptuous African women wearing not much swayed to the Hawaiian strains of a Zairian band. A central theme seemed to be lacking, but Mobutu was theme enough.

He somehow had known Mariana would be at Fish Day, and we were astonished to find ourselves seated at his table. Mariana was to his right and I next to her. Her place card read "Madame Brandon," and she saved it. Fresh from Washington, she felt transported to a different world. Mobutu was in an ebullient mood, his spirits lifted by Fish Day, which he talked about from his own perspective.

During the meal I inadvertently caught the eye of the French ambassador seated at a distant table. He outranked me on the protocol ladder and found Mobutu's breach of diplomatic etiquette disconcerting, as did several of my other colleagues and, I should add, their wives. Yet this was our fate as ambassadors in the heart of Africa celebrating Fish Day at Mobutu's Chinese pavilion. We had become distracted for the moment by seating arrangements and proximity to The Leopard, setting aside our awareness of the shocking nature of the man himself, of the occasion as farce, and of the sources of the riches that brought it off, Mobutu-style.

Finale

In 1997 Mobutu, toppled from power and living in exile, wasted and incontinent, died in Morocco of prostate cancer. This had been a long and tragic journey for the colonel who received a nod from the United States. He had seen Laurent Kabila succeed him in a rebel victory and restore the name of Congo, but little else, to his country. Years of violence and chaos would follow. For Mobutu this was the end he dreaded: his corpse moldering in the sands of the Sahara rather than in the fertile, fragrant earth of the bygone Zaire of his creation. His place in history, like King Leopold's, was no longer susceptible to change.

19

TRAINING

1988 to 1992

Early in 1988, after my three years as ambassador to Zaire, George Shultz offered me the directorship of the Foreign Service Institute (FSI). No previous secretary of state was as committed to training as Shultz, and I was delighted. His deputy, John C. Whitehead, and the department's senior manager, Ronald Spiers, a highly experienced Foreign Service officer, supported Shultz's commitment.

We had before us, thanks to the efforts of my predecessors Stephen Low and Charles Bray, the prospect of building a campus for FSI at nearby Arlington Hall in northern Virginia. A sprawling army installation since World War II, Arlington Hall had been used for code work and was no longer needed. The Cold War was winding down. Here was an opportunity to construct a modern, high-technology facility to provide governmentwide training in foreign affairs, in courses ranging from managing an embassy's budget to negotiating with the Chinese in Chinese.

Well-meaning friends warned that FSI would be a step sideways in my career and I would end up going missing in the asphalt jungle of Rosslyn. They pointed out that the FSI directorship until then, despite the caliber of its incumbents, had been a dead end leading to retirement. Accomplishments at FSI would speak for themselves, I said. One evening during an intermission at the Kennedy Center, Mariana and I came across a State Department friend who asked where I would be working next. When I told him about FSI, he replied: "Well, *somebody's* got to do it!" That summed up a view of training widely held in the Foreign Service of those days. From another colleague I had heard that "training is for dogs."

As it turned out, my four years at FSI engaged me in some of the most exasperating, disappointing, and punishing experiences of my career. My struggles over FSI's future with Ivan Selin, the State Department's new administrator under James Baker, had the unnerving quality of a bad dream and would demoralize those working with me. Selin's inability to understand the place of training in enabling professionals at all levels to do their work properly was unforeseen.

Surviving in Rosslyn

As I took up the reins, two high-rise office buildings in Rosslyn, Virginia— a soulless, treeless pile of Lego blocks on the far side of the Potomac—accommodated the Foreign Service Institute. One was a narrow fourteen-story structure we occupied entirely. The State Department also rented one-third of a similar building two long blocks away. Anyone needing to proceed on a rainy day from consular training to a language class in Urdu got wet. In the main building we senior managers were located on the top floor, isolated from other operations in appearance and in fact. Our offices had unmatched views of Washington across the river but were in the wrong places.

Both buildings were overcrowded. Their halls were dingy and their walls needed paint. Classrooms were either too hot or too cold. Furniture was scarred and worn. Our A-100 course, conducted in the second building, occupied a cavernous windowless room with blue walls that reminded me of a cargo hold in the USS *Cambria*. Small elevators were maddeningly slow. Despite such conditions, the institute had an enthusiastic staff of some 550 people, more than half of whom were engaged in teaching sixty-three different languages as native speakers themselves. The challenges at a human level included persuading a young instructor to move with his family from Ulan Bator to a high-rise apartment in Rosslyn. We needed him to teach Mongolian to a handful of students, among them the future ambassador and his wife.

FSI had a discretionary annual training budget of more than $16 million beyond the fixed costs of salaries and expenses. It provided 1.6 million hours of instruction every year. On a given day we were training about twelve hundred students from the State Department's Civil and Foreign Services and some forty other U.S. government agencies engaged in foreign affairs. We maintained four schools abroad for language and area studies in Chinese, Japanese, Korean, and Arabic. Our training focused on skill-building.

But FSI also enhanced professionalism, the competencies and motivations that emerged from being engaged in exacting and worthwhile work, with clear objectives, standards, and rewards, that wasn't just another job. No element of the State Department was better positioned to define and transmit the core values of the Foreign and Civil Services, their ethos and spirit, and we understood this.

At FSI we portrayed the Foreign Service as it was and as we wanted it to become. Its members were evolving from people who had been committed through decades to the rough terrain of the Cold War and had felt subservient to "the system" and relatively powerless within it. In contrast to earlier generations of diplomats, the current generation, by and large, was a more self-centered and self-promoting group with sharper elbows. They learned their values in the sixties and bore a certain cynicism from America's defeat in Vietnam. Too few of this generation saw the Foreign Service as a shared institution requiring sacrifice, nourishment, and loyalty. The prevailing frame of mind in seeking assignments and promotions was everyone for herself or himself. The question became: "How can I manipulate the system to give me what I want and know I deserve?" (In fairness, many employees were routinely asked by "busy" supervisors to write their own efficiency reports for their supervisor's signature.) Too many of our diplomats were seeing themselves not as future ambassadors who would walk with kings and command generals, but as bureaucratic agents content to drift through their careers propelled by the winds. We seemed to have swung from one set of professional attitudes nearly to the opposite.

As I looked at the Foreign Service of that era, despite its superstars—many of our diplomats were among the world's best, but except for language skills the best were largely self-created—the institution seemed less than the sum of its parts ought to have been. A creaking personnel structure was flawed in nearly every way. Class-action lawsuits on the part of women and minorities were progressing successfully through the courts. Missing at a human level was a broader commitment by the service's members to an institution offering careers and lives of surpassing interest and value. One could count during a graduated career path on changing supervisors and responsibilities every few years; on access to an amazing array of intellectual challenges, people, and places; and on spiritual and family experiences of a lifetime. There was also the honor of serving one's country. This really *was* a privilege and needed to be understood that way.

Few leaders of the State Department, however, thought of FSI as obliged to address professionalism or seemed to care about perpetuating a common core of attitudes, standards, and expectations or, beyond countless notebooks of administrative regulations, about what these might be. No overhaul of a dysfunctional personnel system was in prospect. In the eyes of most senior managers, training needs resided in disciplines such as languages, office management, consular work, advanced economics, and computer skills—worthy subjects well taught at FSI.

But wasn't something lacking here? How different this approach was from our military services, where a four-star general like Colin Powell spent six of his thirty-five years in the army being trained, large parts of his instruction devoted to leadership skills. Motivation through effective leadership and training was, and remains, the main reason our armed services perform so well. The State Department was no different in this regard, but in my day it all too rarely taught leadership skills. Finally, in 2000, a School of Leadership and Management was established at FSI, where necessary work is being done.

Minting Better Diplomats

Three aspects of training shaped the quality of our embassies, and I concentrated on them. I viewed the ambassadorial and DCM seminars, along with the A-100 course, as a training triad. Participants in each needed to understand the needs and concerns of the other two and to learn how they were commingled.

The content and delivery of the A-100 course, forever a work in progress, remained a primary interest of mine. These months of training introduced people to their Foreign Service careers, FSI providing the gateway through which fresh recruits embarked upon what could be a lifetime of service. Through a series of first impressions, planned and unplanned, A-100 set the tone for life and work in the Foreign Service. Remembering how subdued my own experience had been in the aftermath of McCarthyism, I welcomed each new class and met with them again after they received their first assignments. I remembered the thrill of hearing Mike Gannett say to me, "Grove—*Abidjan!*"

As part of their lessons, these diplomats-to-be were staging mock receptions to understand the protocol of receiving lines and how to entertain official guests at an ambassador's residence. Beyond the courtesies, they were learning to focus on guest lists, the reasons for holding an event at taxpayers' expense, and what such an event should accomplish. Students taking the mandatory consular course following A-100 gathered at FSI's jail—yes, we built one—with iron bars and graffiti on the walls in languages I longed to understand. They were engaged in playing the roles of an American prisoner and his foreign interrogator—an American vice consul would show up to negotiate the prisoner's release. They visited a hospital morgue in Washington to view bodies stored in metal drawers with name tags on their toes, preparing our students for what they would encounter, in more grisly surroundings, attending to deceased Americans abroad. When I described this aspect of training to James Baker he looked at me in disbelief, but later he took pride in citing it as an example of a robust Foreign Service.

Joining the DCM Seminar on its opening day at a lodge in West Virginia called The Woods, I spent an afternoon and dined with these prospective deputies to ambassadors at our largest and smallest posts. We discussed their future roles and relationships in this most intimate pairing in diplomatic life, other than marriage itself. I told them of John and Lorraine Cooper and our exploits while I was Cooper's DCM in East Berlin. Ambassadors were permitted to make only two staff choices themselves—their deputies and their personal assistants. Charles "Chip" Bohlen, one of the Cold War's great American ambassadors, liked to express this more graphically: they were allowed to pick their DCMs, their secretaries, and their noses. The largest Foreign Service graveyard was filled with DCMs. Although these officers managed our embassies, they were notoriously poor executives, because the system rewarded political, economic, and policy skills, not those of leadership. The future DCMs attending the seminar, by then seasoned Foreign Service officers, had their own tales to tell and examples of lessons learned the hard way. They were good company, hearty raconteurs, and we laughed a lot. Many would later take their places among the best of our ambassadors.

For prospective ambassadors, whether career or politically appointed, FSI offered a mandatory two-week seminar to explain the current iteration of the State Department as seen from an ambassador's perch. This was never easy work. I led the seminar during the first Bush administration, remembering my distant predecessor Shirley Temple Black as I did so. Working alongside me was Langhorne A. "Tony" Motley, a businessman, former ambassador to Brazil, and former assistant secretary of state for Latin America. Coming from the private sector, Tony impressed political appointees—most of them fellow businesspeople—with particular force. A dapper, ruggedly handsome man and a fanatic golfer, he was funny, penetrating, realistic, candid to a fault, but above all persuasive. Whether spelling out what an ambassador's relations with a CIA station chief should be or lauding Foreign Service professionals, he came from a different corner and reinforced what I, a career man, was saying. Both of us stressed the importance of leadership in running an embassy as one of the main lessons to retain from the seminar.

FSI provided these ambassadors and their spouses two days of media training in its television studio, with experts coaching them on how to look and talk their best while parrying hostile questions. Our ambassadors-designate spent an afternoon at CIA headquarters being briefed on spycraft. For a further dose of reality, we took them to a security training base outside Washington. On a military flight their airplane was hijacked by "terrorists" who had come aboard as repairmen in white overalls, no one noticing that they had remained on board. After takeoff they burst out of the lavatories, waved their pistols, and shouted orders to the startled group. Later, agents at the training base shot up vehicles like theirs with terrorists' weapons. Prospective "excellencies" got whipped around in the backseats of cars, their crash helmets tightly fastened as evasive driving techniques were demonstrated by experts at the wheel. All of this made for an unsettling afternoon but also, we hoped, ambassadors better prepared for a tough world.

Building a Permanent Home

The design and construction of Arlington Hall to replace Rosslyn became my passion. I remembered my Princeton roommate, Norval White, and what I had learned from him about the excitement of architecture. The sketch of a topographical footprint for the new buildings and the funds required were at hand. Our architect was an energetic and visionary young man, Alan Greenberger, from the Philadelphia firm of MGA Partners. He began designing a five-hundred-thousand-square-foot complex that would cost an estimated $86 million. He craved light. Where rectangular windows didn't fit, Alan drew round ones. William Dawson, the consul general who presided over the one-room schoolhouse when George Kennan entered the Foreign Service, would have been pleased.

The administration of the newly elected George H. W. Bush brought with it unexpected difficulties for FSI and the Arlington Hall project in particular. For months those of us on the far side of the Potomac failed entirely to understand the magnitude of change, or that our construction plans were headed toward derailment. Overconfident that the momentum under Shultz would continue, and unable to imagine that it wouldn't, I was not listening carefully to new and unaccustomed voices, shutting them out when they didn't make sense to me. I was slow to accept that what had been obvious to George Shultz's team—the need for better training at a newly built Arlington Hall—was viewed differently by Ivan Selin, who had succeeded career diplomat Ron Spiers as the department's top manager.

Selin was one of Robert McNamara's "whiz kids," the young, creative, and impatient systems analysts at the Pentagon during the war in Vietnam. In 1989

James Baker, Shultz's successor, recruited him for the State Department from American Management Systems, a company Selin cofounded. He was to bring greater efficiency to Foggy Bottom. Ivan, however, had little foreign experience or knowledge of the State Department. At fifty-two, he was a fit and wiry man of medium height with sharp features and black hair receding in a widow's peak that gave prominence to his forehead. He was a forceful person with a store of factual knowledge. Intense, inward-looking, blunt, and intellectually arrogant, Ivan spoke crisply and with overbearing authority. He was not disposed to listen to others and did not tolerate dissent. Lacking warmth, he rarely seemed at ease in dealing with people. He preferred using conceptual models formed before arriving on the scene to shape his decisions, no matter how forcefully reality should have intruded on some of his preconceptions.

Once in office and despite my urgings, Selin waited months before visiting FSI, and then arrived one day to find out how well he would fare in a Russian language test. I began getting his message. Selin viewed training as a process of rote and routine, the teaching of nuts-and-bolts skills for practical use, "dirty fingernails work," as he confided to me. Its needs therefore were modest. In this assessment he was not alone in the State Department's plodding culture, where suspicion of anything with an intellectual cast ran deep.

During his first senior managers' retreat at The Woods, Ivan said Arlington Hall did not occupy a high priority in the State Department's building programs. I argued that construction of this facility, already underway, was an opportunity dropped into our laps by Shultz to meet new and pressing needs. Congress had agreed to fund the project subject to an annual review, and the money could not be put to other uses. To abandon FSI's prospects would be foolish. Others in the room saw I was marching out of step. In this discussion there was much to be lost, and I was busy losing it.

I was not included in Selin's staff meetings; he said he wanted them kept small. He did not, as a consequence, receive firsthand reports of FSI's work or its problems. At the same time, I had no systematic ways of learning what his priorities were, much less Secretary Baker's, or what implications for training his meetings would yield. Selin visited the construction site two or three times but remained unconvinced of the project's value, although by then demolition of the army barracks was completed, asbestos was expensively removed, and funds were committed. Feeling like conspirators over many a lunch in the State Department's cafeteria, my deputy, John T. Sprott, and I discussed our concerns in lowered voices, glancing around to see who was seated at tables nearby as we talked about creating a modern training center at Arlington Hall.

The State Department was obliged annually to renew its requests for congressional funding, providing FSI's opponents in Ivan's fiefdom, suspicious of anything not running in a groove, opportunities to make trouble. Twice Ivan challenged the further need to fund construction at Arlington Hall: once in 1989, and again in 1991. The second threat looked fatal.

I attended a budget meeting in Selin's office during which he announced his decision to drop the department's request for more funds to build Arlington Hall. FSI could make do in Rosslyn, he said, and the land would be put to other government uses. There seemed no better reasons than these. My objections were politely heard but ignored. In an hour, Selin would be going to a meeting in Deputy Secretary Lawrence Eagleburger's office at which he would present the State Department's budget for approval. I would not be there. George Shultz's vision of Arlington Hall was over, and the State Department's own managers were killing it—not the scalpel wielders in the president's Office of Management and Budget, nor a supportive Congress.

Dilemma

Or was it over? For the only time in my career I debated whether to challenge the person whose instructions I was responsible for carrying out by going to his superior to make my case in an argument I had lost. In professional terms this would be disloyal, and I winced at the thought. The State Department was hierarchical. Although no one wore a uniform, its culture was based on a ladder of command, with upward loyalty expected at every rung.

With less than an hour before Selin's budget meeting and facing an ethical dilemma, I agonized over what to do. The stakes as I saw them were high, and Selin's decision was wrong. Few outside the realm of training, however, cared much about Arlington Hall.

On its face the issue involved a line item in State's construction budget already assured of funding, and in those terms Ivan's argument was baseless. Deeper down, the controversy went to what FSI should become: more of the same, marching in place as the world spun faster, or a haven from which to anticipate and support America's role in uncertain times following the Cold War? This wasn't the sort of challenge over which George Kennan did battle, but fate decreed it to be *my* challenge. Neither alternative—to salute and accept this state of affairs or to go behind Ivan's back—seemed obvious. My own training had come in conflict with the training needs of my government, for which I now was accountable. What was the answer?

I walked down the hall to Eagleburger's office to talk with him. Finding him engaged with visitors, I asked his secretary for paper and an envelope. We had not worked together, but I knew Larry over the years as a colleague from Milwaukee and one of our nation's most deeply experienced Foreign Service officers: a stout, chain-smoking, vest-wearing, gruff, joshing, and outspoken diplomat of unyielding integrity who listened to operas in his office. Near the end of the Bush administration, with Baker's reluctant departure to work on the president's flagging reelection campaign, Larry would be the first Foreign Service officer to become secretary of state, if only for a short time.

Sitting at the long table in the deputy secretary's conference room that I had entered for the first time as a staff assistant to Chester Bowles, I took out my pen, and as I paused my career flashed before me like a drowning man's life is said to do. An issue affecting the quality of our diplomacy was to be decided during his budget meeting, I wrote Eagleburger. The outcome could not be left to chance. If we failed to take advantage of the opportunity at Arlington Hall, we would not find a comparable site because there was none, nor would we get from Congress the funding now at hand for which Shultz had fought hard. Two rundown and overcrowded buildings in Rosslyn were not answers to what an unknowable future required, as he had seen in his own training there. I asked Larry's secretary to give him my note before his budget meeting began.

I left the State Department feeling like a faceless functionary in a Kafkaesque tale slouching homeward from the ministry. Should I ask for early retirement, I wondered. My career had begun with an A-100 course in the "gritty green garage." Now it was ending in failed efforts to create a sophisticated facility at Cold War's end to train people throughout our government in the conduct of foreign relations. In a moment of lapse, ignoring years of acquired wisdom, I had difficulty believing something this goofy could be happening. The world had changed, but not the State Department it seemed. I never heard a word from Larry or Ivan. Someone who'd been at the meeting told me the following morning that Eagleburger had not hesitated in reaching his decision.

Soon I was working nearly full-time on the design and construction of Arlington Hall. (Fourteen years later, during the war in Iraq, plans were being drawn up to provide two new classroom buildings and a day-care center.) My contribution to this effort became for me the culminating, visible realization of my career. Getting buildings built was not the customary measure of achievement for a diplomat, but I liked all those bricks.

If you were to view the George P. Shultz National Foreign Affairs Training Center from the air, you would find its buildings forming a large letter A tilted on a woodland plot. They were designed entirely for learning. Thinking of Rosslyn, I wanted them connected by glassed-in bridges creating an atmosphere of cohesion in training and eliminating problems of weather. My successor's office on the ground level was at the heart of FSI's activities. Nearby was the A-100 suite for America's newest diplomats about to enjoy their first moments of having world enough and time.

20

SOMALIA

1992 to 1993

On a brisk and sunny November day in 1992, while working at Georgetown University as a diplomat-in-residence on a nine-month assignment to the university's School of Foreign Service, I received a call from Frank Wisner, under secretary of state for security assistance, science, and technology. We had worked together several years before while he was in the Africa bureau and I in Zaire.

Frank asked whether I would be willing to take charge of a State Department interagency task force to deal with Somalia. General Colin Powell, chairman of the Joint Chiefs of Staff, had persuaded President Bush to appoint Robert Oakley, a retired Foreign Service officer and former ambassador to Somalia, to be the U.S. special envoy in Mogadishu, Somalia's capital. The country was falling apart as a result of widespread starvation and the chaos created by warring factions at each other's throats. This state of affairs was no longer acceptable to the United States, to the United Nations, or to the world at large. I thought for a moment about the pleasures of academic life at Georgetown, but then I heard the fire bell clanging at the station house and knew I was headed for whatever Somalia would bring.

The task force I agreed to assemble would coordinate policy in Washington. We were to support civilian operations in the field aimed at bringing the leading factions in Somalia to the table and enabling food supplies to flow unhindered. If necessary, force could be used to open up the way for relief. The United States would be taking the initiative in Somalia, and we would be able to prepare our actions in advance, a rare advantage in crisis management.

Success would depend on working side by side and harmoniously with our military colleagues in every aspect of what we were about to do. Frank, Bob, and I knew each other as Foreign Service friends and had long histories of involvement with the military, mine through my time in the navy and daily association with army people in Berlin. We felt comfortable with men and women in uniform and were disposed to like and respect them as we set about breaking new ground in the course of a humanitarian engagement in Somalia without precedent.

Somalia Background

By 1992 the Cold War was over and we were no longer competing with the Soviet Union for a presence and influence in this small but strategically positioned country on the Indian Ocean. An insurgency that began in the late 1980s toppled the autocratic government of Mohammed Siad Barre early in 1991. Not long afterward, as clan leaders took over, U.S. Gulf War helicopters were sent to Mogadishu to rescue the besieged staff of the American Embassy from the building's rooftop.

Arms provided by both sides during the Cold War left local clan leaders with an arsenal from which to help themselves as they fought each other and stole or sold emergency food supplies before these could reach their destinations. In widespread pillaging, the clan leaders were joined by militias and roving bandits brandishing AK-47 assault rifles. Much of Mogadishu had been scarred in the fighting. At midday, young Somali men began chewing khat, a mild amphetamine that looked like watercress. They roamed the streets in "technicals," utility vehicles with .50-caliber machine guns bolted down in back, their afternoon highs on khat intensified by an African sun. Governance no longer existed. An estimated three hundred thousand deaths from starvation and disease had already occurred, and people were continuing to die at a rate believed at its peak to be as high as ten thousand a day. The chief economic activity in Somalia, nevertheless, remained stealing donor-contributed food.

In his memoir, the Soviet Union's durable ambassador to Washington, Anatoly Dobrynin, made the Cold War linkage to this disaster explicit: "Even when American marines were sent to Somalia in 1992 by George Bush to join United Nations forces to help feed the starving there, no one in the U.S. Government and only a very few in the press remarked that the seeds of the anarchy then prevailing in Somalia had most probably been planted by the great powers' engagement there fifteen years before. Somalia was only one of a number of countries whose local quarrels became enmeshed in the Cold War—Angola, Ethiopia, Afghanistan, among them, and all of them worse off for their involvement with the two superpowers."

Television was bringing Somalia's famine into the living rooms and family kitchens of a global audience. The actress Audrey Hepburn would visit Somalia on UNICEF's behalf during a well-publicized day dramatizing the plight of starving children, fleshless youngsters she held and caressed while they stared blankly at the camera and flies indulged themselves in the moisture around their open mouths and eyes. Hepburn was dying of colon cancer, and her gaunt, sweet face and wasting body seemed in a sad way to locate her more naturally in surroundings of despair. Flows of relief food, like Somalia's government, had dried up. Inadequate Pakistani and other UN forces in Mogadishu were helplessly pinned down by clan militias. The situation called for effective relief bolstered by military support to guarantee delivery and end the pillaging. These measures could only succeed under U.S. leadership and through the United Nations and would require the president's approval.

What happened in Somalia thereafter is a cautionary tale relevant as a foretaste of future international engagements. The record in Somalia is one of success in delivering emergency food supplies and of failure in subsequent attempts to impose governance and quick-brew democracy on people of different beliefs, traditions, and aspirations, who for the most part knew nothing about democratic ways and at best would be slow learners.

Somalia became the first international conflict after the Cold War to take its participants beyond the traditional disputes over familiar and accepted issues such as sovereignty, security, borders, economic interests, the safety of one's citizens, and self-defense. Classic seventeenth-century diplomatic and military calculations had formed the basis for the actions of a broad military coalition responding, in 1991, to Iraq's assault on Kuwait. Somalia's collapse the following year occurred at a pivotal point in American foreign policy. Determined to act, the United States found itself without a fresh strategic view in a post–Cold War world without new order. Would Somalia contribute to the development of such a view?

To alleviate famine in Somalia, the United States decided to insert itself under UN auspices into a local and centuries-old struggle among warring clans. At the outset the reasons for dispatching U.S. forces, once the United Nation's relief efforts had stalled, were humanitarian. Other nations readily joined in this commitment. Our leaders in Washington knew that in Somalia we had the military capability to provide safe and secure deliveries of adequate relief supplies to people dying of starvation. Knowing this, and in the glare of the media, we asked ourselves how in good conscience could we *not* go in?

Bush Decides

By mid-1992 the suffering in Somalia, characterized by our government as catastrophic, was being addressed in Washington, and modest steps were taken to increase the delivery and protection of food supplies. On November 24, a meeting of National Security Council deputies (rather than the president and his cabinet officers) considered a memorandum with three choices to offer President Bush. The most pressing challenge was to provide enough security in Somalia to permit food supplies to reach the starving. The heart of the matter, stated in the third and most robust option, was whether to create a UN coalition of mainly American troops, led by the United States under a Chapter VII mandate. Chapter VII of the UN Charter concerned peace enforcement and authorized the use of lethal force to accomplish necessary objectives. The State Department's representatives came into the room favoring that option, and so, it turned out, did U.S. military leaders. This is where matters stood when I left Georgetown's campus to become immersed in Somalia's needs.

At around Thanksgiving time the yellow leaves of Washington's ginkgo trees illuminate a chilly autumn and splash sunlight on the burgundies and reds beside them. On sidewalks the fallen leaves make a glowing path during the satisfying, meditative fall season. The days are shorter, preparations for winter made. The time has come to celebrate families and abundance, to snuggle in a warm bed.

The deputies' memorandum reached President Bush on the day before Thanksgiving, an accident of timing that mattered. The spiritual purpose of this holiday is to voice gratitude, but the image is of gluttony. In proclaiming the first modern Thanksgiving in 1864, President Lincoln said, "It has pleased Almighty God to prolong our national life another year." Americans by now were emulating Norman Rockwell's ample dinner table in the 1943 poster illustration of one of Roosevelt's four freedoms entitled "Freedom from Want." (Rockwell once said of his work, "I paint life as I would like it to be.") The moral issues in Somalia came into focus during a celebration of bountiful family reunions while Somali infants were dying on television in the arms of mothers unable to nourish them. The media's depiction of starvation in Somalia during Thanksgiving celebrations in America was unsettling. This was how life was being lived on the Horn of Africa.

Few of us expected Bush's decision, so late in his presidency, to settle on the most ambitious option that called for the greatest degree of U.S. involvement. It would be dubbed "Operation Restore Hope." Americans were about to go into Somalia haunted by scenes of famine on television. In the end, we would be driven out by television images of an ignominious defeat at the hands of a mob.

Bush's decision was made after an election Bill Clinton had won on economic and social issues at home. The president had successfully launched and ended the Gulf War and, for a while, soared in popularity. New and highly effective use of overwhelming force may have emboldened him to take the risks entailed in a major U.S. commitment to provide relief to a remote African country. None of us at State or Defense knew at first that the president believed his Somalia operation would be over by January 20, 1993, the end of his one-term presidency. It appeared that Bush intended to leave office with a foreign policy flourish setting a worthy precedent as "the New World Order" emerged. Foreign policy had been his strength, and here was an opportunity for one more win by doing the right thing. We learned from the NSC staff that Bush had consulted president-elect Clinton, who supported his decision. Bush believed the operation could be completed without saddling a new administration with a military commitment he had made in his waning presidency.

Few outside the Oval Office found this goal realistic. The Defense Department, which carried out the operation, did its best to accommodate the deadline. It soon recognized, however, that the United Nations could not possibly achieve a secure environment in the southern 40 percent of Somalia by January 20, 1993, given a limited commitment of U.S. forces and loosely defined objectives. Somalia would be handed from Bush to Clinton as a potential foreign policy time bomb.

Heavy-Handed at the United Nations

On December 3, 1992, the Security Council passed Resolution 794 creating UNITAF (United Task Force) as a Chapter VII operation to establish a secure environment for delivering humanitarian supplies. The resolution provided U.S. commanders in the field the flexibility they would need. On the following day, President Bush made a brief address to the nation explaining his decision. On December 9, two weeks after the president had made his choice, the first UN forces under the command of Lieutenant General Robert Johnston, U.S. Army, landed in Somalia. Television viewers across the world watched as U.S. Navy SEALS with greasepaint on their faces carried out what was intended to be a surprise night landing on the beaches of Mogadishu. The visibly dismayed invaders found not the enemy awaiting them, but floodlights and camera crews.

Frank Wisner asked me to lead U.S. implementing negotiations at the United Nations. I regularly flew to New York with State Department and military representatives on our team to talk with Kofi Annan, the Ghanaian undersecretary-general for peacekeeping operations. He would later succeed, as secretary-general, the prickly Boutros Boutros-Ghali, a sour Egyptian whose annoyance with U.S. positions on Somalia was public and unrestrained. One day he summoned me to his office, along with our ambassador to the United Nations, to complain sharply about Oakley's activities in Somalia independent of UN (his) supervision. He was not listening to my reply.

Annan understood the reasons behind Bush's January 20 deadline that were making our task more difficult and straining credibility. Tactfully, he never discussed them with me. A wise and courteous man of dignity and soft-voiced charm, he was deeply experienced in UN diplomacy in the most difficult area of peacekeeping. Universally respected as a man of principle, he made it a habit to listen and reflect on what he heard. He had a soothing calm and confidence that brought civility to the table. Maintaining his side of the argument in a low and steady voice, he was certain of his brief and could adjust course without needing further instructions. In a Ghanaian habit of speech conveying a certain warmth, Annan habitually dropped his g's at the end of a word, asking me, for example, "When shall we have our next meetin'?" I admired him but found it difficult to penetrate his controlled and politely diplomatic exterior, or even his gentle sense of humor, to reach the less dispassionate and more emotional man beneath.

This was my first experience in negotiating with UN officials in New York, and at times I felt uncomfortable. In the Security Council, representatives of our mission in New York pushed through draft resolutions on Somalia written at the State Department and were not often disposed or authorized to accommodate the views of others. The support of our allies, except for the French, was taken for granted; French diplomacy reflected, as it tended to, a singular passion for choosing its own course. In another example of the U.S. attitude toward the United Nations, we were about a billion dollars behind in paying our dues.

Riding roughshod over others to have our way seemed unnecessary to me. Diplomats were expected to carry out their instructions, yet the manner in which they did so inevitably became part of the message. Washington was also capable of reversing gears and blaming the United Nations when things went awry, as the Clinton administration and Congress did in the second, nation-building phase of the Somalia venture that followed famine relief. Nation building under U.S. leadership was a failure largely of our own making under a Security Council resolution we initiated and pressed to have passed. There must have been a wiser and less arrogant way to achieve our objectives at the United Nations.

Building a Task Force

At the State Department, interagency task forces are assembled to deal with international crises and operations of unusual scope. Normally they are created by the National Security Council through directives requiring the department and agency heads whose responsibilities are affected to send their representatives to meetings led by an official at the State Department. For more than a year, the coordination of Gulf War policy engaged a large interagency task force led by Ambassador Mary Ryan. Overseas plane crashes with many Americans on board, an earthquake in Mexico City, a terrorist attack on an embassy—all were events too overwhelming to be addressed according to traditional lines of authority on organizational charts.

At the White House, Richard A. Clarke was the NSC staff member responsible for Somalia. His customary brief included political-military issues and counterterrorism. As we worked together on Somalia, I found him driven and controlling, someone who had long ago figured out what made the wheels of government spin. Dick had acquired a great deal of knowledge about his issues and, just as important, about the decision-making process itself. He thought and spoke with precision, a quality I admired in anyone. He had a wry sense of humor. No bland bureaucrat, Dick Clarke was a person whose leadership included elements of brilliance and breadth, discourtesy and arrogance, impatience, persistence, and discipline. His temper and his propensity to dress people down icily in front of others were famous. Engrossed in making progress in Somalia, he reminded me of a boxer: gloves up, muscles taut, dancing around to find an opening for a jab. Some people working with him felt intimidated by his tension, his brusqueness, and the burdens on them of his demands, wondering whether he ever relaxed or went home—or even, they quipped, had a home. I found him responsive and supportive, albeit while looking over my shoulder. Clarke was the best crisis manager I ever met—this in spite of, and to some extent because of, the very traits that could make him difficult to work with.

We talked on the telephone several times a day, and Clarke held secure video conferences with key players at four in the afternoon. Cameras at the State Department, Pentagon, CIA, and White House were trained on one or two senior people around their respective tables. Clarke sat alone and insisted his meetings be kept small to pinpoint responsibilities, discourage leaks, and foster openness. At State my answer to such (in my view, anyway) needless curtailing of expertise was to create a nether world of specialists on particular aspects of our work. Artfully concealing themselves on the floor below camera range, they wrote notes to me as needed and passed them up while someone else was on the screen. When at the end of my task force stint I called him up to say good-bye, Dick warmly replied, "The White House thanks you." An odd formulation and a bit presumptuous maybe, but I understood what he meant and felt pleased.

A Japanese proverb warns that an inch ahead lies darkness. Events during crises move swiftly, especially at the outset, and the unexpected derails the best of plans. Early reports are confusing and often wrong. A central location is needed for sorting information and dealing with it. People cannot be telephoning each other from different offices in Washington, trying to decide what to do before going home for dinner. They need to be in the same room working in shifts around the clock with someone in charge.

And so, in times of international emergencies, the authorities and responsibilities of various departments and agencies, many determined by law or regulation, are carried out by their task force representatives gathered around a long conference table in one of the crisis management suites of the State Department's Operations Center, where global communications systems are permanently in place. Usually these people have not known each other before, all of them having other duties from which they have been plucked. The task force director begins building a team by defining objectives, procedures, assignments, and responsibilities. Plans are made for contingencies: what will we do if...? Today is always yesterday's tomorrow.

The task force setting is antiseptic, space not wasted. Secure phones and fax machines keep members in touch with their bosses and colleagues in Washington and with the rest of the world. Maps of different scales are taped to the walls, some of city streets like those of Mogadishu, others of continents. CNN runs mutely on the overhead set until it focuses on the emergency at hand, when all stop working to hear what's new and how events are being covered, or what the White House and Defense Department spokespersons are saying. In the task force suite, plastic status boards record pending items, time lines, phone and fax numbers, and seemingly endless checklists. Clocks on a wall display the hours in different time zones of the world: in Mogadishu it is eight hours later than in Washington. People talk quietly into their telephones, write telegrams, and produce situation reports. When much is going on, the atmosphere is tense and hushed; conversation is clipped, as in any well-run control center. People are disciplining themselves to remain calm and think clearly.

The Operations Center on the State Department's seventh floor maintains a global watch that never shuts down. The secretary of state might walk the few steps from his or her office to be briefed, ask questions, pat a back, or provide instructions. Secretary and Mrs. Kissinger dropped by one New Year's Eve in black tie and ball gown to wish the lonely watch happy times ahead. For a task force there are likely to be intervals of boredom when nothing seems to be happening, as in endless hours of watch standing on military duty. Around the table people catch up on office work, read newspapers, chat, doze, eat food that is not permitted in the area, call their families, or simply stare at the television set. And suddenly, something unexpected. Oakley is on the speakerphone from Mogadishu. One of our vehicles has hit a land mine, and there are casualties. The task force pounces on the problem.

I began assembling a task force of about twelve men and women who would be working on Somalia around the clock in three shifts. No two crises were ever the same, and task forces differed in responsibilities and human chemistry. If one thought of the Somalia effort as a pie cut into wedges, the responsibility of the task force was to keep the policy rim intact and the wedges in proper proportion. At the outset I selected a full-time deputy, David Shinn. He was a broadly experienced Foreign Service officer from Yakima, Washington, an ambassador with extensive knowledge of the Horn of Africa, and he was a top-flight manager. David was someone with a pleasing voice and manner who remained cool under pressure and kept a steady eye on the objectives. Choosing him was the wisest management decision I made. It allowed me to step back from the action and think ahead, to roam and talk with others involved in Somalia beyond the task force itself—or simply to go for a walk outside the building.

Beyond their bureaucratic relationships, and to be fully effective, members of our task force needed to understand each other in human terms. Instinctively, they searched for common ground. As people got to know one another, the mood relaxed; trust built, and humor relieved boredom. Pictures of children were passed around. An artist among them began drawing cartoons, letting caricatures of everyone brighten a wall. I was particularly cartoonable. Pressures of work in windowless confinement inspired bonding surprising in its warmth and openness. One's sense of real time got blurred. People felt themselves on a shared journey during their shifts, sometimes staying on for companionship or the compelling interest of a drama unfolding. The best in themselves and their skills emerged naturally and generously. There was an instinct to find common ground. Task force members in these ways were like jurors on a panel deliberating for a long time in confinement: initially collegial and striving for consensus, but prepared to do battle over disagreements that mattered.

On Christmas Eve I sat alone and uninterrupted, watching Jimmy Stewart on television in *It's a Wonderful Life*. At midnight the watch in the operations center defied the rules and popped a bottle of champagne. David Shinn relieved me at 2:00 a.m. for his own shift. Even in Mogadishu all was quiet.

Exceeding Our Reach

Toward the end of March 1993, the new secretary of state, Warren Christopher, closed down our task force, believing its crisis management functions were no longer required, now that the relief phase was essentially over. I agreed. The time had come for the State Department and other agencies to return to their normal ways and deal with the next steps in Somalia through customary channels. The humanitarian phase of the operation ended in May. The relief effort had succeeded. Beyond doubt, hundreds of thousands of lives were saved, justifying the decision made by President Bush. The emphasis shifted from providing secure conditions for delivery of food to peace enforcement and nation building, an enormous, qualitative change. In the public eye the disasters to occur during this second phase would overshadow the humanitarian achievements. *Somalia* would become a buzzword for all that could go wrong in a military intervention aimed at nation building.

Not anticipated by anyone was that the new administration would underestimate the intractability of the Somali situation and at the highest levels fail to recognize how challenging would be the leap from humanitarian assistance to nation building. There had as yet been few combat casualties on the U.S. side, and the Clinton administration did not have a view of how many it was prepared to accept. Africa's problems were low on the policy agendas of State's new leaders. Christopher had no permanent Foreign Service under secretary in the State Department's top echelon or other means to maintain continuity and ensure that serious problems did not get put aside when administrations changed. As a debacle loomed, the only person in the State Department following Somalia full-time was a junior Foreign Service officer on the Ethiopian desk.

There was still no national government in Somalia. Conditions in the hinterland had changed sufficiently to permit achievement of our relief objectives, but chaos ruled in Mogadishu. Clans continued fighting among themselves and harassing relief workers. Support by the United Nations to bolster Mogadishu's police force dwindled to the point that the force was no longer credible. Young men chewed their khat.

We were beginning to make the mistake of demonizing the clan leader Mohammed Farah Aideed as responsible for the problems of the United Nations in Somalia, and thus our own. Personification of foreign policy issues—putting a face on them and making them ad hominem at the cost of addressing root causes—is misleading and dangerous. It tends to equate unequal opponents, in this case Clinton and Aideed, in a zero-sum game in which the gain of one is seen as the corresponding loss of the other. A clash of egos is perceived as the central aspect of the conflict, displacing attention from the underlying issues, and in Somalia we inadvertently made the thug Aideed into a folk hero, while Clinton appeared a loser.

Early in October 1993 eighteen Americans were killed and seventy-eight wounded while responding to the downing of a Black Hawk helicopter. Aideed's ragtag supporters dragged the body of a U.S. Ranger in his skivvies through the streets of Mogadishu, where he was kicked and spat upon before CNN's cameras. Six months later, without further losses, we handed over Somalia to a UN peacekeeping force. This had been a hazardous journey beginning with an American president's humanitarian impulse on a Thanksgiving weekend and ending in national disgrace.

Joy and Amazement

One of Washington's best and least-known sculptures lies hidden among elm and holly trees near the State Department. Robert Berks's 1979 bronze of Albert Einstein has him sitting on the second of three marble steps while gazing at a round sky map before him with 3,000 metal buttons depicting the planets, sun, moon, and stars. Larger than life, Einstein sprawls in sandals, slacks, and a rumpled sweater, oblivious to time. He is a tired old man with hooded, world-weary eyes that stare vacantly at the chart of the universe at his feet. When the afternoon sun catches the sculpture's surfaces Einstein glows in a thousand places. An inscription in his own words reads: "Joy and amazement at the beauty and grandeur of this world of which man can just form a faint notion."

Visiting Einstein in his bower I felt an intruder on his reverie but welcome nonetheless. I went to see him when I needed a quiet spell from Somalia, a few moments in his company to rekindle "joy and amazement."

And Then...

I retired in 1994, at age sixty-five, on the thirty-fifth anniversary of my walk from Georgetown across Key Bridge to join the A-100 course in Rosslyn, a budding diplomat eager to peek under the hood of the international game. A line from a song came to mind as I looked back on my years in the Foreign Service, a tune called "Thanks for the Memories." *You may have been a headache,* the singer acknowledged, *but you never were a bore.*

21

DIPLOMACY

Modern diplomacy encompasses the peaceful means by which governments conduct their relations with one another—whether bilaterally or through international institutions—as well as the substance of their exchanges. Diplomacy is about managing power and influence, and determining how to wield both in a global arena. Its exercise requires alert and constant care, along with an instinct for taking preventive measures.

What do diplomats do?

Diplomats everywhere are the indispensable brokers of international relations. To get their business done, governments need established and authoritative means of communicating with one another. Maintaining such communication is the work of diplomats—women and men empowered to speak and act for their governments and to transact business on their behalf, often through negotiation. The root *ambasse* in Old French signifies "message" and gives us the words *embassy* and *ambassador*.

Diplomats assess their interlocutors and their influence on other peoples and governments in the region and within multilateral organizations. They analyze how foreign leaders determine their own priorities, how they view those of the diplomat, the challenges these leaders face, and their staying power. They recommend courses of action to their own capitals. Diplomats search for common ground on which to improve relations.

America uniquely offers the world its leadership. Through public diplomacy and by facilitating trade, those working at the U.S. embassies and consulates seek to persuade ordinary people along with their governments of the merits of our nation's values and goals, our goods and services, and our behavior. Effective diplomacy reinforces the positive aspects of interdependence among nations, recognizing that no nation can stand alone.

Our representatives abroad look for elements in other societies seeking to harm us and delve into their origins, motivations, alliances, strengths, and vulnerabilities. When diplomacy fails, everyday people are likely to suffer through the use of force as a last resort. When threats are made in diplomacy, they should be carried out, if need be, to achieve declared objectives and preserve credibility.

For diplomacy to succeed, the people working at our posts abroad, at their professional best, should be students of our own and other cultures who see the shadings in a pluralistic world. Instinctively they should be courteous, honoring the dignity and self-respect of others, shunning arrogance precisely because they represent the economically and militarily most powerful nation on earth. This need not happen at the expense of firmness.

Our diplomats should be language buffs and dispassionate judges of character, hardheaded negotiators alert to body language and knowing when and why to compromise. They are charged and put in place to bring knowledge and coherence to our government's work abroad.

The qualities of diplomats should include loyalty, integrity, knowledge, judgment, vision, experience, and moral courage. Good diplomacy requires precision in thought, speech, writing, and especially in timing. The American diplomat Ellsworth Bunker said about negotiations, "Timing is everything." Needed too are a passion for learning and an ability to limn the scenes around them. Diplomats should have a sense of humor, lacking which they might still be successful diplomats but probably not popular or happy ones.

The influence abroad of our diplomats, whether career or politically appointed, depends on the wisdom of what they are instructed to advocate and on their skills, character, ingenuity, intuition, and resilience—and also on a bit of luck, that fickle actor in our lives. "Statesmen need luck as much as they need good judgment," Henry Kissinger wrote about Gorbachev in his classic work on diplomacy.

America's diplomats are ordinary people with exceptional abilities working in a dangerous world. They choose to go into that world to talk with strangers. They hail from Laurens and Bonners Ferry, Swampscott and Yakima, Hillsboro and Milwaukee, and what they do needs to be demystified.

The days of teacup diplomacy are gone, if ever they existed. Some of our diplomats are taken hostage by terrorists, assassinated, or blown up in embassies. Since the Vietnam War, more American ambassadors (seven) than military officers of flag rank have been killed in the line of duty.

Our foreign policies, determined by the president, are rooted in domestic needs and possibilities and are shaped by what the American people and their representatives will support as well as by political constraints within the president's own party. One can become discouraged seeing how Congress deals with international issues substantively and through appropriations, or by observing the influence of pressure groups and a lack of political will in the White House—especially at election time every two years—when the right thing to do abroad seems evident but is in conflict with domestic agendas.

The diplomat should state his case and is obliged to raise concerns. No diplomat, however, should feel confident in judging whether a president's domestic considerations outweigh predictable foreign policy setbacks. In the end, a diplomat's task is to explain and justify to foreign governments and peoples the *why* of his or her country's actions and intentions.

As Prime Minister Nehru lay dying, a Foreign Service friend in New Delhi said to me on leaving for a new post, "I wish I could stick around to see how all of this ends." I have felt that way myself sometimes, but relations among nations never finish. They outwit and outlast a mere diplomat caught, as Nabokov understood, in his own brief crack of light between two eternities of darkness.

EPILOGUE

My Education Continues

Only a parent knows the feeling of dread when a child says, "There's some-thing I have to tell you." The few times I've heard those words my throat tightened and I felt my heart beating in my chest, knowing our lives somehow were about to change. Helpless, I could only listen.

My son Mark has used this phrase twice with me. The first time, at nine-teen, was to tell me he had borrowed my wife's car without her permission to take his sister to the airport. On the drive back he skidded off a road in heavy rain, badly damaging the car. Mariana and I were recently married, and I had brought four children into her life. There would be a dustup, but eventually, with the car miraculously repaired, we would get past that.

The next time, six years later, we were in the room in which I work, Mark's room when he had lived at home. I was slouched at my desk, with Mark in the large tan reading chair facing me. He was on a quick business trip from Boston, where he worked in computer technology, and soon I would drive him to the airport. We were probably chatting about family. After a pause Mark said, "There's something I have to tell you." I froze and looked at the tense face of my son. "I can't believe I'm about to say this, Dad, but I'm gay."

Two reactions. I recognized how difficult this was for Mark to confide, and I saw how little I knew my son. Instinctively I said what I felt, just letting the words out. "I'm glad you told me, and I don't love you any less." We hugged and I said, "Let's talk in the car."

As we drove along the parkway and across Memorial Bridge, Mark told me he had known he was gay since the age of twelve. He was living with his boyfriend in Boston, and we would like him; he was a good person. In answer-ing my questions, Mark said about himself that he wasn't promiscuous, used condoms, and was happy with his life. I hugged him at the airport and told him again that I loved him just as much as ever. Then I watched him pass through the automatic doors, a tall broad-shouldered man with dark hair below his collar carrying a black travel bag. Overwhelmed, I got back into the car and wept.

I drove home in a state of shock. Thoughts tumbled in my head, but I couldn't make sense of them. I marveled at Mark's courage in coming out to me, probably the most difficult thing he had ever done, and was grateful to him. Other reactions, wrong ones I soon realized, were to feel sorry for him, thinking he would never have a family of his own, and then to wonder whether I hadn't lost my son, so deep was my lack of understanding of his sexual orientation. I worried about how my other children would react when Mark told them. And our friends. Would they need to know? *Why would it matter, and only if they asked.* Was this something to hide? *No.* What would Mark's friends be like, I wondered.

Mariana understood. When I told her what had happened, she said she sympathized with how I felt, but this was not a complete surprise to her. In fact, it explained some of Mark's behavior over the past years. He would no longer have to lie and hide or feel sad and isolated. He could be himself and live as he is. His life would go in a better direction with the pain and fear behind him. Mark couldn't help being gay, and he did the right thing in talking to me about it. His telling me was a measure of his love and trust, she said. My children's response was that they didn't care, and his sexuality had nothing to do with how they felt about their brother. It was I who was a mess.

Never had I confronted such a gap in my understanding of life. Where had I been? It had never occurred to me that my son might be gay. How much did Mark's being gay matter to me? If I had been given an opportunity to decide such a thing I would not have chosen homosexuality for him. But that wasn't the issue. Life didn't offer such choices. I became even more deeply interested in my son. I decided that I would learn about gays and the way they looked at the world, and how the world looked back at them. I would make an effort to nourish my humaneness. Through time, Mark's homosexuality concerned me less and less to the point of becoming irrelevant.

Over the next several years Mark recommended books on gays coming out, and beyond our times together we talked on the phone. I had questions, and he answered them directly. His Christmas present was a gay novel I enjoyed reading. I began to understand that being gay was normal. Mark was a happy man at peace in his soul. All of the family met his partner and liked him, taking him in as one of our own during Thanksgiving and Christmas visits from Boston.

I worried about prejudice where Mark worked if anyone found out. He said that while he didn't make a point of being gay any more than someone heterosexual would advertise that, there were other gays and lesbians in his company and no one was having problems. There were other gays and lesbians nearly everywhere. Our family gradually entered his world, learning what it meant to him and sometimes joking with him about it. That was all right for us to do. Outside our circle I became embarrassed watching adults trying to be funny by mocking homosexuals, or hearing gays and lesbians ignorantly disparaged as a group. Mark was teaching me to begin looking through his eyes. I was continuing my education in understanding other people, in understanding my own family.

I suggested to Mark that we tell the story of his coming out to me because this was such a defining moment for both of us. If he agreed, I would write my own section of an epilogue to this book and keep it from him. He would write his, and we would place the two together. The preceding pages are my section.

What follows is what Mark wrote.

This story is about a new beginning for me. It's about reaching a crossroads in my life when I thought that being gay would ruin my relationship with my father. He had raised me as a single parent since I was eleven. The divorce was traumatic for me. Being gay could very well mean that my father wouldn't want me to be part of his life anymore. The thought of losing him haunted me, but the love we shared was so strong that I believed we could survive this.

Homosexuality doesn't define me, but it does affect me. I made many decisions growing up, like dating girls or making fun of "fags," not because I thought I had a choice in the matter, but because I thought those were the only choices available based on how others would accept me. I dreaded the day someone found out I liked guys. I used to think it was so unfair that this had happened to me. Why couldn't I just be like everyone else was a question I began to ask myself in my early teens.

Thanksgiving was around the corner, and I couldn't lie to my father again, telling him I wasn't going to make it home because I didn't feel comfortable around his wife, when in fact it was because I couldn't bring my boyfriend home with me. Trying to build one family at the expense of another was too painful.

One October afternoon the need to see my father became so overpowering that I left my office, flew to Washington, and went to his apartment. I had made the decision not to live a lie, not to hide myself from who I was, not be ashamed of something over which I had no choice. I needed to talk to him about this before either of us might die. There was no going back.

I wasn't sure how I was going to tell him or how I was going to act. In my mind I watched different endings unfold for the life my father and I had shared up to this point. My memories were of a father and son who loved each other very much, growing up together in different corners of the world. I didn't know how this chapter was going to end, or even how I would begin our talk.

As I entered the lobby of his apartment building I was on autopilot. I couldn't catch my breath on the elevator ride. I thought this might be the last time I could come to see him, and I began to panic. Reminding myself that I was there to end the deception, fear, and hiding that had made me so sad for so long calmed and empowered me. It was time to be truthful and perhaps be able to provide my father with some explanation of my actions over the years. A newfound confidence and determination came over me as I unlocked the door to his apartment.

I found my father at his desk in what used to be my room, where he now worked, bookshelves behind him rising to the ceiling. There was a big easy chair in front of the desk. When I saw him I started shaking. I didn't think he could tell because he smiled and said "Hi Mark," as he always did. He wanted to know what I'd been up to. I thought about all the times I'd cried in his arms and was scared because I knew I'd be crying again very soon, but didn't know if it would be out of happiness or great loss. Trying to pull myself together, I said "Hi" and sat down. My voice was quavering. I told him there was something I had to say, and he needed to listen. He knew the news would be serious. "Dad, I'm gay."

For what seemed an eternity, my father looked at me. He didn't say anything. My father didn't say ANYTHING! I had stumped him. Brandon Grove was speechless. Through the sweat on my palms and forehead, I felt a peculiar satisfaction in all of this. That quickly disappeared when he still didn't say anything. Here was, I thought, the beginning of the nightmare I was so afraid of in which I'd lose my father through my confession. "Um, Dad, say something... please..." Trembling, I held my breath.

It felt like an hour had gone by in the moments that passed before he got up from behind his desk and hugged me. He said he loved me and always would, that I was his son and he was proud of me. I heard the words I needed to hear. I felt the blood come back to my face and my body warm. At that moment, the relief that came over me was as if I had just been pardoned from a life sentence in prison—a prison created by the reluctance of society to accept my homosexuality. I realized that we were going to get through this. Then I cried, letting go of years of pain and unhappiness.

Getting out of the car at the airport, wiping the tears off my cheeks, I said good-bye to my Dad and hugged him. I had made the right decision to tell him, and, finally, I was at peace with myself.

My Dad and I took another step together. His was the first of many toward accepting my sexuality. Mine was to become more comfortable and confident as a gay man. After all, being homosexual is no more of a choice than being black, white, male, or female.

Over the years that followed, now eight, we made efforts to include this topic in our conversations. I provided him with books; he asked me questions. We discussed people we knew and liked that were gay, and my boyfriend was included in family events.

My father continues to reach out to me. We educate each other. It's an ongoing process. My relationship with my father has never been stronger. I consider myself so fortunate.

NOTES ON SOURCES

In his autobiography, *Living to Tell the Tale,* the Colombian author Gabriel García Márquez, my age as well, observed that "life is not what one lived, but what one remembers and how one remembers it in order to recount it."

I have sought help. My sources include diplomatic colleagues with shared experiences and other friends. I have drawn upon their knowledge and observations as we discussed chapters of this book. My colleague Roger Kirk reviewed an early draft as a reader for the Association for Diplomatic Studies and Training. I have turned to *Foreign Relations of the United States,* the Ralph Bunche Library at the State Department, Paul Claussen in the Office of the Historian, personal records, expert advice from academics, and the Internet, among other sources. No one cited here saw the manuscript in final form. Any errors are my responsibility alone. Conclusions and interpretations are my own.

Accounts of my youth drew on family records and observations by my brother, Lloyd; by my uncle Henry Grove and his wife, Alice; and by my Polish cousin Wojciech Gasparski. Joan Williams read the section on Faulkner and recalled his breaking ice on a back road in Mississippi. The quotation from his letter to her is from *Faulkner: A Biography,* by Joseph Blotner. A Bard classmate and World War II veteran, Robert J. Mac Alister, has traded insights and opinions with me for more than fifty years. Carter H. Hills and I recalled our harrowing experiences in climbing the Great Cheops Pyramid. Captain Giles L. Kelly, USNR (Ret.), who served as navigator aboard my first ship, the USS *Cambria,* during World War II, commented on navy times. A diary kept during my first visit to the Soviet Union in 1958 provided material for that section. Robert R. Bowie discussed John Foster Dulles in the State Department. The quotation attributed to Secretary Dulles is from Robert A. Fearey's contemporaneous notes and given to me by him as I was writing this book.

William G. Miller, a classmate in the A-100 course for newly inducted Foreign Service officers, reminded me of the warmth of that experience. Donald R. Norland, the American consul at my first post, reviewed the chapter on Abidjan. Marion J. Henderson, our Foreign Service secretary there, was equally helpful.

Thomas L. Hughes, a longtime associate of Chester Bowles and a State Department official at the time; Lucius D. Battle, then the department's executive secretary; and Walter L. Cutler, staff assistant to Secretary of State Dean Rusk and my counterpart when I worked for Bowles, read the chapter on Chester Bowles and George Ball. Cutler shared with me his recollections of the Rusk-Bowles relationship as he witnessed it during troubled months. Others providing their comments were Samuel W. Lewis and Nicholas A. Veliotes, the three of us recalling the first but not the last time we worked together, and my colleague Howard B. Schaffer, author of *Chester Bowles: New Dealer in the Cold War.* James Reston's quotation of George Ball's "giraffe question" is from *Deadline: A Memoir.*

Robert F. Kennedy wrote an account of his 1962 trip around the world on which I accompanied him called *Just Friends and Brave Enemies.* While Evan Thomas was writing *Robert Kennedy: His Life,* he and I exchanged thoughts about RFK over lunch.

Dennis H. Kux, author of *India and the United States: Estranged Democracies, 1941–1991,* Sam Lewis, and Howard Schaffer commented on the chapter about India. Memories of those times were shared with me, as well, by Nicholas Veliotes, R. Marcus Palmer, and Nancy Pelletreau, all of whom had been in New Delhi with me.

The West Berlin chapter was improved by Kenneth C. Keller, a political officer at the time, and by contemporary legal advisers Marten H. A. van Heuven and Arthur T. Downey. Robert Gerald Livingston, an expert on Germany, reflected on our years in Berlin, where he had worked in the Eastern Affairs Section of the U.S. Mission. Sol and Kay Polansky, contemporaries in West and East Berlin, where Sol succeeded me as DCM, were helpful. My colleague and German expert, W. R. Smyser, author of *From Yalta to Berlin: The Cold War Struggle over Germany,* provided his thoughts. Dr. Andreas Daum shared his knowledge of West and East Berlin and offered editorial advice.

Robert B. Sayre and William T. Pryce, both serving in Panama while I was country director, read the chapter on Panama. Colonel Richard A. Wyrough, U.S. Army (Ret.), who devoted many years to our relations with Panama, shared his thoughts on this chapter. Accounts of Torrijos, Lakas, and our conversations are based on notes I made at the time. I profited from reading *The Making of a Public Man: A Memoir,* by the businessman/diplomat Sol M. Linowitz, who also read the Panama chapter.

W. R. Smyser commented as well on East Germany. Gertrude D. "Trudie" Musson, John Sherman Cooper's personal assistant in the Senate and later in

East Berlin, helped me as I wrote about Ambassador Cooper and his wife, Lorraine. Michael Mangan, the Coopers' butler, shared his recollections over a nostalgic lunch at the Metropolitan Club with Trudie and me. Economic officer Alan Parker, another member of our little band behind the wall, gave his views and recollections, as did James Weiner and Aniko Gaal Schott. Ursula Wieland Lambach guided me on East Berlin, recalling inter alia Lorraine's cucumber sandwiches. Gerald Livingston provided advice. My friend the former Soviet diplomat Alexander S. Yereskovsky, at Georgetown University, talked with me about his colleague Piotr Abrasimov, the Soviet ambassador in Berlin during Cooper's time, and about the nature of diplomacy. Material cited on the opening of Berlin's wall was drawn from the Cold War International History Project's *Bulletin* of Fall/Winter 2001, published by the Woodrow Wilson International Center for Scholars, in Washington, D.C.

Richard McCoy, desk officer for Guyana in the State Department at the time of the Jonestown suicides, reminded me of our experiences in Washington as we coped with this tragedy. He reminisced about his work as a consular officer at the American embassy in Georgetown before these events happened. For background I read *Seductive Poison: A Jonestown Survivor's Story of the Life and Death of the Peoples Temple,* by Deborah Layton.

Chapters on Jerusalem and Philip C. Habib were enriched by comments from Samuel Lewis, U.S. ambassador to Israel; Nicholas Veliotes, the assistant secretary of state for the Middle East; Carol Thompson, a junior Foreign Service officer at the consulate general in Jerusalem; Edward Abbington, a successor consul general there; Morris Draper, Philip Habib's deputy in negotiations to expel the PLO from Lebanon and also a successor consul general in Jerusalem; and Michael E. Sterner, a State Department expert on the region. Talal Belhriti, working at the Middle East Institute, offered his knowledge and editorial advice. *Divided Jerusalem: The Struggle for the Holy City,* by Bernard Wasserstein, recounts the history of consulates in that city. While both of us were writing books, I became acquainted with John Boykin, then working on his biography of Philip Habib, *Cursed Is the Peacemaker: The American Diplomat Versus the Israeli General, Beirut, 1982.* We exchanged ideas and information. Colonel James T. Sehulster, USMC (Ret.), wrote to me about his support to Philip Habib during negotiations over the PLO's expulsion from Lebanon.

During our conversations over a country weekend in August 2001, Larry Devlin, the former CIA station chief in Léopoldville, reminisced about his days in the Congo and Zaire. Daniel L. Simpson, my deputy chief of mission in Kinshasa, and his wife, Libby, read this portion of the manuscript and made suggestions. Michela Wrong, author of *In the Footsteps of Mr. Kurtz: Living on the Brink of Disaster in Mobutu's Congo*, gave me her reactions to the chapter. From her I learned about Mobutu's hatter in Paris.

The account of training America's diplomats and building a permanent home for the Foreign Service Institute was sharpened by observations from Dr. John T. Sprott, for many years the deputy director of FSI and deeply involved in creating a rededicated Arlington Hall. Assistance came from Catherine J. Russell, who devoted nearly all of her time to the Arlington Hall construction project and knew more about it than anyone else in government.

Robert B. Oakley, U.S. special envoy to Somalia, commented on the Somalia section. I also drew on his account of those experiences written with John L. Hirsch, *Somalia and Operation Restore Hope: Reflections on Peacemaking and Peacekeeping*. Dan Simpson, who eventually succeeded Oakley, provided his views. David H. Shinn, my deputy on the Somalia Task Force in Washington, made suggestions. For other perspectives on events in Somalia, I drew on Reuters reporter Aidan Hartley's book *The Zanzibar Chest*.

William C. Harrop and E. Allan Wendt, Foreign Service veterans, commented on the concluding chapter about diplomacy, as did our colleagues Arthur T. Downey and Herbert J. Hansell. In my thoughts were the writings of Sir Harold Nicolson and Dr. Henry Kissinger, both of whom produced classics in the modern literature entitled, quite simply, *Diplomacy*. I acknowledge them also.

Others, more briefly, shared their reactions with me. I am grateful to everyone.

INDEX

Page numbers in *italics* refer to illustrations.